Oracle Press

Oracle Business Process Management Suite 11g Handbook

 *Oracle Press*™

Oracle Business Process Management Suite 11g Handbook

Manoj Das
Manas Deb
Mark Wilkins

New York   Chicago   San Francisco
Lisbon   London   Madrid   Mexico City
Milan   New Delhi   San Juan
Seoul   Singapore   Sydney   Toronto

The McGraw·Hill Companies

Cataloging-in-Publication Data is on file with the Library of Congress

McGraw-Hill books are available at special quantity discounts to use as premiums and sales promotions, or for use in corporate training programs. To contact a representative, please e-mail us at bulksales@mcgraw-hill.com.

Oracle Business Process Management Suite 11g Handbook

1 2 3 4 5 6 7 8 9 0   QFR QFR   1 0 9 8 7 6 5 4 3 2 1

ISBN   978-0-07-175449-1
MHID   0-07-175449-0

Sponsoring Editor Wendy Rinaldi	**Technical Editors** Bhagat Nainani Dan Atwood	**Composition** Cenveo Publisher Services
Editorial Supervisor Jody McKenzie	**Copy Editor** Mike McGee	**Illustration** Cenveo Publisher Services
Project Manager Harleen Chopra, Cenveo Publisher Services	**Proofreader** Debbie Liehs	**Art Director, Cover** Jeff Weeks
Acquisitions Coordinator Stephanie Evans	**Indexer** Jack Lewis	**Cover Designer** Pattie Lee
	Production Supervisor Jean Bodeaux	

About the Authors

Manoj Das is Senior Director of Product Management at Oracle, and is responsible for Oracle's BPM Suite of products. Manoj's Business Process Management (BPM) journey started at Siebel Systems, where he was responsible for the next-generation process-centric and insight-driven application platform. Since joining Oracle as part of the Siebel acquisition, Manoj has been a key member of the business integration team, focused on BPEL, Business Rules, and BPM. He plays a leadership role setting BPM and SOA industry standards, especially in BPMN 2.0, BPEL, and Business Rules. He is widely recognized at industry conferences and Information Technology publications and has published articles related to BPEL, BPEL4People, and BPMN. He has also contributed articles to the Workflow Management Coalition's yearly handbooks, including those on Social BPM. Manoj has a BS in Computer Science from IIT Kanpur and an MBA from UC Berkeley. He has held senior Product Management, Development Management, and Product Development positions at Oracle, Siebel, Mentor Graphics, and others.

Dr. Manas Deb, a Senior Director in the Fusion Middleware (FMW) core product group at Oracle HQ, currently leads outbound product management for all of the Business Integration Products within the FMW family, worldwide. These products include Business Process Management Suite, SOA Suite, Complex Event Processing, and Governance. Manas's charter is focused on market growth, revenue generation, and the strategic adoption of these products. Manas has worked in the software industry for more than 20 years, most of which was spent in software product management/marketing and on architecting and leading a wide variety of enterprise-level application development and business integrations and process management projects in a wide variety of industries. Manas is an engineering graduate of IIT Kharagpur. Manas attended post-graduate studies at Memorial University in St. John's, Canada and the University of Texas at Austin. He has an MS in Engineering, a PhD in CAM (Computer Science, Applied Mathematics and Engineering), as well as an MBA with a specialization in international business.

Mark Wilkins started his career with a large Systems Integrator, and has more than 20 years consulting experience with a wide variety of clients, spanning the health care, banking, and telecommunications industries.

Business Process Management has been a reccurring theme throughout this journey, taking many twists and turns along the way. Currently working as Enterprise Architect for Oracle's Global Enterprise Architecture Program, Mark has a renewed focus on BPM, working across product lines to develop BPM architectural strategies and methodologies. Mark joined Oracle from BEA where he was instrumental in developing Service Oriented Architecture methods and service offerings, enabling a new strategic consulting practice. Mark holds a Bachelor of Science degree in Pure and Applied Physics from the University of Manchester, England. Originally from the UK, he now lives with his all-American family in close proximity to the Rocky Mountains in beautiful Colorado.

Contents at a Glance

Contents

PART I
Introduction

PART III
Essentials of Oracle BPM Methodology

Foreword

This book holds many opportunities if you choose to read it and leverage what you've learned. The authors have put together a comprehensive backgrounder on Business Process Management (BPM) and potential.

If you are interested in learning what BPM is all about and why it matters to your business, then you have picked up the right book.

If your goal is to better understand the adoption patterns and methodologies applied by others in their usage of BPM, then you've come to right place.

If you are looking for specific information on how Oracle's BPM 11*g* release helps you solve your business process needs with a detailed overview of key features, then this book is what you are looking for.

BPM 11*g* represents a tremendous milestone for Oracle. We've acquired a lot of products over the years to build out our Fusion Middleware stack, but we've always held the belief that it is only through integration of these disparate products that the customer experiences something greater than the sum of the collective parts. BPM 11*g* is a complete rewrite of our BPM product and shares the same micro-kernel–based runtime architecture that drives our SOA Suite of products.

What does this mean for the customer? Many things, actually.

BPM 11*g*'s BPMN 2.0 process execution shares the same engine used by our BPEL product in SOA Suite. This means it has been proven to scale and perform to the highest standards by thousands of Oracle customers on hardened code.

By extending a common platform we make the user experience across the products consistent.

BPM 11g users have ready access to all the features of BPEL, the Service Bus, adapters, Business Activity Monitoring, B2B, and the rest of the SOA Suite.

In practice, this means that, by using Oracle BPM 11g to solve your business process challenges, you have opted into a full solution stack that can span any business or process needs you may have. This comes as welcome news to both IT and the lines of business as each has potentially different requirements for what they need from an enterprise software solution. Subject matter experts in the line of business can stay within the tools that are comfortable to them and create solutions without having to involve IT. Enterprise Architects and IT can use other tools within the stack to augment content from the line of business, add BPEL process flows to a solution, or anything else you wish to do with the full breadth of the SOA Suite.

BPM's greatest value is bringing subject matter experts in the line of business into the design and implementation of a business process in a meaningful way so the end result is a solution that truly meets users' needs because they actively engaged in the creation process. Building your solutions on Oracle's BPM 11g extends that value proposition by layering BPM on top of the SOA Suite stack, allowing the full spectrum of solution options to your enterprise in a seamless stack. The whole is definitely better than the sum of the parts.

So, if you have an interest in BPM, you have some interesting reading ahead of you.

My thanks to the authors for putting together a great book that really shows what is possible with BPM and how to put yourself on the best possible path to successful process solutions.

Enjoy the read!

Michael Weingartner
Vice President of Development
Oracle's Integration Products

Acknowledgments

To start with, I am extremely grateful to the development, product management, and quality assurance team responsible for bringing BPM 11*g* to the market. The product, and hence this book, owes its existence to the tireless commitment and extreme professionalism of this team. It is a pleasure and a privilege to be a part of it. Within this great team, I would like to specifically thank Yogeshwar Kuntawar, who is always ready to roll up his sleeves and look into an issue, and whose timely help proved critical in creating this book. I also want to thank Ravi Rangaswamy for his input on Chapter 7.

I am also very thankful to the technical reviewers of this book—Bhagat Nainani and Dan Atwood. Their review, inputs, and comments have helped shape this book's content, focus, and readability. I am also very thankful to Duncan Mills and Frank Nimphius for their review of Chapter 8. Much of what I know about ADF I owe to Frank's articles and his and Lynn Munsingner's book "Oracle Fusion Developer Guide: Building Rich Internet Applications with Oracle ADF Business Components and Oracle ADF Faces" (McGraw-Hill, December 2009). Niall Commiskey also did a very in-depth review of Chapters 6 and 8 and I am extremely thankful for it.

I am extremely blessed to work with the BPM product management team, each and every member of which is an exceptional professional. In the context of this book, I would like to especially thank Heidi Buelow for her review of Chapter 4, Meera Srinivasan for her review of Chapters 4 and 5, and David Read for his advice. Writing a book of this nature over a period of six to seven months can be a daunting task, and I had my moments of disillusionment. I am very thankful to Meera for her words of encouragement—learning that even she found the content useful motivated me to stay focused in getting the book done.

I am thankful to the McGraw-Hill editorial staff for their patience with us and their help in completing the book. Also, I am thankful to my co-authors for their cooperation; in particular to Mark Wilkins for his timely reviews and edits.

Lastly, and most importantly, I am extremely thankful to my wife, Kakali, for her patience and tolerance. Writing this book has consumed an inordinate amount of personal time over the last half year or more, and I understand that no amount of thanks can compensate for that.

—Manoj Das

No one would have said that contributing to a book while handling an often-more-than-a-40-hour workweek and extensive business travel across the globe would be easy—and this writing wasn't either. However, in many ways, the expected usefulness of the ultimate result and the enthusiastic support and collaboration of many along the way seem to have made the extra effort worthwhile.

My heartfelt thanks go to my colleagues at Oracle Product Management and Product Engineering for doing the hard work of bringing a visionary product like BPM Suite to life. As I planned my chapters and detailed them, I benefited immensely from discussion with my co-authors, Manoj Das and Mark Wilkins, and my Product Management teammate, Prasen Palvankar, and I thank them all. Comments from my technical reviewer, Bhagat Nainani, were always pertinent and to the point, which helped me improve my chapter drafts—I owe my sincere gratitude to him. I would like to thank my manager at Oracle, Michael Weingartner, for his encouragement and support toward completion of this book.

The editorial teams at McGraw-Hill, the Oracle Press team, and the legal team at Oracle, all deserve my sincere thanks for their guidance, input, and facilitation of this book project.

Last but not least I would like to gratefully acknowledge the love, support, and good humor of my daughter, Chaarushena, and my wife, Sanghamitra, in absence of which my work on this book would not have been possible.

—Manas Deb

There is no doubt that writing a book is a very challenging experience, but it has also been very rewarding, giving me an opportunity to work more closely with some very smart people—my fellow authors in particular. I have worked with various incarnations of BPM throughout my career, but I believe it is only now that we finally have all the pieces of the puzzle in place to actually make it truly do what we have always hoped for. There are still challenges, as with any new technology, but I believe these have been addressed sufficiently enough here to at least establish a framework for the successful execution of business process automation projects.

In addition to my thanks to Manas and Manoj, I would like to thank Prasen Palvankar for his support and long discussions about BPM methodology, and of course the wonderful team at McGraw-Hill for their patience and expertise in helping us bring this book together.

—Mark Wilkins

Introduction

This book is targeted at people involved in implementing and managing Business Process Management (BPM) initiatives—BPM developers, process architects, consultants, and project managers. Business analysts should also benefit from the explanation of BPM concepts. They may need to skip some of the more in-depth details and focus on the concepts, use cases, and best practices.

Our goal in writing this book was to help with the successful implementation of BPM projects using Oracle BPM 11g. We designed this book to focus on explaining the concepts underlying Oracle BPM 11g. Oracle BPM 11g has a very broad set of features and we have tried to cover nearly the complete range of it, explaining not only the functionality of the feature, but its broader context, including when to use it, how it relates to other similar features, and any best-practice considerations.

We have not attempted to provide step-by-step instructions on product usage. We believe that the product is rather easy to learn and use, and once armed with the conceptual understanding, one can easily figure out the step-by-step procedures. Also, Oracle's product documentation does a good job in providing detailed step-by-step instructions. We have included pointers to the relevant chapters and books within Oracle's product documentation online bookshelf. Oracle's product documentation online bookshelf can be accessed at www.oracle.com/technetwork/indexes/documentation/index.html. Documentation for BPM 11g and related components referenced in this book can be found under *Oracle Fusion Middleware* grouping. Also, in many cases complete projects and other supporting material related to the examples used in the chapters can be accessed from the web site for this book.

This book has been organized into three parts:

- **Part I: Introduction** This part provides an introduction to the discipline of Business Process Management, including its historical context, some of the frameworks and theoretical concepts fueling the field, and the standards shaping it. This part also introduces the architecture and functionality of Oracle BPM 11*g*.

- **Part II: Mastering Oracle BPM 11*g*** This part provides a detailed explanation of the concepts underlying BPM 11*g*, feature usage, and best practices. As the name of the section indicates, the goal of this section is to help the reader master the usage of Oracle BPM 11*g*.

- **Part III: Essentials of Oracle BPM Methodology** This part explains how to address the broader issues associated with adopting and expanding BPM within an organization and identifies the frameworks and skills necessary for successful BPM.

Part I: Introduction

This part consists of Chapters 1 through 3.

Chapter 1: BPM: Background   This chapter sets the overall context for the book and the discipline of Business Process Management (BPM). Starting with the evolution of BPM from the 18th-century's Factory Model to today's comprehensive Business Process Management Suites (BPMS), the chapter goes on to define BPM and explore its characteristics and benefits. It delves into high-level techniques on how BPM can aid the execution of business strategies and help business-IT alignment. It identifies BPM's roles and relationships with business architecture, Service Oriented Architecture (SOA), and packaged application integration and customization. The chapter also provides introductory discussions on the BPM life cycle and strategies for successful BPM adoption.

Chapter 2: Standards in BPM   This short chapter starts with a discussion of the types of standards needed to support the wide variety of activities and assets involved in typical BPM projects. The chapter is then devoted to the description of some of the key events in the evolution of BPM standards and captures the essence of the standards involved.

Chapter 3: BPM Suite 11*g*: An Overview   This chapter is sort of an introduction to Part II of the book—Mastering Oracle BPM 11*g*. It begins with a short history of Oracle's offerings and acquisitions, and how the BPM Suite 11*g* effort started. After exploring the requirements of a modern BPMS, the chapter discusses the goals and guiding principles behind the making of BPM Suite 11*g*, including the main product architectural themes. In the remainder of the chapter, important features of BPM Suite 11*g* are covered in an overview fashion, while the details are deferred to Part II.

Part II: Mastering Oracle BPM 11*g*

This part encompasses Chapters 4 through 8, starting with a broad but rapid introduction to Oracle BPM 11*g* concepts and continuing with a deeper dive into key elements of the product.

Chapter 4: The Quick Learner's Guide to Oracle BPM 11*g*   The intent of this chapter is to provide enough information for the reader to successfully get started with an Oracle BPM 11*g* project. This chapter explains BPM projects, BPMN 2.0, Human Tasks, Business Rules, Service Tasks, and Process Monitoring and Analytics. While the main focus of the chapter is from the developer perspective, it also covers Simulation and Process Composer, which are of interest to business analysts and Workspace, the application used by end-users to interface with Oracle BPM 11*g*.

Chapter 5: Business Process Modeling and Implementation Using BPMN 2.0
BPMN 2.0 is at the heart of Oracle BPM 11*g*, and this chapter provides a detailed explanation of its proper and effective usage. While this book is targeted at Oracle BPM 11*g*, this chapter may benefit anyone interested in

understanding the implementation aspects of BPMN 2.0. The chapter includes process modeling best practices. It covers BPMN 2.0 concepts including Subprocesses, Events and Exceptions, and Conversations (that is, interprocess communication). This chapter also reviews many common process patterns and explains how BPMN 2.0 can be used to address them.

Chapter 6: Mastering Business Rules   Business Rules should be an integral component of every process application. This chapter takes a close look not only at Oracle Business Rules 11g but business rules in general, explaining the use cases for business rules as well as the workings of the Rete algorithm, the core of most modern rule engines. This chapter also describes some recommendations and best practices in using rules effectively. It covers Oracle Business Rules 11g in great detail, including Rule Organization, Rule Data Model, Functions, and Testing Business Rules. It also explains business rules—both if-then and decision tables—in significantly more depth than Chapter 4, including advanced mode, tree mode, aggregates, and more.

Chapter 7: Advanced Human Tasks   While Chapter 4 provides sufficient coverage of human tasks for many readers and use cases, this chapter takes a much deeper look at task metadata, including task stakeholders, users and roles, notifications and deadlines, task payload and the usage of flex fields, and more. It also explains advanced routing capabilities available within Oracle BPM 11g, including the concept of declarative participant list builders, integration with business rules, overriding of task routing in task models as well as by users on an ad hoc basis, and more. This chapter also introduces the concept of Activity Guides.

Chapter 8: Developing Rich User Interfaces for BPM with ADF   Being easy to use, productive, and having rich end-user interfaces are an integral part of winning end-user buy-in to BPM project and maximizing the productivity improvements. Oracle Application Development Framework (ADF) provides a rich set of capabilities for building user interfaces for BPM and other applications. This chapter provides in-depth coverage of ADF, especially from the perspective of usage in the context of BPM.

Part III: Essentials of Oracle BPM Methodology

Chapters 9 through 11 make up the third part of the book, encompassing strategic planning, business analysis, and an IT perspective on process automation projects. For a rapid start in a BPM initiative, in which time constraints may preclude strategic planning, it is reasonable to start with business analysis (in other words, reading Chapter 10 before 9) since this includes a detailed approach for process identification and selection. In this way, the more involved strategic approach (in Chapter 9) can be revisited as the BPM program gathers momentum.

Chapter 9: Planning BPM Adoption   Starting with the broadest view of enterprise BPM planning, this chapter looks at all aspects of BPM in an organization, discusses the importance of assessing the organization's readiness, and explains how to create a roadmap for successful BPM adoption. Along the way, a set of important frameworks and methods are identified, and of these, business process selection and BPM project delivery strategies are described in detail in succeeding chapters.

Chapter 10: Strategic Analysis, Process Selection, and Design   Choosing the right business processes for automation (or even distinguishing business processes from other types of orchestration) is never simple, but it is always critical to a successful BPM. This chapter describes the Oracle approach to selecting processes for automation based on relevant criteria and alignment with strategic objectives.

Chapter 11: Technical Design and Project Delivery Strategies   While BPM fosters valuable communication and cooperation between the business and IT, it is still necessary to delineate responsibilities in a BPM project. This chapter describes the key roles of a BPM project and focuses on the organization of the technical activities necessary to realize effective process automation. The BPM project life cycle is introduced to ensure that all activities, their dependencies, and associated skills can be integrated with the project delivery strategy of choice.

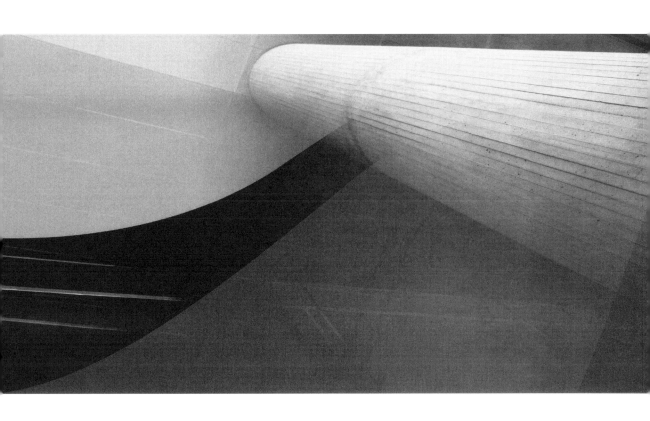

PART
I

Introduction

CHAPTER 1

BPM: Background

n September 2010, ebizQ (www.ebizq.net), an online IT publisher, invited its readers to "describe BPM in one sentence." Responses ranged from BPM being something that allows us to "take control of all work activities" to a "way of thinking," with all the usual definitions in between. Interestingly, in all the explanations that the responders provided, one theme was consistent—BPM (Business Process Management) helps an organization do its job better. The reason for this belief would not be hard to understand if we consider that BPM involves comprehensive management of "business processes" that are, in turn, articulations of activities that a business does to conduct its operations.

The idea of taking control of the activities of a business, and thus enforcing a variety of disciplines to increase the quality of execution of such activities is not new. We can trace certain aspects of BPM to as early as the 18th century when the famous economist Adam Smith noted a more than two orders of magnitude increase in productivity at a pin factory via the use of the ideas of division of labor and work specialization. Of course, this "factory model" would be too simplistic for most of today's businesses. In their book *Business Process Management; The Third Wave* (Meghan Kiffer Press, 2006), authors Howard Smith and Peter Fingar have captured the evolution of BPM in three waves:

- **First Wave**   This began in the early part of the 20th century and was focused on deriving higher efficiency in the day-to-day operations of businesses. The work of Fredric Winslow Taylor in theorizing disciplined approaches to achieve such goals was pioneering. The practices in Ford Motor Company's assembly line were also stunning examples of efficiency.

- **Second Wave**   This coincides with the pervasive adoption of packaged enterprise applications like ERP (Enterprise Resource Planning), SCM (Supply Chain Management), CRM (Customer Relationship Management), and HR (Human Resource) systems, and the utilization of business processes embedded in such applications as a way of guiding business execution.

- **Third Wave**   This refers to current efforts to recognize BPM as a holistic endeavor that a business engages in to gain efficiency and agility in its operations while creating sustainable competitive advantage.

While early IT systems took a data-centric approach to supporting business needs (epitomized by evolutionary steps through mainframe "number crunching," the invention of the spreadsheet, and database management systems), the second wave provided IT with a functional view of business operations, and many organizational structures are modeled around this functional view. Fingar's Third Wave removes the compromises and contortions imposed by prior technological constraints and allows the business to take control at the highest level—the business process. This removal of IT constraints has far-reaching implications, not the least of which is the opportunity for enterprises to become *process-centric* organizations.

As the notion of BPM was maturing, the use of statistical analysis to improve pertinent worker activities came into vogue in a variety of TQM (Total Quality Management) efforts. The Toyota Product System (TPS) and Six Sigma, pioneered at Motorola and popularized at General Electric, are noteworthy examples. It turned out that TQM procedures utilized strategies and artifacts that would be similar to many aspects of BPM as we describe it today.

Earlier scopes of BPM (or BPM-like) initiatives were very narrowly focused. Operational efficiency was the main focus and business processes were conceived as a collection of relatively simple tasks. In fact, in the late 1990s, there was a significant effort in operational efficiency improvement by the so-called "Business Process Reengineering (BPR)" initiatives, which aimed at both reducing the execution time and the cost of activities, and also pushed for the elimination of many activities altogether. The various mechanisms of discipline enforcement combined with the elimination of certain activities to maximize efficiency gain had its problems, however. After a few iterations, improvements in efficiency gains were diminishing, the processes had become hard to change, and the conspicuous reduction of the work force generated ill-feeling towards BPR and associated "automation." Also, most of the automation of these processes were largely hardwired by technical staff, and implementations were inflexible. The difficulties of translating business requirements to IT functionalities while keeping the technical systems abreast of the evolution of the business itself became a big challenge contributing to the harmful "business-IT" gap.

Modern BPM initiatives typically encompass a much broader scope in terms of activities and participants; their goals go beyond mere operational efficiency and include the flexibility to cope with business change, intelligent exception handling and enhanced customer satisfaction, the facilitation of predictive analytics, and the triggering of cross-sell and up-sell opportunities. The technology platforms and products supporting modern BPM initiatives also benefit from the great advancements in computation and communication technologies as well as human adoption of digital collaboration.

BPM in a Nutshell

BPM, as the name suggests, is all about managing business processes (BP), typically with an aim to maintain or make better certain aspects of the performance of the business. Business processes, in turn, refer to collections of activities that a business does. As can be expected, many definitions of BPM and BP exist, varying in their scope and points-of-view. Later in the book we will delve into the finer details of BPM and BP, but in an attempt to provide some formal structure for the ongoing discussions, we will adopt the following nontechnical working definitions for them:

- **BPM** is defined as a strategy for managing and improving the performance of a business through continuous optimization of business processes in a closed-loop cycle of modeling, execution, and measurement. BPM activities span conception and discovery through deployment and management of the execution of business processes within some appropriate governance framework.

- A **business process** is a set of linked activities performed by people and systems that deliver some business value to internal or external customers.

Thus, we embrace a comprehensive scope for BPM spanning a complete life cycle and including continuous process improvement. We recognize this as a management discipline that goes beyond software development activities or the mere use of software applications. We also include related governance as a necessary element of BPM. We believe that adequate governance is required to ensure quality BPM adoption that is capable of sustained competitive advantage.

In the case of the definition of a business process, we purposely avoid the restriction of any structured association of business activities. In structured processes, steps of the process and their sequence are known *a priori,* at least within a specified set of possible options. For many business processes this restriction does not pose any real difficulty and, in fact, makes the computer realization of the business processes simpler. A straightforward order-to-cash for simple goods, a provisioning of a telephone service, supporting back-end business processes for most Internet purchases would fall under the structured business process category. However, today's businesses need to both improve and guarantee the quality execution of business transactions that involve rather ad hoc collections of activities where the exact number of tasks, and the exact nature of their association, including apparent task flows, are not known *a priori.* Business processes evolve depending on the specific context of a particular business transaction, and are based on intermediate results. As opposed to the strict sequence and prespecified branching of task flows, these transactions are guided by higher-level business norms, rules, and policies. Such transactions could also include the relatively free-form collaboration of *knowledge workers* as opposed to ordered human tasks familiar to traditional workflow systems. Management of these transactions can be formulated using what are called unstructured processes. Many case management activities, as well as pharmaceutical R&D and complicated risk analysis, are examples of unstructured processes.

We would like to point out that business processes can and do exist within packaged applications like ERP, CRM, HRM, and SCM, and they can also be created in *middleware* that usually surround such applications. While cross-application business processes clearly sit in the middleware, situations often arise where multifaceted design and operational considerations are needed in determination of the best place for creation of a business process. Oracle BPM Suite is a middleware product (in fact, it is a part of Oracle's Fusion Middleware family of products) and can be used to create independent business processes that can integrate with, or extend, packaged applications.

It may also be useful to note that the abbreviation "BPM" is also commonly used for Business Process Modeling, Business Process Monitoring, and Business Performance Management. The first two are included in our definition of BPM, while the third is concerned with financial measures of business performance to which our BPM should ultimately contribute.

Why BPM?

Presently, most companies are highly interested in adopting BPM across their organizations to help better their organizational performance. Few companies have yet achieved maturity in their BPM initiatives, while most others are grappling with early stages of adoption. Frequent reports by leading analyst firms like Gartner, Forrester, and IDC have been indicating that the improvement in process management has been one of the top concerns of senior management for the past few years and will remain so in coming years. Analysts estimate the annual BPM spend to be in the range of 5–6 billion USD and is projected to grow at the rate of 30–40 percent per year (compare this with the projected growth rate of 5–10 percent for most other business integration software markets). All in all, BPM appears to enjoy a strong positive momentum at the present time. Thus, it would be worthwhile to dig a little deeper to see why BPM is regarded as being so beneficial to a company.

BPM Benefits

As we have already noted, BPM is about managing business activities in a comprehensive way. While adopting of BPM offers many benefits, the primary motivation for using it in a given company could differ. For example, some companies may be focused on executing their activities more efficiently— that is, producing the same output with less resources like time, money, goods, and labor—while others may be more interested in creating higher business agility in order to respond better to changing market conditions. In some cases, process management may be necessary to produce sufficient visibility and create audit trails across a chain of activities so as to meet a variety of regulatory compliance requirements. Such benefits of BPM, generally speaking, can be classified as either internal or external. Internal benefits are typically efficiency, as well as worker empowerment and satisfaction, while external benefits help customers and partners derive better value from the company's products and services.

BPM delivers increased business operation efficiency by delivering integrated processes that span distributed IT functionalities and human workers.

An increase in the transaction execution automation level due to computerization of the process activities decreases process execution time, provides higher transaction volume capacity, and reduces human-generated errors. Collaboration facilities (as included in Oracle BPM Suite 11*g*) make complex exception handling much easier and cheaper, thus contributing toward higher productivity and efficiency.

Better visibility over a business transaction requires adequate monitoring of the underlying process. A process may be monitored at the top level to get general health-check data about the transactions relating to that process—for example, how many transactions are underway and how many are at what state of completion, ranges of process completion times, and fall-out percentages. Often these are the types of information that senior management are interested in. The process designers or those interested in continuous process improvement, on the other hand, would also like to track several performance parameters associated with the individual activities and responses of the performance of the edge applications that the process connects to. IT operations teams are generally concerned with system level performance of software and hardware, information regarding quick fault detection, and providing the expected level of service of the running systems for support of business continuity. Sales and marketing people would be interested in up-sell and cross-sell opportunities associated with a customer and his or her transactions. Explicit and digital description of the process showing all associated activities, rules and end systems, and events generated by the running business process instances are great facilitators of process visibility. Once all the activities in a process-based transaction are tractable, the creation of audit trails or the generation of alerts for use with compliance procedures also becomes easy. Process analyzers built into the BPMS (as in Oracle BPM Suite 11*g*) or companion tools like Business Activity Monitoring (for example, Oracle BAM) or Business Intelligence (for instance, Oracle BI) can be used to visualize a variety of process information easily.

High business agility has become an essential quality of the winning companies in today's globally competitive marketplace. Agility has to do with responding to planned and unplanned changes in business execution quickly; business processes are often an ideal place to orchestrate such changes. Collaborating business and IT participants can quickly modify existing processes as may be needed by the change imperatives. Also, reuse of either subprocesses or services (at process end points) can greatly reduce the response time to handle change. Use of externalized and hot-deployable business rules that can alter some aspects of the process execution (as is possible in Oracle BPM Suite 11*g*) is another way to increase business agility since some of the process changes can be incorporated directly by the business analysts without requiring long and expensive IT development projects.

Figure 1-1 summarizes the key BPM benefit categories, along with some of the typical metrics that can be used to monitor the benefit levels actually achieved.

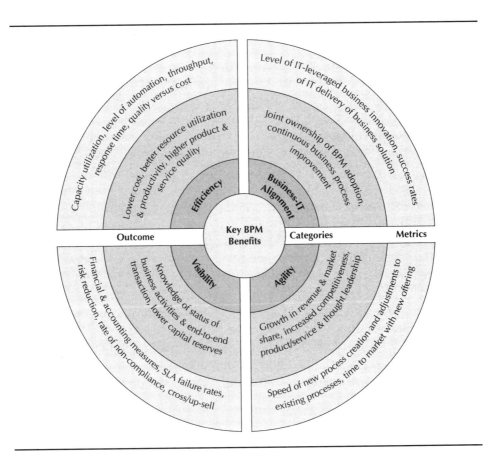

FIGURE 1-1. *Key BPM benefits*

BPM and Business Strategy

The notion of business strategy, made formal and popular by Michael Porter in the 1980s, refers to the set of concepts and prescriptions that a business adopts in order to maintain healthy growth and to generate sustained competitive advantage. For example, a business may want to provide the best price for products and services in its industry, or may excel in customer satisfaction, or may differentiate itself as an innovator in a niche market. Whatever the strategy of the business, ultimately proper management of its business processes is critical in achieving strategic goals. Hence, it is essential that BPM adoption aligns with the business strategies.

One approach to keeping BPM aligned with the execution of overall business strategies is to ensure that BPM supports and enhances the *value creation* activities and processes of the business (where value is something that the customer is willing to pay a price for). This approach is derived from Michael Porter's idea of enterprise value chains (*Competitive Advantage: Creating and Sustaining Superior Performance*, Free Press, 1985)— that is, the chain of business activities that incrementally add value on top of certain input in order to produce the output delivered to the customer (see Figure 1-2 for a schematic of an example of Porter's value chain for a software vendor).

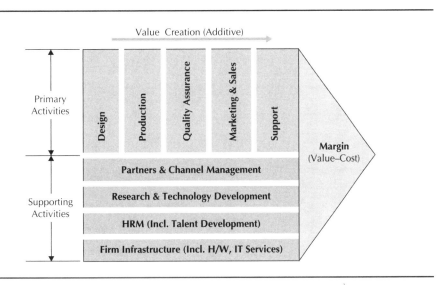

FIGURE 1-2. *An example of Porter's value chain for a software vendor*

Another approach stems from the work of Michael Treacy and Fred Wiersema around the mid-1990s. They held the view that a business has to focus on one of the following—(i) product leadership, (ii) customer intimacy, or (iii) operational excellence—to stay ahead of the competition. Treacy and Wiersema based their theory on a classification of customers based on their (the customers') main expectations from a company. Product leadership is achieved by superior and innovative product offerings. High-quality customer service and high levels of customer satisfaction are the central goals of customer intimacy. Operational excellence translates to higher efficiency and continuous improvement, and thus lower cost of products and services. BPM initiatives can align themselves to the corporate strategy by targeting business processes that serve the chosen corporate focus. As most modern businesses deal with diverse products and services in a wider demography, they may be required to excel on all three of the focus areas, albeit at different levels. As shown in Figure 1-3, it is natural to expect companies to have differing focus profiles depending on their high-level corporate goals and strategies.

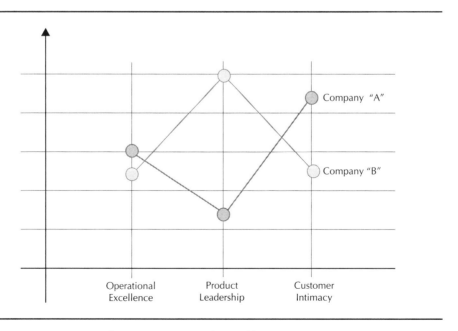

FIGURE 1-3. *Areas for organizational excellence*

In 1992, Robert Kaplan and David Norton introduced the idea of the Balanced Score Card (BSC) as a way to monitor (and help manage) the growth and leadership of a business. BSC sought to balance four perspectives of business strategy, for example, *financial, customer, internal processes,* and *learning and growth.* In the late 1990s through the early 2000s, Kaplan and Norton popularized the concept of *strategy maps* as an aid to the creation of BSCs. A strategy map is a network of value-generating strategic objectives showing cause-and-effect relations between them (the objectives). These strategic objectives are classified along the four BSC perspectives and thus provide a way to drill-down from a higher-level financial goal to, say, strategic objectives that need to be attained in the execution of business activities (the internal process perspective). The generic strategy map, following Kaplan and Norton, has four process themes: operations management (for example, supply-chain, production, distribution), customer management (such as CRM), innovation (for instance, R&D), and regulatory and social (for example, SOX or Basel-III compliance, safety, or community processes). Companies following BSC and strategy maps can align their BPM initiatives with corporate strategies by focusing BPM to improve the various process thematic strategic objectives.

BPM and IT Application Integration, Customization, and Modernization

Modern businesses rely heavily on IT and packaged (enterprise) applications like the generic ERP, SCM, HRM, CRM, and industry-specific applications like the provisioning, metering, and billing applications (for instance, in the communications or utilities industries). These applications process and store a great deal of information generated by, and passing through, the business. In order to support enterprise value chains, these silo-ed packaged applications have to be integrated for data exchange. Older enterprise application integration (EAI) practices used direct integration between applications (also called point-to-point or P2P), thus creating implicit business activity chains. This implicit nature of cross-application business processes greatly reduces the end-to-end visibility of business activities and prevents the tracking and auditing of business transactions. Also, in this type of EAI style, more and more P2P integrations are introduced as business requirements increase or are changed, leading to *integration spaghettis* that are very hard to maintain. Thus, the old style P2P EAI eventually consumes most of the IT budget and attention, and often becomes a source of errors in the execution of enterprise value chains.

While packaged applications do enable most of the information management in a business, simple out-of-the-box (OOTB) application implementations are almost nonexistent. In order to fit the packaged applications into a company's environment, some level of customization that go beyond configuration file changes are almost always necessary. These customizations, typically done by writing scripts or adding one-off coded extensions, are not cheap—some estimates put them at around 20 percent of the cost of the effort of the original implementation of the packaged application, on average, each time a packaged application is installed or upgraded. In fact, these customizations are usually the biggest bottlenecks during application upgrades; in some cases excessive customizations prevent timely upgrade of applications, thus preventing the users of the applications from realizing the benefits of progressive releases of the software. A far better approach to handling the business requirements not provided by OOTB functionalities of packaged applications is to capture them in the process management layer implemented using middleware (such as Oracle BPM Suite) outside the packaged applications. In this approach, smaller units of application functionality are packaged and exposed as *services,* which are then combined together along with additional business logic in the process layer (Service Oriented Integration, or SOI). In most cases, this approach produces solutions that have a far lower total cost of ownership (TCO) over the life of the applications, provides a mechanism to easily incorporate changing business requirements, and automatically helps with the challenge of end-to-end tracking and monitoring of business transactions, particularly when the transactions span multiple applications. Figure 1-4 illustrates the basic ideas behind P2P and BPM/SOA-based application integration styles.

Businesses have become a lot more attentive to the quality of business transactions, whether it is an external facing delivery of product or services to the customer or it is an internal supporting process. In order to provide timely service to customers, businesses are vigilant about system performance bottlenecks that could disrupt customer service level agreements (SLAs). To improve the quality of service, businesses also want to better empower their knowledge workers. In order to identify potential up-sell or cross-sell opportunities, businesses are looking for greater intelligence from their business transactions, some even in (near) real-time. Such advanced requirements are commonly met by what are called composite (business) applications that are composed over several traditional packaged applications. Often these composite applications either include, or are supported by, business processes as the components that are

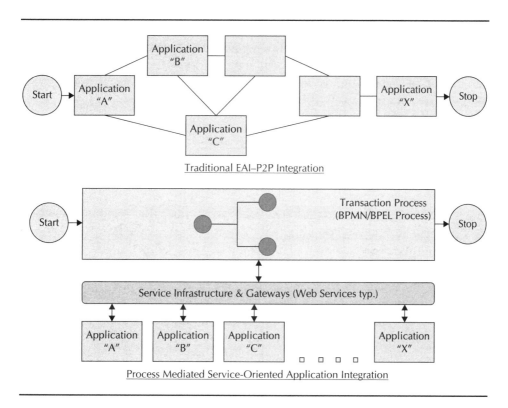

FIGURE 1-4. *Traditional and BPM/SOA-based application integration*

primarily responsible for business logic execution. Of course, besides process management, additional software components like the Web 2.0–style UI platform, business intelligence modules, and business activity monitoring and complex event processing capabilities are also typically required to build modern composite applications.

Businesses that have been around for a while are often somewhat burdened by legacy IT applications such as those on mainframes computers. Several decades ago, these legacy applications surely provided high operational efficiencies and some competitive advantages, but in modern times with high-quality yet cheap commodity hardware and significantly more flexible software platforms, these legacy applications and platforms are seen as too expensive to run and maintain, and too large and too rigid to admit business-driven changes cheaply and quickly. While most legacy applications are closed—that is, they are black box monoliths (or at least behave like one)—currently, there are many options available to expose various portions of their functionalities as services. Once this is done, the legacy applications can essentially be treated as (relatively) modern packaged applications for the purposes of creating BPM-based composite applications.

BPM and Business-IT Alignment

The alignment between business and IT teams has long been a topic of great interest. As shown in Figure 1-5, a true business-IT alignment should be bidirectional—in other words, IT delivers accurately, efficiently, and in a timely manner, specific technology-based capabilities that the business needs to execute on the company's long-term vision, as well as its day-to-day operations (business-to-IT). The business is also proactive in creating strategic and innovative projects based on the broad capabilities of modern IT infrastructure (IT-to-business). The benefits of good business-IT alignment are well-known. At a summary level, good business-IT alignment plays a critical role in helping companies achieve sustained competitive advantage and produce high shareholder value, often five to ten times higher than the average performer in its industry, and at average IT-spend levels. However, it takes strong management commitment, changes in organizational behavior,

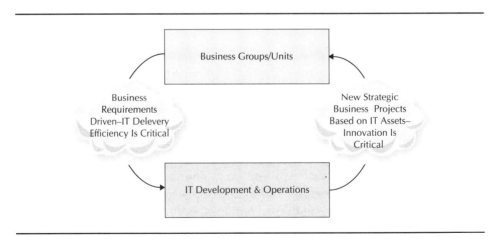

FIGURE 1-5. *Business-IT bidirectional alignment*

correct technology exploitation strategies, and some initial investment to achieve better-than-average business-IT alignment. A successful BPM adoption can go a long way in delivering this goal.

BPM, by its very definition, involves participation and leadership from the business more than most other technology projects. The functionalities of a typical BPM-based application are directly recognized by business groups, and they are typically much more eager to see BPM adoption be successful. A full-featured BPM suite such as Oracle's BPM Suite 11*g* provides multiple ways in which IT and the business can collaborate throughout the life cycle of BPM applications, starting at the conceptual and requirement gathering phases through the feedback gathering and continuous business process improvement stages. From a BPM platform perspective, this translates to providing easy and role-specific access to view various BPM assets, such as process models and business rules, performance indicators, process-related documents, and in facilitating collaborative generation and modification of such assets.

Today, business requirements change rather quickly, and traditional software development styles cannot cope up with such fast-paced changes. This leads to frustration over inadequate IT capabilities to sustain and grow the business. A suitable combination of comprehensive BPM methodology, software tools that allow rapid application development and tuning, and incremental (shorter delivery cycles of four to six months) and iterative project delivery styles that can adapt to changes rapidly and economically are necessary to minimize the business-IT gap that can arise from long and waterfall-style software development projects. Another key contributor to the business-IT gap is the communication impedance between business and IT. Using collaboration features of BPM and associated software, adopting a model-based execution strategy supported by appropriate BPM software (for example, Oracle BPM 11*g*), and by using vernacular clearly understood by all involved parties along with a suitable governance model that spans both business and IT, this gap can also be substantially reduced or even eliminated.

Business Process Types

As we have indicated before, processes are comprised of a collection of activities and information about how these activities are executed. For a process to be called a business process, it must have some relevance to the overall working of the business. Based on the type of functionality a business process delivers, it can be classified under one of the following three (see, for example, *Business Process Change,* 2nd ed., Paul Harmon, Morgan Kaufmann Publishers, 2007):

- **Core processes**   These business processes carry out the main activities of the business that typically have interactions with the customers and produce revenue. These processes are often derived from, or are closely related to, *enterprise value chains* (*EVCs*). The ability to execute core business processes correctly and efficiently has direct implications on customer satisfaction and operational efficiency. An order-to-cash business process (a process triggered by a customer order and terminating in collecting payment after the goods or services have been delivered) would be an example of a core business process.

- **Supporting processes**   These business processes, generally speaking, support core business processes, directly or indirectly, by helping execute certain activities of those core business processes. For example, if the order-to-cash core process had high-level activities like "design product" or "manufacture product," then these could in turn be accomplished by specialized business processes supported by the design groups or the manufacturing groups within the business.

- **Management processes**   These business processes mainly create the underlying capabilities that are necessary for core or supporting processes. For example, financial planning or budgeting processes, partner recruitment processes, and supply chain optimization processes are examples of management processes. There are also administrative processes like employee on-boarding and employee system access provisioning that may be viewed as special management processes. Management processes generate or support broad capabilities and are not usually tied to a specific business transaction.

The American Productivity and Quality Center's Process Classification Framework (see www.apqc.org) classifies core or value adding processes as operating processes and the rest of the processes as management and supporting processes—this appears to follow Porter's value chain model described earlier.

Business processes have also been characterized by the type of activities they handle. For example, *human-centric* processes were used to guide human worker activities (this is the traditional workflow type); *document-centric* processes handled and automated, where possible, the movement of documents and the further processing of some of the information in those documents (a faxed order analyzed by an OCR-based system and automatically creating a purchase order record in a company's order management system would be an example of this type of process); and *decision-centric* processes facilitated multistage and multiperson decision making (a process to determine the appropriate insurance premium for a complex risk will fall under this category). Such categorizations were helpful to keep the focus on process work and encouraged software vendors to deliver high-quality, albeit very specific, software solutions. Current approaches to BPM adoption tie higher-level business processes to value chains and to the mechanism of value creation, which have broader scopes than any of the human-centric, document-centric, or decision-centric processes. Thus, modern BPM requires the ability to handle more than one of the preceding process types simultaneously.

Generally speaking, processes that are well-known (or essentially standardized) in a given industry can contribute toward better organizational performance or some level of competitive advantage, mainly via process efficiencies. Innovation opportunities are higher in processes that are not as public and can provide a substantial competitive advantage. Clearly, a business process design, as well as creation, deployment, management, and monitoring considerations would depend on the type of process, as well as the business goals behind it.

Capturing a Business Process

One of the basic activities in modern BPM is to describe the business process in a computer-understandable fashion. Over the years there have been many efforts to come up with modeling notations that aimed at balancing the ability to capture business requirements, the ease of expression, and the syntactical adequacy required to ultimately create executable, process-based software applications. At this time, two standards, Business Process Modeling Notation or BPMN (www.omg.org) and Business Process Execution Language or BPEL (www.oasis-open.org) are receiving the highest industry adoption, both from software vendors and from user communities. While BPMN specifies both execution semantics and graphical notations to be used in depicting a process, BPEL restricts itself to process execution. Thus, vendors have come up with their own graphical representation of BPEL modeling elements. We will discuss BPM notations in more detail later in the book. Here we would like to capture the essence of a typical business process using basic modeling elements, without insisting on high-tech rigor.

An executing business process is associated with particular business transactions (for example, a new mobile phone order or a request to cancel previously ordered books). This transaction-specific business process is an instance of a predefined business process model executing within some BPM engine or server and carries information obtained from the customer as well as additional information it generates in the process of carrying out the business transaction. Some of the information associated with a business process instance is transient (that is, they are retired by the time the process execution is completed, while some others persist for a variety of durations. A business process is kicked off as a result of the receipt of a starting trigger or a triggering (business) event—for example, as a result of an interaction with a customer. After the required processing (that is, the completion of all the tasks involved in handling the associated business transaction), the process reaches a state of completion. Thus, a process has at least one start and one end state. Multiple starts, as may be the case where the starting input could be received via different channels and at different levels of preprocessing, and multiple ends that may signify different completion alternatives, including aborted processing, are of course possible.

Tasks, chunks of actual work associated with a business process, can be either automated or manual. Automated tasks are handled by one or more computer applications using messaging mechanisms between the process instance and the applications. Manual tasks are completed by human process operators who may receive the request for completion of such tasks either directly from the BPM application or indirectly via other intermediary applications such as e-mail or a web application. When a task is completed, depending on the guiding rules incorporated in the business process model, the next set of tasks is taken up for completion, and the process execution progresses. Communications to and from a process can be either *synchronous* or *asynchronous*. Thus, to describe a process we will need the ability to represent different types of tasks and their executors, transition paths from one task to another, rules and decisions associated with such transitions, and messaging in and out of the process.

Business events associated with a business process are part of the definition of a process. Events are signatures of something that either happened or did not happen (in other words, after the wait time for something to happen expires) and are communicated as special messages. A business process can be subject to triggering events (for example, start processes, interrupt processes, and so on); the process itself can generate events for its own working (such as timer and calendar events indicating when some task must be undertaken or aborted) or for the benefit of process users (for instance, possible fraud alert, likely up-sell or cross-sell opportunities, and others).

Often we can have situations where a process must either complete all of the tasks in a given set (of tasks) or none at all. For example, if some money is transferred from one bank account to another, both accounts must be modified, holdings in one decreased and in the other increased essentially at the same time so as to keep the overall accounting states consistent. If one of the account modifications fail, both the accounts must be returned to their states before the process started and the process itself must be aborted—some remedial actions could of course follow after such an abnormal termination of the process. These two account updates are considered to be within a *transactional* boundary and the action returning all concerned systems to their original states is called a *roll-back.* A process may have several such transactional scopes and this is an important type of information that needs to be captured while describing a business process.

Just as in the case of use case descriptions, we need to cater for *exceptions* that may occur while a business process is executing. Exceptions signify deviations from the normal or ordinarily expected path of process execution (sometimes called the *happy-path* or the *sunny-day scenario*). Exceptions can occur due to data errors (for example, data types or values that cannot be understood or handled by the business process) or can be raised depending on certain data values of task states (such as loan applications above a certain amount with an applicant of less-than-adequate creditworthiness may require some human approvals where the human tasks can be raised as exceptions in the business process). Exception handling involves rework or manual work which is expensive, can lead to delays in process execution completion, and can result in the loss of income or profit and the erosion of customer satisfaction. Thus, intelligent and efficient exception handling needs to be part of a process definition.

A variety of operational policies including security policies like access control, and process performance indicators such as execution response times for the overall process and some selected task levels, are also important information that should be captured as part of a business process definition.

In order to keep the details of a business process manageable, in case of nontrivial business processes many activities in a process can be formulated as processes themselves—thus, the higher-level activity is realized as a lower-level subprocess. This leads to a hierarchical composition of business processes. Such hierarchical decomposition also helps partition the business process into groups of closely related activities, thus affording the benefits of modularity, the separation of concerns, and in many cases the reuse of existing functionalities.

Written text and visual representations are used to capture a process description. A business context diagram like the one shown in Figure 1-6 can provide a high-level summary of a process description. While common flow chart–like techniques have been used to visualize high-level pictures of business processes, the job of adequately capturing a business process goes far beyond what can be described by flow charts, and what's required are more sophisticated process analysis and modeling tools, and practices.

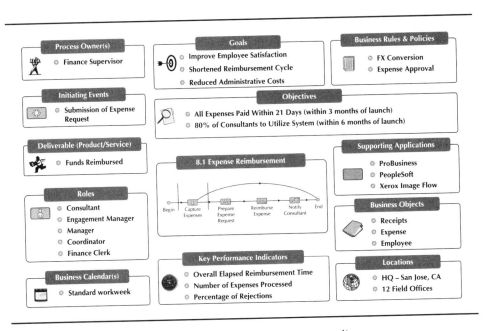

FIGURE 1-6. *An example business process context diagram*

Business Process Architecture and Frameworks

Just as Business Architecture (BA) lays out the way business operates via its organizational structure and employee actions, and just as Enterprise Architecture (EA) describes the way organization units and technology systems work in order to execute business operations, Business Process Architecture (BPA) defines the high-level architecture of all the key business processes of a business. The scope of BPA is much broader than process diagrams or models and includes the knowledge of all the subprocesses and business activities that roll up to some value chain, the interaction between the process and various internal and external human and machine resources, key performance indicators of the process, and process governance (see Figure 1-7). As may be expected, BPA is closely related to EA and BA, and depending on the scope and definitions of EA and BA in an organization, BPA may have some overlap with components of EA and BA.

BPA connects, by design, business strategies with business processes and activities that occur within the business or with its partners and customers.

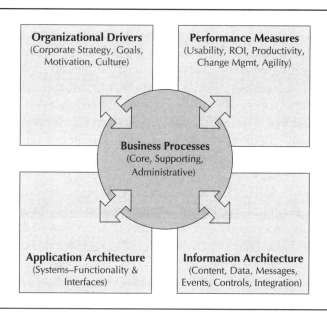

FIGURE 1-7.   *Components of Business Process Architecture*

BPA facilitates the alignment of IT and HR resources, and of business policies and rules. BPA is an essential starting point of the broader enterprise adoption of BPM and guides overall process excellence and various quality improvement initiatives like Six Sigma and Lean. Done right, BPA becomes a valuable corporate asset that can be used by senior management, line managers, and employees to gain a better understanding of how their business really works and to suggest possible improvements to their business execution. Software products like Oracle Business Process Analysis Suite (OBPA) can be used to create, document, and publish BPA models.

A business process framework is part of BPA and describes how the critical value chains of an enterprise are expressed via networks of business processes. These process networks are often hierarchies of subprocesses. Process hierarchies are generally delineated using *Levels*, with Level 0 typically denoting the top-level process directly matching some value chain. Individual tasks are usually found at lower levels—for example, 4 and 5. We will delve more into process leveling later in the book (see the BPM Methodology section). In the meantime, it is worthwhile to point out here that a process framework provides a useful structure to organize business activities and to create business process performance measures at different process levels.

Enterprise architects and process architects usually have the responsibility of coming up with process frameworks that are suitable for a business, and this is not always an easy task. Many aspects of business processes must be considered, along with the diverse interests of relevant stakeholders. Fortunately, in some cases, industry community organizations have already created such frameworks, which can be used at least as a reference by individual companies. The *SCOR framework* from the Supply Chain Council (SCC, www.supply-chain.org) and the *eBusiness Telecom Operations Map* (*eTOM*) from the TeleManagement Forum (TMF, www.tmforum.com) are a couple of popular examples.

As shown in Figure 1-8, SCOR captures the business execution required to support a value chain in three levels. While SCOR starts with a supply chain as its highest level process, usually the supply chain is one of the processes of a yet higher level value chain, such as Order Management or Fullfilment. With the value chain being designated as Level 0, SCOR's highest-level process, the supply chain then becomes a Level 1 process. According to SCOR, a supply chain is made up of three basic types of activities: Source (S), Make (M),

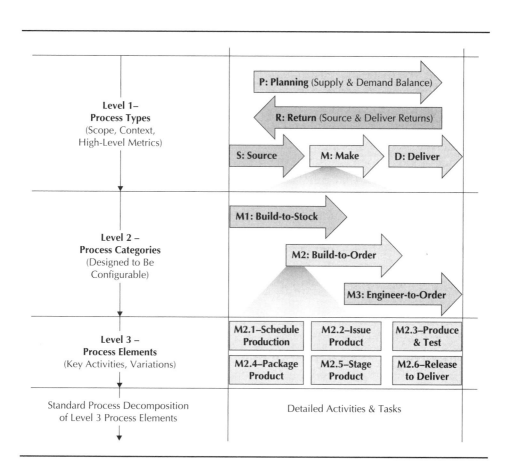

FIGURE 1-8. *Process classification using SCO*

and Deliver (D). Many types of S, M, and D exist, and these are specified in Level 2 of a SCOR framework. Level 3 indentifies the different variations for each of the S, M, and D types in Level 2. Strictly speaking, this is not a traditional hierarchical top-to-bottom decomposition, but rather a relationship diagram. SCOR does not define levels finer than Level 3—those details are left to the individual companies adopting SCOR.

Since SCC has around 700 member companies, many of whom collaborate in the extended value chains (for example, supplier-manufacturer-distributor),

SCOR's usefulness goes beyond the boundaries of an individual company. It unifies process terminologies making inter-company collaboration easier. SCOR is also able to provide industrywide process performance measures that can help a company compare its own performance against its industry peers and make business process improvement decisions to stay competitive. A SCOR *thread diagram* is a convenient and easy-to-interpret depiction of a supply chain going across multiple companies and geographies connecting input resources to output products for the customer.

SCOR framework is also helpful in mergers-and-acquisitions (M&A) situations, where the creation of the merged business execution can often be a substantial challenge. An example of the highly successful use of SCOR is noted in Harmon's book *Business Process Change,* where after the merger of HP and Compaq, the merger team was able to establish the merged business processes in about a month using the SCOR framework. Although originally designed for optimization of supply chains, the ideas behind SCOR are generally applicable to many higher-level processes and value chains, and in fact, efforts are currently underway to explore such possibilities.

The eTOM framework, developed and popularized by TMF, a telecom industry forum, is designed specifically for handling the unique requirements of telecommunications (and by extension, most communication) companies. IT and network-based technologies are heavily used by telecoms to provide their services to customers and communicate with their partners, and this is reflected in the eTOM framework. At the top level, eTOM takes a matrix view of the organizational and functional divisions (see Figure 1-9). The rows and columns of this matrix designate the high-level processes (for example, Fulfillment, Assurance, Billing, and Operations Support) and the management categories (such as Supplier/Partner, Resources, Service, and Market/Product/CRM), respectively. The individual cells of the matrix then define the next level of detail. For example, the "Supplier/Partner (S/P) Management–Billing Process" cell of the eTOM matrix contains capabilities or functionalities like "S/P Settlements and Billing Management" and "S/P Interface Management," or the "Service Management–Fulfillment Process" cell has "Service Configuration and Activation" as key functionalities or capabilities. The eTOM framework does a good job of identifying the key capabilities a telecom must master and excel in, however, it does not explicitly depict, particularly for non-telecom experts, how these capabilities relate to the more

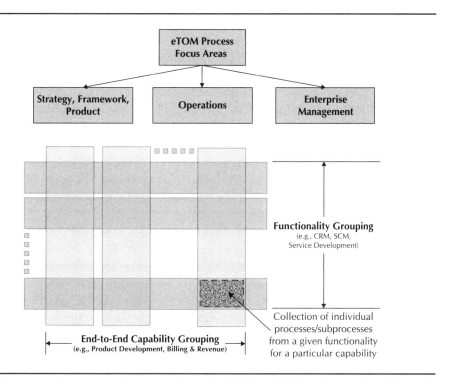

FIGURE 1-9. *eTOM process architecture strategy*

traditional notion of enterprise value chains. One would have to select the relevant group capabilities and their supporting business processes needed for a typical value chain (for instance, a Phone Service or Broadband Service offering) for any value chain type analysis.

Besides SCOR and eTOM, there are several other industry consortia led initiatives to create business process frameworks. The ACORD framework for the insurance industry is an example (see www.acord.org). It is clear that as industry groups adopt standard process frameworks, intra- and intercompany BPM adoption will speed up. However, this appears to be a work-in-progress. In the meantime, enterprise architects and process architects have the responsibility to provide their companies with process frameworks that best fit those companies. Of course, they can and should consider the pros and cons of existing frameworks like SCOR and eTOM at least as inspirations for their process framework development work.

The BPM Life Cycle

Most engineering methodologies follow similar sequences of activities spanning analysis, design, implementation, and deployment. In modern software engineering methods, these activities are applied iteratively while making incremental changes. The life cycle of an executable business process is, in many ways, similar to traditional software development methodologies, but with a particular emphasis on inbuilt monitoring and analysis driving the iterative cycles of continuous (incremental) improvement. The diagram in Figure 1-10 shows the business process life cycle with a more detailed sequence of activities in the cycle of continuous business process improvement.

In the case of business process engineering, analysis occurs in two separate activities, shown in Figure 1-10 with the labels "identification" and "define/refine." These are separated because of the different activities involved in getting started with process automation. In order to enter the continuous improvement cycle, an analysis activity is required to identify business processes and select those most appropriate for automation. Identification involves describing the process only at the highest level in order to understand its current ("as-is") state, while process selection applies analytical techniques to evaluate the process for automation. The details of business process identification and selection are described in more detail in the BPM Methodology section.

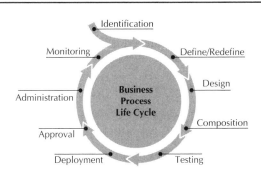

FIGURE 1-10. *BPM life cycle phases*

On entering the cycle for the first time, the business process undergoes further analysis (definition) to describe it at the next level of detail and to apply the first iteration of improvements (refinement). Subsequent iterations through the cycle focus on refinement since most of the definition exists, while analysis efforts are concerned with incremental improvements. These subsequent iterations also benefit greatly from the analytical information provided by monitoring previously deployed processes.

Design is a technical activity that explores the IT capabilities and determines the feasibility of the implementation of the process model as an executable process. Where possible, existing services are identified for use in subsequent implementation activities, but where gaps exist they must either be filled through software (or service) engineering or the process specification is returned to the previous step for rework. This is an example of various loops that can occur within the main business process life cycle.

Implementation is replaced with business application composition and associated testing. Unlike implementation in software engineering, composition involves the mostly declarative coding of business rules and the graphical "wiring" of messages between service components.

Business process administration and monitoring are closely linked in the traditional sense of OA&M (Operations, Administration, and Management) since monitoring provides information for process control dashboards; however, monitoring plays an important role in the business process life cycle since it also drives the analysis needed as part of the next iteration of process improvement.

As we will describe later in the book, the Oracle Business Process Engineering Methodology elaborates on this outline while providing a business-focused approach that is intended to augment, rather than replace, existing software engineering practices.

The BPMS and BPM Ecosystem

A complete yet minimalistic BPM tool set would include a process modeler to define the process and a process engine to execute many instances of that process. Business process execution captures and generates a lot of valuable information. As lower-level processes get connected up to high-level value chains, many different stakeholders, from IT's technical people to operations groups to senior management become interested in information about and within the business processes. For example, a head of a business unit may want to see high-level statistics on the order management processes to get an idea of sales volumes and seasonal trends, while an operations person may be interested in knowing how healthily the business process engine (server) is running at a given time. A business analyst may be interested in altering certain behavior of some executable processes via editing business rules, while a process architect may want to relate aspects of enterprise architecture or business architecture to specific business processes in order to align organizational structures, roles and responsibilities, and success measures across divisional boundaries. As should be apparent by now, the minimalistic tool set that we mentioned at the beginning of this paragraph will not be adequate to serve the needs of all the BPM stakeholders and thus a richer definition of a BPM software system is required. So, a few years ago the notion of Business Process Management Suites (BPMSs) started becoming popular to describe this expanded BPM software system.

As an example of the capabilities of a BPMS, we can inspect Gartner's list, which includes the modeling and analysis of structured and unstructured processes and associated information with adequate richness to do the following: model most practical process situations; process change management in both design and execution stages with the *round-tripping* (that is, keeping in sync bidirectionally) of design and the executable versions of the process; manage interactions between humans and systems along with the associated content; use and manipulate business rules that drive decisions associated with processes; monitor and report the processing of information and events; generate a framework to connect to technical end-points of the process (for example, web services); and manage various process assets throughout the life cycle of the process.

A BPMS should, according to Gartner, support at least four key BPM use cases, namely, implementation of an industry or business-specific process application or solution, support continuous process improvement, facilitate process-based Service Oriented Architecture (SOA) service design and service consumption, and provide tooling support of business-IT collaboration, particularly in business transformation initiatives. As will be described later in the book, Oracle BPM Suite 11*g* is a BPMS that supports capabilities similar to Gartner's list and includes either as part of its own install or as a closely connected product, Oracle Business Process Analysis (OBPA), Oracle Business Rules (OBR), Business Activity Monitoring (BAM), collaborative and Enterprise 2.0 (E2.0)–style process portals using Oracle WebCenter, a complete application integration layer and a rich business-to-business (B2B) integration layer via Oracle SOA Suite features, and a wide variety of business event generation, capture, and processing features (also known as Complex Event Processing or CEP).

BPM and SOA

Service Oriented Architecture (SOA) is currently a popular paradigm to develop, package, deploy, and consume IT functionalities that could be either capabilities coming from enterprise applications like ERP, CRM, HRM, and SCM, or homegrown software modules. These packages of functionalities are termed *services* that can be utilized or consumed by other applications like a BPM application. In fact, such services just become the end-points of business processes. Also, in most cases a BPM application itself can be exposed as a service, thus allowing yet other applications to leverage such BPM applications—for example, a web application could connect to a BPM application via service interfaces. As Figure 1-11 illustrates, agility delivered by SOA-enabled BPM spans both business and IT.

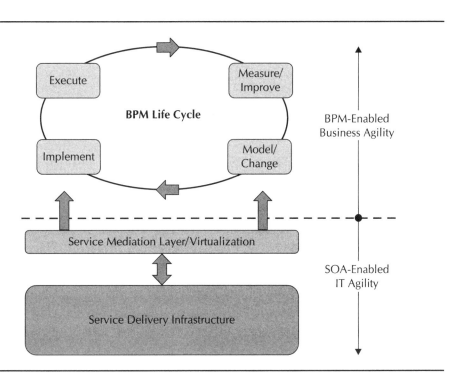

FIGURE 1-11. *BPM with SOA—top-to-bottom agility*

SOA provides a loosely connected technology platform where the service consumers (such as a BPM application) do not need any knowledge of the implementation and deployment of services in order to consume them. SOA service providers are obligated to provide service functionalities and quality-of-service (QoS) in accordance with service contract specifications used by the service consumers. When created on top of a SOA, the robustness of the overall BPM application increases due to proven and tested functionalities of the services. BPM, along with SOA, also enhances the agility and change resilience of the BPM application. Reuse of IT functionalities via published services speeds up BPM application development. A BPM application on SOA also provides a good separation of concerns: when a change is required in the BPM application, process logic level changes can be easily incorporated via edits to the process itself or by altering the associated business rules, often by business analysts or process architects without much involvement from IT developers, while changes required in service functionalities can be done behind the service interfaces by IT developers. Using versioning, it is possible to incorporate such changes into the business process without impacting existing applications. On the flip-side, process analysis phases sometimes produce requirements for new service development—this service identification helps SOA efforts focus on services that have immediate utility. Thus, a combined SOA-enabled BPM approach offers benefits greater than what either SOA or BPM could individually provide. Of course, in order to adopt SOA-enabled BPM, the appropriate modifications to methodology and practices are necessary during the planning and engineering phases. Also, SOA-enabled BPM challenges can be greatly eased by software platforms where the modelers and developers can move between BPM and SOA layers easily. Oracle's BPM Suite 11*g* is built on top of Oracle's SOA Suite infrastructure and provides great tooling support for SOA-enabled BPM.

Succeeding in BPM Initiatives

As with anything else, the success of BPM initiatives in a company depends on the expectations of the stakeholders and the chosen success measures associated with the initiatives. Both the expectation and the success measures vary depending on the scope of a particular BPM initiative. Broadly speaking, such initiatives could be either *strategic* or *tactical.* Strategic BPM adoption success requires appropriate focus in organizational culture, software and hardware tools, and adoption methodologies, and involves adequate planning (see Figure 1-12). Such BPM projects are motivated by an overall vision of excellence of a company and enjoy the substantial commitment and participation of senior management. These projects directly align with enterprise value chains and strategy maps, support implementation or improvement of core business processes and span many organizational divisions. Successful strategic BPM initiatives help companies raise their *BPM capability maturity* to handle increasingly difficult and mission-critical processes. At higher levels of BPM maturity, a company evolves into a process-centric organization; the management and employees of the company are then quite adept in leveraging BPM for operational excellence and sustained competitive advantage—this is depicted in the structure of the organizational units and their interplays, and in the way business problems are expressed in terms of BPM components. Strategic BPM is aimed at longer-term results. Executed along an appropriate strategic BPM roadmap,

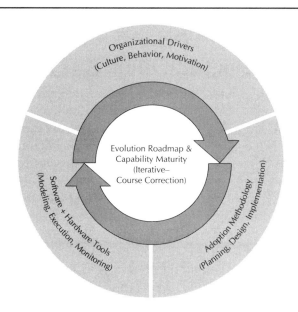

FIGURE 1-12. *Focus area for BPM adoption success*

companies achieve high BPM maturity usually in two to four years. Some of the key success measures of strategic BPM are business agility, leadership in product innovation, excellence in customer service, a better ability to execute on business transformations and M&As successfully, and high employee satisfaction.

Tactical BPM projects, on the other hand, tend to focus on solving near-term and apparently isolated problems—for example, a few known processes needing improvement or some process defects requiring correction. Such projects are usually of short duration, say, on the order of four to six months each, often involve only a few organizational units, and may not necessarily have or require senior management level visibility. It is quite common to see processes handled in tactical BPM projects as those supporting core and higher-level business processes or coarse-grain activities therein. Some of the key success measures of tactical BPM projects are the reduction in process cycle time, the level of visibility and transparency of business activities, an increase in the level of automation, the reduction in human effort, improvement in error-rates and exception handling, and the degree of abstraction of process control to business users.

A company adopting BPM at a strategic level will create an enterprise-level BPM adoption roadmap and framework for architecture and governance for the participating organizational units to leverage and share. Within or associated with strategic BPM adoption, a company should and will undertake many BPM projects, and the outcome of these projects will yield solutions to specific business problems, thus providing the incentive for the company to continue investing in such initiatives. Seen in isolation, most of these projects (under the strategic BPM adoption program) would look very similar to tactical projects. However, process implementation projects under strategic programs differ from those under tactical programs in significant ways. For example, in the context of strategic BPM programs: (i) projects will receive strong commitment and high-level guidance from senior management; (ii) business groups will own the project goals, either by themselves or in partnership with IT; (iii) individual BPM projects will be subjected to strategic guidelines and governance; (iv) where applicable, individual projects will be required to produce reusable assets for the benefit of other projects; and (v) a special organizational structure like a BPM center of excellence (CoE) or a center of competence, either virtual or dedicated, will be active in facilitating, collecting, and disseminating organizational learning related to BPM, thus help sustain and increase the

BPM maturity of the company. Also, under a successful strategic adoption program, as the BPM maturity level of the company goes up, success measures for individual projects will also steadily improve.

In order to better the chances of success of BPM programs, a company must pay close attention to a set of success enablers or critical success factors (CSFs). Some of these CSFs are:

- **Clarity of BPM program goals**   Clear statements regarding program goals, stakeholder benefits, possible challenges and corresponding solution approaches must be adequately communicated to all program participants.

- **Identification and assignments of program participants**   BPM initiatives involve a wide variety of participants that may include senior management, program directors, architects, analysts, operations people, and end-user experts. At different stages of the BPM life cycle, these participants will have different roles and responsibilities that must be clearly understood by all participants. Program and process owners have the additional responsibility of driving the overall success of the program.

- **BPM methodology and program governance**   Adherence to a suitable BPM methodology is important for successful BPM adoption. Such a methodology outlines the activities to be performed at each of the BPM life cycle phase and prescribes best practices for executing them. In case of a combined SOA and BPM adoption, this methodology should also indicate the necessary touch-points between SOA- and BPM-related activities and specify activities that bridge SOA and BPM initiatives. A BPM methodology must also facilitate iterative project delivery strategies for BPM implementation. For BPM adoption, comprehensive and adequate program governance becomes even more critical due to the wider range of participants and activities. BPM governance must span both business and IT participants and cover both the design-time and runtime aspects of BPM implementation. (See Part III of this book for some discussion on BPM methodology and governance.)

- **Appropriate success measures**   In order to monitor and guide BPM adoption to success, appropriate success measures are highly important.

These measures must not be too numerous yet must cover the interest of different stakeholders of the program—for example, senior management, business sponsors, technical experts and IT developers, IT operations, and end-users.

- **Scope management** As with most projects, project scopes must be managed with respect to the amount of functionality and time lines. It is essential that process selection ties to prioritized business requirements and the scope of individual projects are kept small enough for easier project control yet are adequate for delivering real business value.

- **BPM maturity and adoption roadmap** For a company that intends to evolve toward a process-centric organization, it needs a framework for systematically developing its BPM competency. BPM capability maturity models provide such a framework (see Part III of the book). For example, Oracle's BPM maturity identifies of the order of a hundred BPM-related capabilities, ranging from business and organizational concerns to IT development and operations tasks. These capabilities are grouped under eight labels (for instance, Architecture, Operations Administration and Management, and so on) and five levels of maturity are defined for them. The spread of the capabilities assures comprehensiveness of the overall BPM competency development, and the maturity levels indicate an organizational ability to undertake projects of a certain complexity and mission-criticality. Adoption roadmaps combine immediate and long-term needs of the company with respect to BPM maturity with BPM investment ROIs, and help guide the BPM adoption.

- **Funding model** Mechanisms that fund BPM adoption programs at project and enterprise levels can be leveraged to guide the evolution of such programs. For example, a business group funding a particular BPM implementation project becomes naturally interested in the successful completion of that project and is willing to participate more closely with the IT teams, or the program directors looking to include activities that produce sharable benefits and increase organizational BPM maturity should find some corporate budget or shared pool of resources to help accomplish their goals.

- **Change management** Since business processes impact business operations including the day-to-day work of employees, BPM adoption invariably causes a certain amount of change in the activities that are done and the way they are done. In order to avoid the usual resistance to change, adequate communication regarding the benefits of such changes and employee retraining become critical to BPM adoption success.

A primary goal of BPM is to improve the state of the business. In this regard, an organizational culture where business and IT are bidirectionally aligned provides the right environment for a successful BPM adoption. Such a culture is a deeper attribute of an organization and is one of the most difficult things to achieve. Organizational development and management techniques do exist that can help in overcoming this challenge. While a comprehensive discussion on such techniques are deemed outside the scope of this book, we can point out that effective collaboration between all program participants can go a long way in closing the business-IT gap.

Finally, we would also like to make some remarks regarding the importance of a proper BPM technology platform that support activities of participants through the BPM life cycle phases in successful BPM adoption. For example, such tools must make collaboration easy and effective. They must provide role-based tool interfaces and common metadata for process assets so that business users as well as technical developers can find the right environment to work in. When deployed, these systems should be scalable and reliable, and offer adequate visibility of the running process as well as provide policy-based management of such processes. As will be shown later in the book, Oracle BPM 11*g* fulfills these requirements nicely.

Summary

In this chapter, we provided an overview of different aspects of BPM and its adoption in a company. Currently, interest in BPM is quite high, resulting in a lot of BPM-related activities by software vendors, analysts, consulting companies, industry organizations, and end-user communities. Thus, it is expected that BPM as a discipline is likely to mature rapidly in the near future.

From BPM technology and solution architecture points of view, we are likely to see a greater use of collaboration and social media, E2.0-style portals as the face of BPM applications, the leveraging of events to manage processes as well as to derive additional value from process transaction, and increased adoption of SOA-enabled BPM. Also, contemporary momentum around cloud computing will impact the way BPM tools and engines are developed, packaged, sold, and used.

CHAPTER
2

Standards in BPM

s in other technologies, standards play a vital role in BPM adoption. They help with fostering skills, lead to better and more consistent products and vendor offerings, aid in the interoperability with other technologies, reduce vendor lock-in, ease implementations with patterns and best practices, and facilitate the reuse and longevity of assets. As BPM and related technologies have been evolving over the last two decades, so have the various attempts to create standards applicable to BPM, especially in the area of notations and executable meta-models. While some of these attempts did not survive the test of time because they either failed to generate enough interest in the industry or got absorbed into other emerging initiatives, the standards that have taken hold are well situated to become as ubiquitous as SQL is to database programming. This is rapidly leading to vendors and user communities focusing their efforts on increasing BPM adoption through maturing product offerings and implementation practices.

Although a typical technology user does not always need to be highly knowledgeable about the finer details of all the applicable standards in order to use the technology, an understanding of the most frequently encountered standards can surely help the user appreciate the nuances of the technical platforms, and thus better leverage the strengths and avoid the weaknesses of such platforms. This section presents an overview of the evolution of BPM notations and standards and points out the usefulness of the currently popular ones in the context of different activities related to BPM adoption.

The Need for Standards in BPM

Ease of communication among various stakeholders and project participants, portability and interoperability of engineering models in the presence of heterogeneous technology platforms, and cross-industry benchmarking of application performance are some of the key drivers behind the use of commonly accepted standards specifications. The creation of standards is relatively easy and adoptions are usually pervasive for simpler technologies that often have one or few specific usage patterns. Standards like IP, HTTP, and DNS are such examples. BPM, on the other hand, is often regarded as multi-disciplinary, an aggregate of many activities and artifacts, making the task of formulation of standards and their broad acceptance challenging. Also, a typical BPM application has, besides process and rules definitions, connections to a wide range of computer applications, user interfaces, and monitoring dashboards. Hence, several standards, some regarded as core and the rest supporting, are needed to adequately represent BPM. Naturally, these standards progress at different levels of maturity at any given time.

One approach to identifying the type of standards needed to support BPM is to recall the business process life cycle mentioned in Chapter 1, and then take some of the key phases like design, composition/implementation, deployment, and administration/monitoring, and investigate the type standards required for each of those phases to guide the related activities and artifacts.

For example, in the design phase, the main focus is around creation of the diagrams representing the process flows, and possibly high-level specifications of human interfaces (for, say, human tasks) and business rules. Here, standardized graphical notations that are rich enough to capture the process descriptions, yet are sufficiently business-friendly so as to facilitate business-IT collaboration, are of primary importance. Often the so-called "process models" may have to be shared between BPM project participants who may use different tools to view (and in some cases, modify) these models. So, standards enabling platform-independent process model exchange are relevant as well.

In the composition/implementation phases, additional technical details are added to the process models to create process-based business applications that can be executed. Hence, standards pertaining to process execution are most relevant here. Since process-based applications involve integrations with other computer applications, B2B gateways, and others—as well as the creation of user interfaces, dashboards, and portals—standards related to these functionalities become important supporting standards. The core standards applicable here focus mainly on the ability to create unique and streamlined execution instructions, as well as on interoperability among various connected systems, and focus less on the ability to exchange all or part of the BPM application between different BPMS platforms.

Once a BPM application has been composed, it is then deployed in some execution (or runtime) environment like a J2EE application server so as to realize the functionalities of the BPM application. Standards for such runtime environments are currently quite mature. Finally, signals and events from executing BPM applications are collected, analyzed, and displayed for the purpose of monitoring and administering these applications. Enabling administration or monitoring features of a BPMS are usually provided at a platform level and are usually customized as needed for a specific BPM application; commonly practiced standards are also available for the implementation of such functionalities. While the standards supporting deployment, monitoring, and administration are clearly important for an executing BPM application, for the purpose of the current discussion, we will regard them as playing supporting roles and will not delve into them in further detail.

Figure 2-1 summarizes the type of standards required to support the key BPM life cycle phases as discussed here. The figure also references the names of several standards, which are introduced in the next section.

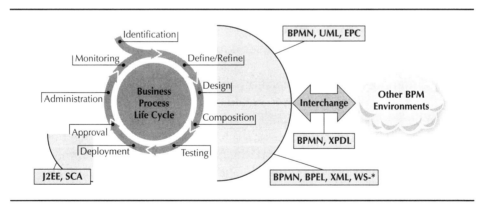

FIGURE 2-1. *A sample of standards needed to support selected BPM life cycle phases*

The Evolution of BPM Standards

As we noted earlier, the range of activities and types of participants in a BPM project is wider than most software projects. Thus, approaches to the creation of standards supporting BPM have had varying roots and styles, from computer sciences to management sciences, from semi-formal to rigorous, from skeletal to comprehensive, depending on the background and primary focus of the parties proposing the standards. While some notable activities relating to BPM standards did start in the early 1990s, the momentum started picking up in the late 1990s and early 2000s. Technical aspects of BPM systems were usually the target of proposed standards. However, in recent years there has been an equally strong interest in the standardization of (business-friendly) graphical notations so as to facilitate easier collaboration among interested parties in a typical BPM project.

One of the most notable early efforts in the standardization of BPM systems began with work done by the Workflow Management Coalition (WfMC), an industry consortium formed in 1993 with the aim of standardizing the interoperability of workflow management systems. The Workflow Reference Model specification (see www.wfmc.org/standards/docs/tc003v11.pdf), defined by WfMC in 1995, identified the key components of a typical BPM system such as the process definition tool, process execution engine, administration and monitoring tools, and the primary interfaces like those between the tools and the engines, between engines and the client or back-end applications, and between engines. The WfMC Workflow Reference Model provided the inspirational framework for some of the early BPM standards, including WF-XML, an XML-based interface specification proposed in 1997 for handling communications between process engines.

As alluded to earlier, in the last dozen years or so, there have many standardization efforts that could be related to BPM practice. Synergies with other important technology standards such as XML and WS-* helped some of the BPM standards gain faster adoption. It is not our intention to provide an exhaustive chronology of all such efforts. Rather, we will offer some essential background information on a subset of such efforts that may be directly or indirectly relevant to a BPM Suite 11*g* user. For the sake of clarity, we will provide these summaries in the following sections under three headings: graphical notations, execution, and interchange.

Graphical Notations

Graphical notations are highly important during modeling and review phases. The removal of ambiguity results from standardized notation and reduces errors in the communication of intent and semantic errors within and across teams (for example, business and IT). With notation standardization, the development of modeling tools and modeling skills become easier as well.

The introduction of flow charts (credited to Frank Gilbreth in 1921) to express process flows was possibly the first noteworthy notational style relevant to today's business process modeling. Using simple symbols to represent process elements like start, end, input/output, tasks, decisions, conditionals, flow direction (arrows), branching (forks, joins), and conditionals, flow charts are able to document processes and algorithms, and remain highly popular among technical and nontechnical people even today. In fact many modern efforts for creation of business process notation borrow substantially from flow charts. Flow charting may be adequate for describing simple business processes, but it is not rich enough to handle general business process representations. Many standards for flow charts exist, some from organizations like ISO and ANSI. Many consider UML Activity Diagram (discussed later in the chapter) symbols from OMG as a flow chart standard. Since flow charts are used for a variety of purposes, no one standard is adequate for all flow charting needs. Also, extensions and additions to such standards are quite common in the practical use of flow charts.

Designed specifically for business process modeling, the Event-Driven Process Chain (EPC) specification was introduced in 1992 by Professor August-Wilhelm Scheer and others from the University of Saarland, Germany. An EPC-based model is essentially an ordered and connected graph with nodes representing events, functions, and logical connectors. The EPC specification includes logical operators like OR, AND, and XOR, and supports parallel process execution. EPC was relatively easy for nontechnical users to understand and use—this aspect was pioneering and was important in seeking collaboration with nontechnical stakeholders (for instance, business analysts) at the process model level. In later years, EPC was adopted with some extensions as the modeling notation for the ARIS modeling tool set from IDS Scheer, a company started by Professor Scheer.

EPC's focus was in creating graphical representations of business processes and it found good support from customers wishing to document business processes for communication purposes. While a pioneering effort of sorts, and popular within the ARIS community, EPC did not get universal acceptance because graphical notation for processes stayed a specification and did not become a standard.

Unified Modeling Language (UML) standards from OMG (2004) were originally designed to support the needs of object-oriented design and development. Many have used use case documents, sequence diagrams and activity diagrams of UML to capture various aspects of business processes. Activity diagrams were often the preferred choice for the UML-based graphical representation of business processes. UML combines flow charting style and the idea of states and state transitions, and it supports some notion of events and subprocesses. All in all, UML activity diagrams are capable of handling most of the workflow patterns and associated data objects, but lack the ability to naturally capture some of the key aspects of many business processes such as resources, organizational roles, and system interaction. Notational deficiencies and the technical modeling style of UML left the industry looking for still better alternatives. Today, UML continues to be used for use case diagrams and data modeling; however, its use for process and activity modeling is no longer mainstream.

As we have mentioned before, serious BPM initiatives involve many stakeholders—for example, business analysts, process designers, and system and software engineers. Business process representations may involve multiple levels or granularities of activities, and the assignment of resources and execution responsibilities. Thus, a great need existed for a graphical notation that is business-friendly yet provides the means for IT developers to add execution-related details and is simple enough for simple business processes (as flow charting is, for example) yet has the capability to capture the details of complex business processes; the Business Process Modeling Notation (BPMN) standard from OMG is now becoming the *de facto* choice that fulfills these needs. Interestingly, work on BPMN started over a decade ago with the Business Process Modeling Initiative's (BPMI) creation of the Business Process Modeling Language (BPML) standard, which focused on the execution aspects of business processes. BPMI released the specifications of BPMN 1.0 in 2004.

In 2005, BPMI and BPM-related activities of OMG merged to jointly develop and promulgate BPMN. BPMN 1.0 was then adopted as an OMG standard in 2006. The BPMN 1.1 and 1.2 versions were released by OMG in 2008 and 2009, respectively. While BPMN 1.x generated great interest and respectable industry adoption, it was not the complete answer that the BPM community needed from a standards point of view. BPMN 1.x was strong in graphical notation, but lacked execution semantics and a serialization format (that is, an executable process language); industry coalitions with heavy involvement from leading vendors like Oracle, IBM, and SAP continued working on the next version of BPMN with a goal to remedy these deficiencies. A beta release of OMG BPMN 2.0 occurred in late 2009, and in early 2011 the BPMN 2.0 standard became the latest version. The 2.0 release added, among other things, execution semantics, serialization for interchange and extended support for choreography. Choreography is intended to support the interactions or collaborations between multiple processes executing relatively independently and syncing up only at some certain predefined milestones. The addition of execution semantics, while not critical from a graphical notation point of view, made it possible for BPM tools to directly execute BPMN models without the need for intermediate translations.

At a high level, BPMN notation has a flow chart–like style that makes it easier for nontechnical BPM project participants (for instance, business analysts) to understand and use. The key structural elements of BPMN (see www.omg.org) are flow objects (events, activities, gateways), connecting objects (sequences flows, message flows and associations), artifacts (data objects, groups, annotations), and swim-lanes (lanes, pools). Some of these structural elements, such as activity, event, gateway, and so on, have many variants. BPMN can support process decomposition and representations at different levels of granularity. This is very helpful when one wants to, for instance, only look at the high-level view or focus on the finer-grain details of an activity.

BPMN also facilitates progressive modeling (that is, starting with a skeletal representation of the process and then adding details in successive modeling passes). For example, one could start with the "happy path," typically the simplest version of the process flow modeled with the basic set of symbols, and then add all the exceptions iteratively where more advanced notational concepts may be necessary. In his 2009 book, *BPMN Method and Style,* Bruce Silver described a top-down three-level BPMN modeling methodology based on this idea of progressive modeling. These levels are termed *descriptive, analytical,* and *executable.* The descriptive phase is when business analysts document the essential process using basic BPMN symbols. Employing more advanced shapes and symbols from BPMN, the analytical phase expands on the work done in the descriptive phase, adding more complex details such as exception handling, compensation, and so on. At the end of analytical phase, specifications from business to IT are expected to be fully incorporated. The executable phase then picks up the functionally complete process model from the analytical phase and delves into the details required to make the graphical process an executable one—XML manipulations, data associations, service calls, and completing the creation of human tasks are the key focus points of this phase. Such a progressive modeling provides a disciplined divide-and-conquer strategy that is helpful in managing the modeling complexity and skills required at different phases. Furthermore, BPMN 2.0 provides a foundation to enable all this in a single model, without the need for the transformation or migration of any form.

Execution

In order to realize the actual functional benefits, graphical process representations have to be converted to computer executable applications. Standardization of execution semantics is critical for ensuring accuracy of the executable process vis-à-vis its graphical representation, and for the creation of robust and performant process execution engines. While many tools have been developed over the years to interpret and convert graphical process representations to executable code, prior to the release of BPMN 2.0, most noteworthy efforts to create standard language for process execution were the BPML from BPMI, and BPEL from the OMG. BPML and BPEL are both XML-based languages meant for web services–based BPMS and essentially competing efforts. BPML specification covers graphical notations that include constructs like loops and parallel paths as well as block-structured constructs that make BPML amenable to execution (elements within a block are executed serially). BPEL is mainly block structured with limited capabilities for free form flow chart style modeling, but it enables easier modeling of fault handlers, event handlers, compensation, and so on. Formally, the BPML effort started in 2000 and was led by open-source promoters like JBoss and Intalio while work on BPEL specification was inspired by IBM's Web Services Flow Language (WSFL) and Microsoft's XLANG process orchestration initiatives. In 2002, BPMI released BPML specification 1.0, and Microsoft and IBM submitted their BPEL4WS 1.0 to OMG. With added support behind BPEL4WS from other big software vendors, OMG's BPEL4WS 1.1 was released in 2003 and forms the basis of today's top BPEL-based process engines. BPMI merged with OMG's process-related activities in 2005 and BPMI discontinued work on BPML. This cleared the path for BPEL to be recognized as the winning standard for process execution language. OMG renamed BPEL4WS to WS-BPEL; WS-BPEL 2.0 (or BPEL 2.0) was released in 2007 and is the latest version.

The originators of BPEL envisioned two distinct types of process descriptions: executable processes that define implementation logic and abstract processes that describe message exchanges between process participants. BPEL process representation includes activities, partner links (for interactions with external elements), variables, and event handlers. BPEL also includes participant roles and message correlation information (useful in case of asynchronous interactions between the process and its endpoints). BPEL is a high-level programming language for processes and is amenable to graphical composition, supports transactions and exceptions, and is meant for use with web services via WSDL (Web Services Definition Language) and popular XML-based messaging protocols like SOAP (Simple Object Access Protocol), and has become the language of choice for web service orchestration. BPEL traditionally lacked support for human tasks. As a remedy to this shortcoming, in 2007 a group of leading software vendors, including Oracle, proposed a BPEL4People specification to OMG that included a WS-BPEL 2.0 extension for people activities, thus extending the interactions of a BPEL process beyond web services and the use of WS-HumanTask specification (www.oasis-open.org).

Inclusion of serialization and execution semantics in BPMN 2.0 has added an interesting twist to the standards landscape for BPM. As mentioned earlier, it is now possible to use BPMN to specify the required technical details so as to make a graphical representation of a process into an executable (similar to BPML or BPEL). This was labeled as the executable phase of a process modeling.

Interchange

Process model interchange is necessary whenever the process model is to be shared between different tools, especially if they adopt different technologies, or when the graphical process model needs to be converted into an executable format by a separate software tool than the one that produced the graphical representation. XML-based Business Process Definition Metamodel (BPDM) from OMG, and XML Process Definition Language (XPDL) from WfMC, are the two most noteworthy efforts thus far in the creation of the process model interchange standard. OMG's goal in creating BPDM was to formulate a technology agnostic process model representation covering both graphical descriptions and execution-related details. With the original RFP issues by OMG in 2003, the 1.0 version of BPDM was released in 2008. BPDM standard is deemed quite rich, but is also complex, which is a likely reason for the low interest by software vendors. Lack of industry adoption and the apparent absence of momentum to push BPDM further raises serious questions about its long-term viability. On the other hand, XPDL, somewhat limited in scope compared to BPDM and mainly focused on capturing process model descriptions, has been enjoying good industry adoption for over a decade.

Cast in the context of supporting one of the five key interfaces of WfMC, namely the interface for process definition exchange between workflow management systems, work on XPDL began in the mid-1990s as Workflow Process Definition Language (WPDL). As XML emerged and started gaining popularity in the late 1990s and early 2000s, WfMC adopted XML as the interchange format for WPDL—hence the name XPDL. WfMC released XPDL 1.0 in 2002, followed by 2.0 and 2.1 releases in 2005 and 2008. Today, most BPM software vendors support process model import and export based on XPDL. As BPMN 2.0 also specifies serialization of the process model, it will be used for interchange as well, and consequently it will be interesting to see what impact it will have on XPDL's popularity.

Figure 2-2 shows the timeline of the evolution of core BPM standards.

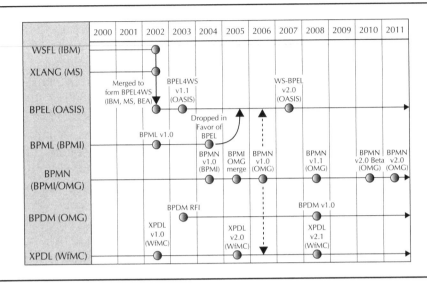

FIGURE 2-2. *Evolution timeline of core BPM standards*

Summary

In this chapter, we provided a short account of the evolution of the standards and specifications relevant for a general BPM practitioner. As such, Oracle BPM Suite 11*g* supports BPMN 2.0 and BPEL 2.0 natively. Oracle BPM Suite 11*g* also supports the XPDL 2.0 interchange format.

CHAPTER
3

BPM Suite 11g:
An Overview

PM Suite 11g is a key product offering within Oracle's Fusion Middleware (FMW) product family and is a result of a great amount of R&D work. This represents the unification of BEA's Aqualogic BPM (ALBPM) product and Oracle SOA features (such as human workflow, business rules, and process orchestration) into a unified BPM suite that is included in the Oracle FMW family of products.

Oracle has always regarded process management as an important discipline to pursue. Around a decade ago, Oracle released Oracle Workflow, which helped customers manage traditional workflow chores and connect information flows between human workers and computer applications. It was essentially a database application with a tool, the Workflow Builder, for modeling these workflows. This workflow product was subsequently embedded in the Oracle EBusiness Suite applications for managing workflows within the ERP application. Over time, demands on process management software tools increased and standards for process modeling and execution emerged. In June 2004, through the acquisition of Collaxa, Oracle added the industry-leading BPEL-based (Business Process Execution Language; www.oasis-open.org) process manager (BPEL PM) to its portfolio of Middleware offerings. Oracle continued investing in BPEL PM in order to maintain its market leadership in features and performance. As Oracle completed its product offering for SOA (Service Oriented Architecture), currently called SOA Suite, BPEL PM became the main vehicle for service orchestration.

In 2008, Oracle acquired BEA and gained ALBPM, then a market leading product for business-friendly process modeling and optimization. Post-acquisition, Oracle significantly increased its investment into the development of ALBPM and its unification into the FMW family of products. Besides excelling in process modeling, this unified BPM platform would also be capable of handling a diverse set of BPM use cases for modeling, execution, analytics, and optimization while handling extreme performance requirements, supporting complex UI and application integration challenges, and providing a platform that was easy to deploy and manage. The end result of this R&D exercise was BPM Suite 11g.

In this chapter, we will introduce the BPM Suite 11g product. We will start with a quick examination of the goals and challenges of a modern business process implementation and describe the architecture and the functionalities of BPM Suite 11*g* within the context of such goals and challenges. Of course, this being an overview chapter, all treatment will be at a very high level, with the details deferred to subsequent chapters.

Building a Modern Process-based Business Application

As we mentioned in the last chapter, business processes are at the heart of how companies conduct themselves. They are key enablers of operational efficiency, are responsible for employee and customer satisfaction, and support business innovation and agility. In short, business processes are the foundations of healthy growth and sustained competitive advantage for companies. How do business processes solve such multidimensional business problems? Let's explore this via an example from the credit card industry.

A credit card company is faced with solving the problem of handling requests for increases in credit limits from its customers. The current way of handling such requests in that company is mostly manual and often takes too long, thus frustrating the customers to the point where they either stop using their cards or switch to another credit card company. Sometimes credit limits are granted to undeserving customers, leading to an eventual loss of money to bad credit. This credit card company decides to undertake a BPM project to improve the situation.

At a basic level, the problem of granting additional credit to existing customers involves checking whether the customer are in good standing, adjusting their account, and informing them. However, real-life scenarios bring in additional considerations, some of which could be nontrivial. For example, in the case of this credit card company, the process improvement sponsors laid out certain success measures for the project that implied that the new process must significantly improve the level of process automation, manual steps must be resource-optimized so as to meet preset customer-facing SLAs (service level agreements) while keeping the operational costs down, and process logic must be such that the number of bad or faulty decisions will be significantly reduced. The project goals also mandated process invocations over multiple channels, such as customer self-service via the Web, phone call requests via call centers, and batch requests via B2B (business-to-business) channels from their business customer accounts and from their resellers. Visibility into the process transactions was another area that needed to be improved. In fact, requirements included visibility at different levels—for example, management dashboards, system-level reporting for the operations people, transaction-level drill down for process workers, and process completion status reporting to customers. All in all, this was about raising a critical business capability of the credit card company, namely, the credit limit increase service to a much higher level.

As the business analysts and process architects went to work designing a suitable solution, there were more things to take care of. In order to create the target (or the *to-be*) process, information about the current way of working (the *as-is* process) had to be gathered and analyzed for possible improvements, and a series of discussions needed to be held with all the stakeholders ranging from business groups to IT developers to operations teams to finalize the internal design and external features of the future solution. For such collaboration to be useful and disciplined, different participants would need different levels of access to the design assets, some would be able to modify them and some only review. It was clear that different participants preferred different interaction styles: business people liked lightweight web browser–based no-need-to-install software types of tools and were focused more on the process model and business logic, while the IT developers required access to more technical artifacts of the process. It also seemed highly desirable that discussions among the participants could be recorded when required so that design decisions could be easily revisited if necessary.

In order to ensure that only the right amount of credit increase is granted to a requesting customer, a whole set of rules involving credit usage history was deemed necessary. In trying to eliminate fraudulent transactions, signs for *possible* and *probable* cases needed to be identified. A variety of exception handling strategies had to be incorporated into the solution; some routine ones would require approvals through organizational hierarchies, while some others needed multiple people to collaborate to resolve the issue. The process needed to have the ability to handle events like interruption or suspensions, say, due to a call from a customer while his/her transaction is in flight or when an impasse is reached during a manual exception handling.

A wide variety of graphical elements like UIs and notification dashboards needed to be developed in order to present different kinds of information to different participants involved in the execution of the process; these ranged from alerts on multiple devices to management dashboards to worker task lists. In many cases, these graphical display and interaction elements needed to be a part of a bigger web portal or an E2.0-style *mash-up* or *collaborative workspace.*

Of course, the process had to exchange information and in some cases triggering transactions within various enterprise applications. Consequently, security concerns around user access and data were highly relevant. The company identified several occasions where the process workers needed to look up documents associated with a particular process instance or to reference the company's operating practices. In other words, integration with their document management system was also necessary. Additionally, the analysts and designers needed the ability to play out several *what-if* scenarios with respect to the process model, business logic, and resource assignments. There was also a concern as to how the process should be designed so as to make it resilient to change, particularly when certain decision logic would change in the future. Figure 3-1 captures, at a high level, the building blocks of a comprehensive BPM application.

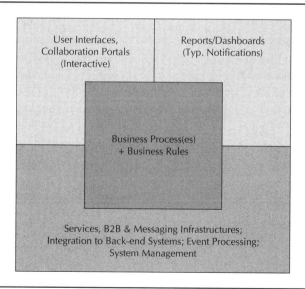

FIGURE 3-1.   *The building blocks of a comprehensive BPM application*

The business problem and its associated business process under scrutiny here is of only modest complexity. Yet, the task of creating a business-friendly, effective, and efficient solution would require a toolset that goes far beyond a process designer—it would need a *full-palette* business process–based application builder, a solution architecture and building blocks that afford easy change-edits, and an overall solution implementation methodology. Oracle BPM Suite 11*g* is such a platform—it is an enterprise-grade BPMS (Business Process Management Suite, as coined by the analyst firm Gartner) that is feature-wise comprehensive, provides *role-* or *persona*-based user interfaces and design environments, and has the ability to handle change efficiently. In order to better appreciate the capabilities of BPM Suite 11*g*, let's first examine the design goals and guidelines that were used to build this product.

Design of BPM Suite 11*g*: Goals and Guiding Principles

After the acquisition of BEA, during the unification phase of BEA's BPM product (then called ALBPM) into the broader FMW ecosystem, Oracle significantly increased BPM R&D investment in order to create a BPMS that would preserve and strengthen the popular and unique features of ALBPM, but would also add a set of forward-looking capabilities. As a component of the FMW family, this unified BPM would be guided by the core guiding principles of FMW R&D:

- **Complete** The offering provides a comprehensive set of features so the designers or developers would not have to bounce from tool to tool to get their job done. In case of BPM Suite 11*g*, this requirement translates to providing all the features and tool interaction styles necessary for a variety of participants, ranging from business analysts to IT developers, capabilities to handle different types of process types (for example, human-, document-, decision- and integration-centric processes, departmental and enterprise scopes, and so on), and support for different modeling components (such as BPMN, BPEL, rules, human tasks, and others).

■ **Integrated**   The offering is not a loose cluster of tools, instead the tooling components are pre-integrated. This would benefit both development and operational activities. Designers or developers will not have to manage additional integrations to keep track of their work and the work-products (artifacts) as they move through multiple tools or modules during the course their work; IT operations will have a simpler platform to administer and manage. This requirement led to the unified development environment and execution and management infrastructure of BPM Suite 11*g*.

■ **Open**   Where applicable, products adhere to leading industry standards and, in spite of pre-integration between product components, remain modular so as to provide customers with adequate choices for creating best-fit solutions. Additionally, the open platform will make it easy for customers to find a skilled work force. Consequently, BPM Suite 11*g* natively supports BPMN 2.0 (see www.omg.org), BPEL and other relevant WS-* standards, and XML-based manipulations. Also, where appropriate, it provides a rich library of Application Programming Interfaces (APIs) and facilitates connectivity to other applications via web services, messaging, and data imports/exports.

■ **Best-of-breed**   Each component of the offering, on its own, is a best-in-class offering. This puts the focus on making the components and features of BPM Suite 11*g* comparable or ahead of market leaders in this industry segment.

Besides the preceding guidelines, BPM Suite 11*g* also added the following focus points in its product design considerations:

■ **Leverage collaboration**   In today's "age of digital interaction," we increasingly use online media to engage in ad hoc interactions via electronic forums, chats, and web-based collaboration portals. BPM Suite 11*g* leverages these trends to facilitate fast and effective collaboration among diverse BPM participants.

- **Single model through entire BPM life cycle** While collaboration among various participants is very beneficial to BPM adoption, it also brings forth the challenge of maintaining concurrency of all the process artifacts at all times. For example, it would be highly undesirable if modifications made by business analysts were not exactly conveyed to IT developers or vice versa, since the analysts and developers may use different interaction interfaces of the BPM toolset. Or, for example, the runtime version of the process turns out to not be exactly the same as the design-time version. BPM Suite's design strategy is to adopt a common process model with a "What-You-Model-Is-What-You-Execute (WYMIWYE)" paradigm in order to avoid these so called lost in translation or roundtrip problems.

- **Built for adaption** Due to the need of responding to ever-increasing competition in the marketplace, the redistribution of work between in-house and outsourced work forces, dynamic supply chains and distribution chain management, and the constant need to improve operational efficiency, business processes must evolve continually. Design considerations for BPM Suite 11*g* include many capabilities that help companies make their business processes change-resilient, make it easy to introduce changes to existing processes, and help them reuse assets from existing processes to create brand new ones rapidly. In addition to these design-time changes, it may sometimes become necessary to alter the actual execution steps of a business process from what it was originally designed for. For example, depending on the data associated with a particular process transaction, an approver may feel the necessity of adding additional approvers, or an exception handler may invite other experts to help resolve a special situation. These conditions reflect the runtime adaptability of the process. BPM Suite 11*g* provides capabilities that could handle such runtime changes as well.

- **End-to-end management and monitoring** A great amount of value that business processes yield comes from the fact that these processes integrate, explicit or implicitly, many diverse computer applications and human user interfaces. However, such integration also poses the challenge of keeping track of the evolution of the process transactions, end-to-end, and providing adequate visibility of the transactions to various process participants. BPM Suite 11*g* facilitates the monitoring of process transactions at multiple levels: transaction summaries, business events and activities, and system.

- **Built-in process analytics**   A set of design goals of BPM Suite 11*g* has to do with *easily* extracting useful information from business process transactions and presenting them to the interested subscribers in a timely manner. These may range from information leading to historical perspectives of transaction variables via traditional business intelligence applications to real-time information initiating additional human or system action. BPM Suite 11*g* facilitates the creation of process Key Performance Indicators (KPIs) by defining business indicators and process measurements at modeling time. Often such information is helpful in identifying cross-sell or up-sell opportunities, in taking proactive actions so as to avoid breach of SLAs, and in pursuing continuous process performance improvement.

- **Leverage SOA Suite and FMW**   Service Oriented Architecture (SOA) is a software application architecture based on loosely coupled packages of software functionalities termed "services." SOA facilitates rapid assembly of composite applications functionality reuse, and insulates service consumers from modifications to portions of an application. A BPM application is often an ideal candidate to leverage SOA concepts, assets, and application building styles. Wherever applicable, BPM Suite 11*g* is designed to leverage SOA intrinsically. BPM Suite is part of the broader FMW family of products, which offers many tools that can be helpful in the context of building a comprehensive process-based business solution—for example, content management, security, business intelligence, portals, and the like. BPM Suite 11*g* is designed to either directly incorporate, or make it easy for the implementers to leverage, other relevant FMW components while designing or building their BPM solutions.

■ **Enterprise-grade** While some BPM projects may start small with low complexity, departmental scopes, or non-mission-critical applications over a relatively small period of time, larger multidepartment or enterprise-scope complex and mission-critical projects are sure to follow. It would be desirable to have the BPM technology platforms scale smoothly from the smaller to the larger projects without having to change products or project execution styles. Projects may scale due to the need for higher throughput or higher concurrency of user requests. Hence, a BPM Suite 11*g* design criterion is to include necessary features typical for high-quality enterprise-grade software tools, giving high performance, scalability, and reliability.

As depicted in Figure 3-2, the BPM Suite 11*g* product design essentially captured the preceding requirements in three architectural themes: persona or role-based tooling, social BPM, and unified process foundation. The remainder of this chapter will provide an overview of how BPM Suite 11*g* has implemented its features so as to deliver on the product design requirements and the architectural guidelines discussed thus far.

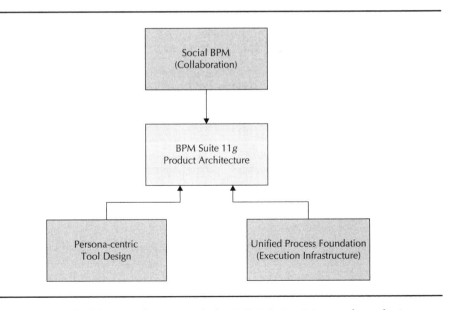

FIGURE 3-2. *Architectural approach for BPM Suite 11g product design*

BPM Suite 11*g*: Product Architecture and Functionality Overview

As mentioned before, BPM Suite 11*g* is a member of FMW, Oracle's middleware and application infrastructure family of products. The FMW breadth ranges from application servers and messaging products to business integration, identity management, business intelligence, content and user interaction management, and enterprise performance management (see Figure 3-3). BPM Suite 11*g* installed on top of SOA Suite 11*g* provides BPM Suite 11*g* with a rich application integration capability often demanded by BPM applications.

The main purpose of this section is to provide a quick overview of how the BPM Suite product is composed and to summarize its important feature functionalities. Later chapters in this handbook go into deeper details of the functionalities and usage of BPM Suite 11*g* features.

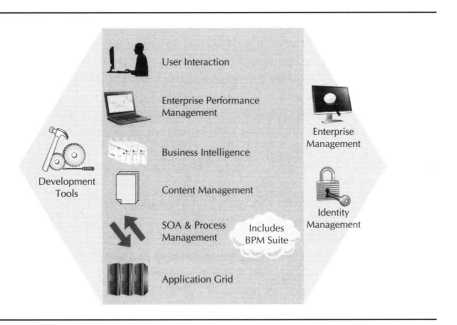

FIGURE 3-3.   *Oracle FMW and BPM Suite 11g*

Modeling and Simulation Tools

As we noticed in the credit card company example earlier, a typical BPM project requires several additional features besides the basic process flow. For example, incoming requests need to be mediated to figure out the expected follow-up actions within the BPM application; business rules are needed to derive a variety of decisions from available facts; groups of software services (often web services) may have to be orchestrated to create additional functionality; many heterogeneous computer applications and complex human tasks must be connected; and so on. In the following, we will briefly describe the key BPM Suite 11g modeling and simulation features and the philosophies behind them.

A BPM Project and Model-based Solution Architecture

Given the wide number of building blocks employed in a typical BPM solution, a high-level solution architecture philosophy is needed to guide the composition of the BPMS toolset and to provide a discipline for solution construction. BPM Suite accomplishes this challenge by recognizing a set of modeling components or constructs such as BPMN, BPEL, human workflow, business rules, and others and provides the realization of the final solution as a composite of these interrelated modeling components. Each modeling component is supported by the necessary modeling interfaces that are integrated within the BPM Suite development environment. This allows the modeler or the developer to focus only on the modeling interfaces necessary for their immediate work without the burden of all the modeling interfaces at once.

BPM Suite achieves this persona-based modeling by supporting two modeling and development front-ends: BPM Studio and Process Composer. BPM Studio is installed as a plug-in to JDeveloper, the Oracle FMW Integrated Development Environment (IDE), and provides all the modeling and development features of BPM Suite. Process composer, on the other hand, is a web browser–based interface that is designed mainly for business analysts for relatively higher-level interaction with the process artifacts. Composition of the BPM solution can start either from BPM Studio or from the Process Composer, and can be modified, refined, and enriched in either interface, often through the iterative cycles of modeling and development activities. Use of a common metadata store (MDS) ensures the work done either in BPM Studio or Process Composer is applied to the same process model (see Figure 3-4). Once the implementation level details are incorporated, typically through BPM Studio, the process model is ready to be deployed to an application server instance (for example, Oracle WebLogic Server) and administered by Oracle Enterprise Manager.

BPM Studio

As already mentioned, BPM Studio is installed as a plug-in to Oracle FMW's standard IDE framework, JDeveloper. It provides a comprehensive modeling and development environment for process-based applications. Its wide range of features includes the creation of artifacts related to process models based on BPMN 2.0 and BPEL languages, business rules, human tasks, and organizational models. Application analysts and designers can carry out what-if analyses and resource-optimize the solution using the simulation capabilities in BPM Studio. Leveraging the common infrastructure that BPM Suite shares with SOA Suite, BPM Studio also provides features for interaction with external and internal web services, request mediation and routing, data manipulation, user interaction via rich UI components and connectivity to Java components, files, databases, and applications. BPM Suite 11*g* uses a Business Catalog, which is a categorized list of assets and resources available to the BPM modeler and developer in the BPM Studio,

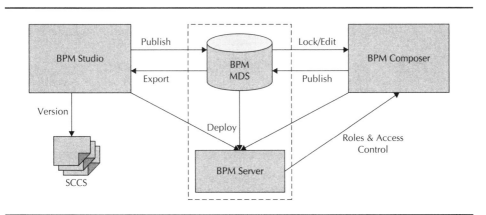

FIGURE 3-4.   *BPM Studio and Process Composer*

as well as to the web-based Process Composer. Assets are created by a process developer using the BPM Studio and include Process models, Human Tasks, Business Rules, and Services (web services, adapter services, and others). Figure 3-5 shows a screenshot of BPM Studio.

BPM Suite 11*g* supports modeling and execution of BPMN 2.0 models natively. BPM Studio supports this by providing all levels of BPMN modeling perspectives, namely Descriptive, Analytical, and Executable. BPM Studio provides mechanisms to assign different roles to different tasks consistent with the BPMN standard; the roles themselves can be mapped to physical groups and users which may be stored in an identity store such as LDAP. It supports persona-based profiles—for example, a process analyst persona gets access to only the BPM modeling features, while a developer

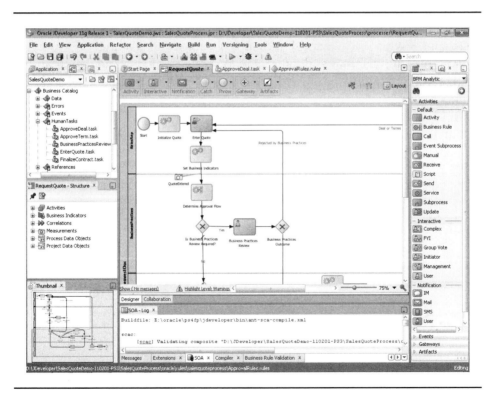

FIGURE 3-5. *A screenshot of BPM Studio*

persona also gets access to more technical features like XML manipulation, web services interaction, and Java components.

Process Composer

The web browser–based Process Composer component of BPM Suite 11g exposes modeling aspects that are typically of interest to business analysts, like the BPMN model, business rules, and task features of BPM Studio. Process Composer is designed to cater to project contributors who do not need to deal with IT system–oriented features or artifacts. This tool is also highly useful for accessing and browsing process models during collaboration sessions. Using its role-based access features, a business analyst can share and review the process models with various collaborators who may be granted a read-only access to the artifacts. Figure 3-6 presents a screenshot of Process Composer.

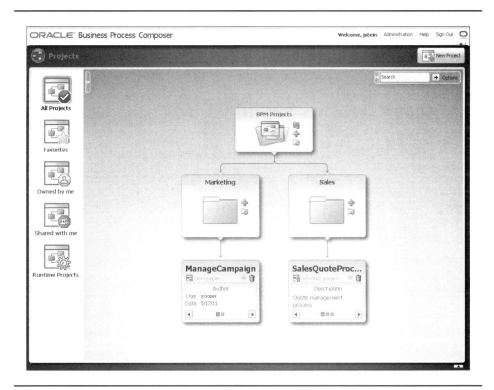

FIGURE 3-6. *A screenshot of Process Composer*

Process Simulation

Often, what-if analysis of as-designed processes from the points of view of expected cost, performance, and resource utilization is necessary for design refinements. BPM Suite 11*g* provides a rich process simulation tool, currently accessible through BPM Studio, to accomplish this task. Simulation scenarios can be created by assigning probability distributions of various process events and resource and cost models. Multiple scenarios can be simulated simultaneously. Simulation outputs include charts of cost, time spent, and queue build-ups. Queue build-ups are overlaid on the process diagram (see Figure 3-7) for easy interpretation of the results; resources can be dynamically adjusted to resolve queue build-ups.

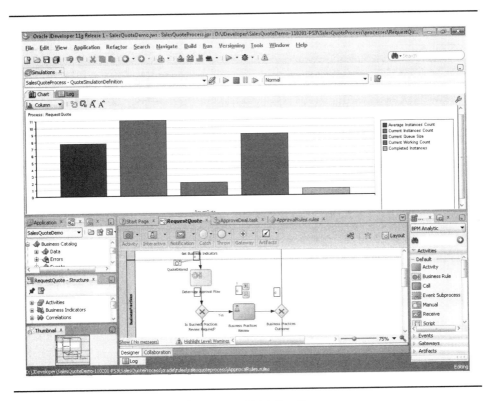

FIGURE 3-7. *Process simulation in BPM Studio*

UI Components and Use of ADF

Oracle Application Development Framework (ADF) is a comprehensive UI development framework based on the model-view-controller (MVC) paradigm for building enterprise-class web applications. ADF is also Oracle's strategic UI framework and is used for Oracle's next-generation web browser–based UIs across a wide range of applications, such as Fusion CRM, Fusion HCM, Oracle Enterprise Manager, and so on. ADF is also the foundation for Oracle WebCenter—Oracle's portal and collaboration product.

ADF is a JSF–based UI framework that allows for visual and declarative development of complex web applications. It extends the JSF framework and adds a number of features, such as drag-and-drop designer, along with a rich selection of interactive controls and data visualization elements like charts, graphs and trees, transaction management, callable page flows (using ADF Task Flows), ADF binding, and so on. Figure 3-8 shows a high-level schematic of ADF.

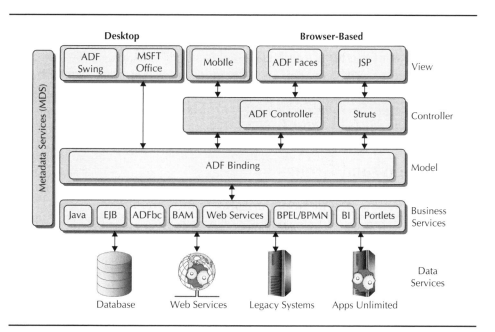

FIGURE 3-8.   *A high-level schematic of Oracle ADF*

All of the Oracle BPM 11*g* UI components, such as Process Composer and BPM Workspace, are also built using ADF. BPM Studio provides design-time tooling based on ADF that can be used to generate or custom-design human task forms (see Chapter 8, "Developing Rich User Interfaces for BPM with ADF," for additional details of use of ADF in the BPM Suite 11*g* context.)

Business Rules

Use of business rules has increasingly become a necessary element in process-based application development. In many instances, business rules can easily capture decision-making mechanisms; they can help model business or process flow control logic including human task assignment. Rules tend to be more business-friendly than graph-based process models and thus can be easily understood and modified by business participants. By externalizing business rules—that is, setting them up outside of the usual procedural process model, execution behavior of a process-based application can be changed without having to redeploy the BPM project, consequently often avoiding the need for additional IT projects. Thus, business rules enhance the agility of process-based business applications.

BPM Suite 11*g* includes a richly featured business rules component with an easy-to-use user interface that is available via BPM Studio as well as through Process Composer. This business rules component can model both *if-then-action* as well as the *decision table* (collection of logical conditions) style specification of rules (see Chapter 6, "Mastering Business Rules," for an in-depth discussion of BPM Suite 11*g* business rules capabilities).

Roles, Users, and Groups

While Oracle BPM Suite 11*g* leverages users, groups, and organizational hierarchies maintained in an organization's preferred identity store, process-specific roles can also be defined within BPM Suite 11*g*. In addition to process-specific roles, BPM Suite allows the definition of Calendars and Holidays. Roles in BPM are used to define initial participants in human tasks in the process. Roles are of two types: Application roles that are based on a BPM project, and Enterprise roles that are defined externally in an LDAP store. A BPM role (that is, an Application role in the context of BPM Suite 11*g* projects) has one or more users or groups (from the organization's identity stores) assigned to it. These assignments can be done either during

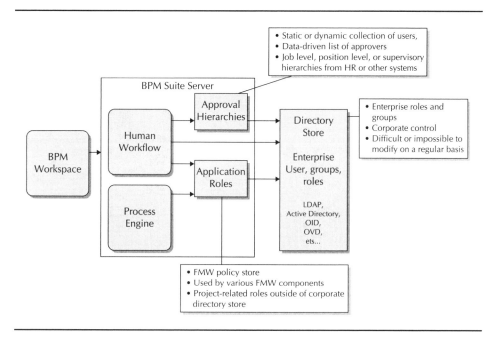

FIGURE 3-9. *Roles, users, and groups concepts used in BPM Suite 11*g

design time or at runtime using the BPM Workspace application. The actual users and groups are defined in an enterprise directory such as LDAP. Role definitions are shareable among BPM projects. Figure 3-9 presents a schematic showing these relationships.

Human Tasks and Workflows

Human tasks and workflow support in BPM Suite 11*g* is aligned with the WS-Human Task (a subspec of what is popularly known as BPEL4People) specification (see www.oasis-open.org). Accordingly, it separates the components that handle the execution of tasks from the process flows, connecting the two by a service interface for invocation and call-back (see Figure 3-10). Within the execution infrastructure of BPM Suite, human task components (called Human Workflow or HWF) are handled by a separate service engine. Thus, HWF components can be called by any of the other components or can be used directly. For example, BPMN and BPEL processes can invoke the same HWF components.

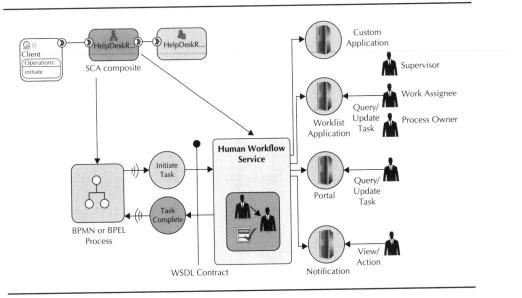

FIGURE 3-10. *HWF component of BPM Suite 11g—high-level schematic*

For task assignment and routing, business rules can be invoked from HWF; the integration between HWF and business rules offers the flexibility of decision making based on specific participants interacting with the human tasks. Oracle Unified Messaging Service (UMS) is used by HWF to deliver notifications through channels based on user preferences. Actionable e-mails capable of handling task interaction via inbound e-mails are also supported by HWF. (Refer to Chapter 7, "Advanced Human Task," later in this book for more related details).

Forms for Human Tasks
BPM Suite 11g uses Oracle ADF as the default technology to create the human task forms or UIs. BPM Suite 11g includes wizards for automatic or user-guided generation of ADF Views and Task Flows. These UI elements can either be used as is or further modified in the ADF Designer.

The workflow service engine exposes a rich set of APIs, abstracted through ADF Data Control (ADF DC), for accessing and interfacing with the human tasks. In the ADF designer in BPM Studio, using ADF DC, designers can bind UI elements to human task data by simple drag-and-drop. Using ADF DC, designers can also create Microsoft Excel interfaces without the need for writing any code. The underlying APIs are also available in Java or as web services for designers wishing to create task UIs in technologies other than ADF or Excel. See Developing Rich User Interfaces for BPM with ADF for more details on how to create forms for human tasks.

Agility with BPM Suite 11*g*: Handling Change

Change imperatives are inevitable in business; they are increasingly more frequent due to the fast-changing competitive playing field. Business processes, therefore, carry the burden of handling many of these changes. An agile organization needs to have the ability to change affected business processes correctly and rapidly. BPM Suite 11*g* provides many capabilities that could be utilized to change existing business processes easily.

As already mentioned, BPM Suite 11*g* allows pervasive use of business rules for decision making, the dynamic binding of process activities that can capture process variances due to differences in process parameters like geography or product, and for human task assignment and routing. Using business rules, processes can be made change-resilient. Since rules can be changed outside of the core process and hot-deployed (in other words, done without the need for redeployment of the whole BPM project), the impact of change on existing processes is greatly minimized.

Rules provide a way to handle planned change patterns. In some situations, for example during some of the nontrivial exception handling, ad hoc changes to certain functionalities of business processes can be very helpful. BPM Suite 11*g* allows appropriately privileged process workers to reassign current tasks and reroute current or future tasks, including the addition of more participants. Additionally, process owners can alter the flow of in-flight process instances and also change certain data variables in-flight if they have appropriate privileges.

Of course, there can be changes that require modification to the basic definition of the process. As discussed earlier, Process Composer can handle incorporation of most such changes rapidly. Use of Process Composer facilitates easier participation of business users and analysts in incorporating the changes to the existing process; these changed processes can be also be deployed without IT's involvement, thus reducing time and cost. A built-in governance mechanism in BPM Suite 11g can be used to specify who-can-change-what, thus preventing undesirable modifications to the process definition.

Process Analytics and Business Activity Monitoring

Insight into the working of processes is often required to assess the process design or to track process performance, starting at the business activity level. Such insight and visibility are helpful in process design refinement and for correlating process performance with related business activities and KPIs. As depicted in Figure 3-11, BPM Suite 11g incorporates an audit service that can continuously audit a variety of process metrics and user-defined business indicators. Depending on the user's choice, such audit information is pushed to a Process STAR schema and/or as events to Oracle Business Activity Monitoring (BAM), where they are captured in BAM Data Objects. Standard and customized dashboards can be built on top of the Process

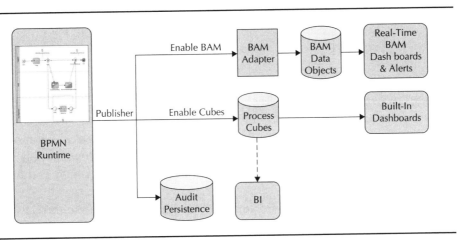

FIGURE 3-11. *The BPM Suite audit service and process analytics*

STAR schema, or the information can be consumed by external business intelligence tools such as Oracle Business Intelligence Enterprise Edition (OBIEE) and others.

Oracle BAM includes a set of out-of-the-box dashboards for standard process metrics. For example, monitoring and visualization of overall process performance, the number of running or faulted instances, completion times of processes and process activities, the frequency of invocation of specific activities (for example, high-cost manual versus low-cost automatic), bottleneck trends within or across processes, and so on are provided out-of-the-box. Further customizations can be easily done using Oracle BAM Studio in order to create special visualizations and additional indicators, or to generate real-time actionable alerts. Figure 3-12 shows a sample BAM dashboard.

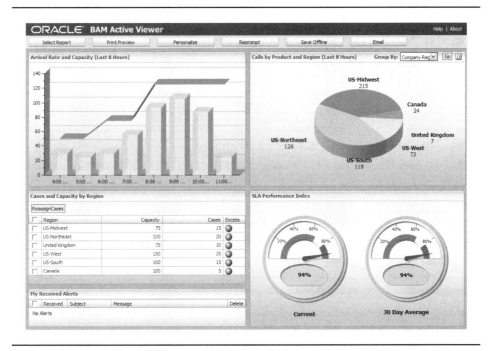

FIGURE 3-12. *A sample BAM dashboard*

Collaboration Components: Process Spaces

BPM Suite 11*g* leverages Oracle WebCenter for providing a collaboration framework as well as out-of-the-box collaboration facilities. The E2.0 features requirement discussed before is supported through a set of WebCenter Spaces called Process Spaces. WebCenter is a comprehensive platform for enterprise portals, web portals, and composite applications that is integrated with social media, collaboration, and content management infrastructure. WebCenter Spaces (sometimes referred to simply as "Spaces") is built on top of the WebCenter framework and allows for creating dynamic online communities.

BPM Suite 11*g* provides three, Spaces out-of-the-box: one for design-time collaboration among the wide range of process modeling participants called *Modeling Spaces,* and two run-time spaces, namely *Process Work Spaces* and *Process Instance Spaces* aimed at mainly facilitating collaboration during process execution.

Process Modeling Spaces

Process Modeling Spaces provides a collaboration environment for the design and modeling phase of the BPM project. Process Modeling Spaces integrates the web-based modeling tool, Process Composer, with discussion, document management, calendar, to-do lists, and more. Once Process Spaces is installed, one Process Modeling Spaces is created out-of-the-box that can handle multiple projects and communities. If needed, customers can create additional Process Modeling Spaces using the provided template. Figure 3-13 shows a screenshot of a Process Modeling Spaces.

Process Work Spaces

Process Work Spaces is an out-of-the-box WebCenter Collaborative workspace that facilitates collaboration among various business workers who are interacting with the process. Often when working with processes, process participants exchange information using a variety of channels such as e-mail, instant messaging, and others. These interactions may also include exchanging documents that are relevant to the process being discussed, including currently applicable policies, expert tips for problem resolution, and so on. Also, frequently it is difficult to get a single view of the progress of the process and the related interactions.

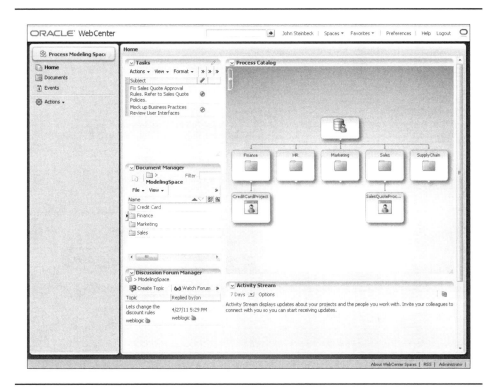

FIGURE 3-13.   *Screenshot of a Process Modeling Spaces*

Process Work Spaces provides a customizable single interface for collaborative business process management. The Process Work Spaces mash-up brings together a wide variety of information such as an active task list, a calendar showing a participant's to-do list based on the progress of the business process, a dashboard showing business process metrics, and others. To aid collaboration on a business process, it also provides discussions, document attachments, and other items that are tightly integrated with the business process.

Similar to Process Modeling Spaces, installation of Process Spaces creates one out-of-the-box Process Work Spaces; process workers sign into this Spaces to access items related to their work and preference. Figure 3-14 shows a screenshot of a Process Work Spaces.

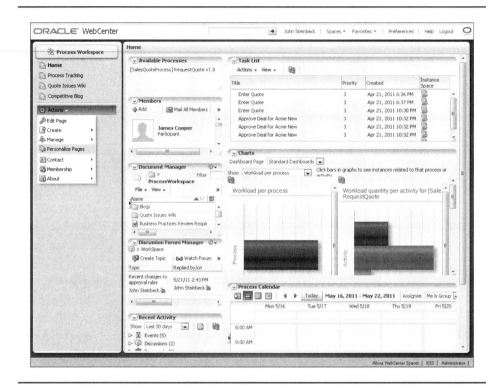

FIGURE 3-14. *Screenshot of a Process Work Spaces*

Process Instance Spaces

Process Instance Spaces is a dynamically created WebCenter Spaces for collaborating on a specific instance of a business process. A process worker can spin off an Instance Spaces for a particular process instance they may be working on. For example, in a home loan approval process, each loan application may require significant collaboration between the loan officer, the mortgage broker, the load processor, internal auditors, and others. There may be active discussion among these participants to decide whether to approve the loan or resolve certain details of the closing costs. In the event that a senior manager may have to approve the loan, say as an exception, (s)he may need quick access to the work of the other process participants in one place. Process Instance Spaces is an ideal solution for such requirements; it can help the participants pursue joint investigation activities, facilitate

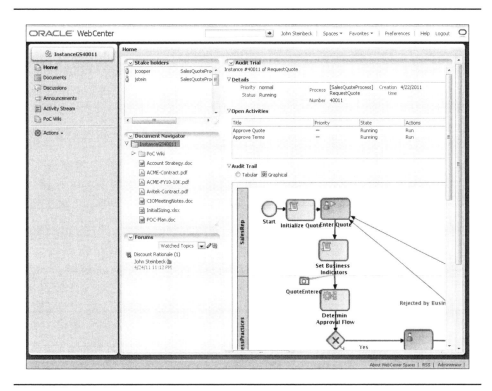

FIGURE 3-15. *Screenshot of a Process Instance Spaces*

discussions and keep track of an evolving case for a specific loan application process instance.

Figure 3-15 presents a screenshot of a Process Instance Spaces.

Infrastructure Tools and Features

One of the goals of a BPM project is to streamline business activities, making them simpler to work with and track. In many cases, BPM projects are undertaken to solve fairly complex business problems. As seen in the example from a credit card company (discussed earlier in this chapter), a BPM project may connect together a diverse set of modeling components such as BPMN- and BPEL-based process models, business rules, human tasks and workflows, document handling, event processing, the exchange of information with several computer applications, and the incorporation of security and other operational policies. Thus, ordinarily speaking, process-based applications could become complex integration challenges of their own with consequential difficulties in modeling, development, execution, and maintenance of such integrated applications. BPM Suite is industry's first solution that comprehensively addresses this challenge by providing a uniform process foundation that executes on a service-oriented execution infrastructure.

Assembling a BPM Application—Use of SCA

The first strategy that BPM Suite 11*g* employs in simplifying the creation of a BPM application is to leverage the *assembly* concept from the Service Component Architecture (SCA) standard (www.osoa.org). Per SCA, an application is *composed* from a set of *components,* and thus the application is termed an SCA *composite.* Figure 3-16 shows a schematic of an SCA component. It essentially consists of details corresponding to some

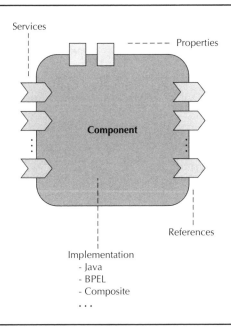

FIGURE 3-16. *Schematic of a generic SCA component*

modeling paradigm (for example, in the case of BPM Suite 11*g*, BPMN, BPEL, business rules, and so on) as its body; and on the periphery, *services* and *references* as a means for invocation from multiple channels or components and connecting to multiple-end systems or components, respectively—along with a mechanism to parametrically alter the behavior of the component via *properties.* As shown in Figure 3-17, a SCA composite is simply *wired* from a collection of components. A SCA composite can include one or more of a particular component type. SCA provides a cleaner discipline to pursue either a top-down or a bottom-up approach to application design and to manage the resultant application across a range of its life-cycle phases. Use of SCA also simplifies deployment and versioning as the application is captured and dealt with as an assembly. BPM Suite 11*g* uses a metadata store (MDS) to collect and preserve the SCA artifacts.

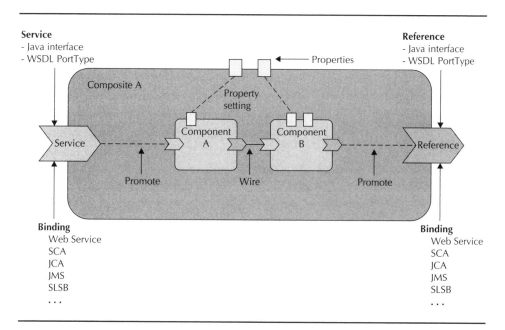

FIGURE 3-17.   *Schematic of a generic SCA composite*

BPM Studio's SCA Editor automatically creates and maintains the necessary SCA artifacts and this may be totally transparent to process analysts using Process Composer. SCA components created in BPM Studio get included in BPM Suite's Business Catalog and become available to process analysts as modeling components in BPMN models.

Figure 3-18 shows an SCA composite for a BPM project in the SCA editor. Here a BPMN process component invokes one or more of the other components like human task, business rule, BPEL process, and mediator. Of course, any of these invoked components could also invoke one or more BPMN processes. In fact, the modeler has the flexibility to define as many of any of the allowed components, and connect (or wire) them, as the solution demands. The composite itself can be invoked in more than one way; the figure here shows two different invocations using two services it exposes. Also, the composite can connect to other services such as technology or application adapters or web services.

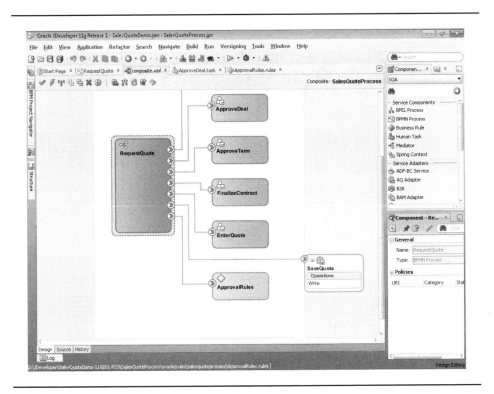

FIGURE 3-18. *A BPM application as an SCA composite*

Unified Process Foundation and Service Infrastructure

As shown in Figure 3-19, BPM Suite 11*g* uses a common execution infrastructure (also known as the Service Infrastructure) where plug-in service engines natively execute specific modeling components; BPMN, BPEL, Rules, Human Tasks, and Mediator are examples of such service engines used by BPM Suite. An application server like Oracle WebLogic Server provides the final runtime environment that hosts these service engines.

Using SCA and the common service infrastructure BPM Suite provides a foundation to unify all the modeling components like BPMN and BPEL process models, business rules, human tasks, and so on. This strategy yields very high modeling and development flexibility, and eases the task of tuning and managing the resulting BPM application. Also, this unified infrastructure helps in providing better design-time and end-to-end visibility into the application and the associated services and end-points.

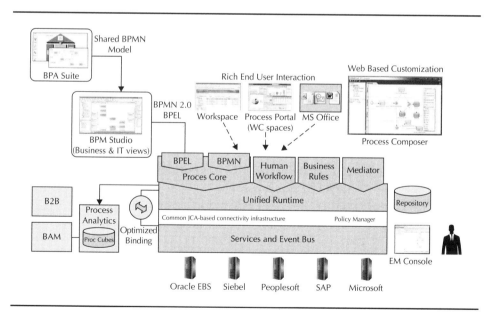

FIGURE 3-19. *Unified process foundation and service infrastructure of BPM Suite*

Since BPM Suite shares the service infrastructure with Oracle SOA Suite, it automatically provides a rich collection of application integration features supporting the connection to Oracle Service Bus, application adapters, web services, service repositories, imaging and content management, Oracle Business Activity Monitoring (BAM), Oracle Complex Event Processing (CEP), Oracle Real-Time Decisions (RTD), and Oracle Security. Using this unified service infrastructure, BPM Suite also delivers an enterprise-grade operational platform that is highly performant, available, and reliable.

Enforcing Security

Security aspects of applications built with BPM Suite 11g can be classified under two main categories: the first is about user authentication and authorization, and the second is about access to services and data. As discussed earlier, BPM application–specific users and roles ultimately are mapped to corporate identity stores. BPM Suite uses Oracle Platform Security Services (OPSS) for integrating with identity directories such as Oracle Internet Directory (OID) Active directory, and any LDAP compliant directory. Consequently, the OPSS layer handles the configuration of identity providers for authentication and authorization. Oracle BPM web applications are also certified with multiple Single Sign On (SSO) providers—for example, Oracle SSO, Oracle Access Manager, Windows Native Authentication, and others.

For managing access to services and data including data encryption, BPM Suite 11g adopts a policy-driven approach. Oracle Web Services Manager (OWSM), a built-in component of the service infrastructure, manages the enforcement and auditing of security policies. In BPM Suite 11g, the creation of security policies can be separated from functional development and deferred to security experts. This strategy also allows security policies to be changed without requiring redeployment of the BPM Suite project. A BPM Suite application enables policy specification, enforcement, and audit. BPM Suite 11g supports the relevant WS-* standards for security policies that include access to services, passing of credentials between services, and data encryption. Security policy definitions are created in FMW Control of Oracle Enterprise Manager (the overall unified management console for FMW applications), while either BPM Studio or Oracle Enterprise Manager can be used to attach those security policies to target interfaces. In addition, the configuration of credential stores and roles can be done at Enterprise Manager Console. One-way or two-way Secure Socket Layer (SSL) protocol can also be used in BPM Suite applications; however, OWSM provides additional security capabilities like Security Assertion Markup Language (SAML) for identity propagation, and Kerberos, username, or X509 tokens for authentication.

Operations, Administration, and Systems Monitoring/Management

Often IT solutions get rejected or considered failures if they pose a high operational complexity and cost. One of the key goals of BPM Suite 11g has been to provide a relatively simple framework to handle the operation, administration, and management (OA&M) chores for BPM applications. In the following, we will provide some highlights of the OA&M features of BPM Suite.

Oracle Enterprise Manager

Staying fully compliant with the core guiding principle of an integrated stack, BPM 11g is managed through the single monitoring and management console provided by Oracle Enterprise Manager (EM). Oracle FMW Control, part of the Oracle Enterprise Manager, allows system administrators to monitor and manage the health of the Oracle BPM 11g system—from the servers running BPM Suite 11g to individual instances of every process. FMW Control also provides runtime life-cycle management, such as deploying and un-deploying BPM applications (also known as composites per SCA vernacular), and starting, stopping, and retiring a specific version of the composites. Figure 3-20 shows a screenshot of Oracle Enterprise Manager.

Exception Handling

Exception handling in BPM Suite 11g can be done by either explicitly modeling business exceptions and associated process paths (that is, using BPMN constructs such as "catch" and "throw" events, even subprocesses, and patterns generated using such constructs) or using policy-driven declarative exception handling.

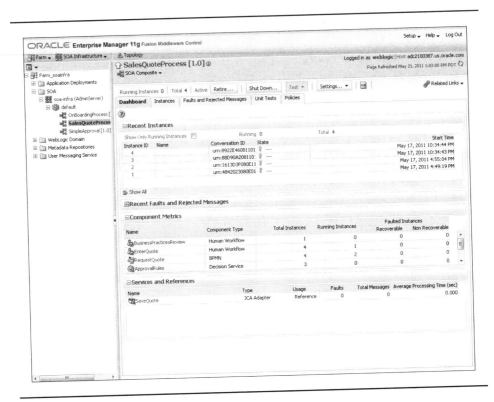

FIGURE 3-20. *Screenshot of Oracle Enterprise Manager*

An exception handling policy, called the Fault Policy, contains one or more policies that define exceptions to be caught and the actions to be taken when such exceptions occur. The exception handling framework provides a choice of various actions such as retry, abort, and human intervention via Oracle Enterprise Manager, and custom actions created using Java. Fault Policies are generic and are not specific to any process. Process developers can attach appropriate policies during build time so that they are part of the deployment unit.

The exception handling policies are stored as XML files that define how different types of faults should be handled. This allows for nonintrusive exception handling that is completely separated from the process.

Typically, system errors and exceptions such as network and database errors can also be handled using this framework. Oracle FMW Control (part of Oracle Enterprise Manager) is also used to manage faults and exceptions occurring during the execution of a process. It provides the administrator with options to abort, resume, fix data errors, and restart process instances.

It is worthwhile to note here that the policy-based exception handling strategy is typically well suited for system level exceptions, while business exceptions including situations where compensation logic may be needed are usually better handled via the BPMN-based patterns and applied where the exception is raised from.

Deployment

From a small single server deployment, suitable for development environments, to multiserver clustered deployments, Oracle BPM 11*g* is quite flexible in the ways it can be deployed. BPM 11*g* fully leverages high-availability and failover features provided by the underlying WebLogic application server. The supported deployment topologies include both active-active and active-passive patterns.

Oracle BPM 11*g* provides a set of command-line tools for automating the compilation, building, and deployment of BPM composite projects. The deployment tools can use a Configuration Plan that provides an easy way to modify environment specific values such as file system paths, network port number, URLs, database connection information, and others. A configuration plan is external to the composite application and applied to the composite application JAR file at deployment time. This allows for easy migration from one environment to another—for example, from test to production.

BPM Suite Interplay with Related Technologies

As we have shown thus far, BPM Suite 11*g* is a feature-wise comprehensive offering. However, there are many related technologies, both from Oracle stack as well from external vendors, that can also be leveraged along with BPM Suite to deliver yet higher value. In this section, we will explore some of them.

Visio and Other Modeling Tools

While BPM Suite includes a rich BPMN 2.0 process modeler, many customers would have existing process models in Visio and other process modeling tools. BPM Suite 11*g* includes a business process converter to import these models using XPDL 2.0 as an interchange format from Visio and other modeling tools that can export XPDL. It is widely expected that as BPMN 2.0 matures, different modeling tools and BPM Suites will be able to exchange BPMN 2.0 models without needing XPDL as an interchange format.

Decisioning

While BPM Suite includes a very capable and easy-to-use business rules component (which we have already mentioned briefly here and will be described in detail later in this book), there are scenarios where different decisioning technologies may be used with BPM 11*g*. Some of these decisioning products are:

- **Complex Event Processing (CEP)**   Oracle CEP (which from the packaging perspective is included in BPM Suite 11*g*) may be used alongside Oracle BPM Suit 11*g* to detect interesting business scenarios by looking for patterns in events emanating from BPM and elsewhere over windows of time. The BPM processes cannot only feed events to the pattern processor, but they can also be designed to adjust accordingly as different scenarios are detected or anticipated (Gartner calls this *Scenario Based Planning*). For example, a credit card issuer may relax its credit approval rules if it detects that a slowing economy is going to adversely impact the volume issued; if the company detects a continued deterioration of the economy in conjunction with increased defaults, it may put in place rules designed to weed out potential defaulters.

- **Real-Time Decisions (RTD)**   Oracle RTD (a separately licensed component) is a predictive analytics product that allows real-time intelligence to be instilled into business processes. Based on modeled objectives and observed outcomes, RTD can suggest decisions and actions to process participants. As the process unfolds and the outcomes of decisions become available, BPM can communicate it back to RTD, which then evolves its decision making.

For example, if a credit card issuing company wants to optimize its credit card issuing decisions to maximize business while minimizing defaults, it can use RTD as the recommendation engine powering the card issuing process.

- **Oracle Policy Automation (OPA)**   Oracle Policy Automation (a separately licensed component) can be used to address the following scenarios:

    - Creating rules from existing policy documents (in Word or Excel).

    - Implementing guided questionnaires—for example, a set of rules may be used by a credit card issuing company to decide what information it needs to collect from various applicants.

    - Conclusion-driven reasoning (also known as backward-chaining), where a conclusion such as "Customer is eligible for credit increase" is supported by conditions.

Content Management

Oracle Universal Content Management (UCM) (restricted use license included) is integrated with Oracle BPM 11*g* so that:

- Task and process attachments can be specified to be stored in UCM

- UCM can be configured to kick off a process based on UCM events

- Process Spaces is pre-integrated with UCM and provides the community-based creation and sharing of documents, wikis, and blogs (which are also UCM content)

Business Intelligence

As mentioned earlier, Oracle BPM 11*g* includes a rich BAM product for end-to-end monitoring and alerting. However, certain types of analysis may require the capabilities of a business intelligence product. Also, as indicated before, Oracle BPM 11*g* provides views on top of its STAR schema to facilitate analysis by Oracle Business Intelligence (a separately licensed component) or other BI tools. Oracle BI also supports the concept of actionable insights—kicking off BPM processes from BI dashboards to take corrective or other actions. Oracle BPM 11*g* can invoke BI to get a report included as part of a human task form so that the decision maker has the necessary insight to make a good decision. Finally, just as BPM Suite 11*g* is integrated with WebCenter Spaces, Oracle BI is integrated with WebCenter Spaces, too. A customer using these products from Oracle can very simply create composite portal interfaces—this is a business-user targeted task completed from the web interface itself using drag-and-drop editing of pages.

Summary

In this chapter, we provided a high-level overview of BPM Suite 11*g*. We covered the essentials of the product architecture and the drivers behind it, key product functionalities, and the ways this toolset could benefit those seeking to adopt BPM. As we described here, using the principles of social and collaborative interactions, role-based tooling, and unified execution infrastructure, BPM Suite 11*g* provides excellent capabilities to create, deploy, and manage full-featured, process-based business applications efficiently. Business empowerment, development agility, and operational ease are some of the immediate benefits of BPM Suite 11*g*. Along with insightful simulation, the use of business rules, multilevel monitoring and analytics, and its what-you-model-is-what-you-execute paradigm, BPM Suite 11*g* is an ideal product to handle incremental changes to existing processes and to pursue continuous process improvement. In the following chapters, we will delve into the finer details of many of the topics covered in this chapter.

PART
II

Mastering Oracle
BPM 11g

CHAPTER
4

The Quick Learner's
Guide to Oracle
BPM 11g

his chapter briefly introduces the concepts and technologies of the Oracle BPM Suite 11*g*. The intent of this chapter is to provide a quick tour through Oracle BPM Suite 11*g*, providing readers with enough information to get started with a BPM project, leveraging its rich set of model-driven technologies, such as BPMN, human tasks, services, and rules. Therefore, the focus of the chapter is on developing BPM projects. In a typical BPM life cycle, process analysts would start first to model and simulate the process and then engage developers in implementation details; however, to give readers a quick immersion into BPM components, this chapter starts with a developer focus. The business analyst tooling—Business Process Composer—is also introduced and explained at a depth sufficient for quick learners to be able to start using it. BPM WorkSpace, one of the end-user interfaces, is briefly explained so that readers following this chapter can use it to execute and use their business processes. Process Monitoring and Analytics is also introduced so that quick learners may start leveraging its capabilities, including integration with Oracle Business Activity Monitoring (BAM).

BPM Projects

A BPM project is the container for business processes and other supporting artifacts constituting a process application. A new BPM project can be created from BPM Studio's new gallery (the *New* submenu of *File* menu) by selecting either *BPM Application* from *Applications* (within *General*) as shown in Figure 4-1. If you are adding a BPM project to an existing application, select *BPM Project* from *BPM Tier*.

NOTE
BPM Studio refers to Oracle JDeveloper with BPM and SOA extensions installed. In this chapter, JDeveloper is used to refer to the base capabilities of JDeveloper.

A BPM project within BPM Studio can contain the following artifacts:

- Business Process Modeling Notation (BPMN) 2.0 processes
- Business Process Execution Language (BPEL) processes

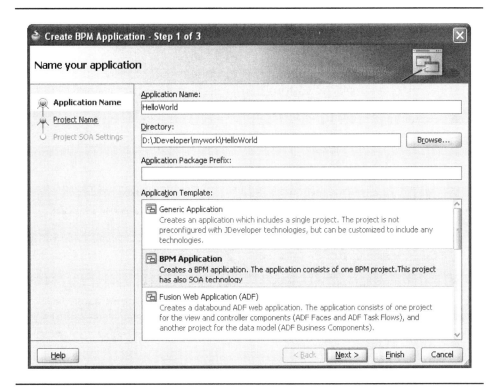

FIGURE 4-1. *The new application gallery in BPM Studio*

- Activity guides to overlay milestones and related information on BPMN processes to provide end-users with a guided navigation path through the process
- Human Tasks
- Business Rules
- Organization Model
- Simulation Scenarios

In addition, a BPM Project is layered on top of an SOA Project and can contain all SOA artifacts including:

- **Service references**   External web services used within the project or services exposed by various components within the project

- **Schemas**   XSDs for data types defined within the project

- **Transformation maps**   XSLT files for specifying complex data transformations between various XML types

- **Mediator components for mediating**   Routing, filtering, and transforming data—between multiple service and event endpoints

- **Spring context components**   For including services implementing Java interfaces in BPM projects

- **Service adapters**   Includes ADF-BC (Oracle Application Development Framework Business Components) Services, File Adapter, Database Adapter, and so on

- **Application adapters**

The BPM Project Navigator

In addition to JDeveloper's standard *Application Navigator,* BPM Studio features a *BPM Project Navigator* that provides a process-centric view of a BPM project. A BPM analyst or developer may find this navigator more conducive to accomplishing their tasks; falling back to *Application Navigator* only to access details abstracted away by the *BPM Project Navigator.*

Business Catalog

BPM Projects also feature a *Business Catalog* that contains business object (data type) definitions, various implementation artifacts including human tasks, business rules, events, exceptions, services implemented within the project, and external services referenced within the project. The catalog is a sharing mechanism between developer and analyst, and enables the developer to organize catalog elements, as well as make these elements more business-analyst friendly by documenting and customizing their presentation, such as selecting appropriate operation names and so on.

Deploying a BPM Project

A BPM project may be deployed by right-clicking the project node in the *Application Navigator* panel and selecting *Deploy*. Readers familiar with JDeveloper will realize that this action deploys a deployment profile defined in the project settings. For BPM projects, a deployment profile of the correct type is automatically created during new project creation; interested readers may note that the deployment profile type used by BPM projects is *SOA-SAR* (Service Archive), which is the same as SOA projects. The deployment of projects to a server also requires that a connection to a server is defined within the *Resource Palette* by selecting menu *New Connection* and submenu *Application Server*. A BPM project may have associated web projects containing the user interface elements; these projects may be deployed by right-clicking the application node (the dropdown) in *Application Navigator* and selecting *Deploy*. User interface projects are discussed in greater detail in Chapter 8.

BPMN 2.0 for Quick Learners

Business Process Modeling Notation (BPMN) 2.0 is a graphical, flow-based process modeling language that can be refined with enough implementation details to make the model itself an executable process. This enables Oracle BPM 11*g* to provide a what-you-see-is-what-you-get (WYSIWYG) experience, leveraging standard semantics that facilitate high-fidelity business-IT collaboration and business traceability. A sample BPMN 2.0 process is shown in Figure 4-2.

The important concepts in BPMN 2.0 are:

- **Swim-lanes**   Swim-lanes are a visual way of organizing the process by participant. A new swim-lane gets created in Oracle BPM 11*g* when a new human activity is dragged and dropped outside of any existing lanes. In BPM 11*g*, a swim-lane implies assignment—human activities in the lane are assigned to the swim-lane role; however, such implied assignment may be overridden.

- **Activities**   Activities are the tasks performed by a process. BPM 11*g* features, among other things, the following type of activities: *Interactive* (that is, human), *Business Rules, Service* (that is, system),

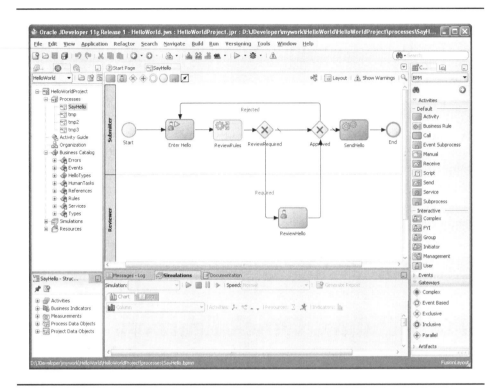

FIGURE 4-2. *A BPMN 2.0 process in Oracle BPM Studio (JDeveloper)*

and *Script.* Activities are added to a process diagram by dragging and dropping them from the *Component Palette.* BPM 11*g* is a zero-code environment and the implementation of an activity is specified through the *Implementation* tab of its *Properties* window, which can be launched by double-clicking the activity. Properties are also available from the *Property Inspector* window of BPM Studio.

■ **Sequence flows** The sequence in which activities are performed is specified by sequence-flow connectors. An activity is executed when it receives a token (that is, an internal control message indicating that the prior activity is complete) from an incoming sequence-flow, and when it is completed successfully it sends a token through its outgoing sequence flow. Sequence-flow connectors may be added by dragging and dropping them from the palette or by right-clicking the source activity and selecting the action to start a connector, as shown in Figure 4-3. Sequence flows may be conditional, in which case a conditional expression can be specified in the *Properties* window of the connector.

NOTE
A new connector is added as a straight connector that can be dragged to convert it into an elbow connector. To add the Rejected connector in Figure 4-2, move one of the activities, convert the connector into an elbow connector, and then move the activity back.

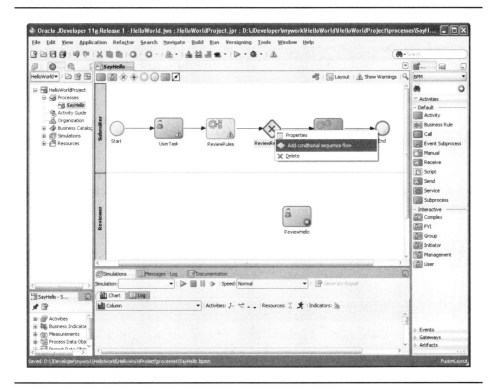

FIGURE 4-3. *Right-click to start a connector*

- **Gateways** Gateways allow richness in a process flow beyond simple sequential order. The two most commonly used gateways are *Exclusive,* also known as XOR, and *Parallel,* also known as AND. An exclusive gateway is the equivalent of switch statements in programming languages and sends a token to (that is, executes) one of its multiple outgoing connectors. A parallel gateway is the equivalent of fork statements in programming languages and sends tokens to all of its outgoing connectors. Gateways are added to the process and connected the same way as activities are.

- **Events** *Start* and *End* events model how the process starts and ends. *Catch* events model handling of exceptions including faults and timeouts. *Throw* events enable a process activity to raise an exception.

Process Simulation

One of the important benefits of BPMN process modeling is that the BPM processes can be simulated even before they are implemented so that certain validation of the process model can be done early on. There are two concepts in using simulation:

- **Simulation Model** A simulation model captures the assumed execution characteristics of a BPMN process. Multiple simulation models may be created for a process modeling different scenarios representing different business conditions. Simulation models are created from *BPM Navigator* by navigating to *Simulation Models,* child of *Simulations* node in the navigator, finding the node for the BPMN process within it, and right-clicking to create a new simulation model. Some of the characteristics captured in the simulation model are:

  - **For Activities** The statistical model for time taken to complete the activity, resources to use, and costing model.

  - **For Gateways** Probabilities for different conditional paths.

  - **For Events** Statistical model for instance creation (start event) and probabilities of events (intermediate events).

■ **Simulation Definition**   A simulation definition defines which
   processes to include in a simulation run, and for each process to
   include, which simulation model to use. Since multiple processes
   may share resources and be impacted by each other, the ability to
   simulate multiple processes together provides a more realistic view.
   Simulation definition also allows defining resources to assume during
   simulation, including what percentage of a resource to assume.

A simulation model and a simulation definition, along with the result of
a simulation run, are shown in Figure 4-4. The result of a simulation run can
also be exported as an HTML report or be sent to Excel for further analysis.

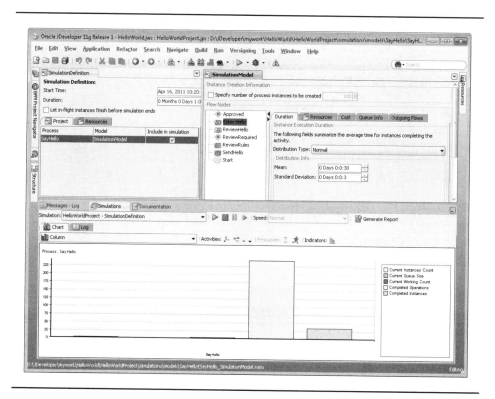

FIGURE 4-4.   *A BPMN 2.0 process simulation*

Process Data

Process data is held in Data Objects, which are the equivalent of variables. Data objects may be based on simple types such as *String*, or they may be based on Business Objects, which are the equivalent of complex type definitions. Business objects may be based on an existing XML Schema (XSD) or created from scratch in BPM Studio.

NOTE
Careful readers may note that the attribute needed in Figure 4-5 is of the type String *instead of* Boolean. *XPath's handling of Booleans is not always intuitive and it may be simpler to use strings and string comparisons where possible.*

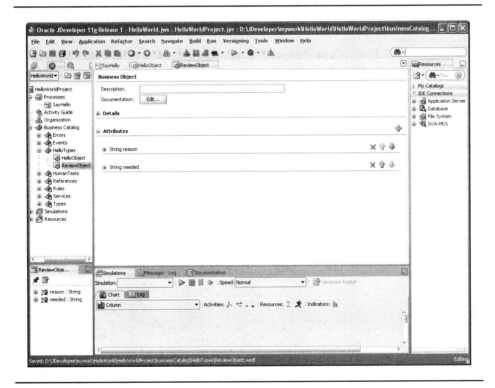

FIGURE 4-5. *The Business Object editor in BPM Studio*

Process data is passed to invoked activities inputs and the activities outputs are stored back in the process using input and output data association. Data associations are available from the *Implementation* tab of the activity's *Properties* window and are created, edited, and viewed in the Data Associations editor, as shown in Figure 4-6.

As shown in Figure 4-6, the Data Associations editor has three panes: the source pane on the left, the target pane on the right, and the mappings pane on the bottom. The source pane displays the data elements available as a source for the associations, while the target pane displays the target

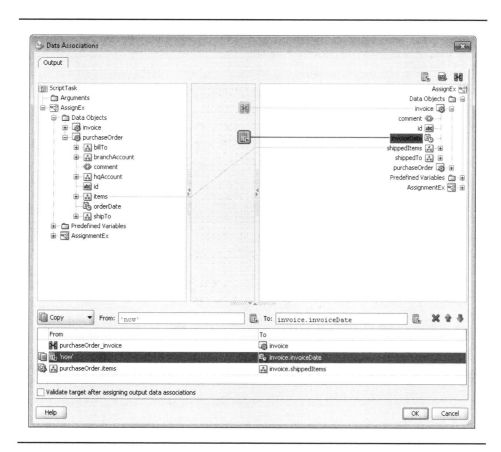

FIGURE 4-6. *The Data Associations editor*

data elements. The mappings pane displays the current mappings to target data elements in an ordered fashion; the mappings are also visually indicated in the canvas area between the source pane and the target pane.

New mappings can be added by dragging and dropping data elements from source pane to data elements in the target pane. Also, at the top right of the target panel are three icons representing expression, literal, and XSLT (left-to-right). These icons can be dragged and dropped to target data elements to assign them an expression value, literal value, or the result of an XSLT transformation. Both the expression and literal assignment bring up the expression editor where a simple expression, XPath expression, or a literal value can be specified. Expressions may, and typically will, include source data elements; however, this relationship is not visually shown.

The XSLT assignment option enables running an XSLT transformation on one or more source data elements and assigning the result to the target data element. BPM Studio includes a visual drag-and-drop XSLT editor that can be used to create the XSLT mapping. This option is needed when the structure of the source and target are quite different, and more complete transformation capabilities—including constructs such as *for* and *if*—are needed.

The mapping pane lists all the mappings and enables deleting and reordering mappings. At runtime, the mappings are executed in the same order, and since multiple mappings can assign to the same target element— either directly or through a hierarchical relation (that is, mapping to a parent data element)—ordering is important. Some scenarios where this multiple mapping capability is needed are:

- The target data is almost a copy of the source data; however, one or two attributes need to be different. This is achieved by first copying the source data element to the target data element and then specifying the overriding mappings for the attributes that need to be different.

- The target data needs to collect values from multiple-source data elements.

Once a mapping is created, it can be edited from the mapping pane either using the expression boxes on the top of the mapping pane or by clicking the mapping to bring up the expression editor.

In addition to the default Copy operation, which copies a specified value to the target data element, the following operations are supported:

- **Copy List** In this option, both the source and the target expressions can return multiple nodes (elements or attributes). All nodes pointed by the target expression are removed. If there are left over sibling nodes of the target nodes, then the source nodes are inserted before the next sibling of the last node in the target expression. Otherwise, the source nodes are appended.

- **Append** Append the content of the source expression to the existing content of the target.

- **Insert Before** and **Insert After** Insert the content of the source expression before or after the specified target.

Watch Out for Implications of Loops in the Process Flow

When a process flow has a loop, special attention must be paid to ensure the business logic is correct. For example, in the process shown in Figure 4-2, the loop back to *Enter Hello* user activity on *Rejected* causes two issues that need to be handled:

- Unless input data association is specified for *Enter Hello* activity, each re-invocation of the activity will present the user with empty data. This is easily addressed by specifying the process data object as the input data association for this activity.

- If the first time the reviewer selects *Reject* and on the second loop the business rules determine that the review is not needed, the earlier reviewer's selection would continue to stick. This can be addressed by resetting the outcome to the desired default value in each loop. One way to accomplish this is to use the output data association for the rules activity as shown in Figure 4-7.

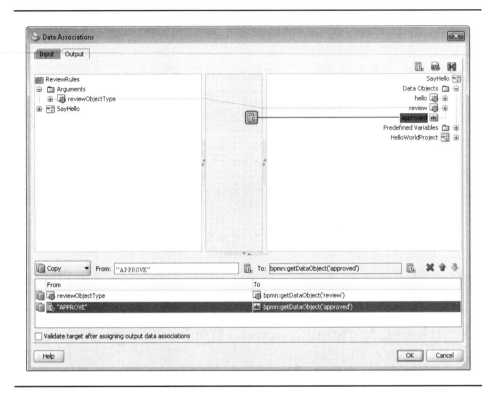

FIGURE 4-7. *Resetting an approved data object using custom assignments*

These additional options are particularly useful when working with repeating data elements such as arrays and lists. One of the preceding operations can be selected using the pick-list at the top-left corner of the mapping pane, after which the selected operation is visually indicated in the first column of the mapping. For example, in Figure 4-6 the third mapping has an icon with a plus sign in the first column, indicating usage of the *Append* operation.

Script activity in a BPMN process enables specification of data associations outside of any activity's input or output.

Expressions

Expressions are needed in conditional connectors as well as in some situations in data associations. BPM 11*g* supports two flavors of expressions: Simple and XPath. The difference between the two is only in presentation;

FIGURE 4-8.   *Expression Builder—simple expressions mode*

underneath, even simple expressions use XPath. Expression Builder in simple mode is shown in Figure 4-8.

Learning simple expressions is straightforward using the Expression Builder. Simple expressions use *dot-notation* to reference data; the variables panel of the expression builder allows graphical selection of data and generates the *dot-notation* reference. Simple expressions also feature many functions for string, number, and time manipulation. The *Function* panel of the *Expression Builder* allows for browsing and using the functions listed in the panel. In addition, simple expressions support the following operators:

- Logical Operators:

  - *and* for conditional, *or* for conditional and, *not* for negation

  - == for equal, *!=* for not equal, > for greater, >= for greater-or-equal, < for less, and <= for less-or-equal

- Arithmetic Operators:

  - + for adding numbers, concatenating strings, and adding intervals to date and time types

  - - for subtracting numbers, and as an interval value from date and time types

  - * for multiplying, / for dividing, and *rem* for calculating remainders of numbers

  - (and) for ordering precedence

XPath expressions support many more functions than simple expressions, and XPath as an expression language is significantly richer than the capabilities exposed in simple mode. Therefore, XPath mode is useful for advanced requirements. XPath is widely documented and explained on the Internet, including at www.w3.org/TR/xpath/. Moreover, similar to simple expressions, *Expression Builder* facilitates the writing of XPath expressions using select-and-click.

Process Start and End

A start event is used to indicate how a BPMN process is started; common options include:

- **None** A business analyst would typically start with a *None* start event that the developer may then refine to another type. An implementation ready process may continue to use a *None* start event in the following two scenarios:

  - The *None* event handler followed by an *Initiator* (*Interactive*) activity signifies that the process will be started by a user who has been granted the *Initiator* role. These processes are typically invoked from a form submitted by the user from BPM WorkSpace.

- Otherwise, it signifies a subprocess that will be invoked by another process using *Call* activity.

- **Message**   A message event signifies that the process will be invoked as a service. The Implementation tab of the event's *Properties* window allows the interface to be specified.

- **Signal**   A signal event specifies that the process will be invoked based on the receipt of an event, which is useful in decoupling the process from the invoker.

- **Timer**   A process may be started based on a timer; however, in most cases the use of an external scheduler may be preferred.

A process may end normally with a *None* end event or a *Message* end event. A *Message* end event signifies that the process ends with the sending of a reply or invocation of the callback interface. A process may end abnormally by raising an exception with the *Error* end event or terminate immediately with the *Terminate* event.

A Process's Service Interface

A service interface is automatically created for a process based on its start and end events.

While a BPMN process will typically be asynchronous, the synchronous pattern is supported as well. When creating a new process, BPM 11*g* supports specifying the pattern: asynchronous, synchronous, and so on. However, if the process was created by a business analyst, it will typically be created with *None* start and end events; developers can easily change the event types to *Message* by right-clicking the corresponding event in the BPMN editor. In this scenario, asynchronous versus synchronous behavior is specified in the *Advanced* section of the *Implementation* tab of the event's *Properties* window, as shown in Figure 4-9. Note that a synchronous start event must have a corresponding message throw or end event.

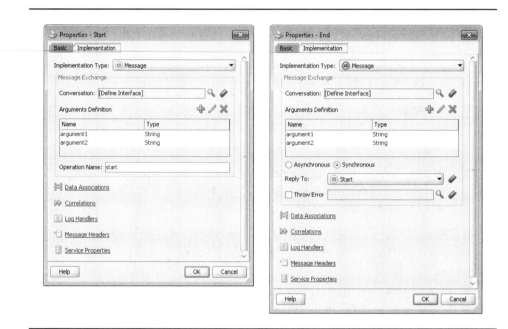

FIGURE 4-9. *Implementation properties for a matching start and end event*

The generated service interface creates a request-reply operation for synchronous processes and a combination of the request and callback operations for asynchronous processes. By default, BPM 11*g* uses WS-Addressing to correlate the request and callback operation ensuring the requesting process is the one receiving callback. In addition to these operations, using a message end event, with implementation type *BusinessException,* results in the generation of fault definition in the operation (note that faults apply only to synchronous request–reply operations).

In addition to the typical synchronous and asynchronous patterns, sometimes a combination is desired; for example, to get an acknowledgement synchronously from an otherwise asynchronous process. This is achieved in Oracle BPM 11*g* by using a message throw event matching the synchronous message start event. The process can continue its flow after the throw event. This is discussed in greater detail in Chapter 5.

BPMN and BPEL

In addition to BPMN 2.0, Oracle BPM 11*g* also supports Business Process Execution Language (BPEL). Under the covers, both types of processes are executed on a common process core and work with the same surrounding components, such as human tasks, business rules, mediators, and so on. This means that, independent of the process technology used, customers can expect similar characteristics. At its core, the difference between BPMN and BPEL boils down to the fact that the former is graph-based (as in flow charts), whereas the latter is block-structured (as in most programming languages). Following are some of the guidelines that may be used to determine which technology is best suited to any given process:

- **Audience**   BPMN appeals to business analysts and business users and should be used if it is desired to include them in the BPM life cycle. The block structured nature of BPEL, on the other hand, is more familiar to developers.

- **Process Flavor**   BPMN with its swim-lanes and related concepts is better suited for human-centric processes. BPEL, on the other hand, with its block-structured exception handling semantics, is better suited for integration subflows or straight through processing.

- **Flow Patterns**   BPMN, being graph-based, can handle loops and similar patterns that may be difficult to model in a block-structured language.

A good rule of thumb is to use BPMN as the top-level process modeling language, as well as for the human-centric and document-centric aspects of the process, and to use BPEL for the underlying integration subflows. Another scenario for which BPEL is well suited is service orchestration, where coarse-grained business services are composed from fine-grained services, usually in a transactional manner.

While most of the preceding discussion has been focused on the process of exposing a service interface based on its definition, BPM 11*g* also supports leveraging existing interface definitions (WSDL). In this scenario, the interface to be used can be specified in the *Implementation Properties* of the start and end events.

Human Task for Quick Learners

Consistent with the Web Services for Human Tasks (WS-Human Task) architecture, Oracle BPM 11*g* uses a separate workflow component (service engine in the Service Component Architecture terminology) to manage the life cycle of interactive or human activities. Within the modeling environment, this component is called Human Task and the artifact is stored with a ".task" suffix; a sample human task is shown in Figure 4-10. From a runtime and administration perspective, the component is also called a Human Workflow component.

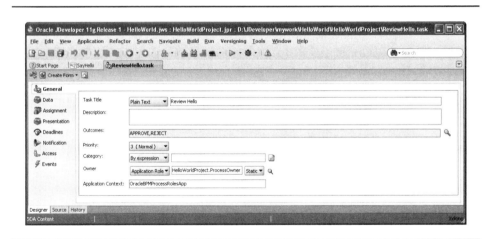

FIGURE 4-10. *Human Task definition in BPM Studio*

The Human Task component includes definitions of:

- **Task Header Attributes**   Attributes such as title, description, outcomes, priority; outcomes are the task-specific actions available to task performers.

- **Data**   Task-specific data available to task performers, including whether such data is read-write or read-only.

- **Assignment**   Task performers, as well as reviewers, owners, and error assignees. This is discussed in more detail later in this section.

- **Deadlines**   Task deadlines, including escalation and expiration conditions. Escalation by default follows the management chain hierarchy in the identity store (LDAP, OID, and so on). A custom escalation hierarchy may be specified by plugging in an extension Java class.

- **Notification**   Notify users or groups of changes to the task state and assignment. You can specify what notification to send, to whom, and when. Note that the channel by which notification is delivered is an end-user preference. E-mail notifications may be configured to be actionable; in which case, the recipient gets an e-mail with links for the actions, and clicking the actions composes a reply message that the BPM server can understand and thereby further the process. This enables end users to work their processes even when working remotely.

- **Access**   Who has access to which actions and which data. The most common scenario for using this is to grant different predefined actions (called system actions), such as reassign, suspend, and so on, on a selective basis. You can also control what parts of the task data are visible to different participants in the workflow.

Human Tasks and BPMN

The BPMN editor in Oracle BPM 11*g* exposes human tasks using the following flavors of interactive activities:

- **User**   This is the simple flavor and would be the most common one to use. When this pattern is used, the task gets assigned to the grantees of the role associated with the swim-lane that this task sits in.

- **Initiator**   This is a special task type that is used to expose the ability to start a process to users. Users granted this task see a link to initiate the process in the *Applications* panel of their workspace. Note that a process may loop back to this step as in Figure 2; the subsequent invocations of this task behave the same as *User* task.

- **FYI**   This is similar to *User task,* with the exception that this task is a notification-only task and the process does not wait for the user's action. While users can dismiss the *FYI* tasks manually, it is a good idea to use expiration settings to automatically expire *FYI* tasks.

- **Management Chain**   This flavor encapsulates the management chain routing pattern in a single activity. The routing starts based on the swim-lane that the task resides in, similar to *User* task. The task is further routed up the management chain of the first performer based on the specified number of levels up to the top approver (optionally) specified. Note that the management chain is tied to the first actual performer and not to the swim-lane role.

- **Group (Vote)**   This flavor encapsulates the group-vote pattern where multiple people work on a task in parallel, and the task may be deemed complete based on a certain quorum. All grantees of a swim-lane role get this task as a parallel task (and not shared tasks as in *User* and others) and can vote on the outcome.

■ **Complex**   This flavor delegates assignment and routing completely to the task metadata and leverages the full power of the human task component. Here you can specify any combination of the predefined patterns and create complex approval workflows based on process data and business rules.

Advanced Task Routing

As mentioned earlier, the human task component supports specification of sophisticated or advanced routing within itself. An example is shown in Figure 4-11.

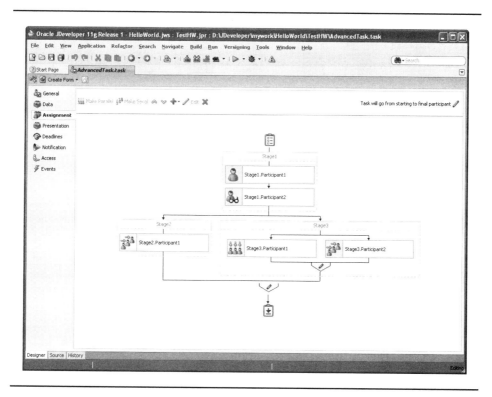

FIGURE 4-11.   *Advanced task routing within Human Task*

Multiple participants can be arranged in a combination of sequential and parallel blocks to specify the routing flow. Each participant in turn could represent a routing pattern such as management chain, group vote, and so on. Participants may be specified as users, groups, roles, expressions based on task data, or business rules. The routing flow may be further organized into stages; in addition to serving as an organization mechanism, a stage can be made to repeat in sequence or parallel based on collections in the task data (for example, line items in a purchase order).

In addition to using business rules to assign participants, business rules may also be used to override the specified routing flow. In this scenario, after every participant acts on the task, the specified rules are invoked and these can decide to override the routing flow and, among other things, complete the task or route it to a different participant.

Roles and Users

Oracle BPM 11*g* has two primary concepts concerning roles and users:

- **Users and Groups** These are accessed from an identity store, which may be Oracle Identity Directory (OID), LDAP, Active Directory, or something else. The configuration of the identity store is done at the Oracle Platform Security Services (OPSS) layer using the Web Logic console application.

- **Application Roles** Application roles are a feature of the Oracle Fusion Middleware policy store that enables the definition of roles outside the corporate identity directory. These roles can be granted to users and groups in the corporate identity store as well as other application roles. Application roles are defined in the context of an application—for example, the *soainfra* application is seeded with SOA and BPM policy–related roles such as *BPMAdmin*. BPM 11*g* allows tasks and other privileges to be granted to application roles, thus avoiding the need to modify the identity store.

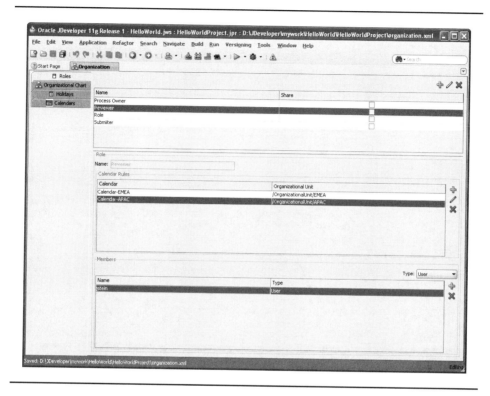

FIGURE 4-12. *An Organization definition for a BPM 11g project*

A BPM 11g project also has an *Organization* definition, as shown in Figure 4-12. A role defined inside a BPM *organization* definition is essentially an application role stored within the *OracleBPMProcessRolesApp* application.

As seen in Figure 4-12, roles may be associated with business calendars, which will be used to calculate due-date, expiration, and other timers. Also seen in Figure 4-12 is the ability to grant the role to users, groups, and other application roles from within BPM Studio. However, these grants would typically be managed by a business administrator from the workspace (end-user interface) application, as shown in Figure 4-13.

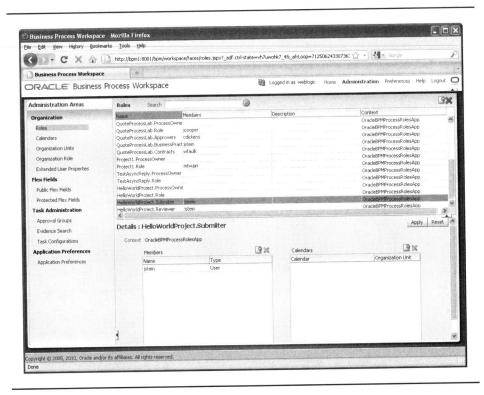

FIGURE 4-13. *Roles and organization management in workspace*

Process Owner and Other Special Roles

In addition to the performer of a task, BPM 11*g* supports the following roles for a task:

■ **Process Owner**   Typically, the process-owner has business admin privileges, including the ability to act on others' behalf or reassign tasks. A BPM project has a special pre-seeded role called *ProcessOwner* and by default this role is granted the process owner role for all tasks in the project. Interested readers may note that this default granting is accomplished by setting the *Owner* attribute within the *General*

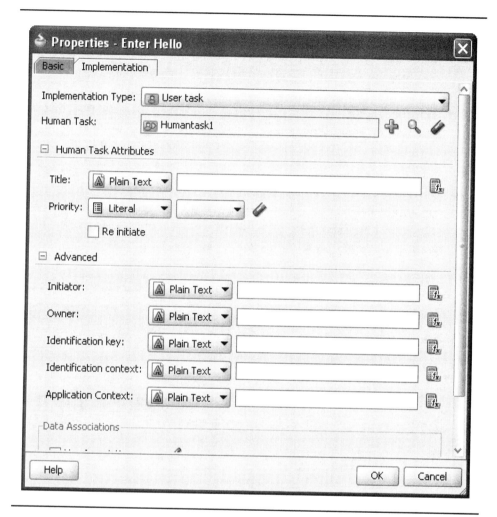

FIGURE 4-14. *Advanced implementation properties for an interactive activity*

section of the human task definition to *<ProjectName>.ProcessOwner.* This role may also be granted on an instance basis by specifying a value for *Owner* in the advanced section of an interactive activity's implementation properties as shown in Figure 4-14.

■ **Initiator or Creator**   This is the user who is defined as the initiator of the process containing the task. The creator, by default, has view, delete, and withdraw privileges. For the *Initiator* interactive activity, the creator is automatically set. For other interactive activities the initiator property needs to be set in the advanced implementation properties, as shown in Figure 4-14. If the process is initiated by an *Initiator* activity, then its *creator* attribute may be the appropriate value to set as the initiator for other tasks; this value can be accessed in the output data association for the *Initiator* activity within the *execData* node.

■ **Reviewer**   Typically user(s) granted this role have review-only capabilities. This role is granted from the *Configure Assignment* dialog which pops up by clicking the pencil icon next to *Task will go from starting to final participant,* as shown in Figure 4-15.

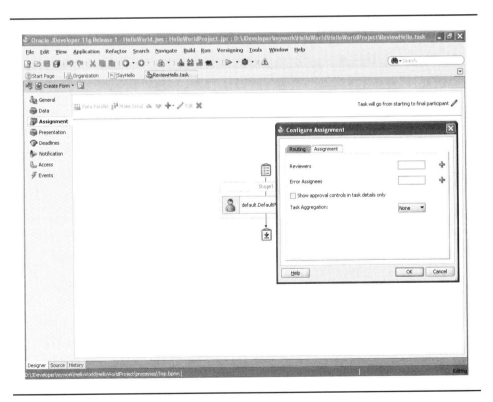

FIGURE 4-15.   *Configure Assignment of reviewer and error assignee*

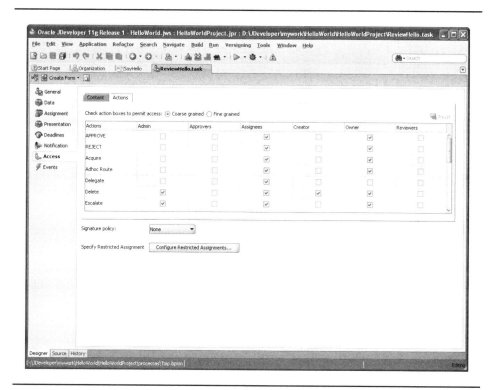

FIGURE 4-16. *Access rules for Human Tasks*

- ■ **Error Assignee**   This specifies who the tasks should be assigned to if they run into errors. This is specified in the same place as *Reviewer* as shown in Figure 15.

The default privileges of the roles mentioned here can be viewed and modified within the Access tab of the Human Task editor, as shown in Figure 4-16.

Careful readers may note in Figure 4-16 two roles not discussed in the previous paragraphs: *admin* and *approvers.* The former refers to the application role *BPMAdmin* in *soainfra* application. Typically, the overall administrator (*weblogic*) is granted this role as well, and the latter refers to all previous participants in a task's history.

Forms (User Interfaces) for Human Tasks

BPM 11*g* by default uses Oracle Application Development Framework (ADF) for task forms—the user interfaces presented to task participants. ADF UI projects can be automatically generated using either a one-click generator or a wizard that provides for more flexibility. The generators can be accessed from the BPMN editor, as shown in Figure 4-17, or from the Human Task editor.

The forms are generated in a separate ADF project that contains a data control abstracting bindings to BPM data and actions, a task flow, and JSF pages. The generated pages may be used as is or can be easily customized or extended in the ADF JSF/JSP editor within BPM Studio, as shown in Figure 4-18.

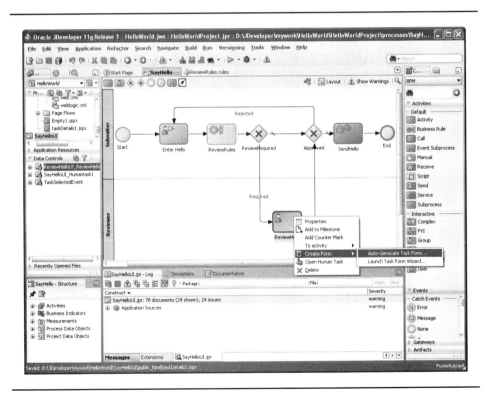

FIGURE 4-17. *Generate Human Task forms (ADF user interface)*

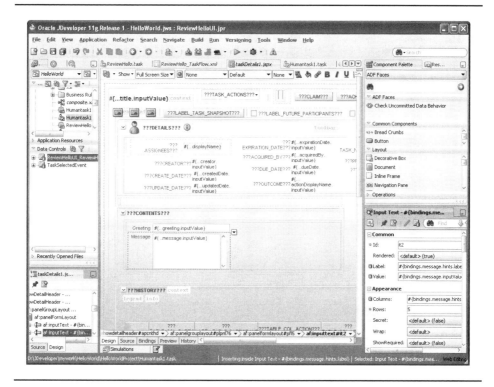

FIGURE 4-18.   *Using the ADF JSF/JSP editor to extend or customize Human Task forms*

Business Rules for Quick Learners

Oracle Business Rules is an integral component of Oracle BPM 11*g* and enables the abstraction of business rules and policies outside of procedural and business process logic in an easy-to-understand-and-modify declarative representation. It supports two metaphors for expressing business rules:

- **If-Then Statements**   In this metaphor, each rule is expressed as an independent if-condition-then-action statement.

- **Decision Table**   In this metaphor, a logical collection of rules is expressed in a table format, as shown in Figure 4-19.

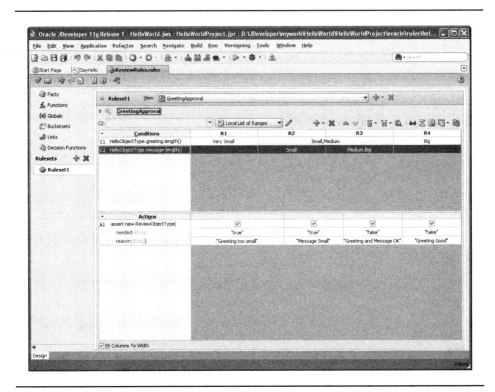

FIGURE 4-19.   *A sample decision table*

Rule Actions

Both flavors of business rules take as input some set of rule facts from the process and support the same set of actions. The common scenario when using business rules from BPM 11*g* is for the rules to return results and for the process to act upon the results. In other words, no action per se happens within business rules other than the creation or manipulation of the result.

In these scenarios, most commonly the *Modify* action will be used; it modifies the state of an existing fact. Note that if there are other rules whose condition tests for the modified fact, a modify action will cause such conditions to be retested. Interested readers may note that this automatic reevaluation of dependencies is commonly known as inference and is a salient feature of Rete rule engines.

Two other fact manipulation actions that are not as commonly used as *Modify* but are useful to understand are:

- **Assert New** Creates a new fact. This is one of the common strategies for creating new result facts. This is the action being used in the example shown in Figure 4-19.

- **Retract** When a fact no longer holds, it may be explicitly retracted, causing conditions testing for the fact to be reevaluated. (Oracle Business Rules uses optimizations to minimize the reevaluations.)

Another commonly used action is *Call,* which may be used to invoke a *Function* that abstracts a set of other actions such as one to facilitate authoring, as well as to invoke Java methods as actions, where such behavior is needed (although the recommendation is for business rules to only create and modify results.) For Java methods to be invoked as a *Call* action, corresponding Java classes need to be imported as Java Facts.

Rule Dictionary, Rulesets, and Other Concepts

Rules of both flavors are contained within *Rulesets.* A ruleset is the unit of inclusion within decision functions—within Oracle Business Rules, rules are never individually invoked or used, instead usage is always at the ruleset level. A rule file (or artifact) is known as a *Rule Dictionary,* which contains one or more rulesets as well as:

- **Facts** Facts are the objects that rules reason on. When using business rules from BPM 11g, facts are set up by the business rules wizard. However, it may be useful to edit the fact definitions and turn off visibility for elements that will not be useful for rule authoring, as well as provide more business-friendly aliases.

- **Globals** Globals are variables that may be final or non-final. Final globals may be used in rule conditions, thus effectively parameterizing them, enabling business users to change rules by simply changing the value of the global. Non-final globals can be used to hold the outcome of rules evaluations.

■ **Functions** Functions are procedure definitions. They may be used to provide an easier-to-use action abstraction by encapsulating the details of other actions, and a more language-like representation for Boolean expressions in conditions. They are also useful as utilities for testing and diagnostics.

■ **Bucketsets** Bucketsets are essentially a named set of ranges. These will be explained later along with decision tables.

■ **Links** Links enable linking multiple dictionaries into one virtual dictionary. This allows sharing and reuse—for example, facts and functions may be in a common dictionary. Also, since a dictionary is a physical artifact, and therefore a unit of change and versioning, dictionary linking is also a mechanism to achieve finer-grained change and version management.

■ **Decision Functions** A Decision Function wraps a sequence of one or more rulesets with an input and output definition, providing an interface that may be invoked as a service or through Java API.

Working with Business Rules

New Business Rule dictionaries may be created from the Implementation properties of a *Business Rules* activity in BPMN editor. The *Create Business Rules Wizard* prompts for the specification of process data objects as rules input and output, as shown in Figure 4-20.

NOTE
Business Rules interfaces are limited to XSD elements—that is, either business objects defined within BPM or business objects based on XSD elements. In particular, this means that simple types such as strings, as well as business objects created based on XSD complex types, cannot be used. For the latter, the workaround is simple—define an XSD element based on the XSD complex type and create a business object based on it.

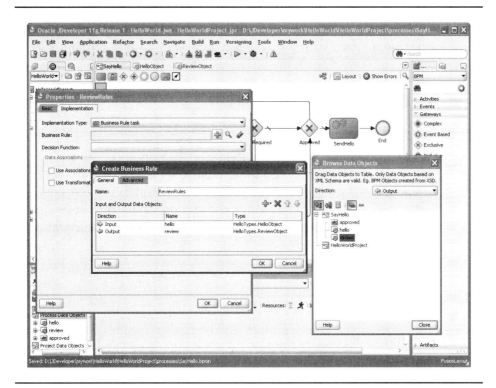

FIGURE 4-20. *The new Business Rules wizard in BPMN editor*

The wizard generates a new dictionary with facts defined for the input and output types, one decision function created and exposed as a service, and an empty ruleset. New rulesets may be created by clicking the green-plus icon next to the label *Rulesets* in the left panel, as shown in Figure 4-19. Since the generated decision function is set up to include only the generated ruleset, new rulesets must be explicitly added to it. New rules, both If-Then and decision tables, may be created by clicking the green-plus icon next to the pull-down next to the ruleset name at the top of the canvas as shown in Figure 4-19.

Decision Tables

A decision table has two sections—the top section describes conditions and the bottom section describes actions. The way to read a decision table is:

- Conditions

  - Each column (except for the first column) represents a rule.

  - Each row in the top section represents a condition using an expression in the first column, labeled Conditions, and a set of possible values in other columns (rules columns). A condition cell in a rule column is true if the expression in the first column evaluates to one of the values in it. The value '-' in a condition cell indicates "*don't care.*"

  - The condition for the rule is a conjunction (*and*) of all the conditions that are not "don't care."

- Actions

  - If the checkbox on the row for an action is checked, invoke this action when this rule condition is true.

  - For each parameter of the action in the secondary rows, use the value specified in the corresponding cells.

For example, the decision table shown in Figure 4-19 is read as:

- *R1* If *HelloObjectType.greeting.length* is *Very Small,* then assert new *ReviewObjectType* with *needed* = "*true*" and *reason* = "*Greeting too Small*". Note that the second condition row is a don't-care.

- *R2* If *HelloObjectType.greeting.length* is *Small* or *Medium* and *HelloObjectType.message.length* is *Small,* then assert new *ReviewObjectType* with *needed* = "*true*" and *reason* = "*Message Small*".

NOTE
While the preceding discussion assumes that a column represents a rule, it is possible in Business Process Composer to transpose the table rendering each row as a rule.

Bucketsets

The previous discussion assumes that each condition cell in a rule condition is one or more values—in the preceding example, *Very Small*, *Small*, and *Medium.* When the test condition is a continuous value, Oracle Business Rules allows dividing the value into buckets of ranges, as shown in Figure 4-21.

In the earlier example, we defined a bucketset called *Greeting Sizes* that buckets an integer value into *Very Small* if less than 5, *Small* if between 5 and 9, *Medium* if between 10 and 29, or *Big* if 30 or more.

This approach of defining bucketsets first and then using them in decision table conditions may appear to be an extra step to some readers who may be wondering why the ranges cannot be directly specified in the table cells. The rationale behind this approach is that, in addition to providing *bucketsets* as an abstraction that can be independently exposed and modified, by dividing the universe of possibilities into a finite set, it also enables Gap Analysis and overlap checks.

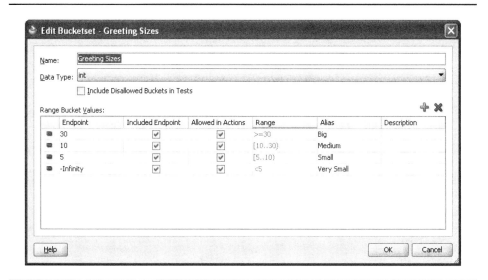

FIGURE 4-21. *Bucketsets for greeting sizes*

NOTE
*Ranges can be typed directly in the condition
cells; a local bucketset is automatically created
or updated.*

Working with Decision Tables

The green-plus icon within the decision table is a dropdown and allows the
creation of new conditions, actions, and rules. Typical steps in authoring a
decision table are:

1. Create a new condition for each condition dimension. In the
   example shown in Figure 4-19, these are *greeting length* and
   message length. After creating a new condition using the green-plus
   icon, double-click the condition to browse the fact tree and select
   the desired fact element, as shown in Figure 4-22.

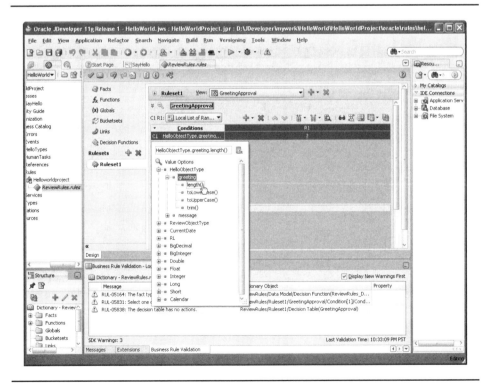

FIGURE 4-22. *Adding a new condition to a decision table*

2. For each condition in the previous step, choose an existing bucketset or define a new one using the dropdown next to the spreadsheet-like cell-address indicator on the top of the decision table.

3. Create a new action for each needed action. Mark the properties of the action that should be set from the decision table as parameterized, as shown in Figure 4-23.

4. Now add new rules. Click condition cells to select one or more of the available buckets. For don't care, right-click or type '-'.

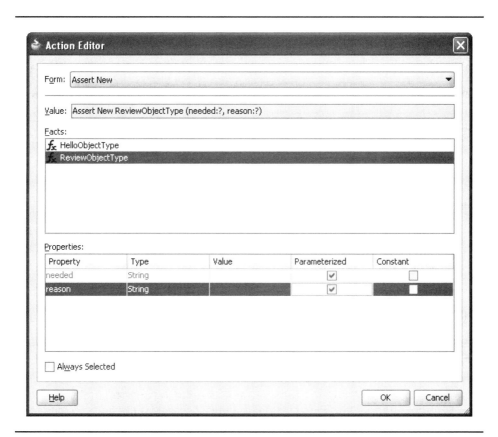

FIGURE 4-23. *Adding a new action to a decision table*

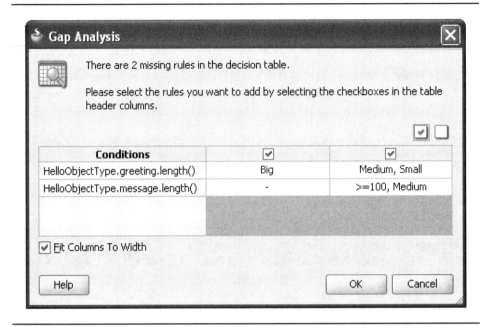

FIGURE 4-24. *Using Gap Analysis to auto-create rule conditions*

5. The Gap Analysis feature is a useful mechanism to automatically create all missing rules, as shown in Figure 4-24.

6. If needed, the decision table, a condition row within it, or a condition cell can be split. In summary, split takes a condition cell and creates sibling cells for all included buckets.

Service Tasks

Service tasks are implemented in Oracle BPM 11*g* by selecting an available service in the business catalog within the *Implementation Properties* for the activity. The looking-glass icon next to the *Name* field in Figure 4-25 launches the business catalog browser and an existing service in the catalog may be selected, causing the *Name* to be set; if the selected service exposes more than one operation, the *Operation* field may be changed using the dropdown. Data from process data objects may be assigned to invoke the service's input and its output may be assigned back to process data objects using the Data Associations editor discussed earlier.

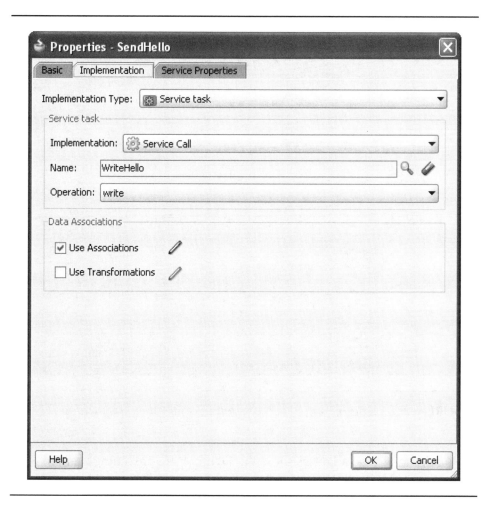

FIGURE 4-25. *Implementation properties for a service activity*

Since the service activity's implementation may be bound only to existing services in the business catalog, implementation of service activities includes population of the business catalog with services. Oracle BPM 11*g* leverages Oracle SOA Suite's rich set of zero-code wizard-driven adapters, including adapters for Web Service, Database, File, JMS, Oracle Applications, and EJB. These wizards may be launched from the *BPM Project Navigator* by right-clicking the *Services* node within *Business Catalog,* as shown in Figure 4-26.

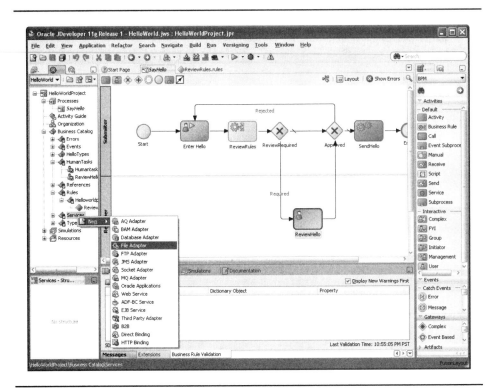

FIGURE 4-26. *Adding a new service definition to business catalog*

In addition to the adapters shown in Figure 4-26, any component in the underlying SOA Composite is also available as a service in the business catalog. This enables the following choices for implementing services:

- **BPEL**   Useful when service implementation is an orchestration of other services. BPEL also enables stateful interactions.

- **Mediator**   Useful for creating services based on message and event route–filter-transform patterns. Mediator may also be used in conjunction with Business Rules to do rule-based dynamic endpoint invocation, enabling an activity in BPMN to be bound to multiple possible implementations based on business rules.

■ **Spring Context**   Enables implementation of services as plain old Java objects (POJOs) leveraging the spring framework capabilities provided by the WebLogic Server Service Component Architecture (SCA).

Oracle Business Process Composer

This chapter has so far assumed that the BPM project is created and developed within and deployed from BPM Studio. However, Oracle BPM 11*g* also includes a web-based business process modeling tool called Oracle Business Process Composer—Process Composer for short—which may be used by business analysts to:

■ Create and model abstract process definitions that can then be shared with BPM Studio for implementation.

■ Modify processes, business rules, and human task definitions for implementation-ready projects and deploy the modified projects. An implementation-ready project is one that has a business catalog populated with implementation artifacts within BPM Studio. (The concept of a business catalog was discussed earlier in this chapter in the section titled "BPM Projects.")

NOTE
Oracle BPM 11g also supports the notion of Templates *where a template project may be defined in BPM Studio, including a business catalog populated with implementation artifacts within BPM Studio. In Process Composer, new projects may be created based on such templates and these projects are implementation-ready. In most aspects, templates are the same as regular projects shared from BPM Studio. However, templates cannot be deployed themselves. Also, templates support capabilities to lock down a process flow or activity that is not yet supported for regular projects.*

Project Sharing via MDS

Oracle BPM 11*g* uses a special partition in the Oracle Metadata Services (MDS) called Oracle *BPM metadata service* (*obpm MDS*), to enable the sharing of projects. Oracle Business Process Composer accesses projects from *BPM MDS* and writes back changes to it. BPM MDS enables multiple users to work together in Process Composer providing capabilities such as locking. BPM Studio integrates with *BPM MDS* via a *BPM MDS Navigator*, which can be defined as a *SOA-MDS* connection in the *Resource Palette* within BPM Studio; typical settings are shown in Figure 4-27 (the left window). On top of the *SOA-MDS* connection, a *BPM MDS* connection needs to be created. This connection adds authentication. To create a *BPM MDS* connection, the *SOA-MDS* connection, as well as the connection to the *soainfra* server that would manage authentication, must be specified. Typical settings are shown in Figure 4-27 (in the right window). The *BPM MDS Navigator* enables publishing of projects from BPM Studio into BPM MDS, as well as bringing down projects from BPM MDS into BPM Studio.

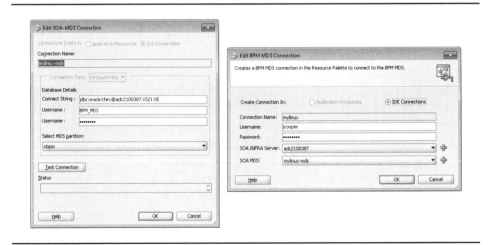

FIGURE 4-27. *A SOA-MDS and BPM-MDS connection*

Roles and Access

Process Composer is a role-based application that enables the granting of different visibilities, including view and edit to different groups and users. As in BPM runtime, actual groups and users and their authentication is managed by an external identity store. Within Process Composer (see Figure 4-28), the owner of the project can grant other users and groups different access to the project. To manage access, the owner of the project needs to click the *Private* (if not shared with anyone yet) or *Shared* (if already shared with others) icons at the top-right corner of Composer when the project is open (see Figure 4-29).

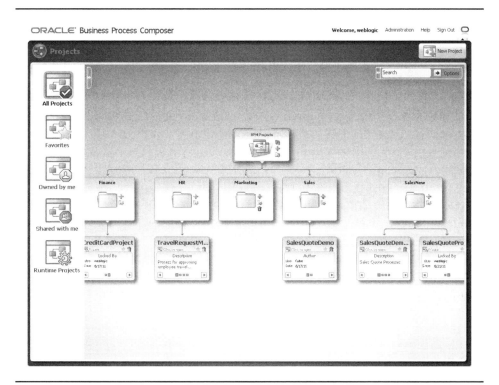

FIGURE 4-28.   *The Process Composer home page*

Working with Process Composer

Process Composer may be accessed using a URL of the form http://bpmserver:
8001/bpm/composer, where *bpmserver* is the name of the server on which
Oracle BPM is running, and *8001* is the port number for the SOA/BPM
managed server (while 8001 is the default, this depends on the configuration
of the installation.) Using the concepts discussed earlier in this chapter in the
context of BPM Studio, working with Process Composer is rather straightforward.
Therefore, instead of a comprehensive discussion on working with Process
Composer, only some noteworthy aspects are covered in this section.

Process Composer Pages

Process Composer has two different sets of pages depending on whether
a project is open or not. At login or when no project is open, Composer
displays a home page shown in Figure 4-28. As can be seen in this figure,
the page displays a catalog view of available processes. From this catalog,
a project can be opened by clicking it, and then new projects and folders
can be created by clicking the plus icon on the parent folder.

When a project is open, the project home page shown in Figure 4-29 is
opened. This page displays summary information about the project, including
versioning details and available snapshots. A user with *Owner* access can
also manage project settings such as approval workflows from this page. The
page includes a list of project artifacts, and from there existing artifacts can
be opened or new ones created. When an artifact is opened, its editor opens
as a new tab (for example, the *TravelRequestManagementProcess* tab shown
in Figure 4-29).

As can be seen in Figure 4-29, the top bar of Process Composer displays
information on the sharing status of the project, including whether the
current user is viewing or editing and who else is viewing the project.

TIP
*Composer's main menu can be accessed by
clicking the circular process icon at the top-left
corner of the Composer window, as seen in
Figure 4-28 and Figure 4-29. This menu
provides access to most actions and operations.*

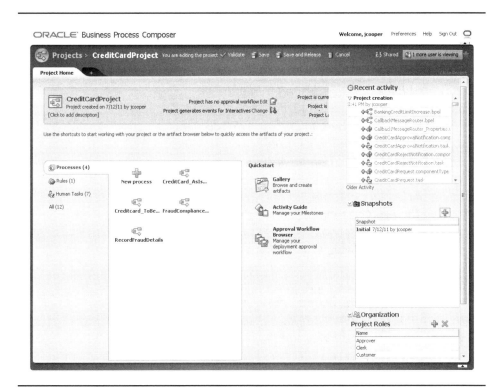

FIGURE 4-29. *A project home page in Process Composer*

Working with Projects

As discussed earlier, projects may either be created in BPM Studio and published to the BPM-MDS to be used within Process Composer or created within Process Composer. New projects may be created within Process Composer from the *Project* menu item by selecting the *Create a New Project* submenu.

Existing projects are displayed hierarchically in the *Project Catalog Browser,* from where a project may be opened by clicking the project node. Within Process Composer, only one project may be open at a time. Opening a different project requires closing the currently open project by clicking the *Projects* link at the top-left corner of the Composer window (to the left of the Composer icon) or using Composer's main menu.

TIP
At the time of writing of this chapter Composer did not allow moving projects between folders. However, a project may be exported and imported back into the desired folder to accomplish this. Editing a project requires entering edit mode by clicking the Edit icon at the top-left corner of the Composer window (to the right of the project name and the "You are viewing the project" text). Only one user can edit a project at one time. If another user is editing the project, then instead of the edit icon a lock icon is displayed alongside the name of the user who is editing Once edits are complete, edit mode may be quit by selecting the Save and Release *icon on the center-top of the Composer window or by closing the project or Composer session. Composer also indicates which other users are viewing the project at any time on the top-right corner. The person editing the project may use this information to decide when to yield the edit mode.*

As has been mentioned before, it is possible to make implementation-ready changes from within Process Composer. Such changes may be deployed using the *Deploy Project* menu item from the main menu. Only users with *owner* access can deploy a project; the *Deploy Project* menu item is not displayed to others.

It is also possible to associate approval workflows within a project that kicks in when the project is deployed from Process Composer. The workflow status can be managed in the *Approval Workflow Browser* tab, which can be launched by clicking the *Approval Workflow Browser* link in the project home tab.

Working with Process Editor

Within Process Composer, new process models can be created, and existing ones can be modified. Unlike typical analyst-targeted modeling tools that stop at high-level modeling and require implementation in a developer tool,

Process Composer features enough functionality for a business analyst to completely implement and deploy a business process, leveraging implementation artifacts available within a business catalog.

Working with process editor shown in Figure 4-30 within Process Composer is almost the same as working within BPM Studio as described earlier in this chapter. A few noteworthy differences are highlighted here:

■ There are two palettes: BPMN and Business Catalog, which may be selected using the pick-list at the top of the palette. The BPMN palette is organized in two tiers: a basic set of activities and a more complete set of activities that include specializations of the basic activities. The *More* and *Less* button at the bottom of the palette can be used to display or hide the detail or specialized activities. When the detail activities are being displayed the list of detail activities changes as mouse hovers on different basic activities.

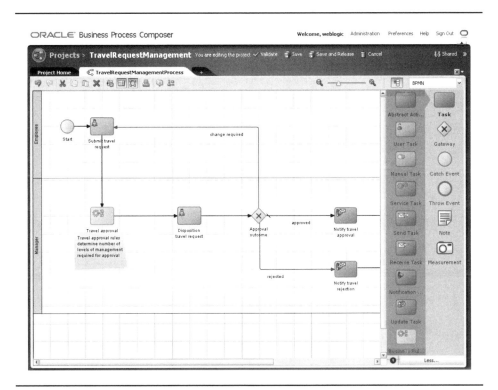

FIGURE 4-30. *BPMN editor in Process Composer*

- In the current version unlike BPM Studio, Process Composer does not feature an Organization editor. However, roles can be viewed and new roles added in the *Organization* section of the *Project Home* tab. New roles can also be created by dragging and dropping a human task on the empty canvas (as in Studio) or right-clicking an existing swim-lane and bringing up its *Properties* window. While these roles may not be granted within Process Composer, the role administration interface within WorkSpace, as shown in Figure 4-13, may be used.

- In addition to selecting implementation artifacts available in the business catalog from the *Implementation* tab (which can be opened by right-clicking an activity and selecting *Implement* menu item), artifacts may be dragged and dropped from the Business Catalog palette onto existing activities, binding that activity to the dropped artifact, or process canvas, and creating a new activity bound to the dropped artifact, as shown in Figure 4-31. Users can also add a web service to the catalog by specifying the WSDL URL for the service.

- Data association for an activity is accessed by right-clicking on it and selecting the *Data Association* menu item unlike BPM studio, where it is accessed from the *Implementation* tab of the *Properties* window. Once the data association editor is open, as shown in Figure 4-31, the *Apply* or *Cancel* buttons may be used to get back to the process editor.

- In the current version, there is no *Structure* window for a process where process data objects may be defined and edited. However, process data objects may be created and modified from the *Variables* panel within the Data Association editor, as shown in Figure 4-31. New business objects cannot be created within Process Composer. New variables defined within Process Composer may be either of simple types or based on existing business objects in the business catalog.

- There is also a documentation panel at the bottom of the process canvas where you can specify documentation for the process, or for specific activities within the process. Two flavors of documentation can be entered—end-user targeted documentation and internal collaboration documentation to communicate intent and details between various stakeholders.

FIGURE 4-31.   *The Data Association editor in Process Composer*

Working with Business Rules Editor

Within Process Composer, new rule dictionaries cannot be created, nor can fact definitions be created or modified. The rules editor within Process Composer enables the definition of new rules and the modification of existing rules once the dictionary and facts are set up within BPM Studio. A rule dictionary may be opened by clicking on a rule artifact either in the *Project Home* or *Artifact Gallery*. Working with the rules editor in Process Composer is almost the same as working with the rules editor in BPM Studio, as described earlier in this chapter. Business analysts may create new If-Then and Decision Tables rules within rulesets. If rules are designed correctly, many scenarios of the business user modification of rules may be achieved simply by modifying *Globals* and *Bucketsets* definitions. In the current version, it is not possible to restrict access to these tabs to desired roles;

however, the UI components are available as reusable components that may be used in a custom UI shell to provide authoring access to only *Globals* and/or *Bucketsets.*

Working with Task Editor

Within Business Process Composer, new tasks may be created from the *Project Home* or the *Artifact Gallery* by clicking on *New Human Task.* The task editor within Composer can be launched by clicking on a task artifact in either the *Project Home* or the *Artifact Gallery.* Within the task editor:

■ The *General* tab allows the specification of participants and the routing flows leveraging the routing concepts, described earlier in this chapter in the section "Human Tasks for Quick Learners," as shown in Figure 4-32.

■ The *Data* tab allows the specification of task data. As in process editor within Composer, either simple types or business objects available within Business Catalog may be used. A form (or user interface) may be associated with a task definition as well.

■ The *Duration* tab allows the specification of deadlines.

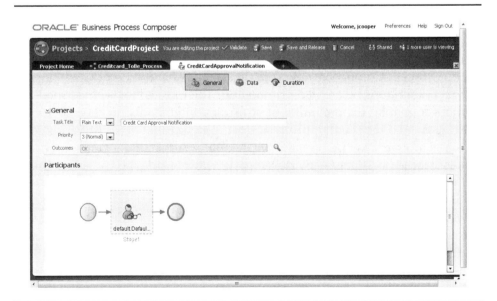

FIGURE 4-32. *The task editor in Process Composer*

A Quick Tour of BPM WorkSpace

Oracle BPM Suite 11*g*'s end-user interfaces come in two flavors: a stand-alone WorkSpace, and a social and collaborative Process Spaces built on top of Oracle WebCenter Spaces application. In this section, a quick tour of BPM WorkSpace is provided to give the quick learners following this chapter enough pointers to test and use the BPM processes.

BPM WorkSpace is typically accessed from a URL such as http://bpmserver:8001/bpm/workspace, where *bpmserver* is the name of the server where BPM is running and *8001* is the port for the BPM/SOA managed server. Out of the box, the WorkSpace application has three main tabs:

- **Tasks**   The *Tasks* tab shown in Figure 4-33 is the primary interface for most users, enabling them to initiate new processes, as well as organize, find, and perform their tasks.

  The *Applications* panel at the top left of Figure 4-33 lists the business processes that the user is granted the initiation privilege to, via Initiator Task, as discussed earlier. Clicking a link in this panel launches the associated form. At the center-top of Figure 4-33 is the *tasklist* panel that, in addition to providing access to tasks assigned to the user, also features tab listing tasks that the user has access to either as an initiator, supervisor, or process-owner. The *tasklist* includes filtering and sorting capabilities; also, such filters including sort conditions and display information may be saved as *views* that may be accessed from the *Worklist Views* panel below the *Applications* panel. The form for the selected task may be displayed in the center-bottom panel, as shown in Figure 4-33.

- **Process Tracking**   The *Process Tracking* tab shown in Figure 4-34 provides process owners and others interested in process tracking, a process-centric view instead of a task-centric view. The process view includes process audit-trail information, both graphical and tabular.

- **Standard Dashboards**   The *Standard Dashboards* tab provides standard process analytic dashboards, including workload and performance dashboards.

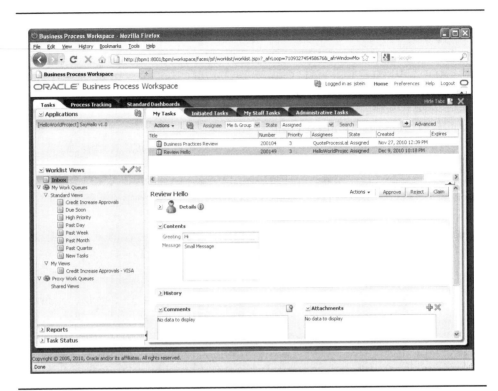

FIGURE 4-33. *The Tasks tab in BPM 11*g *workspace*

In addition, custom dashboards may be created combining dashboards built on standard and custom business indicators, as well as task lists and process instance lists.

■ **Administration and Configuration** The *Administration* page, as shown in Figure 4-13, may be accessed from the *Administration* link, and preferences like vacation rules and group dispatching (that is, work routing) rules may be accessed from the *Preferences* link. The administration section includes the mapping of logical rules in the organization to physical roles in the corporate directory, application configuration, and so on.

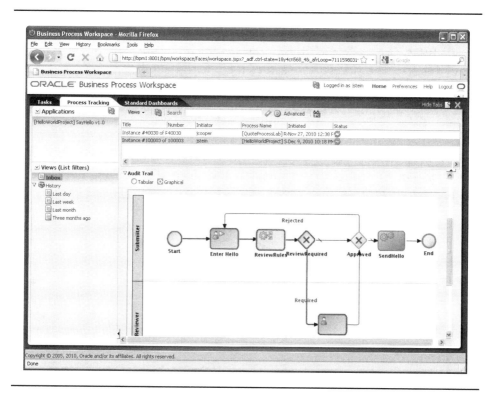

FIGURE 4-34.   *The Process Tracking tab in BPM 11g workspace*

Process Monitoring and Analytics

Oracle BPM 11*g* enables rich process monitoring and analytics capturing standard and process-specific custom metrics that can be sent to an out-of-the-box process STAR schema, as well as to Oracle Business Activity Monitoring (BAM). BPM 11*g* also provides out-of-the-box dashboards, and allows business users to create dashboards leveraging the analytic information in the process STAR schema. This provides an analytic capability similar to most BPM products. Oracle BAM, while requiring an additional server footprint, provides comprehensive real-time business activity monitoring (which includes rich self-service business dashboards and alerts) that is not limited to events and analytic information in BPM (as most other BPM products), but can provide true end-to-end visibility and monitoring (which is a significant differentiation from most other BPM products).

Business Indicators and Measurements

Oracle BPM captures standard process analytic measures and dimensions out of the box. The standard measures include the number of instances and the completion times, and the standard dimensions include the process, activity, and participant. In addition to standard analytic information, often business process–specific information is valuable for process analytics. Process-specific business indicators, both measures and dimensions may be defined in the BPMN editor *structure* window by right-clicking the *Business Indicators* node. Business indicators may be assigned data using the Data Associations editor just like other process data objects, as shown in Figure 4-35.

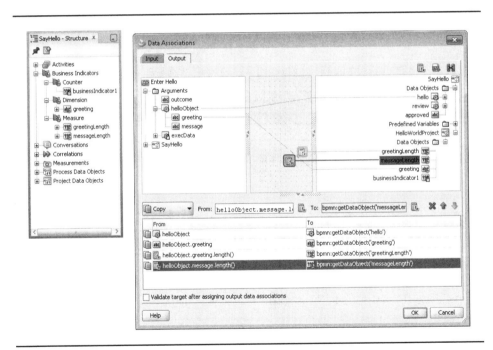

FIGURE 4-35. *Process-specific business indicator definitions and assignments*

Counters are a special type of measure that are used to count the number of times an activity is executed, enabling analysis and scenarios including rework. A counter is associated with an activity by right-clicking the activity in the BPMN editor and selecting *Add Counter Mark*. In the current version, counter marks are added and deleted by right-clicking the activity, but are edited within the *Counter* tab of an activity's *Properties* windows (this tab is available only when a counter has been added).

NOTE
The value of the counter is only available in the context of process analytics. Trying to access it within the process itself will not yield the desired result.

The sampling points—points at which process analytic data is captured—are configured as a project preference, as shown in Figure 4-44. In addition, explicit measurement marks may be added to the process—at a measurement mark, all standard analytic information, all dimensions, and specified business indicator measures are captured. Measurement marks may also be used in a pair—interval start and interval end—to create an interval definition, which may be thought of as a group or compound activity for the purposes of process analytics. Analysis available for an activity such as the number of active instances in the activity and the average completion time may also be performed for an interval defined with measurement marks.

NOTE
Two important settings govern the behavior of process analytic metric capture: CubeUpdateFrequency, which determines how often to compute, and CubeInstanceExpiration, which determines the retention for the workload records. These settings are set from Fusion Middleware EM control, as shown in Figure 4-43.

Oracle Business Activity Monitoring

Oracle Business Activity Monitoring (BAM) is a framework for aggregating and correlating business events from a variety of sources and presenting real-time dashboards and alerts based on them.

Oracle BAM can accept real-time data streams from a variety of sources leveraging technologies, including Oracle BAM Adapter, Java Messaging Service (JMS), Oracle Data Integration (ODI) sources, and Web Services. These feed data to the Oracle BAM Active Data Cache (ADC) in a continuous stream as data changes occur. Oracle BAM ADC maintains the definition for this data as BAM data objects (not to be confused with BPM data objects) and receives transactions (insert, update, delete, and update-or-insert) to its data objects. Data objects may be linked to other data objects via lookups, and ADC propagates changes to all interested data objects. Reports and alerts in Oracle BAM are built on top of BAM data objects, which are defined in a tabular representation, as shown in Figure 4-36.

Layered on the BAM ADC is BAM Report Cache, which is responsible for maintaining the view set in memory and providing real-time updates to open browser sessions, and BAM Event Engine, which is responsible for monitoring complex data conditions and executing specified alerts.

Oracle BAM tooling is completely browser-based and the main console may typically be accessed from a URL such as http://bamserver:9001/OracleBAM, where *bamserver* is the name of the server on which BAM is running and *9001* is the port for the BAM Managed Server (by default, this is 9001, but may depend on the configuration of the installation). It provides access to four components:

- **Active Viewer**   Used for viewing reports; however, reports are URL-addressable and may be accessed directly as well. Oracle BAM reports may also be downloaded as Microsoft HTML (MHT) files for offline viewing.

- **Active Studio**   Used for creating, editing, and sharing reports and alerts.

- **Architect**   Used for creating and managing data objects, as shown in Figure 4-36.

- **Administrator**   Used for administration, including user management.

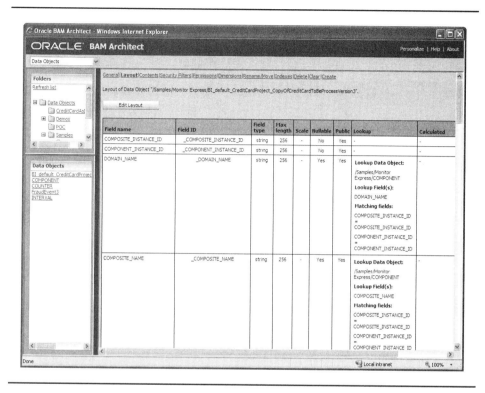

FIGURE 4-36. *A sample BAM data object*

BAM Reports

Oracle BAM Active Studio enables a power business user to declaratively create and edit reports. A BAM report is a collection of one or more BAM views organized in desired layouts. The new report creation wizard allows the graphical selection of a desired layout template. The wizard also allows for graphical selection of a desired view type, as shown in Figure 4-37.

Once a view type is selected, the wizard walks through the steps of configuring the view, including the selection of a data object and the selection of fields within the data object. These configuration properties may be edited later by editing the report and then editing the view inside the report, as shown in Figure 4-38.

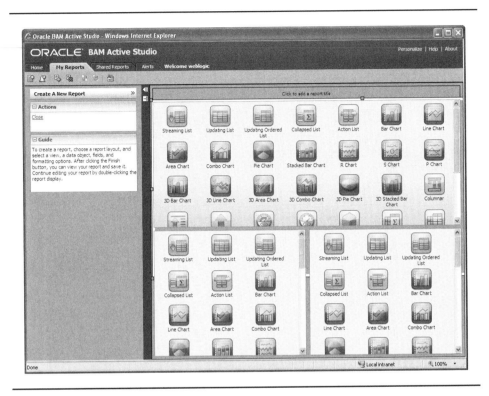

FIGURE 4-37. *The new BAM report wizard*

As part of a view definition, fields within a data object may be rearranged and grouped, summary functions, such as average, may be specified, and calculated fields may be defined. Also, drill-downs and surface prompts including actions may be specified. Within view properties, visual aspects of the view may be specified.

BAM Alerts

BAM Studio also enables creating BAM Alerts that are useful for proactively monitoring for interesting conditions or simply to get a periodic update. Alerts are defined as shown in Figure 4-39.

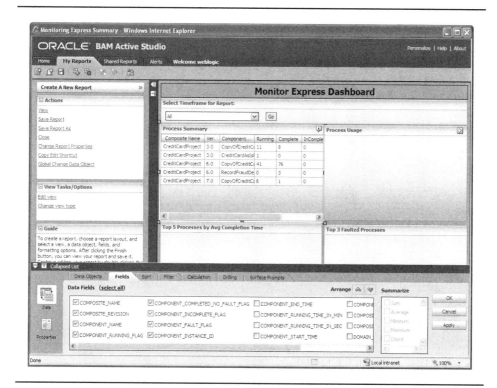

FIGURE 4-38. *Editing a BAM report*

An alert monitors for an event that may be based on time period or schedule, report changes, or data object changes. The event may further be constrained by a condition. The alert also specifies an action, which may include sending a report via e-mail, alerting a user, executing other rules, deleting rows from data objects, and external actions including invoking web services.

BPM and BAM Integration

Oracle BPM and BAM are seamlessly integrated and BPM can automatically create data objects within Oracle BAM as well as publish events to BAM.

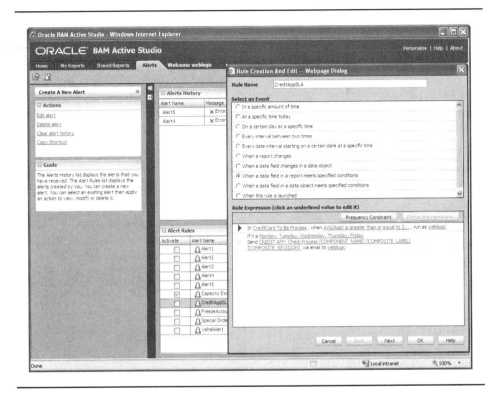

FIGURE 4-39. *BAM alerts in BAM Studio*

However, to enable the integration between BPM and BAM, a few configuration steps are needed:

- **Configure BAM Adapter** The BAM adapter's outbound connection properties need to be configured on the BPM Server to define which BAM Server is integrated with BPM. Steps to configure this follows:

  1. Launch the WebLogic Console application, typically accessed from http://bpmserver:7001/console URL, where *bpmserver* is the name of the server where BPM is running, and 7001 is the port for *Admin* server, which by default is 7001, but may depend on the install configuration.

2. From the left panel, within *Domain* Structure, select *Deployments.*

3. Within the Deployments table, find *OracleBamAdapter,* which is a *Resource Adapter.*

4. Drill down into the *OracleBamAdapter,* select *Configuration* tab and then select the *Outbound Connection Pools* subtab, which lists the outbound connection pool groups and instances, as shown in Figure 4-40.

5. Expand *oracle.bam.adapter.adc.soap.SOAPConnectionFactory* (assuming *SOAP* is to be used).

6. Drill down into *eis/bam/soap.*

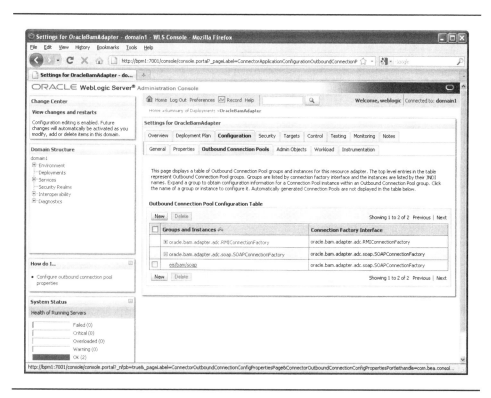

FIGURE 4-40. *BAM Adapter Outbound Connection Pools*

NOTE
Make sure to drill down into eis/bam/soap node and not the oracle.bam.adapter.adc.soap .SOAPConnectionFactory node, which also has the same property settings available.

7. Configure values similar to those shown in Figure 4-41 where *bamserver* is the name of the server where Oracle BAM is running (in this example, assumed to be different from the server where BPM is running, but that need not be the case).

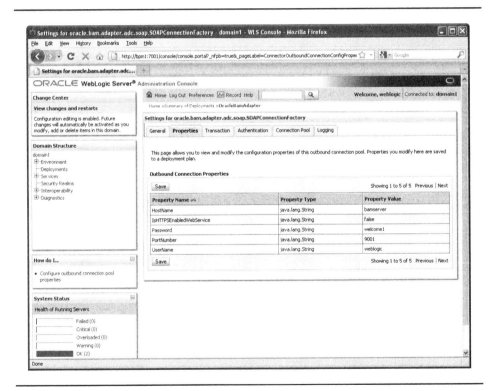

FIGURE 4-41. *BAM Adapter Outbound Connection settings*

■ **Configure BPMN Engine** By default, publication of events to BAM from BPMN engine is off and needs to be turned on. Steps to configure this follows:

1. Launch Fusion Middleware EM control, typically accessed from http://bpmserver:7001/em URL, where *bpmserver* and *7001* are as discussed in previous paragraph.

2. Within the tree navigator in the left panel, expand *SOA* node and then select *soa-infra(soa_server1),* where *soa_server1* is the name of the BPM/SOA managed server.

3. Click the *SOA Infrastructure* dropdown menu (located just below *soa-infra*) and then expand the *Administration* menu and select *System MBean Browser,* as shown in Figure 4-42.

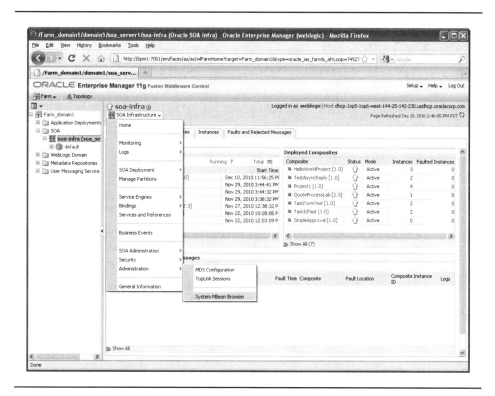

FIGURE 4-42. *Launching the System MBean Browser from EM*

4. Within the *System MBean Browser,* select *Application Defined MBeans,* then *oracle.as.soainfra.config,* then *Server: soa_server1* (where *soa_server1* is the name of the BPM/SOA managed server), then *BPMNConfig,* and then *bpmn,* as shown in Figure 4-43.

5. Select *DisableActions* attribute and clear out its value to empty, as shown in Figure 4-43.

■ **Enable BAM in Project** The project needs to have BAM integration turned on as well. This is configured within BPM Studio by right-clicking the project node in the *BPM Navigator* to bring up the project preferences window and setting the project preferences as shown in Figure 4-44. In summary, checking on *Enable BAM* within *Data Targets,* and specifying the *BAM Adapter JNDI Name* and the *Data Object Path* (values shown in Figure 4-44 may be used as is).

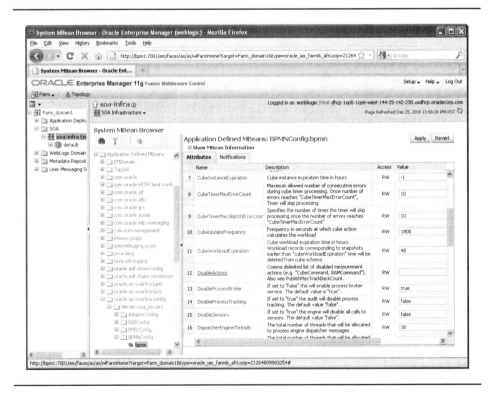

FIGURE 4-43. *Configuring the BPMN engine to send events to BAM*

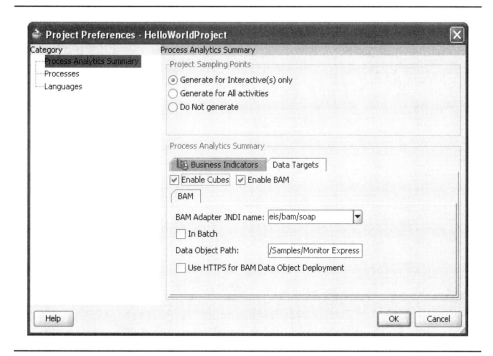

FIGURE 4-44. *Enabling BAM in BPM project preferences*

Once the integration between BPM and BAM is enabled, BAM data objects will be generated when the BPM project is deployed. BAM Architect may be used to add columns and indexes to a generated Data Object; such columns and indexes are preserved during redeployments. The standard BAM dashboards available as part of *Sample Monitor Express* may be used or new dashboards may be defined within BAM Studio, leveraging the generated data objects. Also, alerts may be defined, leveraging these data objects.

Business Intelligence and BPM

Business Intelligence products, including Oracle Business Intelligence, may be used to analyze the process analytic data captured in the process STAR schema. SQL scripts to create view definitions on top of the process STAR schema to facilitate BI queries, along with documentation on the schema, can be downloaded from https://bpmsamples.samplecode.oracle.com.

Summary

This chapter provided quick learners with a guide map through BPM 11g concepts and technologies. Readers should be able to get started with developing BPM processes at the end of this chapter. Many of the topics will be discussed in greater detail in subsequent chapters to address advanced questions that may not have been fully covered in this chapter.

CHAPTER
5

Business Process Modeling
and Implementation
Using BPMN 2.0

usiness Process modeling and implementation is at the heart of any BPM project. With BPMN 2.0 it is now possible to go all the way from an initial business analyst's model of a process to the implementation of an execution-ready business process, all within a single representation of the model. While Chapter 4 should have already given readers enough information to get started with process modeling and implementation, this chapter will provide a much more comprehensive and conceptual understanding of BPMN 2.0, specifically as implemented in Oracle BPM 11*g*.

This chapter assumes familiarity with Chapter 4 and employs the terms and concepts used there without reintroduction. Also, it does not repeat the business process discussion covered there. Please read the section "BPMN 2.0 for Quick Learners" in Chapter 4 before continuing.

Recommended Flow and Practices

This section provides some recommendations for best practices and workflow when modeling business processes. These are not necessarily prescriptive, but can serve as the starting point for every organization's or team's best practices for business process modeling and implementation.

The Flow of Process Modeling

Process modeling should start with a solid understanding of the as-is process, as well as associated pain points and other business drivers. Part III of this book describes the details of how to develop this understanding through interviews and workshops with business stakeholders and so on. Once the goals of the process design are clear, modeling should start top-down. First, the *happy path* of the business process should be modeled; the *happy path* is the simplest form of the process, unencumbered by exceptions and abnormal events, from start to finish. This can be established through interviews with the business owner. Next, the happy path needs to be refined with details from the process participants and subject matter experts. While modeling the process, details such as the constraints and policies forcing a particular behavior or design choice should be captured.

After the happy path is modeled, exception scenarios should be added, one by one, applying many of the same analysis techniques, but typically extending the pool of participants interviewed in order to capture the nuances of the process.

Before the implementation refinements are applied to the process, it may be useful to simulate the process and share the simulation scenarios and the results with the business stakeholders as an initial sanity check on the model of the process.

Design Process Analytics Early

In the very early process modeling steps, the monitoring and analytical aspects of the process should be considered. This may include the interesting performance indicators, service level agreements (SLAs), as well as any business data that would be useful for analyzing, tracking, or categorizing business process performance and managing exceptions. In addition to identifying measurable values (known as "measures" in Oracle BPM), dimensions, along which these values will be sliced and diced, should be defined.

Process Readability

It is important to realize that one of the big advantages of the BPM approach is that the process model serves as a communication mechanism between various stakeholders throughout the life cycle of the process, all the way from discovery, through implementation, to execution, and redesign for process optimization. Therefore, it is important that the process model be designed for readability. Some considerations in keeping the process readable are outlined below.

Naming Convention

A consistent naming convention should be used. While the naming convention to use depends on every organization's practices, a common pattern is to use the *Verb Object* form—for example, *Approve Expense*—for activity names. For conditional gateways, it is common practice to use a question for the gateway name, and the answers for the outgoing sequence flows— for instance, the conditional gateway may be named *Approval Required?,* and the outgoing sequence flows may be named *Yes* and *No.* Business Objects are typically named using the noun form of the object, using uppercase letters to start each word in the name—for example, *Purchase Order.* Process data objects, attributes of business objects, and arguments should be named similarly, typically mirroring the name of the business object, except that the first word starts with a lowercase letter. Also, if there can be multiple instances of a business object, then the name should be prefixed with a qualifier—for example, *shipping Address* and *billing Address.* In addition to applying consistent naming practices within the process model, the model itself should be named in a consistent fashion. In some organizations, the process name may be prefixed by identifiers that place the process within the organizational process taxonomy.

Process Layout

Consistent and standardized layout practices improve process readability. Some common practices include keeping the happy path on a straight line and alternative paths on parallel lines, drawing the process model from left to right in accordance with progression of time, starting back transitions (in the case of loops) from conditional gateways, and minimizing transition crossovers. While the selection of elbow connectors versus rounded connectors may be an individual preference, standardizing on the choice of one over the other may help the readability of processes across users and models. Oracle BPM also supports additional visualization aides such as swim-lane colors and the use of custom icons for activities and swim-lanes; usage of these should be in accordance with agreed guidelines to maintain readability.

Process Size

While users often worry about process size from a performance point of view, the primary consideration in determining the correct process size is readability. Too big a process will not be readable; the readability of the process will be compromised long before any impact on tooling or runtime performance. At the same time, a process should not be unnecessarily split into multiple subprocesses because this can also compromise readability. Another readability concern that should be considered at this stage is the viewpoint of the various stakeholders that will be expected to review and contribute to the model as well as use it during operations (that is, runtime) for tracking, monitoring, or auditing. It is important to keep in perspective the fact that while the analyst, who may be too close to the process, may have a wall full of pasted papers to model the process end-to-end, other stakeholders may need it in more bite-sized pieces to be able to comprehend it.

Process Decomposition

Just like size, process decomposition—that is, the breaking down of a process into subprocesses and activities—needs to be correctly used to maintain readability. While some aspects, such as IT implementation details, are always candidates for pushing inside subprocesses, in other situations there is a trade-off between being able to see process aspects in one glance versus seeing so many things as to obscure the big picture. Where possible, the consumers of process details should be considered while designing—for instance, who will need this level of detail and for what purpose? This line of questioning helps establish the right level of decomposition, such that, a stakeholder with a particular perspective or a specific need will have all the details at one level of decomposition, but these details do not obscure the view of other stakeholders.

Data Considerations

While data design may or may not be considered part of process modeling, it is still an important part of any business process, therefore some recommendations on data design are covered in this section (some further treatment of data can also be found in Chapter 10 in Part III).

Data Definitions

If a business process spans multiple applications, or if the data definition for the process is not already provided by an end application, data definition for the process layer needs to be developed. It is typically a good practice to keep the process layer data definition independent of the back-end applications; this is usually called a canonical object definition. If an enterprise standard for canonical data is not available, definitions from standard bodies, such as the OMG, may be used. Also, Oracle Application Integration Architecture (AIA) includes a foundation pack consisting of canonical object definitions.

Data Master

Whether the process should own the data or the data should be mastered outside should be considered during data design. If the data can be updated independent of the process, if it is shared by multiple processes and services, or if the data needs to be available in perpetuity, it should be mastered outside of the business process. If an application mastering the data is not already available, persistent entity objects and business objects may be defined using Oracle Application Development Framework (ADF) Business Components (ADF-BC) technology, and its associated service interface can be used to retrieve data from the database or store it there. Data may also be kept and read directly in and from database tables using the database adapter included in BPM Suite. ADF-BC provides for business object definition, including validation logic and other business logic, such as computed fields, whereas a database adapter provides an easy mechanism for writing and reading from the database where additional business logic is not needed. ADF-BC and the choice of ADF-BC vs. Database Adpter are discussed in Chapter 8.

Data Size and Scoping

When the process state is saved (dehydrated) or restored (rehydrated) all process variables are written and read from the database. Also, when process variables are assigned to each other or to an invoked service's inputs/outputs, deep copy of data happens—that is, data for all attributes is copied over hierarchically, essentially creating a full duplicate of data. Both of these factors imply that data design may have performance and scalability impacts. Recommended best practices are:

- Don't bring the whole data object into the process unnecessarily. Instead, design it such that minimum data flows through the process. The services and user interface elements that need to access more data can retrieve it from the data master. Data flowing through the process should be limited to the following: (a) attributes that are needed to make routing decisions in the process, (b) primary keys needed to retrieve additional data from the master when making service calls or when presenting it in user interfaces, (c) key business indicators needed for monitoring the process or tracking business exceptions.

■   BPMN supports the scoping of data variables—that is, data variables can be specified to be available at the process scope or only within certain subprocesses. Define variables in the deepest possible scope so that their life cycle is the minimum possible and it is not saved and read from the database unnecessarily.

BPMN Basics

The basic concepts of BPMN 2.0—swim-lanes, activities, sequence flows, gateways, and events—were explained in the section "BPMN 2.0 for Quick Learners" in Chapter 4. The discussion there will not be repeated in this chapter; however, gateways and events need more explanation and will be described in greater detail in this chapter. To explain the execution semantics of gateways and other BPMN elements, the concept of tokens is introduced. Also, a listing of the different activities is included.

Token Flow

The BPMN specification uses the concept of *tokens* to specify the behavior of BPMN elements. This concept of tokens can be used to understand the sequence flow of every process diagram and to analyze whether the flow logic of a process has been modeled correctly. Tokens "traverse" the sequence flows and pass through the elements in the process. The behavior of process elements is defined by describing how they interact with a token as it "traverses" the structure of the process. The process elements execute only when one or more tokens "arrive" at their incoming sequence flows and when an element that is done executing it "produces" one or more tokens on its outgoing sequence flow.

NOTE
A token is a theoretical concept. In the preceding paragraph, the words traverse, arrive, and produce are accordingly in quotes.

During subsequent discussion, there will be examples, including parallel gateways and subprocesses, where the current token is held and new ones are generated. One simple rule of thumb in BPMN 2.0 is that tokens of different types cannot be mixed. This rule will be used in subsequent discussions to explain certain semantics.

Activities

Activities in BPMN 2.0 can have multiple incoming sequence flows and one outgoing sequence flow. From a flow control perspective, all activities execute when a token "arrives" at any of its incoming sequence flows, is "held" while the activity is executing, and is "returned" to the outgoing sequence flow when the activity completes normal execution. This simple description ignores exceptions as well as events, which are explained later in this chapter.

Oracle BPM 11*g* features the following activities:

- **Activity**   A generic and abstract activity. At the time of the writing of this book, an activity of this type needs to be changed to a concrete activity type and implemented before the process can be deployed. This activity enables process implementation by refinement. The business analyst may model the process in abstract by using this generic activity type. The developer or the analyst herself, at a later time, changes the activity to a concrete activity as process requirements become clearer.

- **Service**   Invoke a service or another process.

- **Send and Receive**   Interact with other services and processes using message exchange. Essentially the same as Throw Message and Catch Message. Described further in the section titled "Conversations."

NOTE
When working with services, including sending and receiving messages, it is sometimes necessary to manipulate the information being passed in the Web Services header; such information may include security properties for example. The Service Properties *link in the Implementation tab of the* Properties window *allows access to the header information.* Input *can be used to set header properties for an invocation of a service by the process or an outgoing message, and* Output *can be used to read the header properties in an incoming message or an invocation of a provided operation by a client.*

■ **Call**   Invoke a reusable BPMN subprocess. The concept of a BPMN subprocess and the associated differences in behavior from a regular service activity are described in the section titled "Subprocesses."

■ **Subprocess and Event Subprocess**   An inline subprocess. Event subprocess is a special type of subprocess that is triggered by events. Both are described further in the section titled "Subprocesses."

■ **User and Interactive**   These activities model tasks performed by users and have been explained in the section "Human Task for Quick Learners" in Chapter 4.

■ **Update Task**   Update Task is a specialized service invocation to update an outstanding *user* or *interactive* activity. It supports the following operations:

■ **Update Outcome**   Set the user task's outcome to the specified value and route it to next participant in the task routing, if any, or complete it.

■ **Update Priority**   Change the priority of the user task. One of the scenarios is to use this in conjunction with a non-interrupting timer to increase a task's priority if it is not completed within a specified time, as shown in Figure 5-1.

■ **Reassign**   Reassign the user task to the specified user (an expression may be used as well).

■ **Withdraw**   Cancel the outstanding user task by withdrawing it. One of the scenarios where withdraw is useful is when a process is handling cancellation or compensation.

■ **Suspend**   Suspend the task including all its timers.

■ **Resume**   Resume a suspended task.

■ **Escalate**   Cause the task to be escalated to the next participant in the escalation hierarchy as specified in the task metadata. This is essentially the same as a user selecting the *escalate* system action from a task list.

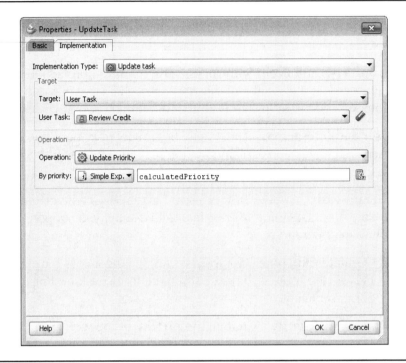

FIGURE 5-1. *Using update task to increase the priority of overdue tasks*

- **Suspend Timers** Suspend the task's timers; however, unlike in *Suspend*, the task itself is not suspended and continues to be available in the task list.

- **Resume Timers** Resume suspended timers.

- **Manual** A manual activity is simply a visual indicator in the process model that a certain activity happens at this point in the process outside the process. It has no execution impact—it simply immediately propagates the incoming token. It is different from the generic activity described earlier because a generic activity is a placeholder that is supposed to be refined to another activity, whereas this is a placeholder for an activity that happens outside the context of the BPM runtime environments (that is, the BPM engine does not execute it).

- **Business Rules**   Models an invocation of a decision function within Oracle Business Rules and is explained in the section "Business Rules for Quick Learners" in Chapter 3.

- **Notification**   Oracle BPM 11*g* also includes a set of notification activities to notify users of any interesting process status changes or updates. The notification activities include *IM, Mail,* and *SMS* to send notification text as an instant message, e-mail, or SMS, respectively, *Voice* to send notification as a voice call where the specified text is read out, and *User* to use the user's preferred notification channel as configured in WorkSpace. Even the *FYI* interactive activity is a way to send notifications—the user sees an FYI task in their task list, in addition to receiving a notification over their preferred channel.

TIP
In Oracle BPM 11g, colors are used to indicate the nature of activities: blue for automatic/ service activities, green for interactive/human activities, and yellow for rules/scripts/data manipulation activities.

Gateways

Gateways add richness to BPMN models by allowing sequence flows to diverge or split and converge or merge. Gateways also serve as synchronization points enabling multiple parallel branches of execution to wait for each other.

Oracle BPM 11*g* supports the following type of gateways: *Exclusive, Parallel, Inclusive,* and *Complex.* Most of these gateways can be diverging or converging. These gateways and associated semantics are explained in this section. An example process using parallel and exclusive gateways that will be used multiple times in this section is shown in Figure 5-2.

Oracle BPM 11*g* also supports an *event-based* gateway, which is explained in the section titled "Events and Exceptions" later in this chapter.

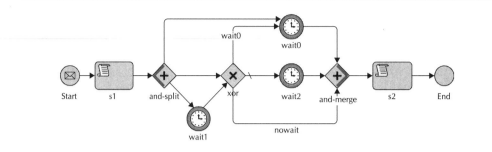

FIGURE 5-2. *A gateways illustration*

Exclusive Gateways (XOR)

In its simple usage, this is essentially a conditional gateway. An exclusive gateway can have multiple conditional outgoing sequence flows (that is, sequence flows that have a conditional expression associated with them, as shown in Figure 5-3) and must have one default outgoing sequence flow (the default sequence flow is indicated with a tick mark close to the source end, as shown in Figure 5-2).

The *outflows-order* property of the gateway, as shown in Figure 5-4, orders the outgoing conditional transitions. When an exclusive gateway receives a token on any of its incoming sequence flows, it evaluates all its outgoing sequence flows in the order specified and passes the token to the first whose condition evaluates to true. If there is none, the token is passed to the default outgoing transition.

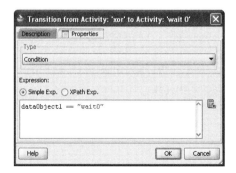

FIGURE 5-3. *Condition specification on sequence flow*

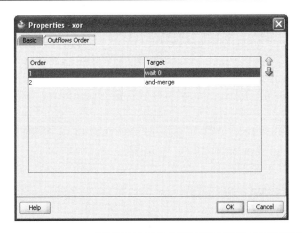

FIGURE 5-4.   *Outflows order properties*

Since the exclusive gateway passes the original token forward, it is legal, as per the rule of thumb on tokens mentioned earlier, for an outgoing transition of an exclusive gateway to go back to an earlier node in the process. That is, an exclusive gateway can be used to create loops or cyclical graphs. As we will see in the following discussion, it is the only gateway that can create loops.

The simple propagation of a token also implies that there is no requirement to balance exclusive gateways and it is the only gateway that Oracle BPM 11*g* BPMN editor allows to be added unpaired.

An exclusive gateway is also the only gateway that can act as both a diverging and converging gateway simultaneously. An exclusive gateway can have multiple incoming sequence flows, as shown in Figure 5-2. As soon as a token arrives at any incoming sequence flow, it is passed on to one of the outgoing sequence flows. For example, in Figure 5-2, assuming default condition, *wait2* will be executed twice.

Parallel Gateways (AND)

In Oracle BPM 11*g*, a parallel gateway can either be a splitting gateway (indicated by shading on the left side) or a merging gateway (indicated by shading on the right side).

A splitting gateway holds on to the incoming token and generates new tokens on each of its outgoing sequence flows. In other words, it forks parallel branches. The splitting gateway must be paired with a merging parallel or complex gateway. The merging parallel gateway waits for a token on all its incoming sequence flows, and once all the tokens have arrived, it releases the original token back to its outgoing sequence flow. In other words, it synchronizes its incoming sequence flows. In effect, this means that all tokens generated on the splitting side either need to flow to an end node or must arrive at the merging gateway.

Inclusive Gateways (OR)

Inclusive gateways are very similar to parallel gateways. The only difference is that the outgoing sequence flows from an inclusive gateway have conditional expressions associated with them (other than the one default sequence flow), just as for the exclusive gateway. A token is sent along to only those transitions whose conditions evaluate to true; a token is sent on the default outgoing sequence flow only if none of the conditions evaluate to true. Since the condition on every transition is tested, unlike the exclusive gateway, there is no concept of the ordering of transitions. A splitting parallel gateway may be thought of as a splitting inclusive gateway with a *true* condition on every outgoing sequence flow. On the merging side, the inclusive gateway waits for only those tokens that were generated on the splitting side.

Complex Gateways

A complex gateway is only a merging gateway and can be used to merge process branches created by splitting parallel or inclusive gateways. A complex gateway allows a condition to be specified, as shown in Figure 5-5.

The complex gateway is activated once the specified condition is true. If the Abort Pending Flows flag shown in Figure 5-5 is checked, the outstanding incoming sequence flows are aborted and activities such as outstanding human tasks are aborted. A special variable—*activationCount*—is associated with a complex gateway and may be used in the condition along with other data objects. The variable *activationCount* indicates the number of incoming sequence flows that have been activated (that is, the number of incoming tokens that have arrived) and can be used in the conditional expression on the gateway to determine how many tokens must arrive from its incoming sequence flows to activate the gateway; additional tokens arriving after the gateway has executed are simply dropped.

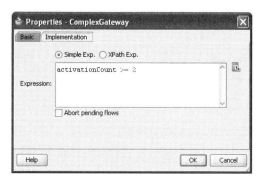

FIGURE 5-5.   *Complex gateway implementation properties*

Pairing Gateways

As discussed earlier, other than exclusive gateways, other gateways must be in matching pairs. The valid Split/Merge pairs are Parallel/Parallel, Parallel/Complex, Inclusive/Inclusive, and Inclusive/Complex.

Using the rule of thumb on dissimilar tokens, a sequence flow from within the splitting gateway and the merging gateway cannot end in a node (other than an end node) outside the graph between the pairing gateways. Another way to think about this is that an implicit *block* structure (similar to a subprocess) exists between the pairing nodes and the graph inside and outside the block cannot mix. An example process with pairing gateways is illustrated with implied blocks in Figure 5-6 (the blocks displayed in the figure are annotations overlaid on the process to depict implied blocks and are not part of the actual process model.)

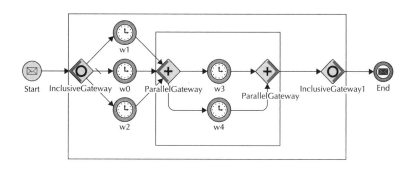

FIGURE 5-6.   *Implied blocks between pairing gateways*

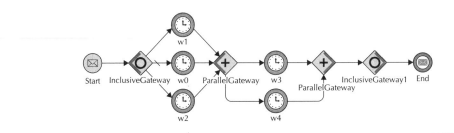

FIGURE 5-7. *A splitting parallel gateway with multiple incoming sequence flows*

As mentioned in the opening paragraph on parallel gateways, a parallel gateway (as well as an inclusive gateway, which behaves the same) can either be splitting or merging. However, Oracle BPM 11g's BPMN editor allows multiple incoming sequence flows to a splitting parallel gateway, as shown in Figure 5-7.

Such a splitting gateway with multiple incoming sequence flows is actually a convenient notation for an Exclusive gateway followed by a splitting parallel gateway—that is, the semantic of the process shown in Figure 5-7 is the same as that shown in Figure 5-8, and in both, the parallel gateway will be activated each time a token comes from one of the incoming sequence flows.

If in the process shown in Figure 5-7 it was desired to actually synchronize the multiple incoming sequence flows and have a single activation of the parallel gateway, the gateways must be balanced as shown in Figure 5-9.

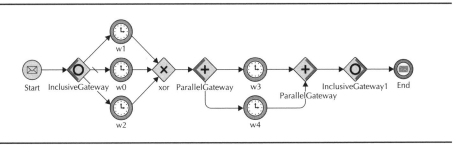

FIGURE 5-8. *The actual semantic of Figure 5-7*

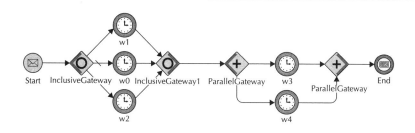

FIGURE 5-9.   *Changing the process in Figure 5-7 to achieve synchronization*

Subprocesses

In process modeling, a subprocess is an encapsulation of a process fragment, typically for abstraction or reuse. In Oracle BPM 11*g,* four important concepts are related to subprocesses:

- **(Inline) Subprocess**   Also known as *Embedded Subprocess*; described in this section.

- **Event Subprocess**   Special purpose inline or embedded subprocess used for events and exception handling and is described in the section titled "Events and Exceptions" in this chapter.

- **Reusable Subprocess**   A process with a "callable" interface that can be called from a parent process. By virtue of being outside the parent process, it can be called from multiple parent processes. *Reusable Subprocess* is described in this section.

- **Peer Process**   Any BPMN (or BPEL) process can be invoked from another using service interfaces. While in popular terminology this is also commonly called a subprocess, it is more accurate to think of these as peer processes. This is described further in the section titled "Conversations."

(Inline or Embedded) Subprocesses

An inline or embedded subprocess is a process fragment residing within the parent process and sharing context with it. In Oracle BPM 11g, any embedded subprocess can be collapsed or expanded by clicking the collapse/expand icon on the subprocess.

In its expanded form, the process within the subprocess can be modeled exactly the same way as a process, with the exception that subprocesses do not have a swim-lane within them; the whole subprocess is considered to be in the swim-lane that the collapsed subprocess activity resides in. Also, an embedded subprocess must start with a single *None* start event; all other start events are invalid in an embedded subprocess (unless it is an event subprocess, which is described later). Figure 5-10 shows an inline subprocess in its expanded form—the fragment between *Start1* and *Bad Credit*, *OK*, and *OK* and containing *Get Credit Score*, *Process Score*, and *Review Credit*. Also seen in this figure are three collapsed subprocesses— *Handle Cancellation*, *Open Account*, and *Start Billing*.

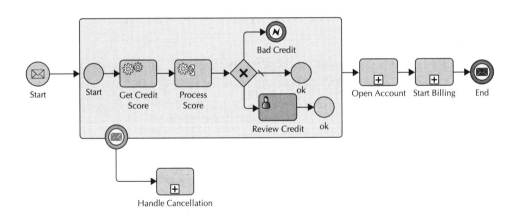

FIGURE 5-10. *An example subprocess*

When a token arrives at a subprocess, it is held and a new token is propagated within the subprocess. When all tokens created within the subprocess have been consumed—that is, all paths within the subprocess, including any attached non-interrupting event handlers, have completed, the original incoming token is propagated to the outgoing sequence flows. According to the law of similar tokens mentioned earlier, no tokens from outside the subprocess can come into the subprocess and no token from within the subprocess can flow outside of it. In other words, a subprocess creates a block structure with only incoming sequence flows being at the start of it and the only outgoing sequence flows being at the end of it. When an inline subprocess has interrupting event handlers attached and the corresponding event is fired, token(s) within the subprocess are consumed, and the original token is propagated to the sequence flow outgoing from the attached event hander. That is, an attached interrupting event handle behaves just like the regular end of the subprocess and sequence flows from it can converge back with the process. Attached non-interrupting event handlers generate new tokens and cannot be merged back into the main process. The behavior of interrupting and non-interrupting events is discussed further later in the chapter in the section titled "Events and Exceptions."

An inline subprocess shares its parent's context and can access the parent's data; however, data objects scoped within the subprocess can also be defined by right-clicking the *Data Objects* node within the subprocess activity node in the structure window.

In Oracle BPM 11*g,* inline subprocesses may be used for the following reasons:

- **Refinement**   When implementation of what appears as one activity to a business analyst involves multiple activities, an inline subprocess should be used to add the implementation details while preserving a single activity view in the process model.

- **Scope for Event and Exception Handlers**   In some situations, certain event handlers need to be scoped—for example, an Order placed at an online retailer may be cancelled only while it is in the billing stage, but not after it starts processing for shipment. Inline subprocesses can be used to model when of these events can be processed in a certain manner. This is explained further in the section titled "Events and Exceptions."

■ **Looping** A subprocess can be set up to execute in a loop, sequentially or in parallel, as described in the following paragraph.

Looping and Multi-Instance Subprocesses

A subprocess can be set up to loop using the *Loop Characteristics* tab of its *Properties* window. Two flavors of loops can be specified:

■ **While or Repeat-Until** This type of loop is specified by selecting the **Loop** option for *Loop Characteristics,* as shown in Figure 5-11. In the BPMN model, this type of a loop is indicated by a loop marker (a circular arrow) overlaid on the subprocess activity. A *Loop Condition* is specified and the loop repeats either while the condition is true (*while* loop) or until it is true (*repeat-until* loop), depending on the *Evaluation Order*—selecting *Before* specifies a *while* loop and unselecting *Before* specifies a *repeat-until* loop. Optionally, a value may be specified for *Loop Maximum;* in this case, the loop will never execute more iterations than the value specified. Among other scenarios, this is useful to avoid an infinite loop due to a logic error in the loop condition. When a subprocess is set up as a *while* or *repeat-until* loop, a special data object, **loopCounter** is available within its scope to indicate the sequence number of the current iteration.

■ **For or For-each** A *for* or *for-each* loop is specified by selecting the **Multi-instance** option for *Loop Characteristics*. In the BPMN model, a multi-instance activity (*for* or *for-each* loop) is indicated by a multi-instance marker (three small parallel vertical bars) overlaid on the subprocess activity. A *for* loop is achieved by specifying the *Loop Cardinality* expression, as shown in Figure 5-12. As in popular programming languages, it behaves like the following:

```
For (int i = 0 to Loop Cardinality) {
       Execute Sub-process
}
```

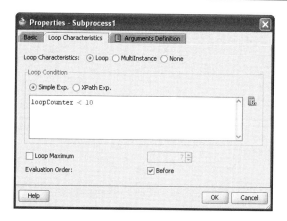

FIGURE 5-11.   *Loop characteristics properties—Loop*

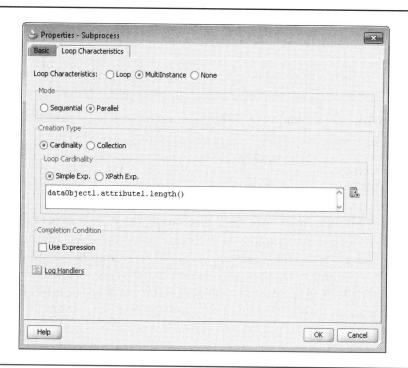

FIGURE 5-12.   *A For Loop specified with Loop Cardinality*

FIGURE 5-13.   *A* For-each *Loop specified with Loop data input*

A *for-each* loop is achieved by specifying the *Loop Data Input* value, as shown in Figure 5-13.

As can be seen in Figure 5-13, in addition to the *Loop Data Input,* a *Loop Data Output* may be specified; this facilitates collection of data produced in iterations of the loop into the specified variable. The *Loop Data Input* and *Loop Data Output* must be collections; within the subprocess special variables *inputDataItem* and *outputDataItem* are available, corresponding to types collected in *Loop Data Input* and *Loop Data Output.* To illustrate these special variables, data associations for a script activity inside a *for-each* loop subprocess is shown in Figure 5-14.

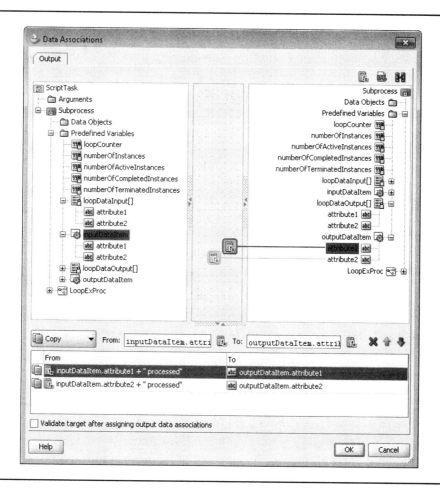

FIGURE 5-14.   *Accessing Loop predefined variables*

The *for-each* loop behaves in the following way:

```
For Each inputDataItem in Loop Data Input {
    Execute Sub-process
    LoopDataOutput [loopCounter] = outputDataItem
}
```

As can be seen in Figure 5-12 and Figure 5-13, a completion condition may be specified for both the *for* and *for-each* loop. Every time an iteration completes, the completion condition is evaluated, and if it evaluates to true, all outstanding iterations are terminated. Also seen in Figure 5-12 and Figure 5-13 is the *Is Sequential* flag, which must be unchecked to achieve parallel iterations.

NOTE
In parallel mode, the number of iterations to execute is determined at the initiation of the subprocess. Any subsequent changes to the loop cardinality or loop data input will not result in additional iterations.

When a subprocess is set up as a *for* or *for-each* loop, the following special data objects are available within its scope:

■ **inputDataItem and outputDataItem**   Explained earlier.

■ **loopCounter**   A sequence number of the iteration

■ **numberOfInstances, numberOfActiveInstances, numberOfCompletedInstances, numberOfTerminatedInstances**   As the name indicates, the total number of instances, number of instances currently active, number of instances that have completed already, and number of instances that have been terminated.

Reusable Subprocesses

Reusable subprocesses are similar to inline subprocesses, but are defined and stored outside of the parent process, enabling them to be used by multiple parent processes. A reusable subprocess is meant to be called only by other BPMN processes using the special *Call* activity, and has the following characteristics that differentiate it from other BPMN processes:

■ Since it is meant to be invoked by another BPMN process, it can only start with a *None* start event; also, the *Initiator* user activity cannot be used.

- It has input and output arguments, which are defined using the *Arguments Definition* tab of the process properties, as shown in Figure 5-15. Recall that regular BPMN processes do not have input and arguments defined for the process; rather, start events or initiator activities assign their outputs to process data objects.

A reusable subprocess is created by selecting the *Reusable Process* type in the new process wizard, as shown in Figure 5-16. Oracle BPM 11g considers a process to be a reusable process if and only if it has a single start event of type *None.* If a process created with a different pattern is changed to fit this, it becomes a reusable process, and bringing up the properties window for the process shows inputs and outputs for it. If a reusable process is modified such that it no longer fits the mentioned criteria, it stops being considered a reusable process.

Call Activity

A *Call* activity is a specialized activity that can be used to call only reusable subprocesses. When a token arrives at a call activity, it is held and a new instance of the reusable subprocess is created. When the reusable subprocess completes, control comes back to the call activity and the token is propagated to its outgoing sequence flows. A *call* activity behaves as other BPMN activities with regard to event handling, exception handling, and so on.

FIGURE 5-15.   *Arguments for a reusable subprocess*

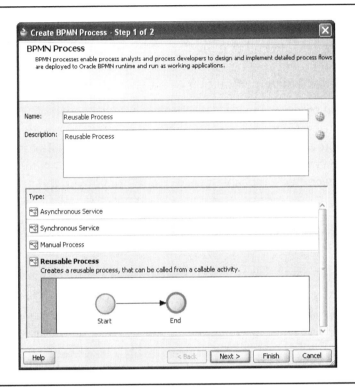

FIGURE 5-16. *Creating a new reusable process*

Passing and Returning Data

As described earlier, a reusable subprocess has input and output arguments defined as process properties. The caller process uses the data association of the *Call* activity to pass data to the input argument of the reusable process and to access the output returned from the reusable subprocess.

To access the input argument within the reusable subprocess, the data association of its start event must be used to assign the value passed by the caller via input arguments to process data objects. Similarly, to return the output to the caller, the data association of the end event must be used to assign values to the output argument.

Reusable Subprocesses vs. Inline Subprocesses

The primary difference between a reusable subprocess and an inline subprocess is that the first exists independently of the parent process and can be reused, whereas the second is defined in place and cannot be reused. The following are the two compared on some other dimensions:

- **Events and Exceptions**   Both behave the same—that is, even for a reusable subprocess, any event or exception thrown within the subprocess can be caught by the parent process. A Terminate end event within either has no impact on the parent—the parent sees it as a regular completion, other than the fact that a special variable—*numberOfTerminatedInstances*—is available in the case of multi-instance subprocesses to indicate how many instances of the subprocess were terminated.

- **Data**   An Inline subprocess has access to its parent's data objects, whereas a reusable subprocess does not, and needs to exchange data through a well-defined interface, as described earlier.

- **Parent Context**   Similar to the case for data, an inline subprocess has access to other parent context, such as conversations (described later in the section titled "Conversations"), whereas a reusable subprocess does not.

- **Swim-lanes**   As mentioned earlier, an inline subprocess cannot have swim-lanes within it, whereas a reusable subprocess behaves like a regular process in this regard and can have swim-lanes within it.

- **Loop**   Only an inline subprocess can be set up to iterate. This is not a significant difference, because a call activity invoking a reusable subprocess can always be wrapped within an inline subprocess and the wrapper subprocess can be set up as a loop.

- **Audit Trail**   The tabular version of the audit trail looks the same for both. In the graphical version, at the time of writing of this book, only the call activity is shown forreusable subprocesses.

Reusable Subprocess vs. Peer Process

As mentioned earlier, even a regular process with a service interface can be invoked from another process, similar to a reusable subprocess, and such processes are considered peer processes. A comparison of the two follows:

- **Events and Exceptions**   The most significant difference between the two is that a peer process has an independent life cycle and events and exceptions thrown within an invoked peer process are not propagated to the invoking process. For synchronous interfaces, a fault message can be sent to the invoker as described in the section titled "Conversations."

- **Control Flow**   When a reusable subprocess is invoked from a call activity, the parent process is paused at the call activity until the called subprocess completes. Whereas, the invocation of an asynchronous interface of a peer-process is invoke-and-continue. The invoking process may wait for a callback from the invoked peer process, as described in the section titled "Conversations."

- **Audit Trail**   Audit trail also reflects the treatment of an invoked peer process as an independent process—the two processes show as independent components in the composite application.

Events and Exceptions

Oracle BPM 11*g*'s BPMN support includes rich support for raising and responding to events. An event is an interesting change in the state of the process or its environment, such as out-of-inventory, customer-cancellation, or database-unavailable. In BPMN 2.0, exceptions, both system exceptions such as system-unavailable and business exceptions such as unauthorized-transaction, are just another type of event.

Events Classification

Figure 5-17 summarizes the various types of BPMN 2.0 events available in Oracle BPM 11*g*, and their characteristics.

As can be seen in Figure 5-17, events in BPMN 2.0 can be classified as *start, catch, throw,* and *end.* Sometimes they are also classified as start,

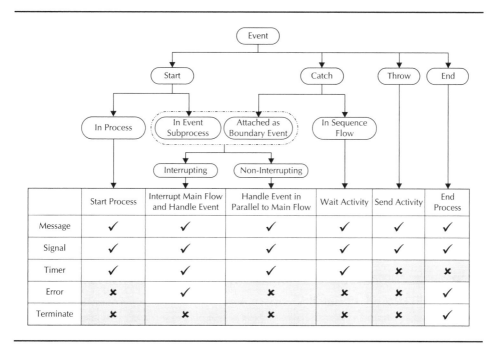

	Start Process	Interrupt Main Flow and Handle Event	Handle Event in Parallel to Main Flow	Wait Activity	Send Activity	End Process
Message	✓	✓	✓	✓	✓	✓
Signal	✓	✓	✓	✓	✓	✓
Timer	✓	✓	✓	✓	✗	✗
Error	✗	✓	✗	✗	✗	✓
Terminate	✗	✗	✗	✗	✗	✓

FIGURE 5-17. *Summary of BPMN 2.0 events*

intermediate, and end; catch and throw being the intermediate events. Start events can be used at the start of a process or at the start of an event subprocess (a concept that will be described shortly). Catch events can be used as boundary events—that is, they can be attached to the boundary of activities, or they can be part of the sequence flow just like activities. The dashed oval in Figure 5-17 indicates that a start event used in an event subprocess behaves essentially the same as a *catch* event used as boundary event. The following is a quick summary of the behavior of these events:

■ **Start (process)** Start the process at the occurrence or receipt of event. Message, Signal, and Timer events can be used.

■ **Start (event subprocess) and Catch (boundary event)** If the event happens while the process is within the appropriate scope, catch it and invoke the event handler logic. There are two flavors of this type of event handling: *interrupting* and *non-interrupting*. As the name indicates, one interrupts the main process flow and the other does not. These concepts are discussed in further detail later in this section. Message, Signal, and Timer events can be handled in both an interrupting and a non-interrupting way. Error events are always interrupting.

■ **Catch (in sequence flow)** The process flow waits for the receipt of the specified Message, Signal, or Timer event. The catch of a Message or Signal in this way is semantically the same as using the Receive activity. The catch of a Timer is essentially a wait or a delay activity.

■ **Throw** Raise a Message or Signal event. Semantically, the same as the Send activity. (The reason there is no Throw Error is that the Error ends the flow and is therefore only an end event.)

■ **End** Ends the process normally with Message or Signal, or abnormally with Error or Terminate.

NOTE
An end event of the type None does not necessarily imply the end of the process. It is just a convenient modeling notation to end a process branch without requiring all branches to end at a common end node. Similarly, it is valid for a process to have multiple Message and Signal end events. In which case, the process sends out all the messages or flows that get activated by tokens flowing into them.

In Figure 5-17 and in the previous discussion, the other dimension to classify BPMN 2.0 events is by:

■ **Message** Message events communicate between processes and services using messages. A message is essentially a one-way web service operation and is specifically directed to a particular recipient. Details of sending and receiving messages and how the identity of the communicating partner is established are discussed in the section titled "Conversations."

- **Signal**   While a message is a point-to-point communication, a signal enables loosely coupled publish-subscribe communication. Details on signals are discussed along with messages in the section titled "Conversations."

- **Timer**   Timers are events that can be set up to fire at the specified time or after the specified duration. Timers are very useful to timeout activities, manage service level agreements, or pause the flow for some time.

- **Error**   Error events are used to raise and catch exceptions. They are discussed in the section titled "Events and Exceptions."

- **Terminate**   Throwing a terminate event allows the process to abort immediately. All outstanding branches and event/exception handlers are aborted. It terminates the process (kills all the parallel flows) and its subprocesses within the current scope; however, it has no impact on the parent. To model an end event that "bubbles up," an error event must be used.

NOTE
In the opinion of the author, a terminate end event should never be used in process models because it can leave the process in an unclean state—for example, tasks may be left open for users even when the process has vanished, as no termination handlers are invoked.

Events Behavior Details

For the following discussion, the process shown in Figure 5-18 will be used as an illustration. In this process, the service invoked in the *Sync Subprocess* activity can throw exceptions *Ex1* and *Ex2,* and the inline subprocess raises exceptions *Ex2* and *Ex3*. These exceptions are caught using different event catching options and logged; *Ex2* is caught and handled inside the subprocess, whereas *Ex3* is raised and caught outside. Also, there is a SLA monitor at the process level, as well as at the inline subprocess level; again, the SLA violation is simply logged.

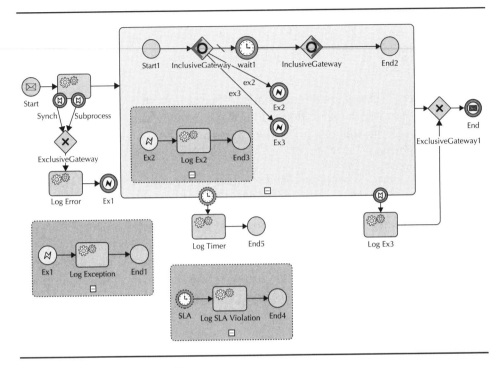

FIGURE 5-18. *Process illustrating event concepts*

Boundary Events

The process shown in Figure 5-18 has two error events attached to the *Synch Subprocess* activity and one error event and one timer event attached to the inline subprocess. Such events are called boundary events and are added by dragging and dropping *catch* events from the component palette to activities on the process canvas.

The scope of a boundary event is the activity or the subprocess it is attached to. That is, while the process is executing the activity or the subprocess, the boundary event is active—if the specified event happens during this time, the modeled handling behavior is executed.

The sequence flow out of the boundary event specifies how the event should be handled.

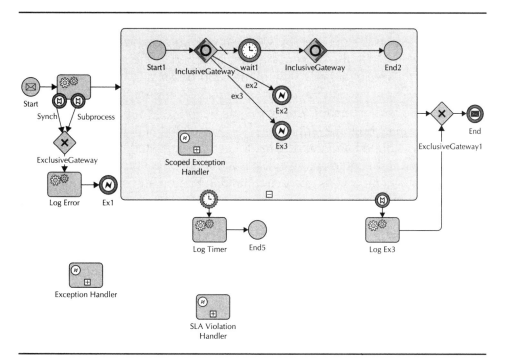

FIGURE 5-19.   *Collapsed event subprocesses*

Event Subprocesses

An event subprocess is a special type of inline subprocess that is visually denoted by a dashed boundary in expanded form, and starts with an event start (whereas a regular inline subprocess has a solid boundary and starts with a *None* start type). In the process shown in Figure 5-18, there are three event subprocesses, starting with events *Ex1*, SLA, and *Ex2*. In the collapsed form, an event subprocess is denoted by an event icon in the top-left corner of the collapsed subprocess activity, as shown in Figure 5-19.

The scope of an event subprocess is the enclosing process or subprocess. That is, while the process is executing the enclosing process or subprocess, the event subprocess is active, and if an event of the specified type occurs, the event subprocess will be executed. In the process shown in Figure 5-18 and Figure 5-19, the *Exception Handler* and *SLA Violation Handler* are active throughout the process scope, and the *Scoped Exception Handler* is active while the process is executing the inline subprocess (between *Start1* and *End2*).

Interrupting Events

Interrupting Events are denoted by solid circular borders. In the process shown in Figure 5-18, the two error events attached to the *Sync Subprocess* activity and the one attached to the inline subprocess, as well as the *Ex1* and *Ex2* start events within the event subprocesses, are interrupting events (as mentioned earlier, error events can only be interrupting).

When an interrupting event occurs, the associated activity, process, or subprocess is stopped and the original token is propagated through the event handler. If the interrupting event is a boundary event, this means that by the law of similar tokens, the event handling path can converge to wherever it would have been legal for the original activity to flow to. In the process shown in Figure 5-18 and Figure 5-19, the event handler for the error event attached to the inline subprocess merges back with the regular process flow after logging the error. If the interrupting event is in an event subprocess, then after the event subprocess has completed executing, if the event subprocess is scoped within a subprocess, the token will be propagated through the outgoing sequence flows of the enclosing subprocess. That is, the behavior of the event subprocess starting with *Ex2* is the same as that of the attached event handler for *Ex3* in the process shown in Figure 5-18 and Figure 5-19.

Non-Interrupting Event

Non-interrupting events are denoted by dashed circular borders. In the process shown in Figure 5-18 and Figure 5-19, the timer event subprocess (*SLA Violation Handler*) and the attached timer event are non-interrupting.

When a non-interrupting event happens, the regular flow continues uninterrupted and the event handler is executed in parallel with new tokens. By the law of tokens, this means that it is not legal for the sequence flow starting from a non-interrupting attached event to merge with the regular flow. Another important aspect to realize is that the associated activity or subprocess is not considered complete until all attached non-interrupting event handlers and enclosed non-interrupting event subprocesses are complete.

Interrupting vs. Non-Interrupting

Message, signal, and timer events offer a choice of whether to be used as interrupting or non-interrupting. Interrupting messages and signals should be used for scenarios such as cancellation, where the normal flow is no longer relevant. Non-interrupting should be used either for queries to the process or for handling events that may impact the process without necessarily making it irrelevant—for example, if a fraud is suspected, the process may need to be paused to investigate the fraud, but if it is determined that there is no fraud, the regular process should be resumed. For timers, interrupting timers should be used for timeouts and non-interrupting timers for alerts.

TIP
It is possible to mix interrupting and non-interrupting behavior, as described in the subsection Conditional Interrupt *within the section* Other Process Patterns.

Boundary Events vs. Event Subprocesses

First, an event subprocess must be used when specifying events at the process scope (no scope to attach a boundary event) and a boundary event must be used when specifying events at the activity scope, other than when the activity is a subprocess. So the choice of whether to use a boundary event or an event subprocess exists when either using an inline subprocess or using a call activity to invoke a reusable process.

From a behavior perspective, a boundary event attached to an inline subprocess or a call activity is essentially the same as an event subprocess contained within the subprocess.

The most important semantic difference between the two is the applicable scope. An event subprocess executes within the scope of the enclosing subprocess (or process), whereas the attached event handler executes outside of the scope of the subprocess it is attached to. What this implies is that:

■ An event subprocess has access to process data (and other context such as conversations) scoped within the enclosing subprocess, whereas the attached handler does not.

■ Any events thrown from within an event subprocess can be caught again by another event subprocess or attached event handler, whereas an event thrown from within an attached handler will not be caught again by event handlers of the subprocess.

A few other differences include:

- For interrupting events, boundary event handlers can be merged flexibly with the main flow. An event subprocess is equivalent to merging only at the immediate outgoing sequence flow.

- A sequence flow starting from a boundary event handler can flow to activities in other swim-lanes in the process. This may be needed when user intervention is required as part of event handling.

Other than the behavior differences listed here, the use of boundary events versus event subprocesses is simply an abstraction choice. Modeling the event handling as an event subprocess makes it part of the subprocess and a detail that is hidden or disclosed along with the subprocess, whereas using a boundary event makes the event handling stand independent of the subprocess details and is shown even when the subprocess is collapsed. Also, when using reusable subprocesses, another consideration is reuse. If every invocation of the subprocess must handle the event in the same way it should be modeled within the subprocess, whereas using a boundary event enables the caller to decide how to handle the event.

Event-based Gateways

Although classified as a gateway, the *event-based* gateway is more like a complex event. Unlike other gateways, the behavior of the event-based gateway is determined in conjunction with elements attached to its outgoing sequence flows. Only *message, signal, or timer* catch events can be the targets of outgoing sequence flows from an event-based gateway. (A receive task is the same as a message catch and can be used as well; however, boundary events cannot be attached to it.) The event-based gateway essentially picks the first event to fire among its target catch events; subsequent event firings are ignored.

From a gateway perspective, an event-based gateway can be thought of essentially as an exclusive (XOR) gateway, but one that works with events instead of data-based conditional expressions. Also, unlike exclusive gateways, there is no concept of a default transition; however, a timer event is the corresponding mechanism in this context—that is, follow this transition if none of the other events fire in the specified time.

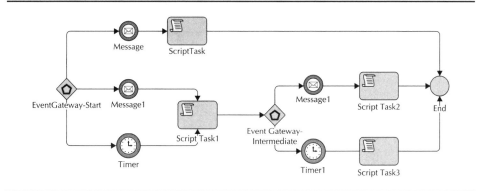

FIGURE 5-20.   *Event-based gateways*

Just as for the exclusive gateway, the incoming token is propagated to the outgoing sequence flow so the outgoing sequence flows from an event-based gateway can be flexibly merged with the process and with each other, as shown in Figure 5-20.

As can be seen in Figure 5-20, an event-based gateway may also be used at the start of the process. In this usage, the *Instantiate* implementation attribute of the gateway must be checked true and there can be no incoming sequence flows. An event-based gateway at the start of a process specifies that the process may be started by the occurrence of any one of the target events.

Exception Handling

As discussed earlier, exceptions are essentially events, and the preceding discussion applies to raising and catching exceptions. In this section, we discuss a few details specific to exceptions.

Business Exceptions vs. System Exceptions

Oracle BPM 11g, classifies exceptions as business exceptions and system exceptions. Business exceptions are essentially user-defined exceptions (see the "Exception Object" section following) and model foreseen abnormal business conditions such as no-stock. System exceptions are exceptions caused by abnormal situations in the underlying platform. A list of system exceptions can be seen in Figure 5-21.

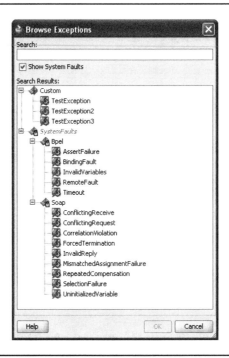

FIGURE 5-21. *System (and business) exceptions*

NOTE
Exceptions in systems that the business process invokes as services are considered as business exceptions, even if they are system exceptions from the perspective of the invoked system.

Exception Objects

Business exceptions are identified by exception objects, which are very similar to business objects. When a service with a fault in its signature is added to the business catalog, a corresponding exception object is automatically added to the *Errors* module of the business catalog. New exception objects can be defined by right-clicking the business catalog and selecting *New* and then *Business Exception,* just as for creating new

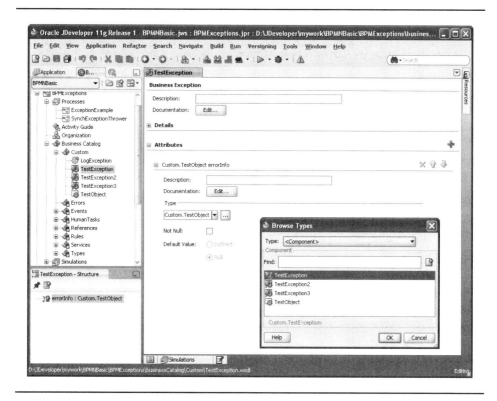

FIGURE 5-22.   *The business exception editor*

business objects. The Business Exception editor is the same as the Business Object editor, but is fixed to a single attribute called *errorInfo* as shown in Figure 5-22. The business exception can be set up to handle custom data types by changing the type of the *errorInfo* attribute to a desired type, as shown in Figure 5-22.

Throwing Exceptions vs. Returning Faults

As discussed earlier, an error end event can be used to raise exceptions. Exceptions raised in this way can be handled in the process or bubbled up to a parent process when invoked as a callable subprocess.

When a process is invoked from another process or service as a peer process, as a *request-reply* operation the invoking process or service expects to be notified of any exceptions that would prevent the reply from being returned. In Web Services terminology, such notification of exceptions is specified with a *Fault* message in the *request-reply* operation's definition.

Fault messages are not created in the process operation definition when an error end event is used. This means that if such an error event is used within the context of a request-reply operation, the exception will be bubbled to the invoking process or service; however, in the absence of a fault definition, it will not be able to catch it, outside of catch-all-business-exceptions.

The correct way to model a return of *Fault* message is to use a message end event, paired with the start just the same way as the reply, and an implementation selected to exception, as shown in Figure 5-23.

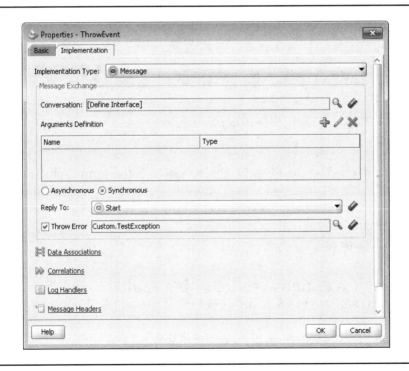

FIGURE 5-23. *An example of returning fault with message end event*

Policy-based Exception Handling

In addition to explicit exception handling, as described in this section, Oracle BPM 11*g* features policy-driven exception handling. Using XML policy files, how to handle different types of faults can be specified using a combination of conditions that can test for fault name and type, as well as any data in fault and actions. Supported actions include retry, terminate, and human-intervention. When human-intervention is specified as the action, the activity is paused and, from Oracle Enterprise Manager, an authorized user can modify variables and then retry the activity, replay the scope, re-throw the error, or abort the process. Policy-based exception handling is described in detail in section 11.4 "Using the Fault Management Framework" of the *Oracle Fusion Middleware Developer's Guide for Oracle SOA Suite,* which is a part of Oracle's product documentation. A fragment of a fault policy file is included next to illustrate the concept.

```
<faultName xmlns:bpelx=http://schemas.oracle.com/bpel/extension
name="bpelx:remoteFault">
  <condition>
    <test>$fault.code="WSDLReadingError"</test>
    <action ref="ora-terminate"/>
  </condition>
</faultName>
<!-- Business faults -->
<faultName xmlns:credit=http://services.otn.com name=
"credit:NegativeCredit">
  <condition>
    <test>$fault.payload="Bankruptcy Report"</test>
    <action ref="ora-human-intervention"/>
  </condition>
</faultName>
```

Conversations

BPMN processes can interact with each other and with BPEL processes and other services using messages and signals. Interactions can be of the following types:

- Request-reply interaction—this is typically used when the invoked process or service is synchronous.

- One-way interaction; also known as fire-and-forget.

- A one-way operation followed by an asynchronous callback.

- A combination of one-way operations and asynchronous callbacks; essentially two processes communicating with each other in a conversational manner.

Also, while typically the preceding interactions would involve one process or service being instantiated based on the interaction, often a process may need to interact with another process or service that is already instantiated. In this section, we will discuss how these interaction patterns may be achieved with Oracle BPM 11g.

Messages

A message is a one-to-one interaction between two processes. The process starting the interaction sends a message using the send activity or throw message event. The process responding to the interaction receives the message using the receive activity or catch message event. It can then reply back using a send activity or throw message event.

Request-Reply (Synchronous) Interactions

Receive (including message start and message catch) and send (including message end and message throw) need to be paired to model a request-reply operation. The *Reply To* implementation property shown in Figure 5-24 allows this pairing to be specified.

For a synchronous process, the request-reply operation is modeled by specifying the reply-to for a message end as the message start, as shown in Figure 5-24. Even a fault is modeled the same way, as shown earlier in Figure 5-23. The invoking process uses a service activity.

Conversation

Conversation is a mechanism for an instance of a BPMN process to establish a message interchange relationship with another process or service instance. Message exchanges between the two instances, initiated from either side, can be accomplished by continuing to use the same conversation—every message send/throw/end and receive/catch/start defines which conversation it belongs to using the *Conversation implementation* property, as seen in Figure 5-24. Under the covers, the BPMN engine uses WS-Addressing-based

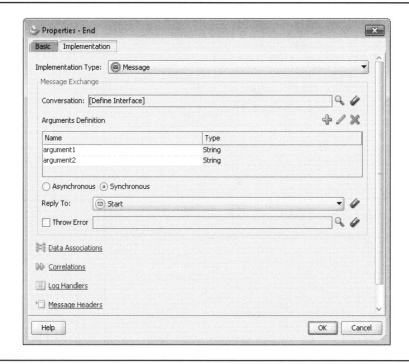

FIGURE 5-24.   *Implementation properties for send, message end, and throw*

correlation, and a unique WS-Addressing Conversation ID is used for each conversation.

BPM 11*g* uses the terms *outbound* and *inbound* conversations to indicate whether the process is starting the conversation (sending the first message) or participating in a conversation started by the partner process, respectively. In the current implementation of BPM 11*g, outbound* conversations use operations defined in a partner's interface and the process includes operations for *inbound* conversations in its own interface.

In certain scenarios, a process instance may need to converse with multiple instances of the same process. For example, there may be two instances of a supplier process and the procurement process may need to interact with both for different items. This is easily modeled by using a different conversation per message exchange instance. Conversations can also be scoped, as shown in Figure 5-25, enabling them to be used in multi-instance subprocesses, where each instance of the subprocess needs to establish a different conversation.

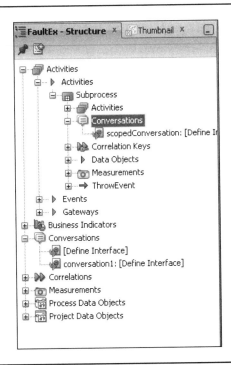

FIGURE 5-25. *Process structure showing conversations at multiple levels*

Correlation

Conversation is sufficient when one of the interacting parties creates a new instance of the other. In this case, the first time it's not needed to determine which instance to route to, and once the first interaction has happened, the two instances can continue to converse using the WS-Addressing Conversation ID.

However, there are situations where a conversation needs to be established with a process instance that is already executing. One common reason such a scenario may happen is that the other party is not designed to maintain a conversational exchange. Another reason is that even if it were possible to design the interaction such that a conversational context is established, doing so would make an unwieldy process design. Example scenarios include those where a change event, in the database, in an edge application, or via customer interaction needs to be communicated to an in-flight process instance.

For such scenarios, correlation, or more specifically message-based correlation, can be used. The concept of correlation is to use one or more elements of the message to match existing in-flight instances. Such correlation is defined using the concepts shown in Figure 5-26 and is described next.

- **Correlation Property**   A correlation property is a mechanism to create a common identifier for related elements in multiple messages.

- **Correlation Property Alias**   A correlation property alias defines which elements of a message map to a defined property. Property aliases may be defined in the WSDL of the message interchange

FIGURE 5-26.   *Correlation keys and properties*

partner, typically if the partner is another BPMN or a BPEL process. In such cases, the definitions in WSDL are used. Otherwise, aliases can be defined from the correlation editor as shown in Figure 5-27.

■ **Correlation Key**   A correlation key is a set of one or more correlation properties, as shown in Figure 5-28.

If the mode of the correlation key is defined as *Uses,* as shown in Figure 5-27, the value of the correlation properties in the incoming message (as mapped via property aliases) is compared against the value of the correlation properties in the correlation key for each existing process instance that has the corresponding receive activity (or catch event) active. If one-and-only-one instance is matched, the message is passed to it; if none or more than one instance is matched, an exception is raised. The value of the correlation properties in a correlation key are initialized from the value of correlation properties in the message if the mode of the correlation key is defined as *Initiates,* as shown in Figure 5-27; they can also be initialized using data associations.

Correlation keys can be scoped just like data objects and conversations, enabling them to be used in multi-instance subprocesses, where each instance of the subprocess can have its own copy of the correlation key.

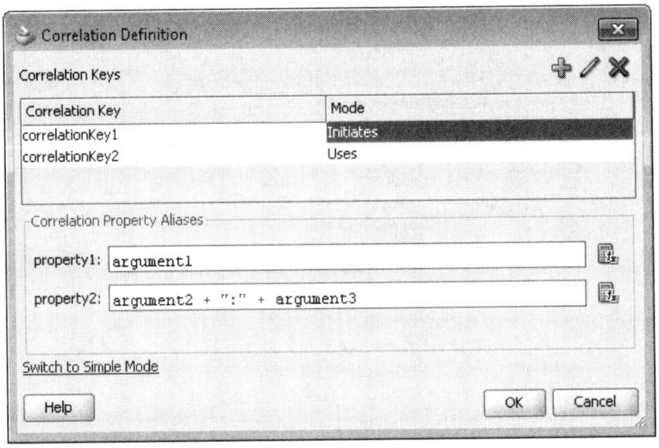

FIGURE 5-27.   *The correlation editor*

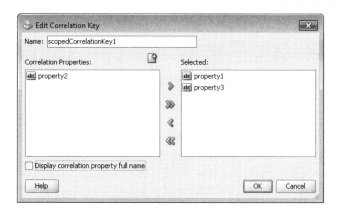

FIGURE 5-28.   *The correlation key editor*

Signals

Signals enable loosely coupled interactions between multiple applications and processes. For example, if a customer changes his or her address, then all processes related to the customer—billing, shipping, mailing—needs to be notified.

The use of signals enables the design of loosely coupled applications. For example, a user interface application and a business process can communicate with each other via signals. This allows the two to be developed and changed independently. Also, since events can have quality-of-service guarantees, including guaranteed delivery, the usage of events as a communication mechanism simplifies error-handling considerations—that is, the UI need not worry about whether the process could be invoked or not.

A *signal* in BPM 11*g* communicates a *Business Event* over the *Event Delivery Network* (EDN), both described next. Multiple BPM process applications can subscribe to a business event. However, within a business process application, in the current version of Oracle BPM 11*g,* a signal is delivered to running instances of the process, just the same as *Message,* and the preceding discussion on *Message* mostly applies to *Signal* as well. This means that correlations must be defined for catch signal events, only one instance of a process can catch the signal, and if multiple instances match the specified correlation, a runtime exception happens.

In BPMN literature, it is common to advocate the usage of a signal to communicate between independently running branches of a process. Given that a signal goes through the EDN and then needs to be correlated back to the instance, this is not a useful pattern in practice. Multiple branches of a process can easily communicate via the state of process data objects instead.

Business Events and Event Delivery Networks

A business event is defined using the Event Definition Language (EDL) editor. As shown in Figure 5-29, an EDL definition consists of a name and content or payload. Typically, business event definitions need to be shared across applications and projects. Similar to other shareable assets such as XSDs, EDL definitions can be deployed to the shared area of Oracle MDS and accessed by applications via the resource palette.

At runtime, business events are published to the Event Delivery Network (EDN), a component that is part of the BPM/SOA runtime infrastructure. Two EDN implementations are supported: DB-based EDN, and JMS-based EDN.

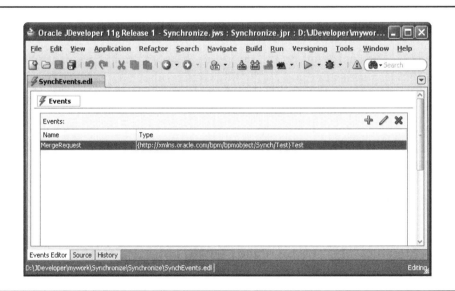

FIGURE 5-29. *The event definition editor*

In addition to BPM/SOA, ADF applications, Java EE applications, and PL/SQL API can raise events, which can be communicated across multiple containers.

For more details on business events and event delivery networks, please see Chapter 39 of the *Oracle Fusion Middleware Developer's Guide for Oracle SOA Suite*, which is a part of Oracle's product documentation.

Workflow Patterns

In the area of Business Process modeling and notation, there is a set of patterns known as the Workflow Patterns that have been broadly used to conceptualize and categorize the process constructs and capabilities of various process languages and their implementations. The Workflow Patterns initiative is a joint effort of Eindhoven University of Technology (led by Professor Wil van der Aalst) and Queensland University of Technology (led by Professor Arthur ter Hofstede), which started in 1999.

The *Control Flow* patterns within the *Workflow Patterns* provide a useful and standard framework for framing the various process constructs discussed earlier. In this section, we list all the *Control Flow* patterns and whether and how Oracle BPM 11*g* addresses them. For the sake of completeness, descriptions of the patterns are reproduced in this section. However, the web site for the patterns, www.workflowpatterns.com/patterns/control/index.php, includes more information, such as flash animation of the patterns. The categorization, naming and numbering, and description for the patterns in this section are from this web site at the time of the writing of this book.

NOTE
The following patterns are not necessarily in sequence because the same ordering and categorization of the Workflow Patterns on the site (www.workflowpatterns.com/patterns/control/index.php) has been used. As noted at this site, additional patterns were added later to the original list of patterns, causing the numbering to get out of sequence.

Basic Control Flow Patterns

This class of patterns captures elementary aspects of process control.

Pattern 1: Sequence Flow

Pattern Description: A task in a process is enabled after the completion of a preceding task in the same process.

Oracle BPM 11*g* Support: Sequence Flow (also called Transition).

Pattern 2: Parallel Split

Pattern Description: The divergence of a branch into two or more parallel branches, each of which execute concurrently.

Oracle BPM 11*g* Support: Parallel (AND) Gateway (splitting).

Pattern 3: Synchronization

Pattern Description: The convergence of two or more branches into a single subsequent branch such that the thread of control is passed to the subsequent branch when all input branches have been enabled.

Oracle BPM 11*g* Support: Parallel (AND) Gateway (merging). Please also see Pattern 7. In BPM 11*g* as in BPMN 2.0, synchronization must be structured as described in Pattern 7.

Pattern 4: Exclusive Choice

Pattern Description: The divergence of a branch into two or more branches such that when the incoming branch is enabled, the thread of control is immediately passed to precisely one of the outgoing branches based on a mechanism that can select one of the outgoing branches.

Oracle BPM 11*g* Support: Exclusive (XOR) Gateway (splitting).

Pattern 5: Simple Merge

Pattern Description: The convergence of two or more branches into a single subsequent branch such that each enablement of an incoming branch results in the thread of control being passed to the subsequent branch.

Oracle BPM 11*g* Support: Exclusive (XOR) Gateway (merging).

Advanced Branching and Synchronization Patterns

These patterns characterize more complex branching and merging concepts which arise in business processes.

Pattern 6: Multi-Choice

Pattern Description: The divergence of a branch into two or more branches such that when the incoming branch is enabled, the thread of control is immediately passed to one or more of the outgoing branches based on a mechanism that selects one or more outgoing branches.

Oracle BPM 11*g* Support: Inclusive (OR) Gateway (splitting).

Pattern 7: Structured Synchronizing Merge

Pattern Description: The convergence of two or more branches (which diverged earlier in the process at a uniquely identifiable point) into a single subsequent branch such that the thread of control is passed to the subsequent branch when each active incoming branch has been enabled. The *Structured Synchronizing Merge* occurs in a structured context—in other words, there must be a single *Multi-Choice* construct earlier in the process model with which the *Structured Synchronizing Merge* is associated, and it must merge all the branches emanating from the *Multi-Choice*. These branches must either flow from the *Structured Synchronizing Merge* without any splits or joins, or they must be structured in form (that is, have balanced splits and joins).

Oracle BPM Support: Parallel (AND) Gateway (merging).

Pattern 8: Multi-Merge

Pattern Description: The convergence of two or more branches into a single subsequent branch such that each enablement of an incoming branch results in the thread of control being passed to the subsequent branch.

Oracle BPM 11*g* Support: Exclusive (XOR) Gateway (merging).

Pattern 9: Structured Discriminator

Pattern Description: The convergence of two or more branches into a single subsequent branch following a corresponding divergence earlier in the process model, such that the thread of control is passed to the subsequent branch when the first incoming branch has been enabled. Subsequent enablements of incoming branches do not result in the thread of control being passed on. The *Structured Discriminator* construct resets when all incoming branches have been enabled. The *Structured Discriminator* occurs in a structured context—in other words, there must be a single *Parallel Split* construct earlier in the process model with which the *Structured Discriminator* is associated, and it must merge all of the branches emanating from the *Structured Discriminator*. These branches must either flow from the *Parallel Split* to the *Structured Discriminator* without any splits or joins, or they must be structured in form (that is, have balanced splits and joins).

    Oracle BPM 11g Support: Complex Gateway (paired with splitting Parallel Gateway).

Pattern 28: Blocking Discriminator

Pattern Description: The convergence of two or more branches into a single subsequent branch following one or more corresponding divergences earlier in the process model. The thread of control is passed to the subsequent branch when the first active incoming branch has been enabled. The *Blocking Discriminator* construct resets when all active incoming branches have been enabled once for the same process instance. Subsequent enablements of incoming branches are blocked until the *Blocking Discriminator* has reset.

    Oracle BPM 11g Support: Complex Gateway (paired with splitting Inclusive Gateway).

Pattern 29: Cancelling Discriminator

Pattern Description: The convergence of two or more branches into a single subsequent branch following one or more corresponding divergences earlier in the process model. The thread of control is passed to the subsequent branch when the first active incoming branch has been enabled. Triggering the *Cancelling Discriminator* also cancels the execution of all of the other incoming branches and resets the construct.

Oracle BPM 11g Support: Complex Gateway with *Abort Pending Flows* checked and completion condition testing for *number of Active Instances = 1.*

Pattern 30: Structured Partial Join

Pattern Description: The convergence of two or more branches (say *m*) into a single subsequent branch following a corresponding divergence earlier in the process model such that the thread of control is passed to the subsequent branch when *n* of the incoming branches have been enabled where *n* is less than *m*. Subsequent enablements of incoming branches do not result in the thread of control being passed on. The join construct resets when all active incoming branches have been enabled. The join occurs in a structured context—in other words, there must be a single *Parallel Split* construct earlier in the process model with which the join is associated, and it must merge all of the branches emanating from the *Parallel Split.* These branches must either flow from the *Parallel Split* to the join without any splits or joins, or be structured in form (that is, have balanced splits and joins).

Oracle BPM 11g Support: Complex Gateway with *Abort Pending Flows* unchecked and completion condition testing for *number of Active Instances = n.*

Pattern 31: Blocking Partial Join

Pattern Description: The convergence of two or more branches (say *m*) into a single subsequent branch following one or more corresponding divergences earlier in the process model. The thread of control is passed to the subsequent branch when *n* of the incoming branches has been enabled (where $2 = n < m$). The join construct resets when all active incoming branches have been enabled once for the same process instance. Subsequent enablements of incoming branches are blocked until the join has reset.

Oracle BPM 11g Support: Complex Gateway with *Abort Pending Flows* unchecked and completion condition testing for *number of Active Instances = m.* Given the requirement to have gateways structurally paired, this is the same as Pattern 30.

Pattern 32: Cancelling Partial Join

Pattern Description: The convergence of two or more branches (say *m*) into a single subsequent branch following one or more corresponding divergences earlier in the process model. The thread of control is passed to the subsequent branch when *n* of the incoming branches have been enabled where *n* is less than *m*. Triggering the join also cancels the execution of all of the other incoming branches and resets the construct.

    Oracle BPM 11*g* Support: Complex Gateway with *Abort Pending Flows* checked. Same as 30 and 31, but with *Abort Pending Flows* **checked.**

Pattern 33: Generalized AND-Join

Pattern Description: The convergence of two or more branches into a single subsequent branch such that the thread of control is passed to the subsequent branch when all input branches have been enabled. Additional triggers received on one or more branches between firings of the join persist and are retained for future firings. Over time, each of the incoming branches should deliver the same number of triggers to the AND-join construct (obviously the timing of these triggers may vary, however).

    Oracle BPM 11*g* Support: Parallel (AND) Gateway (merging). In Oracle BPM 11*g*, as in BPMN 2.0, and-joins exists only in a structured (that is, paired) context.

Pattern 37: Local Synchronizing Merge

Pattern Description: The convergence of two or more branches which diverged earlier in the process into a single subsequent branch such that the thread of control is passed to the subsequent branch when each active incoming branch has been enabled. Determination of how many branches require synchronization is made on the basis of information locally available to the merge construct. This may be communicated directly to the merge by the preceding diverging construct, or alternatively it can be determined on the basis of local data such as the threads of control arriving at the merge.

    Oracle BPM 11*g* Support: Inclusive (OR) Gateway (merging).

Pattern 38: General Synchronizing Merge

Pattern Description: The convergence of two or more branches which diverged earlier in the process into a single subsequent branch such that the thread of control is passed to the subsequent branch when either (1) each active incoming branch has been enabled or (2) it is not possible that any branch that has not yet been enabled will be enabled at any future time.

   Oracle BPM 11g Support: Not supported at the time of writing of this book.

Pattern 41: Thread Merge

Pattern Description: At a given point in a process, a nominated number of execution threads in a single branch of the same process instance should be merged together into a single thread of execution.

   Oracle BPM 11g Support: Embedded subprocesses with multi-instance configuration.

Pattern 42: Thread Split

Pattern Description: At a given point in a process, a nominated number of execution threads can be initiated in a single branch of the same process instance.

   Oracle BPM 11g Support: Embedded subprocesses with multi-instance configuration (that is, the same as 41). Splitting without merging can be achieved by invoking a peer process.

Multiple Instance Patterns

Multiple instance patterns describe situations where there are multiple threads of execution active in a process model which relate to the same activity.

Pattern 12: Multiple Instances Without Synchronization

Pattern Description: Within a given process instance, multiple instances of a task can be created. These instances are independent of each other and run concurrently. There is no requirement to synchronize them upon completion. Each of the instances of the multiple instance task that are created must execute within the context of the process instance from which they were started (in other words, they must share the same case identifier and have access to the same data elements) and each of them must execute independently from and without reference to the task that started them.

   Oracle BPM 11g Support: Invoke a service or a peer process asynchronously from within a multi-instance subprocess.

Pattern 13: Multiple Instances with *a priori* Design-Time Knowledge

Pattern Description: Within a given process instance, multiple instances of a task can be created. The required number of instances is known at design time. These instances are independent of each other and run concurrently. It is necessary to synchronize the task instances at completion before any subsequent tasks can be triggered.

　　Oracle BPM 11g Support: Parallel (AND) Gateway, as well as multi-instance subprocesses.

Pattern 14: Multiple Instances with *a priori* Run-Time Knowledge

Pattern Description: Within a given process instance, multiple instances of a task can be created. The required number of instances may depend on a number of runtime factors, including state data, resource availability, and inter-process communications, but is known before the task instances must be created. Once initiated, these instances are independent of each other and run concurrently. It is necessary to synchronize the instances at completion before any subsequent tasks can be triggered.

　　Oracle BPM 11g Support: Multi-instance subprocesses using variable-based loop specification.

Pattern 15: Multiple Instances Without *a priori* Run-Time Knowledge

Pattern Description: Within a given process instance, multiple instances of a task can be created. The required number of instances may depend on a number of runtime factors, including state data, resource availability, and inter-process communications, and is not known until the final instance has completed. Once initiated, these instances are independent of each other and run concurrently. At any time, while instances are running, it is possible for additional instances to be initiated. It is necessary to synchronize the instances at completion before any subsequent tasks can be triggered.

　　Oracle BPM 11g Support: Multi-instance subprocesses with non-interrupting message handlers to initiate new instances known during runtime. Discussed in detail in the section "Dynamic Creation of Subcases" in this chapter and is shown in Figure 5-36.

Pattern 34: Static Partial Join for Multiple Instances

Pattern Description: Within a given process instance, multiple concurrent instances of a task (say *m*) can be created. The required number of instances is known when the first task instance commences. Once *n* of the task instances have completed (where *n* is less than *m*), the next task in the process is triggered. Subsequent completions of the remaining *m-n* instances are inconsequential; however, all instances must complete in order for the join construct to reset and be subsequently reenabled.

Oracle BPM 11*g* Support: Multi-instance subprocesses with a loop completion condition specified, as shown in Figure 5-30. At the time of writing of this book, outstanding instances are canceled—that is, instead of this pattern, Pattern 35 is supported. However, it is expected that a flag to control whether outstanding flows should be canceled or not, similar to the *abortPendingFlows* flag in Complex gateway, will be added to support this pattern.

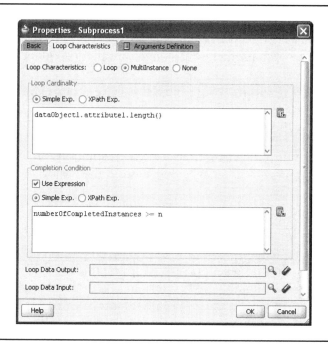

FIGURE 5-30.   *A multi-instance subprocess with completion condition*

Pattern 35: Canceling Partial Join for Multiple Instances

Pattern Description: Within a given process instance, multiple concurrent instances of a task (say *m*) can be created. The required number of instances is known when the first task instance commences. Once *n* of the task instances have completed (where *n* is less than *m*), the next task in the process is triggered and the remaining *m-n* instances are canceled.

Oracle BPM 11g Support: Multi-instance subprocesses with a loop completion condition specified, as shown in Figure 5-30.

Pattern 36: Dynamic Partial Join for Multiple Instances

Pattern Description: Within a given process instance, multiple concurrent instances of a task can be created. The required number of instances may depend on a number of runtime factors, including state data, resource availability, and inter-process communications, and is not known until the final instance has completed. At any time, while instances are running, it is possible for additional instances to be initiated, providing the ability to do so has not been disabled. A completion condition is specified, which is evaluated each time an instance of the task completes. Once the completion condition evaluates to true, the next task in the process is triggered. Subsequent completions of the remaining task instances are inconsequential and no new instances can be created.

Oracle BPM 11g Support: Supported the same way as Pattern 34.

State-based Patterns

State-based patterns reflect situations for which solutions are most easily accomplished in process languages that support the notion of state.

Pattern 16: Deferred Choice

Pattern Description: A point in a process where one of several branches is chosen based on interaction with the operating environment. Prior to the decision, all branches represent possible future courses of execution. The decision is made by initiating the first task in one of the branches—in other words, there is no explicit choice but rather a race between different branches. After the decision is made, execution alternatives in branches other than the one selected are withdrawn.

Oracle BPM 11g Support: Event-based gateway.

Pattern 17: Interleaved Parallel Routing

Pattern Description: A set of tasks has a partial ordering defining the requirements with respect to the order in which they must be executed. Each task in the set must be executed once and they can be completed in any order that accords with the partial order. However, as an additional requirement, no two tasks can be executed at the same time (that is, no two tasks can be active for the same process instance at the same time).

    Oracle BPM 11*g* Support: Parallel execution with ordering can be achieved using an inclusive gateway inside a loop; the conditions on the transitions to activities should check whether the activity is enabled (partial order), as well as whether it has been already performed. The loop condition should check that all activities have been completed. At the time of writing, it is not possible without custom handling to disable other activities once one activity is started.

Pattern 18: Milestone

Pattern Description: A task is only enabled when the process instance (of which it is part) is in a specific state (typically a parallel branch). The state is assumed to be a specific execution point (also known as a *milestone*) in the process model. When this execution point is reached, the nominated task can be enabled. If the process instance has progressed beyond this state, then the task cannot be enabled now or at any future time (in other words, the deadline has expired). Note that the execution does not influence the state itself—meaning that unlike normal control-flow dependencies, it is a test rather than a trigger.

    Oracle BPM 11*g* Support: Accomplished by enabling the task at the start of the state and withdrawing it (if pending) at the end of the state.

Pattern 39: Critical Section

Pattern Description: Two or more connected subgraphs of a process model are identified as "critical sections." At runtime for a given process instance, only tasks in one of these "critical sections" can be active at any given time. Once execution of the tasks in one "critical section" commences, it must complete before another "critical section" can commence.

Oracle BPM 11*g* Support: A process data object can be used as a semaphore to achieve this; each subprocess should check that the semaphore is not acquired, acquire it, and then release it when done.

Pattern 40: Interleaved Routing

Pattern Description: Each member of a set of tasks must be executed once. They can be executed in any order but no two tasks can be executed at the same time (that is, no two tasks can be active for the same process instance at the same time). Once all of the tasks have completed, the next task in the process can be initiated.

Oracle BPM 11*g* Support: Although not supported as is, scenarios requiring these may be accomplished by using the parallel routing feature of a human task with supporting logic to wait for a task claim event and suspend other tasks when one is claimed (to ensure that two tasks cannot be executed at the same time).

Cancellation and Force Completion Patterns

Many of the patterns discussed above utilize the concept of activity cancellation where enabled or active activity instance are withdrawn.

Pattern 19: Cancel Task

Pattern Description: An enabled task is withdrawn prior to it commencing execution. If the task has started, it is disabled and, where possible, the currently running instance is halted and removed.

Oracle BPM 11*g* Support: Throw events, complex gateways, and early completion conditions on multi-instance subprocesses are some of the ways these can be achieved. Also, the *Update User Task* activity enables canceling outstanding user tasks from any point in the process flow.

Pattern 20: Cancel Case

Pattern Description: A complete process instance is removed. This includes currently executing tasks, those which may execute at some future time, and all subprocesses. The process instance is recorded as having completed unsuccessfully.

Oracle BPM 11*g* Support: Throwing an error event and not catching the error event in the process will model this.

Pattern 18: Cancel Region

Pattern Description: The ability to disable a set of tasks in a process instance. If any of the tasks are already executing (or are currently enabled), then they are withdrawn. The tasks need not be a connected subset of the overall process model.

Oracle BPM 11*g* Support: Modeling the tasks in a subprocess and throwing an error event from the subprocess will accomplish this.

Pattern 26: Cancel Multiple Instance Task

Pattern Description: Within a given process instance, multiple instances of a task can be created. The required number of instances is known at design time. These instances are independent of each other and run concurrently. At any time, the multiple instance task can be canceled and any instances that have not completed are withdrawn. Task instances that have already completed are unaffected.

Oracle BPM 11*g* Support: Raising an event and catching it as an interrupting boundary event attached to a multi-instance subprocess will cancel all outstanding instances.

Pattern 27: Complete Multiple Instance Task

Pattern Description: Within a given process instance, multiple instances of a task can be created. The required number of instances is known at design time. These instances are independent of each other and run concurrently. It is necessary to synchronize the instances at completion before any subsequent tasks can be triggered. During the course of execution, it is possible that the task needs to be forcibly completed such that any remaining instances are withdrawn and the thread of control is passed to subsequent tasks.

Oracle BPM 11*g* Support: Same way as Pattern 26.

Iteration Patterns

These patterns deal with capturing repetitive behavior in a workflow.

Pattern 10: Arbitrary Cycles

Pattern Description: The ability to represent cycles in a process model that have more than one entry or exit point. It must be possible for individual entry and exit points to be associated with distinct branches.

Oracle BPM 11g Support: Exclusive gateways can be used to create arbitrary cycles.

Pattern 21: Structured Loop

Pattern Description: The ability to execute a task or subprocess repeatedly. The loop has either a pre-test or post-test condition associated with it that is either evaluated at the beginning or end of the loop to determine whether it should continue. The looping structure has a single entry and exit point.

Oracle BPM 11g Support: A subprocess with a *Loop Characteristics* property set to *Loop*.

Pattern 22: Recursion

Pattern Description: The ability of a task to invoke itself during its execution or an ancestor in terms of the overall decomposition structure with which it is associated.

Oracle BPM 11g Support: A calls B, and B calls A; however, as with any recursion, it should be used with care.

Termination Patterns

These patterns deal with the circumstances under which a workflow is considered to be completed.

Pattern 11: Implicit Termination

Pattern Description: A given process (or subprocess) instance should terminate when no remaining work items are able to be done now or at any time in the future, and the process instance is not in deadlock. There is an objective means of determining that the process instance has successfully completed.

Oracle BPM 11g Support: End events other than *Error* and *Termination*.

Pattern 43: Explicit Termination

Pattern Description: A given process (or subprocess) instance should terminate when it reaches a nominated state. Typically, this is denoted by a specific end node. When this end node is reached, any remaining work in the process instance is canceled and the overall process instance is recorded as having completed successfully, regardless of whether there are any tasks in progress or remaining to be executed.

Oracle BPM 11*g* Support: *Error and Termination* end event; if recording successful completion is desired, the error raised must be caught with an event subprocess and logged (or ignored).

Trigger Patterns

These patterns deal with the external signals that may be required to start certain tasks.

Pattern 23: Transient Trigger

Pattern Description: The ability for a task instance to be triggered by a signal from another part of the process or from the external environment. These triggers are transient in nature and are lost if not acted on immediately by the receiving task. A trigger can only be utilized if there is a task instance waiting for it at the time it is received.

Oracle BPM 11*g* Support: Signal event.

Pattern 24: Persistent Trigger

Pattern Description: The ability for a task to be triggered by a signal from another part of the process or from the external environment. These triggers are persistent in form and are retained by the process until they can be acted on by the receiving task.

Oracle BPM 11*g* Support: Message and signal events.

Other Process Patterns

In addition to the patterns included in the *Workflow Patterns,* some process patterns commonly occur. A few are described in this section.

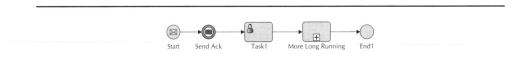

FIGURE 5-31. *An ack-and-continue pattern*

Ack-and-Continue

Though a request-reply operation is typically used for synchronous (or short-lived) processes and a one-way request followed by a callback operation is used for asynchronous (or long-lived) processes, scenarios exist where the client invoking an asynchronous process wants a synchronous acknowledgment back.

This type of a synchronous reply to the initiating client and then continuing on with the process can be accomplished in BPMN using the pattern shown in Figure 5-31. Instead of using an *end message* event, a *throw message* event (denoted in the example as *Send Ack*) is used to reply to the client. This *throw* is set up as a reply to the *start* event, which must be set up as a synchronous operation.

One of the most common items to send in the acknowledgment is the process instance ID, so that the client can later query for the instance. This instance ID is available using the function *getComponentInstanceId()*, within *Advanced Functions* in the data association editor.

Query Operations

In certain scenarios, a process must provide query operation(s) so that other processes or services can query it for its state or process data.

Such query operations can be implemented in BPMN using the pattern shown in Figure 5-32. An event subprocess with a non-interrupting *message start* event is used to implement the query operation and processing. The *start* is set up as a synchronous operation, and a *message end* event paired with the *start* is used to end the event subprocess. Any computation needed to prepare the response can be implemented within the start and the end.

In Figure 5-32, the query event subprocess is defined at the process scope and has access to process scoped data; however, it does not have access to data

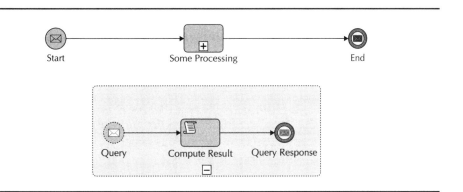

FIGURE 5-32.   *A query operation pattern*

that is scoped within any subprocesses. If needed, a query event subprocess can be defined at any nested subprocess scope. The scoping of the event subprocess determines not only the data accessible to it, but also how long the query operation is available; if it is contained within a subprocess, it is available only while the subprocess is active.

Initializing Process Start Form

As discussed in Chapter 3, Oracle BPM 11*g* features the concept of user-initiated processes, where a user can kick off a process by clicking a link from their workspace application. When the user clicks the link, she is presented with a form where she can enter data needed to start the process. It is a common requirement to be able to initialize this form with some data so the user does not need to enter everything from scratch.

Initialization of the entry form can be accomplished in BPMN 2.0 using the pattern shown in Figure 5-33. The *Initiator* user activity is preceded by

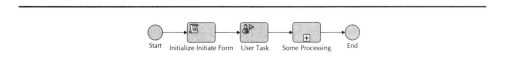

FIGURE 5-33.   *Initializing process start form*

the logic to initialize the data in the form. While in Figure 5-33 a script activity is used, which would commonly be the case, any combination of synchronous services can be used prior to the *Initiator* user activity—for example, if data needs to be read from a database using DB Adapter, it is possible to do so.

While initializing the form, the scenario may require it be personalized for the user clicking the link. The function *getCreator()* in *BPEL XPath Extension Functions* can be used in the data association editor to determine the identity of the user launching the process.

Conditional Interrupt

While BPMN has the concept of non-interrupting and interrupting events, in some scenarios whether the event should be handled in an interrupting or non-interrupting fashion depends on some process condition. For example, whether to close out a service request if no customer follow-up is received within a certain time may depend on the severity of the issue, as well as customer's status.

Conditional handling of an event as interrupting or non-interrupting can be accomplished using the pattern shown in Figure 5-34. An event subprocess

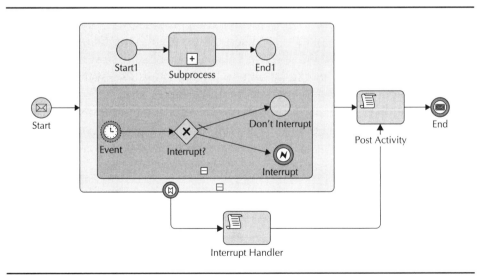

FIGURE 5-34. *Conditional interrupt handling*

is used with a non-interrupting start event. If it is determined that the event should be handled as an interrupting event, then the event subprocess can raise an error event, which can then be handled as an interrupting event. In Figure 5-34, the interrupting event is handled as an attached event; an event subprocess could have been used as well. However, for the non-interrupting event, in this pattern an event subprocess and not a boundary event handler must be used. This is because an event subprocess is within the scope of its parent and any events raised within it can be caught by the parent's event handlers (as explained earlier in the section titled "Events and Exceptions"), as required in this pattern.

Variable Frequency Recurring Timers

BPMN has rich support for timers, including timers that recur at a fixed frequency. However, in some scenarios variable frequency recurring timers are needed. Common examples include exponential back-off—for example, if you are sending reminders to a customer or an executive, you may want to send each reminder at bigger and bigger intervals to avoid upsetting them—and exponential build-up—say, if you are sending reminders to a case worker on an urgent case, you may want to send them reminders more and more frequently as the deadline approaches.

The pattern shown in Figure 5-35 can be used to accomplish the preceding requirements of having recurring timers that recur with variable frequency. In this pattern, the activity or subprocess for which the timer is needed, which is denoted as *Main Task* in Figure 5-35, is surrounded with a parallel-complex split-merge gateway pair. The timer logic is encapsulated in a subprocess on the parallel branch to the primary activity. In this timer subprocess, the interval for which the timer needs to be set is calculated and a *catch timer event* is used to wait for the timer to fire. As noted earlier a complex merging gateway is used to merge the primary path and the timer path—the complex gateway is set up to complete only when the primary path has completed. This means that if the timer does not fire before the primary activity has completed, the timer subprocess is canceled. If the timer fires, the handling of the timer handler logic is in the subprocess following the *catch timer.* The timer subprocess is set up to loop infinitely (that is, while *true*) to make the timer recur.

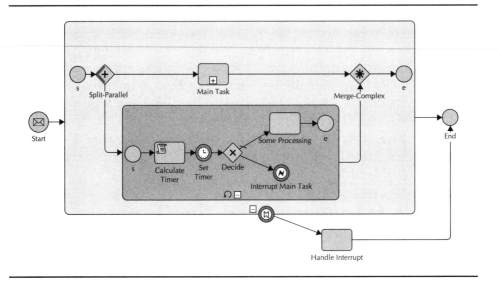

FIGURE 5-35. *Variable frequency recurring timers*

As can be seen in Figure 5-35, the primary activity and the timer subprocess are enclosed in another subprocess. This pattern is used to enable the timer logic to interrupt (that is, timeout) the primary activity. As shown in Figure 5-35, the timer subprocess fires an *error event* that can be caught by the enclosing subprocess, as an interrupting error handler, to achieve the equivalent of a timeout. While not shown in Figure 5-35, even non-interrupting timer handler logic can be modeled this way, instead of embedding it in the timer subprocess, and limiting the timer subprocess to just the setting and firing of the timer.

Dynamically Added Subcases

In this pattern of scenarios, while the subcases of a case (that is, the detail subprocesses of a master process) are being processed, new subcases can be added that need to be processed the same way as the other subcases. The process should not move to the next phase until all subcases have been processed. For example, while a service request (the case) is being processed, a customer can add new incidents and issues (subcases of the case). The service request cannot be closed until all incidents and issues that are part of it have been addressed. As discussed earlier in the "Workflow Patterns" section, this is the same as "Pattern 15: Multiple Instances Without *a priori* Runtime Knowledge."

This pattern is addressed, as shown in Figure 5-36, using a combination of multi-instance subprocesses, event subprocesses, and reusable subprocesses. First, the processing for the subcase is encapsulated in a reusable subprocess and is invoked from the main process using a call activity. As can be seen in Figure 5-36, this allows us to invoke the same processing from two places: the two activities called *Process Subcase.* A multi-instance subprocess is used to process all subcases already available at the time the process completes the *Pre Phase.* New subcases added while the process is executing other subcases—that is, executing the multi-instance subprocess—are handled with a non-interrupting message (or signal) handler event subprocess. As mentioned earlier, the same reusable subprocess is invoked from the event subprocess as in the parent multi-instance subprocess.

Since the event subprocess is within the scope of the enclosing subprocess, any events and exceptions can be handled at the enclosing subprocess consistently for all subcases, independent of the way they were started. The multi-instance subprocess scope is completed and the process moves to the *Post Phase,* only after all subcases, whether started as part of a multi-instance or as part of an event subprocess, have completed.

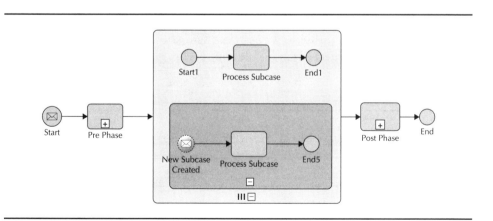

FIGURE 5-36.   *Handling dynamically added subcases*

Merge Independent Instances

In this pattern of scenarios, multiple independently executing process instances need to come together and merge in a single process instance. For example, a process for personnel actions, such as promotions, may start for an employee individually and continue that way until it is approved by an organizational VP. However, executive approval for personnel actions is sought in a batch, and a set of individual personnel actions are collected and approved together. In addition to scenarios where executive approval is sought, this pattern is also common where regulatory approval is needed or an external agency is involved—for example, patent submissions by a development organization may also be collected in batches and sent as a batch to the patent lawyers.

While it may be possible for the independent process instances to synchronize their behavior using sophisticated signaling and acknowledging logic, a much simpler solution to this pattern is available and recommended. The synchronization and merging logic can be achieved by using a database table or files—essentially, any data store where the independently executing process can register their availability to become part of a merged process and from where the merged process can pick up the list of independent instances.

The process pattern in the independent phase of the process is shown in Figure 5-37. In this process, after the independent phase is over, a record is written to a database table to indicate the availability of the instance to be merged—the instance ID of the process and any keys needed for the merged process to retrieve the individual case data will suffice (if the case data is only within the individual instance, the merged process can query the

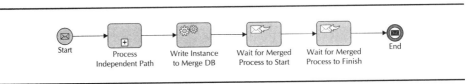

FIGURE 5-37. *The independent process (to be merged)*

individual process instances). Since process stakeholders, such as the manager seeking the personnel action, may have references only to the individual process instance, it is a good design to make sure that the process status is maintained within the individual process. This is accomplished in the example shown in Figure 5-37 by waiting for the merged process to send messages that indicate when it has started and finished.

The process pattern in the merged phase of the process is shown in Figure 5-38. Before starting the processing and after finishing the processing, it sends a notification to the individual independent process instances (if needed, intermediate status updates may be sent as well). To send notification to the individual instances, a multi-instance subprocess that iterates over the instances is used. The *send* message within the multi-instance subprocess can be correlated to the specific independent instance using the instance ID of the independent instance for correlation (as mentioned in the previous paragraph, the instance ID of the independent instance is part of the record written). If needed, the merged process can get the case data from the independent process—another receive-case-data/send-case-date message interaction can be added to the send-start-notification/receive-start-notification message conversation.

The preceding example does not show how the merged phase of the process is initiated. This may be based on any desired strategy, including polling the database for new records, checking on specific dates (for example, the first day of the quarter), or it may be manually initiated (for example, the HR manager pulls all available personnel actions on the day she gets an executive appointment). In addition to the simplicity of design, this decoupling of when to invoke the merged process is a benefit of the proposed solution to this pattern.

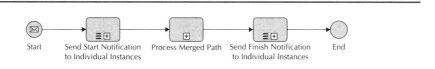

FIGURE 5-38. *The merged process (combining previously independent cases)*

Summary

This chapter, in conjunction with the discussion on business processes in Chapter 4, covered process modeling and implementation in significant detail. Common process patterns were also described. At the end of this chapter, the reader should have mastered the concepts of BPMN 2.0, particularly as applicable to Oracle BPM 11g. For further development of the knowledge acquired in these chapters, readers may refer to samples available online at Oracle's samples site.

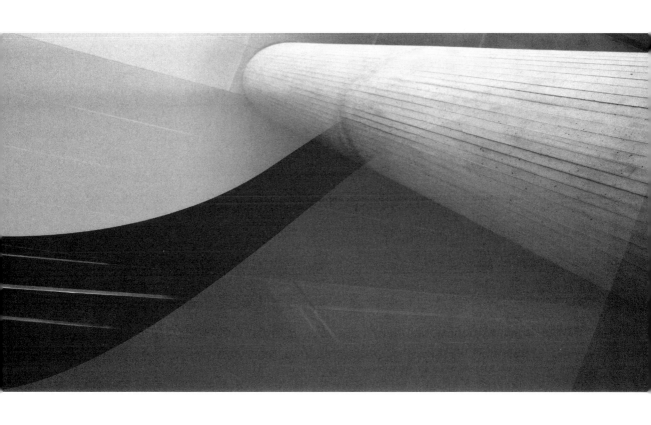

CHAPTER
6

Mastering
Business Rules

hanging markets, increasing competitive pressures, and evolving customer needs are placing greater pressure on businesses to adjust their policies and decisions at a faster pace. Further, there is an increasing desire among business users to get into the driver's seat for defining how the business is run. Moreover, regulatory constraints are increasingly demanding that businesses have transparency and consistency in their decision making and that they are able to certify compliance. Oracle Business Rules 11g is an important tool in the toolbox to address these requirements.

In this chapter, we will take a close look at Oracle Business Rules 11g. The intent of this chapter is to clarify concepts, even where they are typically abstracted by tooling. Therefore, the depth of the detail in some cases may be more than what readers need in order to get started with business rules. However, Chapter 4 should have already provided readers with enough information to get started with business rules.

This chapter assumes familiarity with Chapter 4 and employs the terms and concepts used there without reintroduction. Also, it does not repeat the business rules discussion covered there. Please read the business rules section in Chapter 4 before continuing.

Introduction to Business Rules

Before diving into Business Rules 11g, it is useful to take a step back and understand the rationale behind using business rules, how to identify valid use cases for business rules, and where all business rules can be used. This section provides this context.

Why Use Business Rules

Whether we call them business rules or not, most applications have business rules, which are traditionally implemented just like other aspects of the application in programming languages such as Java. When business rules are implemented in procedural logic, as in Java code, it becomes a difficult exercise to understand the business rules, characterized by the need to navigate complex control flows and invocation sequences. Also, the impact of changing a business rule is difficult to understand because the surrounding control flow may or may not lead to the desired results—for example, the control flow may not be rechecking for other rules that become applicable with this change. Most importantly, when rules are embedded in code, business users have no direct control or visibility into the business rules.

Business Rules technology has emerged as the solution for addressing these problems and the requirements outlined at the opening of this chapter because of the following characteristics:

- **Declarative Specification** Business rules are not buried in procedural logic; instead, they are declared as statements that closely mirror the business intent.

- **Inference and Modular Expression** Most modern rule engines support inference that makes sure all applicable rules are applied regardless of the order in which they are added, modified, or stored. This enables the decomposition of business rules into very granular and modular rules such as:

```
If a customer is a Premium Customer then discount = 40%
If a customer is a Gold Customer then discount = 30%
If a customer has been a customer for more than 3 years then
status = Gold Customer
If a customer is a Gold Customer and spends more than $1000
then status = Premium Customer
```

- **Ease of Change** Business rules are easy to change:

  - New rules can be added and existing ones deleted independent of other rules.

  - It is easy to identify where change needs to happen and what needs to be changed.

  - All rules are in one centralized place.

- **Business Visibility** The business rule expressions, both as if-then statements and as decision tables, mirror the business intent and are easy for business users to understand and, in many cases, manage and modify.

When to Use Business Rules

While business logic is pervasive within most applications, the following considerations may be used to identify the high-value use cases for business rules:

- **Volatility**   Rules that change often are good candidates for implementing with Business Rules technology. The ease of change provided by Business Rules technology will lead to significant cost savings over time.

- **Cost of Implementation Lags**   There may be some situations when the rules don't change that often, but when they do, the business cost of delay in implementation is too high. These high impact rules are good candidates for implementing with Business Rules technology.

- **Ownership**   When business users need to own, author, or edit rules, they are good candidates for implementing with Business Rules technology. Business users relate easily to the declarative and other metaphors supported by Business Rules technology.

- **Compliance**   Rules associated with regulatory compliance requirements are good candidates for implementing with Business Rules technology because they can be clearly seen and managed by those responsible for their governance.

- **Complexity**   Some problems naturally lend themselves to business rules because implementing them in traditional procedural logic would be too complex. Characteristics of such problems include a large number of rules and complex dependencies between them. Examples of this class of problems are product configuration and order decomposition.

- **Variance**   Scenarios where rules vary by business units, products, customers, brands, or other dimensions, Business Rules provide a good mechanism for capturing the variances. For time-based variances, Business Rules support effective dates as a first-class concept.

NOTE
When using business rules, developers should feel comfortable about not controlling the execution flow, but instead, allowing the business rules engine to optimize the execution. If the users feel compelled to control the execution flow, they should consider procedural alternatives such as scripting.

Where All Business Rules Can Be Used

Within a BPM/SOA application, business rules can be used in the following ways:

- **Within Process**   Business rules can be invoked from a BPMN or BPEL process to compute a result, which the process can use. The result may be a calculation, such as, what discount to apply, or a decision, such as whether to follow a manual path or automated path.

- **Within Human Task**   Human Tasks in Oracle BPM 11*g* can invoke business rules to dynamically determine a task participant (instead of statically assigning to a user, group, or role). Also, business rules can be used to override the routing specified in the task definition—for example, complete approval routing if a purchase order is for less than $200 and two approvals have already happened.

- **With Mediator**   Business rules can be used in conjunction with the mediator component to dynamically determine the endpoint to invoke.

- **Stand-alone**   Business rules can be exposed as a service for any service client or business process to invoke.

Figure 6-1 shows a BPM/SOA composite diagram highlighting the usage patterns just described.

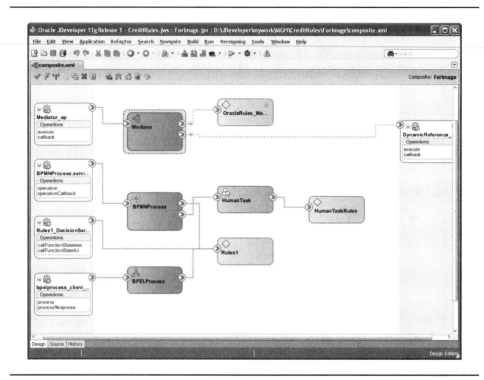

FIGURE 6-1. *Different usages of business rules (within BPM/SOA composite)*

Outside of BPM/SOA, business rules can be used in:

■ **ADF Applications** Oracle Business Rules 11*g* supports Oracle Application Development Framework Business Components (ADF-BC) fact types and can be used to reason on ADF-BC facts.

■ **Java Applications** Traditional Java applications can be rule-enabled by extracting the business rules into a rule dictionary and using the rules engine through Java APIs.

■ **ADF-UI and Other UI Applications** While ADF-UI and most UI technologies feature support for validations, they can benefit from using business rules to complement the built-in validation capabilities, especially where the validation logic is more business-oriented. Capturing business errors early in the entry stage cuts down processing costs.

Business Rules Scenarios

Some scenarios where Oracle Business Rules 11*g* is used are:

- **Approvals**   Who needs to approve what and under what circumstances is naturally expressed via business rules. Also, typically, business owners want to manage and change the approval rules, and the rule changes often.

- **Costing**   Discount and pricing calculations benefit from using business rules as the complexity of the logic becomes much more manageable when expressed in modular rule statements.

- **Order Decomposition**   A complex set of rules governs how an order line item decomposes into multiple service-order and product-order line items.

- **Contracts**   Business rules can be used for template selection and clause selection, ensuring that the correct templates are used and all applicable clauses are inserted, and also used for determining policy violations that can then be flagged to the approver's notice.

- **Dynamic (2-Layer) BPM**   Business rules can be used to dynamically determine the service endpoint or subprocess that should be invoked from a BPM process.

Recommended Flow and Practices

The following sequence of activities and associated practices may be useful to adopt as the best practice for business rules development:

- Clearly identify the decision that needs to be made and what data needs to be returned to indicate what the decision is and how/why it was made. Then, clearly identify what data is needed to make the decision. Data schema or types may already be defined and available to the project. Otherwise, it should be defined using BPM Business Objects, or XML Schema for XML facts, or as JavaBeans for

Java facts. While the data schema may be updated later, the more accurate the starting version is, the more productive the development experience will be.

■ Set up the *Facts*. If business rules are created using the BPM wizard, the facts are already created. Even then, it is beneficial to define aliases and visibility to provide a better user experience (please see the section "The Rule Data Model" later in this chapter). When rules become numerous or complex, a simple data model can greatly simplify the job of writing rules. If there is flexibility to create the data model, some sample rules should be written to iteratively develop the data model. If a complex data model has to be used, a simple wrapper data model using RL facts should be defined as discussed in the section "The Rule Data Model." Initialization rules or functions can be used to assert RL facts based on the original facts.

■ Define the strategy for generating results from business rules. (Please see the section "Strategies for Business Rules Results" later in the chapter.)

■ Set up a test function to test rules. Having this setup upfront will eliminate surprises from rules development. This is especially useful since business rules follow a different paradigm than traditional procedural programming. (Please see the section "Testing Business Rules" later in this chapter.)

■ Consider what actions will be used in business rules. If appropriate, set up some *Functions* to facilitate authoring. (Please see the section "Rule Functions" later in this chapter.) Also, if appropriate, import any supporting Java classes. (Please see the section "Java Facts" later in this chapter.)

■ Plan on how to organize rules into rulesets, as well as whether to use multiple dictionaries as discussed in the following section titled "Rule Organization."

■ Identify what literal values (that is, values such as 500) the business rules may use and consider whether they should be parameterized as *globals*.

■ Develop rules keeping in mind that good business rules are logical and declarative, rather than procedural. For example, to ensure that a decision is made for every product category, think about using a decision table with a rule for each product category, rather than, say, looping over every product category row in a database.

■ Update decision functions as additional rulesets are added.

■ Publish to BPM MDS for business analyst authoring as described in Chapter 4.

Rule Organization

The design elements of Oracle Business Rules 11*g* are shown in Figure 6-2.

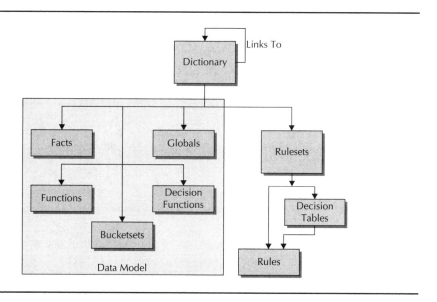

FIGURE 6-2.   *The Oracle Business Rules 11g design element hierarchy*

Rule Dictionary

At the top of the hierarchy is the *dictionary.* A dictionary is an XML file that contains all other design elements. Since each dictionary is an XML file, a dictionary is the unit of versioning. A dictionary contains *facts, functions, globals, decision functions, bucket sets,* and *rulesets.*

Ruleset

In Oracle Business Rules 11*g*, rules always belong to rulesets, which contain one or more rules, including a combination of if-then rules and decision tables. Rulesets are the unit of execution for business rules—that is, individual rules cannot be executed outside the context of a ruleset. Organizing logical groups of rules into rulesets is an important design consideration. Organizing into multiple rulesets addresses the following requirements:

- **Ordering** As explained later in the section "Understanding Business Rules," rulesets are the recommended mechanism for ordering rule firing. The desired sequence of rules can be specified in the decision function. For example, in some scenarios rules may be divided into eligibility rules, computation rules, and then override rules. These can then be ordered to ensure that first eligibility rules are fired, then computation rules, and finally override rules are fired.

- **Specialization** There may be scenarios where some rules may be specialized by customer, product, geography, or other criteria. For example, in processing credit card requests, there may be some rules specific to the credit card brand or issuing bank. Rulesets can be used to organize and include the rules appropriately.

In most cases, decision functions, as explained later in the section "Decision Function," can address the requirements of sequencing, as well as the inclusion/exclusion of rulesets. However, if there are advanced requirements, rule actions and functions can explicitly push/pop rulesets to/ from the ruleset stack using functions *Rl.ruleset stack.push* and *RL.ruleset stack.pop.* (The concept of the ruleset stack is explained later in the section "Understanding Business Rules." For now, it suffices to understand that pushing a ruleset on a stack causes rules contained within it to fire.)

Dictionary Links

A dictionary can include other dictionaries using dictionary links. Facts, functions, rulesets, and other elements of linked dictionaries become available to the including dictionary. If a ruleset of the same name is in both dictionaries, the effective ruleset combines rules from both—that is, rulesets can be striped across dictionaries. Two reasons why dictionary links should be considered while designing rule organization are the following:

- **Reuse** Facts and functions that apply across multiple scenarios can be contained in a separate dictionary that can be linked from multiple dictionaries. For example, the *ReadTestCase* function discussed in the section *Testing Rules in BPM Studio* is contained in a reusable dictionary *TestSupport* that is then linked to from the *CreditApproval* dictionary, as shown in Figure 6-3.

- **Ownership and Versioning** Since a dictionary maps to an XML file and is the unit of versioning, spreading an effective dictionary across multiple physical dictionaries can divide rules and other design elements by ownership as well as provide finer-grained versioning.

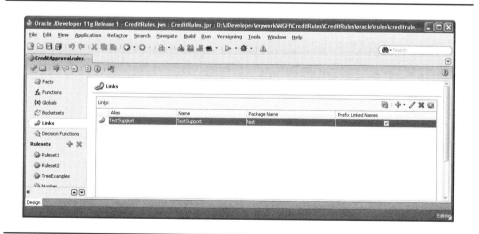

FIGURE 6-3. *Linking dictionaries*

The Rule Data Model

Facts are the objects that business rules reason on. Also, facts provide a mechanism for business rules to invoke Java methods as actions. Oracle Business Rules 11g features the following type of facts: XML facts, Java facts, RL facts, and ADF BC facts.

XML Facts

Oracle Business Rules can import element and type definitions in XSDs and BPM Business Objects as XML facts. To invoke business rules as a decision service from BPM/SOA and other Web Service clients, input and output facts must be of the type XML facts. When a business rule dictionary is created from the BPM business rules wizard, XML facts are automatically populated.

Internally, XML facts are Java facts. Oracle Business Rules uses JAXB 2.0 to create Java types from XSD.

NOTE
If using type definitions from XSD, XML Element must be used for facts that will be used as the input or output of a decision service.

NOTE
The generated classes are stored in ProjectPath/ .rulesdesigner/jaxb_classes, where ProjectPath is the path of the BPM/SOA project. If rules are run outside of BPM/SOA deployment, these classes need to be in the classpath.

Java Facts

Oracle Business Rules can import Java classes as Java facts. When using business rules with Java applications, Java facts provide a convenient mechanism to set up the data model. However, even in a BPM/SOA use case, where the primary data model is based on XML facts, Java facts provide a mechanism to leverage functionality available in Java packages for scenarios such as string processing, time and date handling, and so on.

Considerations in Working with XML Types

When working with XML types, it is important to understand how XML types map to Java types, which is documented by various references, including WikiPedia at http://en.wikipedia.org/wiki/Java_Architecture_for_XML_Binding. Of particular interest is the handling of number types—for example, *xsd:integer* and *xsd:decimal* map to *java.lang.BigInteger* and *java.lang.BigDecimal.* However, Oracle Business Rules 11*g* is preceded with the required Java facts to handle these types, and can also handle working across related types, as shown in Figure 6-4.

The *XMLGregorianCalendar* class is used for all date and time types. Oracle BPM 11*g* includes a helper class *XMLDate* to facilitate handling of the *XMLGregorianCalendar* type, as illustrated in the function shown later in this chapter in Figure 6-10 to calculate *DaysFromNow.*

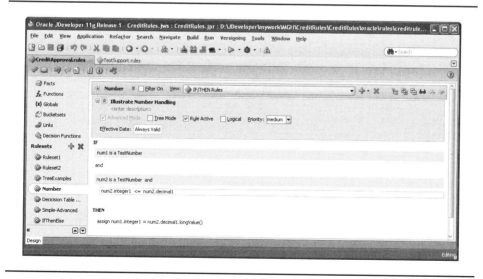

FIGURE 6-4. *Number types handling*

Oracle Business Rules is seeded with a base set of Java facts as documented in Appendix B in the "Users Guide for Oracle Business Rules," which is part of Oracle's product documentation. Additional classes may be imported, as shown in Figure 6-5.

NOTE
Import does not copy the classes or their byte code into the rules dictionary. They need to be available in the classpath when business rules are run.

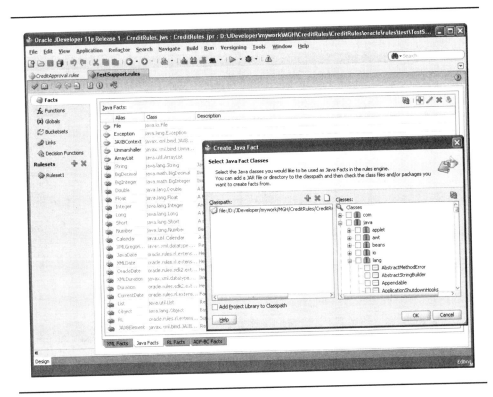

FIGURE 6-5. *Importing Java facts*

If Java facts are used for reasoning (that is, in conditions), it is recommended that they conform to the JavaBeans pattern, and expose getters and setters (if needed) for each property. Even if application data is not available as JavaBeans, it is recommended that the data to be shared with rules is flattened to a collection of JavaBeans that are then shared with the business rules engine.

RL Facts

Rules Language (RL) facts are native fact types for Oracle Business Rules. RL facts are defined completely within Oracle Business Rules and are like Java facts with the exception that they don't support methods. An RL fact contains a list of properties of types available in the data model.

RL facts are a useful mechanism to create intermediate facts, especially when leveraging the inference capability of business rules to accomplish advanced scenarios. Another common use of RL facts is to extend the available XML or Java facts by creating wrapper RL facts—for example, to add a calculated field or to associate different facts together (please see the section "Strategies for Business Rules Results" for an example of the latter). As discussed earlier in the recommended practices, RL facts can also be used to simplify the available data model.

ADF-BC Facts

Oracle Application Development Framework Business Components (ADF-BC) is a framework to facilitate application development as explained in chapter 8 of this book. Business Rules 11*g* supports leveraging the ADF-BC view definitions as facts. Internally, ADF-BC facts are RL facts and therefore do not support methods. In the current version, ADF-BC facts should be used only when business rules are invoked via Java API and not from BPM/SOA as a decision service.

TIP
*Working with facts in Oracle Business Rules
11g is documented in section 3 – "Working
with Facts and Bucketsets" in the "Users Guide
for Oracle Business Rules," which is part of
Oracle's product documentation.*

Refining Imported Facts

Imported facts are usually not optimal as-is for business rules authoring because:

- The fact names and property names may be technically oriented and not intuitive to the business rules analyst.

- The fact may have many more properties and methods than needed by business rules. This may overwhelm the business rules analyst.

Imported facts may be edited in BPM Studio's rule editor to address these issues. Within the rules editor, selecting *Facts* in the left-hand panel brings up the *Facts* tab as shown in Figure 6-6.

Clicking the pencil icon at the top-right corner of the *Facts* tab shown in Figure 6-6 launches the fact editor for the selected fact, as shown in Figure 6-7. *Alias* property should be used to specify business analyst understandable terms for the fact, as well as its properties. The *Visible* property should be used on fact properties to hide unnecessary properties. It should also be used for facts that are not meant to be used in rule conditions, either because they correspond to properties with visibility turned off or because they are helper classes.

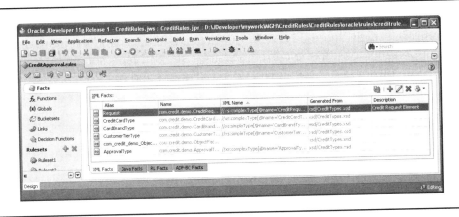

FIGURE 6-6. *The Facts tab in rules editor in BPM Studio*

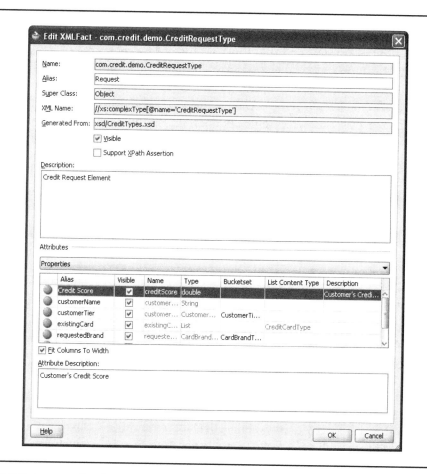

FIGURE 6-7.   *The fact editor for an XML fact*

NOTE
The Support XPath Assertion *property, seen in Figure 6-7, should not be used. It is supported only for backward compatibility. Oracle Business Rules 10g had a feature called* AssertXPath *that is no longer needed.*

Updating Imported Facts

If type definitions are updated in the XSD files or the business objects on which the business rules facts are based, the fact definitions can be refreshed to the new type definition. The icon on the extreme right (next to the red-x icon) at the top-right corner of the *Facts* tab, as shown in Figure 6-6, is the *Upload XML facts from Updated Schemas* icon. As the name indicates, this icon enables refreshing the XML facts to the latest type definition in the source. If the changes are additive or otherwise don't impact existing rules, no further change is needed. If the refresh changes facts and its properties in a manner in which rules or functions are impacted, the impacted rules and its sub elements are flagged with validation errors, which can then be manually fixed.

Rule Functions

Oracle Business Rules 11*g* features *Functions* that allow the sharing of common expressions, typically to abstract a set of expressions needed in an action, as well as to implement supporting functionality, such as reading test cases from files and testing rules leveraging imported Java packages and classes, without needing to add functionality in Java. Functions have parameters, and this makes them more usable than *globals* as a sharing mechanism.

Functions are essentially the same as the *actions* part of rules and can be authored the same way using select-click-select and the expression editor. Readers familiar with Oracle Business Rules 10*g* may be accustomed to writing functions in Rules Language (RL). While the authoring metaphor has changed in 11*g* to provide an easier-to-use and less error-prone experience, RL snippets may still be used in functions using the *RL* action.

Some scenarios where functions are useful are:

- **Providing Language-like Representation** Function names, as exposed in the rules editor, are essentially aliases that can accept business friendly strings with spaces, and so on. This makes the functions a powerful mechanism to wrap condition expressions and rule actions in a business-friendly representation. For example, the Boolean function "*Is Approved for More Than*" as shown in Figure 6-8, tests whether the input card's credit amount is more than the input amount.

This function can then be used in a business rule to provide a business-friendly representation, as shown in Figure 6-9.

- **Initialization**   Functions are useful for initialization, such as setting up globals for holding results or creating wrapper facts. This is discussed in the section "Strategies for Business Rules Results" in this chapter.

- **Test**   Rule editor in BPM Studio allows testing business rules leveraging functions. This is discussed in depth in the section "Testing Business Rules" in this chapter.

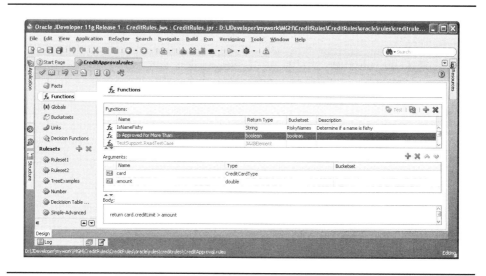

FIGURE 6-8.   *The Boolean function "is approved for more than"*

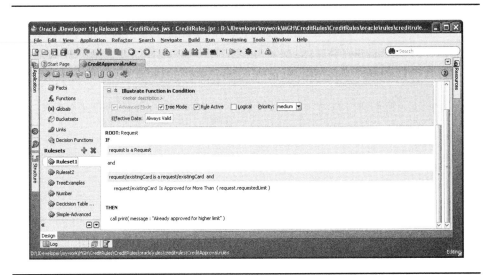

FIGURE 6-9. *The business rule using function "is approved for more than" in its condition*

- **Actions** Functions can facilitate the authoring of rule actions. Some scenarios where functions should be considered are:

  - The rule must invoke multiple actions. Instead of relying on the author to get the sequence of actions correct all the time, a function may be set up to encapsulate the details.

  - The actions must respect some considerations—for example, if a property is used to hold the concatenated impact of multiple rules, it is better to wrap the action in a function, ensuring that concatenation is handled correctly.

  - Use of a function simplifies the authoring experience significantly— for example, if a rule needs to set a property to *n days from now*, it is best to wrap this in a function, as shown in Figure 6-10.

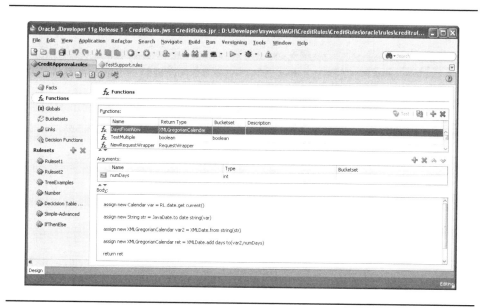

FIGURE 6-10. *The* DaysFromNow *function to simplify rule authoring*

■ **Conditions**   Functions may also be used in rule conditions where available methods are not sufficient to express the condition. An interesting scenario of such usage is in handling bucketsets in decision tables. Bucketsets can be set up to be either a list of values or a simple division of a range into buckets, as explained in Chapter 4. However, in some scenarios buckets must be defined based on regular expression matching or other complex criteria. A function may be set up to encapsulate the criteria and return a value within a list-of-values. In the example shown in Figure 6-11, the function *IsNameFishy* uses regular expression matching to bucket *name* into a list-of-values.

This function can then be used in rule conditions, including in decision tables, as shown in Figure 6-12.

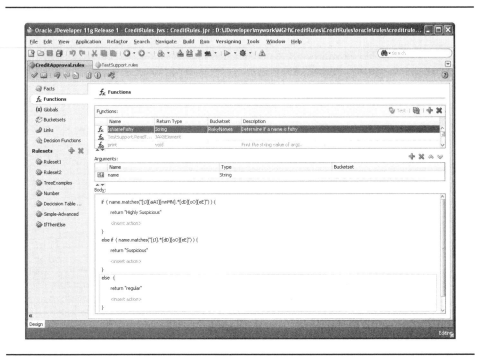

FIGURE 6-11. *The* IsNameFishy *function*

Considerations in Using Functions in Conditions

Methods or functions that have side effects, such as changing a value or state, should not be used in a rule condition. Due to the optimizations performed when the rule engine builds the Rete network (the Rete network and its pattern-matching algorithm are described in the section "Understanding Business Rules Engines" later in this chapter) and the associated Rete network operations that are performed as facts are asserted, modified (and reasserted), or retracted, the tests in a rule condition may be evaluated a greater or lesser number of times than would occur in a procedural program. Thus, if a method or function has side effects, those side effects may be performed an unexpected number of times. Also, in general, functions in conditions should be avoided and rule inference or wrapper facts should be used instead. For example, in the example shown in Figure 6-12, a wrapper fact with an additional property *nameSuspicious* could have been used. The function *IsNameFishy* then would have been guaranteed to be invoked only once per *name.*

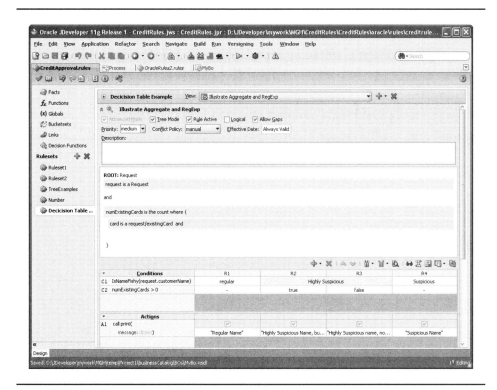

FIGURE 6-12. *A decision table example illustrating aggregates and regular expressions*

Strategies for Business Rules Results

In the example used in Chapter 4, *assertNew* action was used in the rule actions. If multiple rules were to fire, this would cause multiple results to be asserted, which was not the intent. In general, when the result is not part of the rules input, a proper strategy needs to be adopted to generate results, in order to avoid similar issues. Some recommendations follow.

Using Decision Tables

The main considerations in designing the rules strategy are that a result fact is always asserted and multiple rules do not inadvertently assert multiple results. Decision tables help ensure the former with its gap analysis and the latter with its conflict resolution capabilities. So decision tables should be considered wherever viable. The other strategies in this section would be needed if the scenario called for multiple rules to fire but not create multiple results.

Using Global for Holding Results

A global can be defined for holding the result. This global must be defined as non-final. Then an initialization rule needs to be defined, as shown in Figure 6-13.

The initialization rule should *assert* a new fact of the result type and assign it to the global result. The initialization rule must be set up to execute before all other rules, which may be done by either setting the priority of the rule to highest, as shown in Figure 6-13, or by having the rule by itself in a ruleset and then sequencing it as the first ruleset in the decision function.

This strategy has two limitations that must be considered. First, this assumes that only one result is applicable, which is valid if one input is evaluated at a time. However, if at a later date this rule was used in a batch scenario, passing multiple inputs in single invocation, and expecting multiple results, this strategy would become invalid. Second, because the

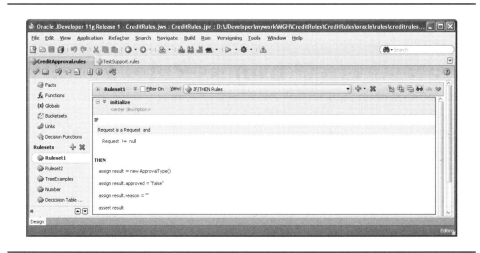

FIGURE 6-13. *A rule to initialize the result*

result fact is a non-final global it is not available to test in rule conditions. If neither of these two considerations is relevant, this strategy provides rule analysts with an easy-to-understand experience.

Using Wrapper Fact to Associate Input and Result

An RL wrapper fact may be defined with the input fact and result fact as its properties, as shown in Figure 6-14. In summary, this achieves the equivalent of a schema design where the input fact is itself designed to contain the result, without needing to modify the input type definition. Since a result is always available for an input, this serves the same purpose as the global result. Further, since it is linked with an input, there are as many result facts as input facts, and the correct one can be easily accessed.

Similar to the earlier strategy, an initialization rule needs to be defined to initialize the wrapper fact and assert it as well as its result property, as shown in Figure 6-15.

While this strategy is more rigorous than the previous strategy and addresses both of the issues with it, rule analysts need to access the input and the result facts by dereferencing the wrapper fact, as shown in Figure 6-16.

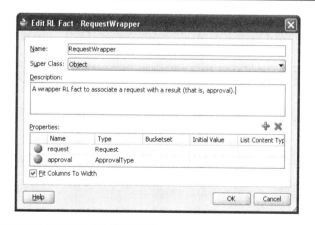

FIGURE 6-14. *A wrapper RL fact associating input and result*

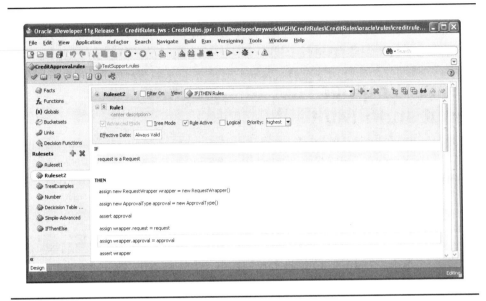

FIGURE 6-15. *A rule to initialize the wrapper fact*

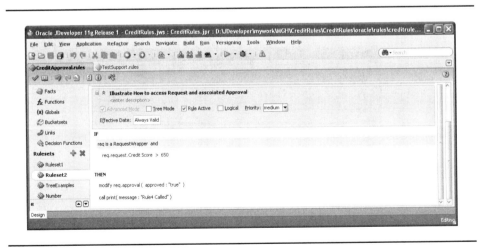

FIGURE 6-16. *An example rule when using wrapper RL fact strategy*

Testing Business Rules

Business Rules can be tested within BPM Studio leveraging functions, or rules deployed to BPM/SOA server can be tested using Fusion Middleware's (FMW's) test feature. The former is useful during development and the latter during runtime rule changes. Also, since business rules provide a rich Java API, custom test suites can be easily developed in Java using tools such as JUnit.

Testing Rules in BPM Studio

A test function can be defined in BPM Studio. Such a function must not take any inputs and must return a Boolean result. A *true* result is interpreted as test passed, and a *false* as test failed. Within this function, inputs should be defined and then a decision function invoked. The returned list contains the results, which may be printed using the *print* function. Figure 6-17 shows an example test function.

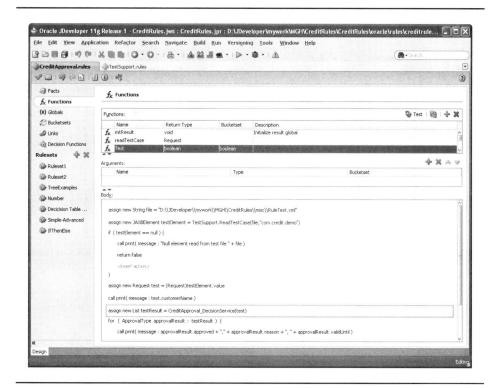

FIGURE 6-17. *An example test function*

In the example shown in Figure 6-17, an input is read from an XML file using the *TestSupport.ReadTestCase* function, *CreditApproval_DecisionService* is called, the result is retrieved from the returned list, and the result is printed. Running the test function by clicking the *Test* icon on the top-right corner of the *Functions* tab produces the output shown in Figure 6-18.

NOTE
If the Test *icon is not enabled, it may be due to an incorrect function signature or validation errors in the dictionary. Validate the dictionary by clicking the green-checkmark icon and fix all reported issues to enable the* Test *icon.*

TIP
Diagnostic tracing can be enabled by calling one of the functions within RL.watch. RL.watch.rules *and* RL.watch.facts *are the most interesting.*

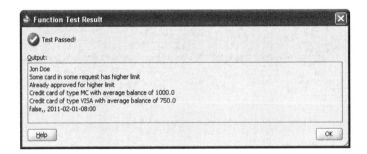

FIGURE 6-18. *Test function output*

The *TestSupport.ReadTestCase* Function

While in some situations an input can be created and assigned in the test function, when the fact is of a type of moderate complexity, it is usually preferable to read the test case from an XML file. The *ReadTestCase* function shown in Figure 6-19 reads an XML file and unmarshals it to a *JAXBElement* that the caller can then cast to the correct fact type, as seen earlier in Figure 6-18.

Since this function is a reusable function, it has been defined in a separate dictionary called *TestSupport,* which is then linked to the user dictionary, as shown in Figure 6-3.

TIP
Readers can download this dictionary from this book's web site and use it in their test functions. A sample XML test case corresponding to the example in this book can also be found at the same location.

This example also illustrates how additional Java types can be easily imported and leveraged in Oracle Business Rules 11*g*. In this case, *javax.xml.bind.JAXBContext, javax.xml.bind.Unmarshaller,* and *java.io.File* are imported into the *TestSupport* dictionary as shown in Figure 6-5.

Testing Using Fusion Middleware Control

Oracle FMW Control for Oracle BPM Suite 11*g* enables the testing of any services exposed from the BPM/SOA application. To leverage this capability to test deployed business rules within the SOA Composite editor of BPM Studio, the decision function that needs to be tested should be dragged and dropped to the left-hand vertical band, where all exposed interfaces reside, as shown in Figure 6-20.

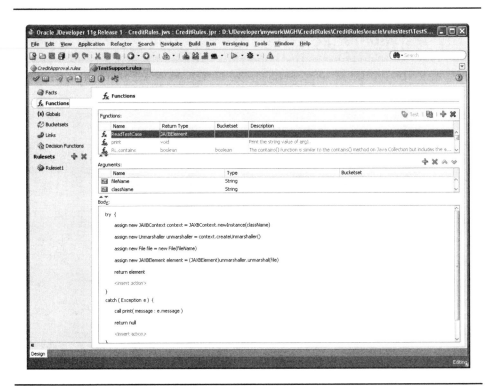

FIGURE 6-19. *The* ReadTestCase *function*

Within FMW Control, in the home page for the BPM/SOA composite (that is, the application), the decision function can be located and tested, as shown in Figure 6-21.

As can be seen in Figure 6-21, the following parameters need to be specified:

■ *name* The name of the decision function. (The "@" in front of the label *name* indicates that it is an attribute of its parent instead of being an XML element.)

■ *bpelInstance* The *bpelInstance* parameter is not relevant when invoking a decision service outside of BPEL. However, since it is defined as a mandatory parameter, any dummy values can be specified to bypass the schema validation, as seen in Figure 6-21.

■ *parameterList* The list of parameters for the decision function.

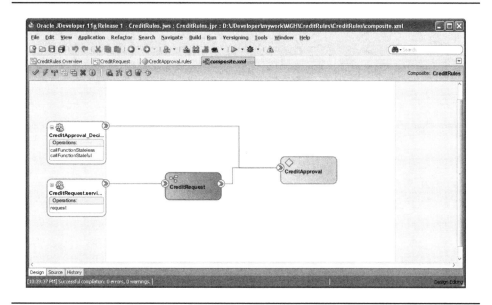

FIGURE 6-20. *Exposing a decision function as a service*

TIP
The XML view of the parameters passed in Figure 6-21 can be downloaded from the web site for this book.

The result returned is reported back, including a link to the audit trail for the rule execution. The audit trail provides tracing information, such as the result for watch functions discussed in the earlier section, as shown in Figure 6-22.

Audit Trails
Like most other components of Oracle BPM Suite 11*g*, Oracle Business Rules provides a graphical audit trail, as shown in Figure 6-22, to aid diagnostics. The audit trail for completed and in-flight instances can be accessed from the page for the BPM/SOA composite in FMW Control. As discussed in the preceding section, when a decision function is tested from FMW Control, the results page also includes a link to the audit trail.

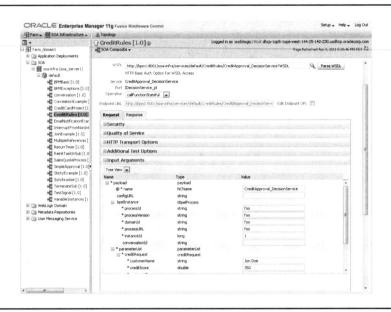

FIGURE 6-21. *Testing business rules from FMW Control*

FIGURE 6-22. *The rules audit trail*

For understanding the terms used in the audit trail, including *rule set stack, activated, asserted,* please see the section "Understanding Business Rules Engines."

Diagnostic Logging

Diagnostic logging for business rules can be configured within FMW Control by navigating to the *soa-infra* child node of the *SOA* node and right-clicking to select *Logs*, and then *Log Configuration.* Within the Log Configuration window, notification levels can be specified for various loggers. The two relevant ones are *oracle.soa.service.rules* and its child *oracle.soa.services.rules.obrtrace.* The notification level of *Trace:32* produces the most information and is a good choice for diagnostics. The diagnostic messages for business rules are logged in *$DOMAIN_HOME/ servers/soa_server1/logs/soa_server1-diagnostic.log,* where *$DOMAIN_ HOME* is the folder location for the BPM/SOA domain, and *soa_server1* is the name of the BPM/SOA managed server.

TIP
The output of print statements in business rules is also sent to the diagnostic log file when the notification level for oracle.soa.services .rules.obrtrace *is set* to Trace:1 *or higher.*

Understanding Business Rules Engines

We have covered the preliminaries of using business rules such as setting up the data model, defining a strategy for generating results, setting up test functions, and so on. Before we dive into defining business rules, it may be useful to have some understanding of the underlying technology, which is the focus of this section. Readers not wanting to get into this depth of detail may choose to skip this section, or revisit it at a later time.

Revisiting Facts

So far we have been using the term *fact* to describe what we should have more accurately termed as a fact type. In this section, the term *fact* is accurately used to refer to an instance of the fact type (that is, the Object for the Class in Java terminology).

The Rete Algorithm

The Rete algorithm was first designed by Dr. Charles Forgy of Carnegie Mellon University in the late 1970s and is at the core of rule engines from major rule vendors. The Rete algorithm is documented by various references, including WikiPedia at http://en.wikipedia.org/wiki/Rete_algorithm.

The Rete algorithm combines rule conditions for all rules into a single network of nodes. There is an input node for each fact definition, and an output node for each rule. In between the input and output nodes are test nodes and join nodes. A test occurs when a rule condition has a Boolean expression. A join occurs when a rule condition ANDs two facts. Fact references flow from input to output nodes. A rule is activated when its output node contains fact references. Fact references are cached throughout the network to speed up recomputing activated rules. When a fact is added, removed, or changed, a fact change reference is pushed through the Rete network that updates the caches and the rule activations with only an incremental amount of work.

NOTE
Because fact references flow from input to output nodes, it implies that only the fact references flowing into the output node are available for rule actions.

A Rete network is shown in Figure 6-23. The nodes with 1-input/1-output in the Rete network are the test nodes, which act as constrictive nodes allowing only matching fact tuples to pass. The nodes with 2-input/1-output are the join nodes, which create new fact tuples that are the cross-product of the incoming fact tuples. Asserted facts are passed to the source nodes. If the tuple makes its

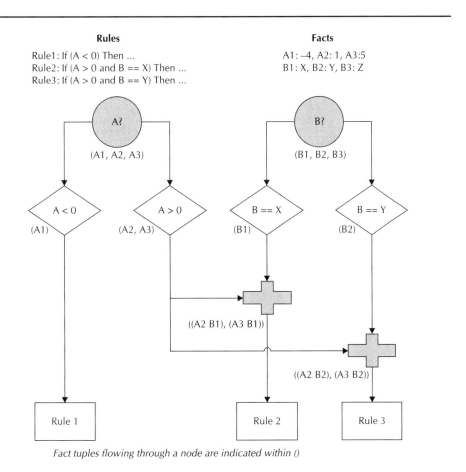

Rules

Rule1: If (A < 0) Then ...
Rule2: If (A > 0 and B == X) Then ...
Rule3: If (A > 0 and B == Y) Then ...

Facts

A1: –4, A2: 1, A3:5
B1: X, B2: Y, B3: Z

Fact tuples flowing through a node are indicated within ()

FIGURE 6-23. *A Rete network*

way through the network to the terminal node, the corresponding rule is matched and is activated with the inflowing fact tuple.

TIP
Interested readers can use the function RL.view rete network *to view the Rete network for their rules.*

NOTE
The process in which a Rete engine automatically evaluates all dependent tests and conditions when a fact is updated is commonly called "inference."

The Rete algorithm provides the following benefits:

- **Independence from control flow** Rules can be added and removed without impacting other rules. This separation of rules from control flow not only provides an easier authoring experience but also a lower cost of maintenance.

- **Modular rules** Rules can be expressed in a modular fashion with the rule engine automatically and implicitly assembling all applicable rules.

- **Optimization across multiple rules** Rules with common conditions share nodes in the Rete network.

- **High-performance inference cycles** Each rule firing typically changes just a few facts, and the cost of updating the Rete network is proportional to the number of changed facts, not the total number of facts or rules.

The Oracle Business Rules Engine

The Oracle Business Rules engine is an implementation of the Rete algorithm described in preceding section. All execution in the engine happens in the context of a rule session. A rule session is comprised of the following:

- **Facts** Instances of the fact types asserted into the working memory of the rule session.

- **Agenda** Explained more fully in the section "The Rules Algorithm" later in this section. Essentially, a set of rules whose conditions are satisfied.

■ **Ruleset Stack** A stack of rulesets. Rulesets can be pushed to and popped from a ruleset stack using built-in RL functions within functions as well as rule actions.

Typical Rule Execution

Typically, business rules will be invoked as a decision function, as described in the section "Decision Function," and as shown later in the chapter in Figure 6-33. To help understand the discussion in this section, the Rules Language [described in the section "Rules Language"] code for the decision function shown in Figure 6-33 is listed next.

```
function MutlipleInputs(java.util.List Input1) returns
java.util.List
  {for (int i = 0; i < Input1.size(); ++i)
    {
      assertTree(Input1.get(i));
    }
    pushRuleset("DecicisionTableExample");
    pushRuleset("TreeExamples");
    pushRuleset("Ruleset2");
    run(null);
    java.util.List _ret$oracle  = new java.util.ArrayList();
_ret$oracle.add(getFactsByType("com.credit.demo.ApprovalType"));
    return _ret$oracle;
  }
```

The preceding code listing illustrates that a decision function essentially does the following:

1. Asserts facts—in this case, using *assertTree.*

2. Pushes rulesets selected in the decision function in reverse order (so that the order in the stack is the same as that in the decision function).

3. Executes *run.*

Rules Algorithm

The execution of the rules engine is described by the following algorithm:

1. As facts are asserted, they are matched against the rule condition of all rules using the Rete algorithm described earlier. Matching happens whenever the state of working memory changes—that is, facts are asserted, modified, or retracted.

2. If a rule's conditions are satisfied, a new activation is added to the agenda. The activation includes the facts matching the rule condition, along with a reference to the rule. *Activations* may also be removed from the *agenda* if the condition is no longer satisfied—for example, if a fact is modified or retracted.

NOTE
Since a Rete algorithm fact references flow from facts to rules, only of whose fact inputs are updated are activated.

3. When a *run* command is executed, rules are *fired* by popping *activations* from the *agenda* and executing the rule actions. As part of rule actions, facts may be asserted, modified, or retracted causing new activations to be added to the agenda or removed from it.

CAUTION
If a rule action asserts or modifies a fact in its rule condition such that the condition is again true, then a new activation *is added to the* agenda *causing the rule to* fire *again, leading to an infinite loop.*

The Ordering of Rule Firing

As mentioned earlier, a rule session has a ruleset stack. The rules engine selects all the activations for the focus ruleset—that is, the ruleset on the top of the ruleset stack. When all activations for the focus ruleset are fired, the rules engine pops the ruleset from the stack and repeats with the new focus ruleset.

Within the set of activations associated with the focus ruleset, rule priority specifies the firing order, with the higher priority rule activations selected to be fired ahead of lower priority rule activations (the default priority level is 0).

Watching the Execution of Rules Engine

Oracle Business Rules provides the capability to watch the workings of the rule engine; watch can be turned on by calling one or more of the functions within the *RL.watch* node. A sample output from executing the decision function (shown in Figure 6-33) with *RL.watch.all* enabled is shown next:

```
==> f-1 com.credit.demo.CreditCardType(averageBalance : 750.0,
brand : VISA, creditLimit : 1000.0, currentBalance : 600.0,
daysOverdue : -1)
==> Activation: Ruleset2.Rule3 :  f-1
==> f-2 com.credit.demo.CreditCardType(averageBalance : 1000.0,
brand : MC, creditLimit : 6000.0, currentBalance : 800.0,
daysOverdue : 20)
==> Activation: Ruleset2.Rule3 :  f-2
...
==> Focus DecicisionTableExample, Ruleset stack:
{"DecicisionTableExample"}
==> Focus TreeExamples, Ruleset stack: {"TreeExamples",
"DecicisionTableExample"}
==> Focus Ruleset2, Ruleset stack: {"Ruleset2", "TreeExamples",
"DecicisionTableExample"}
Fire 1 Ruleset2.Rule1 f-7
...
Fire 2 Ruleset2.Rule1 f-3
...
<== Focus Ruleset2, Ruleset stack: {"TreeExamples",
"DecicisionTableExample"}
```

In the preceding listing:

- Lines starting with "==> f-<n>" report facts as they get asserted or updated.

- Lines starting with "==> Activation" report activations along with the rule activated and the matching fact(s)—for example, *"==> Activation: Ruleset2.Rule3 : f-1"* means that *Rule3* of *Ruleset2* is activated for fact *f-1*.

- Lines starting with "==> Focus" report the rulesets in the ruleset stack—for example, "==> *Focus Ruleset2, Ruleset stack: {"Ruleset2", "TreeExamples", "DecisionTableExample"}*" means that *Ruleset2* is at the top of the ruleset stack and below it are *TreeExamples* and *DecisionTableExample.*

- Lines starting with fire report rule firings—for example, "Fire 1 Ruleset2.Rule1 f-7" means that *Rule1* of *Ruleset2* fired for fact *f-7.*

NOTE
A friendlier and less verbose version of the preceding report is available as an Audit Trail for business rules within FMW Control, as described earlier and shown in Figure 6-22.

In addition to the watch functions, the *RL.show.facts* and *RL.show.activations* functions are available to report the facts and activations on the agenda as needed.

Business Rules

Chapter 4 and the preceding discussion in this chapter have provided enough information for most readers to start using business rules with confidence. In this section, we will take a closer look at business rules, and build a strong understanding of them.

Simple and Advanced Mode

Oracle Business Rules 11*g* by default provides a simple interface, known as simple mode, as shown in Figure 6-24.

There is also an advanced mode interface that can be enabled on a rule-by-rule basis by enabling the *Advanced Mode* checkbox, as shown in Figure 6-25.

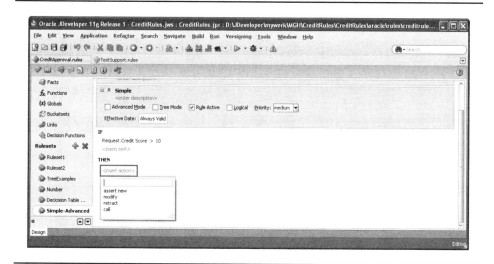

FIGURE 6-24. *The simple-mode rule*

The difference between the two modes is that:

■ ***Is-a* test is implicit in simple mode**   As can be seen in Figure 6-24 and Figure 6-25, the equivalent advanced-mode condition for a simple-mode condition, wraps the simple-mode condition in a test of the type: "variable is a fact type". Also, in the advanced mode, the variable can be named as needed, whereas in simple mode the name is fixed to the fact type name.

■ **More actions in advanced mode**   As can be seen in Figure 6-24 and Figure 6-25, simple mode presents only a small set of actions, whereas advanced mode provides access to all actions.

■ **More patterns in advanced mode**   Advanced mode features additional rule patterns—there is a case, there is no case, and aggregate. These patterns are discussed in the following section "Rule Patterns."

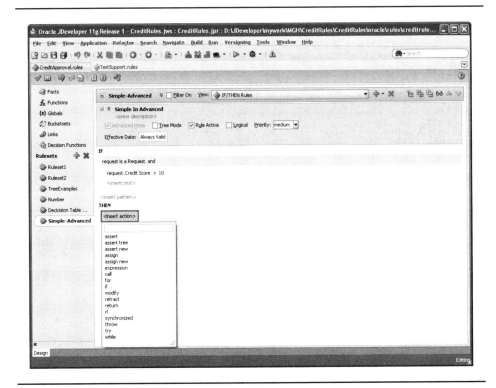

FIGURE 6-25. *The advanced-mode rule*

Since for the same rule, advanced mode just makes the *is-a* test implicit while providing the ability to rename the variable and gives access to more actions, once readers understand this section they may prefer to use advanced mode. Therefore, in this section all examples are shown in advanced mode, although many of them are possible in simple mode as well.

Rule Patterns

Every rule in Oracle Business Rules 11g is based on one of the following patterns:

- **For each** The rule is evaluated for every fact in the rule session that tests positively for the enclosed condition.

■ **There is a case *and* There is no case**   The rule is evaluated if among all the facts in the rule session any or none, respectively, satisfies the enclosed condition.

■ **Aggregate**   An aggregate value is computed for all facts in the rule session that satisfies the enclosed condition. Aggregates are discussed later in this chapter.

For each is the default implied pattern. Other patterns may be used in advanced mode by surrounding the *variable is a fact type* block with an explicit pattern block and selecting the desired pattern, as shown in Figure 6-26.

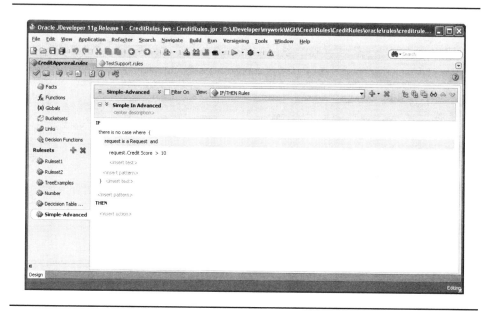

FIGURE 6-26.   *Rule using "there is no case pattern"*

Rule Scope

Earlier in this chapter, in the discussion on the Rete algorithm, it was mentioned that fact references flow from the input (that is, facts) to the output (that is, rules) node of the Rete network. What that implies is that within a rule, after an implicit or an explicit pattern block, within both subsequent tests as well as actions, only the facts matching the pattern block are referenced. From a rule authoring perspective, it implies that fact types that do not correspond to facts that can be potentially matched cannot be used (and are not available) in tests and actions, as shown in Figure 6-27.

The *for each* pattern is the only pattern that flows its matching fact references further. Therefore, only *variables* defined within a *for each* pattern may be used in subsequent tests and actions. *Variables* defined with (and not within) an *aggregate* pattern can be used outside the pattern in the *where* clause following the pattern and in actions. Please see the section "Aggregate" later in this chapter for details.

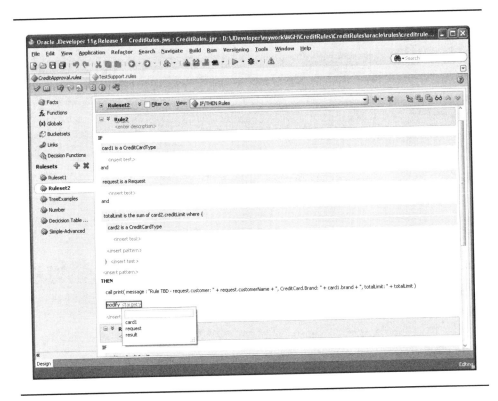

FIGURE 6-27. *Fact types available in actions*

Patterns can be *and-ed*, which does a cross-product or join of the facts matching the patterns, or they can be *or-ed*, which does a union of the facts matching the patterns. Facts corresponding to *and*-ed patterns flow through, but those corresponding to *or-ed* patterns do not.

In addition to facts that are available in tests and actions as discussed earlier, final *globals are available in rule conditions and* non-final *globals* are available in actions. As discussed earlier in the discussion on *strategies for rules results,* defining a global for result therefore enables it to be available in action without adding a pattern matching block for it.

TIP
Final globals are an excellent mechanism to parameterize rule conditions and to enable rule change through a simple change in the global's value. In many cases, changing a global's value is sufficient to enable business user changes. Edits to the global's value can be constrained by associating it with a bucketset.

These concepts are shown in Figure 6-27, where it can be seen that *card1, request,* and *result* are available in the *modify* action—*card1* and *request* because they correspond to the *for each* patterns and *result* because it is a global. *Card2* is not available because it corresponds to an aggregate pattern. However, the aggregate variable *totalLimit* is available, as can be seen in the *print* action (since it is not a fact, *modify* action does not apply to it).

Rule Priority

As explained in the section "The Ordering of Rule Firing" earlier in this chapter, priority can be used to sequence rule firing within a ruleset. The priority for rules and decision tables is highest to lowest, with the higher priority rule or Decision table executing first.

NOTE
Use of priority should be limited because it starts introducing a procedural aspect into business rules. If there is inherent ordering, rules should be organized in rulesets, which can be sequenced in decision functions. If priority is used as a conflict resolution mechanism, decision tables should be considered instead, as they provide conflict analysis and resolution.

Effective Dates

Effective dates can be specified at both the ruleset and rule level. An effective date can be of the from-date, to-date, or from-date-to-date form, as shown in Figure 6-28.

The rule engine maintains an effective date that is used to compare against the effective date specified in the rule or ruleset. By default, the value of the engine's effective date is set to the current system date-time at

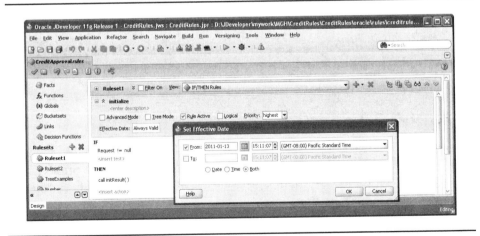

FIGURE 6-28. *Effective dates*

the time when the *run* function (or one of its variants) is invoked (typically, implicitly by decision function, as explained in the section "Understanding Business Rules Engines" earlier in this chapter). The engine's effective date can be manipulated using functions *RL.date.get effective* and *RL.set effective*.

In addition to effective date, the engine also maintains a current date, which is also available as a built-in fact: *CurrentDate.* Since current date is available as a fact, it can be used to explicitly test against current date in rule conditions. Its default value is set the same way as the effective date, and can be manipulated using functions *RL.date.get current* and *RL.set current.*

Tree Mode—Parent–Child References

When a fact type is a hierarchical structure, Oracle Business Rules 11*g* can assert not only the parent fact but the children facts as well. For example, in the scenario being used in this chapter, both *Request* and *CreditCardType* are available as facts. As many examples in this chapter illustrate, this facilitates the authoring of rules on *CreditCardType.*

TIP
The Tree *flag on the* Inputs *section in the* Decision Function *editor causes the entire hierarchy of an input fact to be asserted. This flag is on by default. The rule action* Assert Tree *can also be used to achieve the same.*

As the rule *Incorrect Child Reference* shown in Figure 6-29 highlights, some extra steps must be taken to ensure correct parent–child referencing. In this rule, instead of testing only *credit cards* belonging to a *request,* all combinations of *credit card* and *request* are tested (that is, a request is potentially paired with a card for a different request). To achieve the correct pairing of *request* with *credit cards,* the *Tree Mode* feature can be used. In tree mode, a fact type needs to be declared as root, then *root-fact/child-fact* becomes available as a fact type and should be used to limit the matching of child facts only to those belonging to the root fact. This is shown in the rule *Correct Child Reference* in Figure 6-29, where *request* is declared as the root and *request/creditCardType* is used in the pattern.

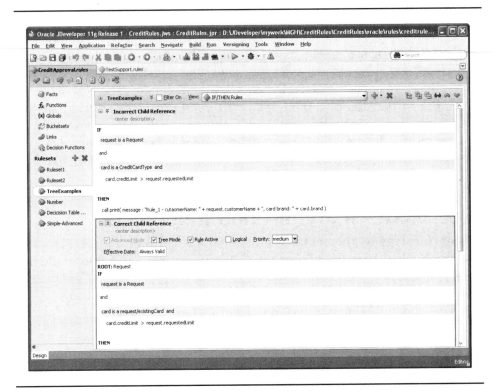

FIGURE 6-29. *Incorrect and correct child references*

Tree mode is simply a UI simplification that adds a test of type
"*parent.childAttribute RL.contains(child)*" within the pattern for the child, as
shown in Figure 6-30, where the *Tree Mode* flag is turned off for the rule
Correct Child Reference shown earlier in Figure 6-29. This type of test can
be manually added to a rule, if the tree mode does not address the rule
requirements—for example, if more than one parent–child references need
to be used.

Aggregate

As described earlier, an aggregate pattern allows an aggregate value to be
calculated for all facts in the session matching the enclosed condition.
A typical aggregate pattern is shown in Figure 6-31.

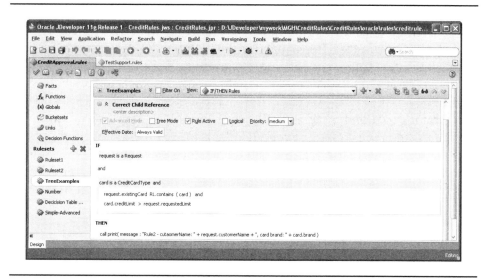

FIGURE 6-30. Tree Mode *under-the-covers*

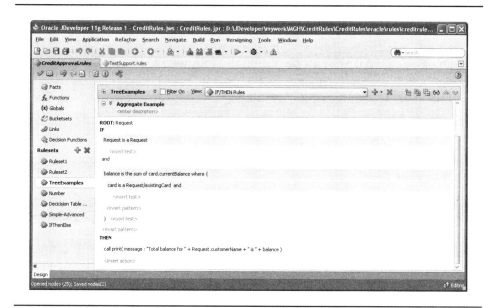

FIGURE 6-31. *An aggregate pattern*

In this example, *balance* is the result of aggregating the expression *card.currentBalance* using the aggregation function *sum,* over all *cards* belonging to *request* (as Tree Mode is used). Within the expression whose aggregate is calculated, variables and facts are available exactly as described earlier in the discussion on patterns (that is, facts in the enclosed for-each patterns, in the preceding for-each patterns, and final globals). The standard aggregation functions available are count, average, maximum, minimum, and collection. Collection collects the expression in a collection element (that is, List); the variable can be assigned to properties or passed to functions expecting the collection type or iterated over in the action using the *for* rule action. The other aggregation functions are obvious from their names.

TIP
User-defined aggregate functions can be used by providing a public Class implementation of oracle.rules.rl.IncrementalAggregate interface. This is documented in Chapter 2 of the "Oracle Fusion Middleware Language Reference Guide for Oracle Business Rules 11g", which is part of Oracle's product documentation.

The aggregate pattern can be optionally followed by a test to filter using the aggregated value—for example, the example shown in Figure 6-31 could have been tested for *balance* above or below a certain amount. The aggregated variable is also available in the following patterns, if any, within test conditions.

If-Then-Else

Users accustomed to procedural programming usually look for the if-then-else construct. The nature of the Rete algorithm, which is based on a network of conditions and rules as described earlier, precludes if-then-else in rule conditions. However, if-then-else as a construct is available in rule actions, as shown in Figure 6-32.

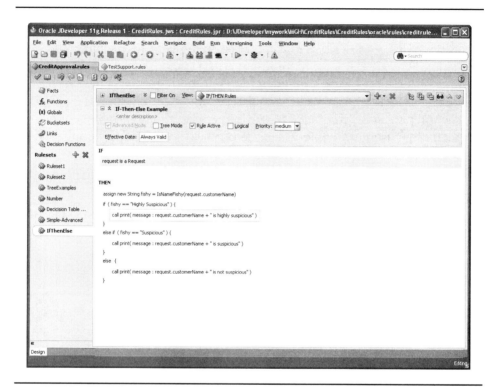

FIGURE 6-32. *An if-then-else example*

When a scenario must have if-then-else, then a common condition should be factored out and included in the rule condition, and the if-then-else logic can be used in the action part.

TIP
Scenarios needing if-then-else can usually be better expressed as decision tables.

Decision Tables

Decision tables, as described in Chapter 4, are an easy-to-visualize-and-conceptualize expression of multiple rules in a spreadsheet-like interface. Since decision tables were explained in detail in Chapter 4, only a few additional aspects will be covered in this section. Readers should first read the section "Business Rules for Quick Learners" in Chapter 4. Since the decision table used in Chapter 4 will be used to illustrate a few concepts in this section, it is reproduced here as Figure 6-33.

Advanced Mode

Advanced mode, including all its patterns, as well as Tree Mode, can be used in decision tables too, as shown in Figure 6-12.

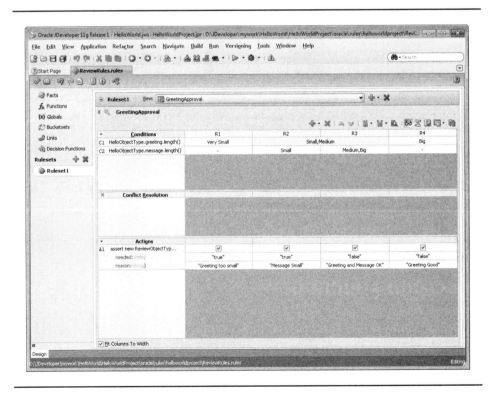

FIGURE 6-33. *A simple decision table*

Irregular Bucketsets

As shown in Figure 6-11, and described in section "Rule Functions" earlier in this chapter, functions can be used to achieve advanced bucketset scenarios, such as when string values need to be bucketed by regular expression matching.

Conflicts

One of the benefits of the decision table interface is that it identifies conflicts in business rules and enables the resolution of them. A conflict means that under certain circumstances more than one rule can fire. A decision table interface shows conflicts in the *Conflict Resolution* row (between conditions and actions) when *Show Conflict* is on. Identified conflicts can be overridden by clicking the conflict cell in the *conflict resolution* row and specifying one of the available resolution strategies, which are:

- **Override *and* Overridden by**   One rule overrides another—that is, if the condition for both rules is true, only the one overriding will fire. The mutual exclusion implied by override is transitive and symmetric—if A overrides C and B overrides C, then, though not apparent, A and B are also mutually exclusive.

- **Run Before *and* Run After**   One rule has a higher priority than another and runs before it.

- **Ignore *or* No Conflict**   Ignore the conflict.

For example, if a new rule *R5* is added to the decision table shown in Figure 6-33 to test for a situation where the *message* is big without caring about the size of the *greeting,* this rule will conflict with existing rules *R1* (because both include *greeting Very Small and message* Big) and *R3* (because both include *greeting Small or Medium and message* Big). These conflicts are detected and reported as shown in Figure 6-34.

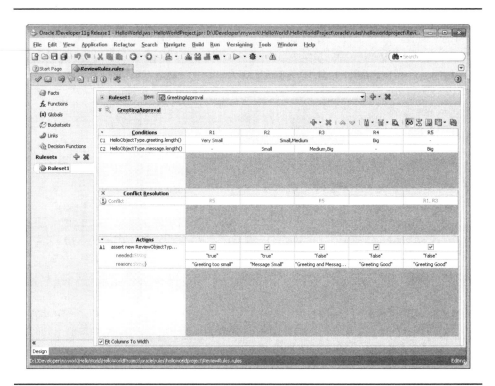

FIGURE 6-34. *Conflict detection for decision tables*

The conflict can be resolved by clicking any of the conflict cells to bring up the *Conflict Resolution* window. For example, clicking the conflict cell in column *R5* in the example shown in Figure 6-34 brings up the conflict resolution resolver shown in Figure 6-35, where an appropriate conflict resolution strategy may be selected. In this case, *R5* may be specified to override *R1* and *R3*.

Conflict resolution can also be specified at the decision table level as manual (default), auto override, or ignore.

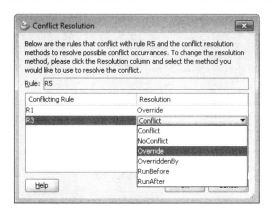

FIGURE 6-35. *Conflict resolution*

Loops

Just like if-then rules, decision table rules can have a loop situation when a fact matched in the condition pattern is asserted or modified (that is, the modify action is used; an assign action does not modify the fact) in the action.

Rearranging Decision Tables

Oracle Business Rules 11*g*, supports the following actions for rearranging decision tables:

- **Split**   Split condition cells into multiple sibling cells, one for each value in the bucketset.

- **Merge**   Merge conditions cells into a single cell with the new cell being a union of the values in the original cells.

- **Move**   Move condition rows up and down. Reordering conditions may lead to a cleaner and easier–to-read table. For example, the result of moving the order of conditions in the decision table shown in Figure 6-33 is shown in Figure 6-36.

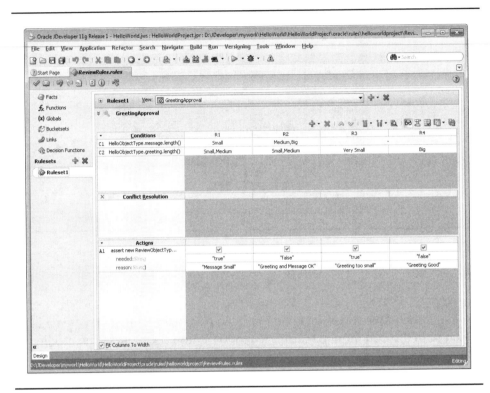

FIGURE 6-36. *The decision table shown in Figure 6-33 with the order of conditions changed*

Business Rules Interfaces

Business rules implemented with Oracle Business Rules 11*g* can be invoked from:

- Within the BPM/SOA application using on-the-wire invocations of decision functions.

- From any web services client using decision function exposed as a web service.

- From any Java program using the Decision Point API to invoke decision functions.

- From any Java program using Oracle Business Rules APIs, including JSR-94 APIs.

These options are described in this section.

Decision Functions

Decision functions are a mechanism to expose a set of rulesets to be invoked with a set of inputs and returning outputs (that is, as a service or function). They must be used if rules are to be invoked from other components within a BPM/SOA application or exposed as a Web Service; they are the preferred mechanism even when rules are invoked from Java clients.

A decision function, as shown in Figure 6-37, specifies the inputs and the outputs for the function and a sequence of rulesets and other decision functions to run in order.

NOTE
The under-the-cover RL code for the preceding decision function is listed and explained in the earlier section "Typical Rule Execution" in this chapter.

Some of the settings for a decision function are:

- **Will Be Invoked as a Web Service**   Needs to be on if the decision function will be invoked from other BPM/SOA components or as a web service. It can be off either when the decision function is meant to be invoked from a Java client or it is meant to be used within other decision functions.

- **Stateless**   Turning this flag off leads to stateful execution, where the same rule session is used for multiple invocations of the decision function from the same process instance.

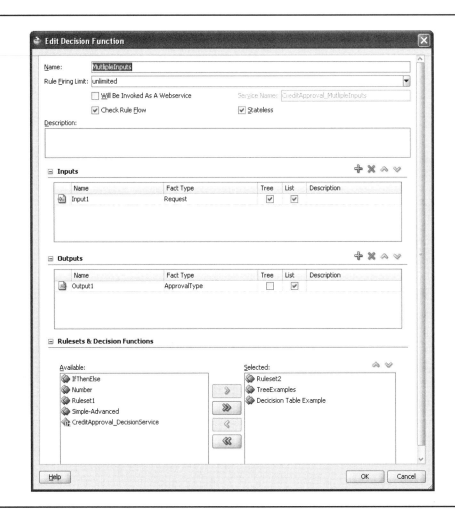

FIGURE 6-37. *A decision function*

- **Check Rule Flow** When this flag is on, design time validations are performed. In some cases, such as when *asserts* are buried in functions, false negatives may be reported and this flag may need to be turned off.

- **Input – Tree** As explained in the section "Tree Mode—Parent–Child References," this flag causes a fact to be asserted hierarchically, leading to a tree of facts. (Output – Tree is only a design-time aide when a decision function is followed by another.)

- **Input – List and Output – List**   Specifies that multiple facts for each input/output will be sent or received. These are collected in a *List*.

Business Rules Java APIs

Oracle Business Rules 11*g* supports JSR-94 interfaces as documented in "Appendix E—Working with Oracle Business Rules and JSR-94 Execution Sets" in the "Oracle Business Rules User Guide," which is part of Oracle's product documentation.

In addition to JSR-94, Oracle Business Rules 11*g* features *Decision Point API* that facilitates the straightforward invocation of business rules. The *decision point API* handles management of rule sessions, including session pooling, as well as the automatic reloading of changed dictionaries. Essentially, it exposes the management and optimization features leveraged by the decision service engine component to the users of the API. This API can work with dictionaries managed in Metadata Services (MDS), taking the fully qualified name as the input, or it can work with a preloaded dictionary, enabling clients to manage the storing and reading of dictionaries. The *decision point API* is documented in "Chapter 7—Working with Rules SDK Decision Point API" in the "Oracle Business Rules User Guide," which is part of Oracle's product documentation.

TIP
When invoking business rules from Java APIs, developers have the choice of whether to use MDS for storing and managing dictionaries or to use a custom implementation.

Oracle Business Rules 11*g* also includes a rich set of APIs that can be used to read and edit rule dictionaries and all their components. Essentially, the APIs used by the rule editors of Oracle BPM 11*g* are also available to customers and can be used to build custom authoring interfaces, reporting tools, or import-export utilities.

Javadocs for all APIs is included in the *Oracle Fusion Middleware Java API Reference for Oracle Business Rules*.

Business Rules Editors

Oracle Business Rules 11*g* includes multiple choices for rule editing:

- **BPM Studio *or* JDeveloper**   BPM Studio (as well as JDeveloper with SOA extensions) includes Rules Editor; all preceding screenshots are from this editor. This editor's functionality is comprehensive.

- **Process Composer**   Process Composer includes business rules authoring along with process and task authoring. In 11*g*, new dictionaries cannot be created in Process Composer; only existing dictionaries can be authored. Also in 11*g*, data model and functions cannot be edited within Process Composer. In addition to authoring rules within (pre-deployment) BPM projects that are shared via BPM MDS as described in Chapter 4, business rules deployed in production can also be edited as what is called runtime-changes. (Oracle literature may refer to this as Design Time at Run Time or DT@RT changes.) Process Composer is typically available using the URL http://bpmserver:8001/bpm/composer, where *bpmserver* is the host name where BPM/SOA server is running and *8001* is the port for the BPM/SOA managed server. Process Composer is shown in Figure 6-38.

- **SOA Composer**   The rule editor in SOA Composer is similar to that in Process Composer, but is limited only to runtime-changes. As shown in Figure 6-39, SOA Composer, being targeted at the runtime-changes use case, includes the functionality to list, commit, and discard (revert) changes.

- **Rule Editor Regions**   The components of rule editor within BPM/SOA Composer are available as ADF Regions and can be used in custom authors. For example, an interface may be provided to author globals for a rule dictionary within the client application.

FIGURE 6-38. *The rule editor in Process Composer*

■ **Custom Editors** As mentioned earlier, Rules SDK exposes all APIs used by the provided editors, and they can also be used to build custom editors.

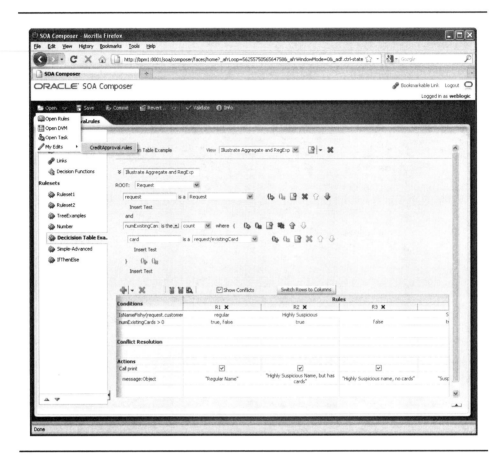

FIGURE 6-39. *Rule editor in SOA Composer*

Rule Language

Oracle Rule Language (RL) is the native language for Oracle Business Rules
11*g*. While the authoring interfaces hide the RL from most users, the Rule
Engine always executes RL, which is interpreted rather than compiled so that
rules may be changed without rebuilding, redeploying, or even restarting
applications. Rules authored in the authoring interfaces (or created with Rules
SDK) are generated into RL at runtime. RL can also be used in functions and

actions using the *RL* action, which allows for RL snippets to be entered or pasted. RL can be run directly using the RL command line interface:

```
java -classpath SOA_ORACLE_HOME/soa/modules/oracle.rules_11.1.1/
rl.jar;BeanPath oracle.rules.rl.session.CommandLine -p "RL> "
```

In the preceding command line, *SOA_ORACLE_HOME* is the folder where BPM and SOA modules are installed and *BeanPath* is the classpath for any needed Java classes.

RL is a full-featured programming language with Java-like syntax and type checking. It differs from Java in the following ways:

- RL includes additional keywords such as *ruleset, rule, fact, aggregate,* and others.

- RL does not support some Java features, including interfaces, forward referencing of methods, bit-wise operators.

- RL facts are not garbage-collected and must be explicitly retracted.

RL is documented in the "Oracle Fusion Middleware Language Reference Guide for Oracle Business Rules 11", which is part of Oracle's product documentation. Please refer to it for a more complete list of RL keywords as well as Java and RL differences. To illustrate RL syntax by using an example, the under-the-cover RL code for the examples shown in Figure 6-30 and Figure 6-31 are listed next:

```
ruleset TreeExamples {

rule IncorrectChildReference {
    if (fact com.credit.demo.CreditRequestType v0_CreditRequestType
&& fact com.credit.demo.CreditCardType v1_CreditCardType && (v1_
CreditCardType.creditLimit > v0_CreditRequestType.requestedLimit)) {
        main.println("Rule_1 - cutaomerName:"+v0_CreditRequestType
.customerName+", card brand: "+v1_CreditCardType.brand);
    } // end action
} // end rule IncorrectChildReference
```

```
rule CorrectChildReference {
    if (fact com.credit.demo.CreditRequestType v0_CreditRequestType
&& fact com.credit.demo.CreditCardType v1_CreditCardType &&
(main.contains(v0_CreditRequestType.existingCard,v1_CreditCardType)
&& v1_CreditCardType.creditLimit > v0_CreditRequestType
.requestedLimit)) {
        main.println("Rule2 - cutomerName: "+v0_CreditRequestType
.customerName+", card brand: "+v1_CreditCardType.brand);
    } // end action
} // end rule CorrectChildReference

rule AggregateExample {
    if (fact com.credit.demo.CreditRequestType v0_CreditRequestType
&& aggregate(fact com.credit.demo.CreditCardType v2_CreditCardType
&& (main.contains(v0_CreditRequestType.existingCard,v2_
CreditCardType))): sum(v2_CreditCardType.currentBalance) var v1_
sum) {
        main.println("Total balance for "+v0_CreditRequestType
.customerName+" is "+v1_sum);
    } // end action
} // end rule AggregateExample

}
```

TIP
Sample code to produce RL code listing for
Oracle Business Rules rule dictionaries can be
downloaded from the web site of this book.

Summary

This chapter, in conjunction with the discussion on business rules in Chapter 4, covered business rules in significant detail, including best practices, scenarios, techniques, and under-the-cover technology. Readers needing to find any missing detail can follow the pointers to the Oracle product documentation provided in this chapter. Readers should be equipped to effectively use business rules to address the requirements of agility and business visibility.

CHAPTER
7

Advanced
Human Tasks

n Chapter 4, we learned how human tasks can be used with BPMN processes. In this chapter, we dig deeper into human tasks, taking a more comprehensive look and exploring some of the more advanced and powerful functionalities. Careful readers may note some repetition of concepts discussed in Chapter 4 in this chapter—certain concepts such as task stakeholders and users and roles have been repeated a bit, because this chapter provides more information and related figures, as well as covers some of the advanced aspects not discussed earlier. We begin this chapter with task metadata that is applicable independent of the complexity of the scenario, then we move on to more advanced concepts, including declarative pattern-based assignment and routing within a human task, runtime re-assignment and re-routing, and an Oracle BPM 11*g* innovation activity guide.

Task Metadata

The human task definition includes task metadata regardless of whether the task is being used as a simple human task from BPMN or a more complex human task. This separation of metadata facilitates reuse (that is, one task can be used in multiple activities in a process or in multiple processes), and enables easier modification (of a subset of metadata including deadlines, escalation policies, notifications, and routing rules) by business users at runtime (from within the *Administration* pages of the *Workspace*).

Task Stakeholders

The primary and most obvious stakeholder is the *assignee*—the user (or users) that need to act on the task to complete and progress it. In addition to the *assignee,* Oracle BPM 11*g* supports the following stakeholders:

- ■ **Owner** This stakeholder is the business owner of the task and typically has business admin privileges, including acting upon the task, as well as reassigning, withdrawing, or escalating it. The owner is specified using the Owner attribute within the General tab of the human task editor. It is typically assigned to the Process Owner role within the BPM project using the value *<Project Name>.ProcessOwner.*

- **Initiator**   The user who is the initiator of the process (or the task). This is typically specified from the invoking BPMN process. The initiator typically has view access so that he or she can track the status.

- **Reviewer**   Reviewers are typically granted only view access and the ability to add comments and attachments. Reviewers are specified within the Assignment tab of the Configure Assignment window, as shown in Figure 7-1. This can be launched by clicking the pencil icon next to "Task will go from starting to final participant" at the top-right corner of the Assignment tab (this tab can be seen in Figure 7-17 where "Use Advanced Rules" is displayed instead of the default "Task will go from starting to final participant").

- **Approvers**   The users who have approved previous steps in the task's routing slip. Approvers get read-only access to the task.

- **Admin**   This is the site admin—users granted the *WorkflowAdmin* role. Unlike the owner, the admin cannot act on the task or add comments and attachments. However, the admin user has administrator privileges and can reassign the task, delete it, and so on.

The access allowed to each of the preceding stakeholders can be managed (strictly reduced and not added) from within the Access tab of the human task editor. The access editor with default settings is shown in Figure 7-2.

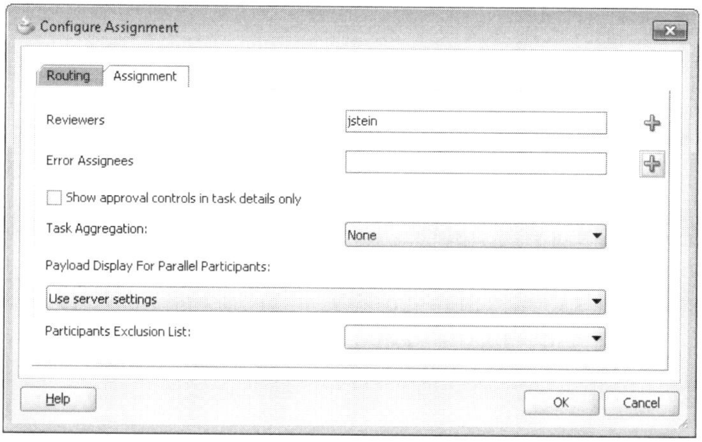

FIGURE 7-1.   *Configure Assignment—Assignment*

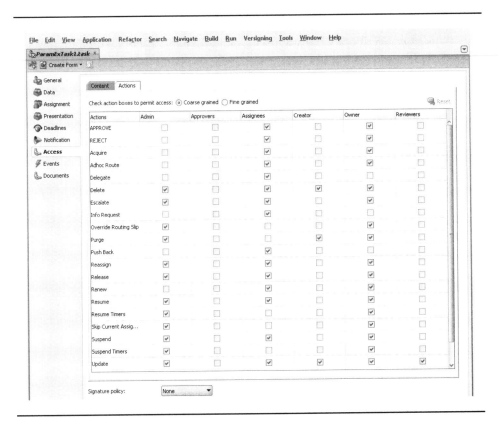

FIGURE 7-2. *The access editor*

Error Assignee

In addition to the aforementioned stakeholders, there is an *Error Assignee* who gets assigned tasks with recoverable errors in the *alerted* state. Common examples of recoverable errors include errors in assignment, such as assigning tasks to an invalid user or group. This stakeholder is different from others in that there is no access enjoyed by this stakeholder other than for *alerted* tasks. Error assignees are specified along with reviewers in the Configure Assignment window shown in Figure 7-1. If an error assignee is not specified, the admin is the default error assignee.

Users and Roles

Tasks can be assigned to the following:

■ **Swim-lane Role**   This is the default for BPMN processes. The swim-lane role is essentially an application role (defined later in this section) contained within the application *OracleBPMProcessRolesApp,* which is a special WLS application to hold all swim-lanes related application roles (the Context column in Figure 7-3 refers to this application). Users and groups (defined next) can be granted swim-lane roles either as part of the process definition in the *Organization* artifact or from the *Administration* pages of the Workspace application, as shown in Figure 7-3.

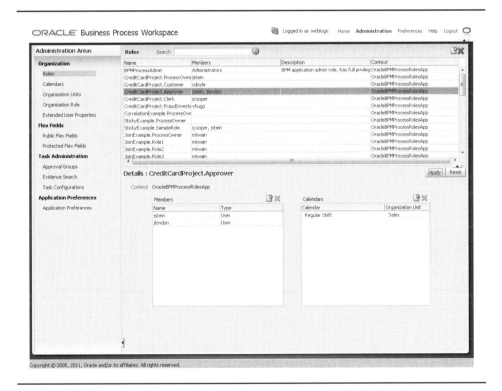

FIGURE 7-3.   *Managing swim-lane roles in Workspace*

- **Users** Tasks can be assigned to users directly. Available users are determined from the identity directory used (that is, LDAP, OID, Active Directory, and so on).

- **Groups** Groups are collections of users and are managed in the identity directory.

- **Application Role** Application roles are roles within an application's policy store and are the more generic version of swim-lane roles. To use application roles from an application, the Application Context property in the General tab should be set to the application name—by default, it is set to *OracleBPMProcessRolesApp,* which is where the swim-lane roles are maintained. Unless working with existing application roles, swim-lane roles should be used instead because they provide more capabilities, including management from within Workspace and the association of calendars and escalation roles.

- **Approval Group** Approval Group is a mechanism to manage a group of approvers. The author recommends against using approval groups and using swim-lane roles instead.

- **Parametric Role** Parametric Role enables the selection of users from an application role based on conditions matching user attributes against specified parameters or values providing a simple mechanism to divide a role into subroles. For example, an insurance company may want to segment their "underwriters" by "customer" and "location" or a support organization may segment support staff by language and product expertise.

  A parametric role is created and managed within the Administration pages of the Workspace application, as shown in Figure 7-4. In this example, the parametric role has three parameters—*language, skills,* and *role*—and selects users granted the *role* application role and whose *LANGUAGE* attribute equals the parameter *language* and whose *TECHNOLOGY* attribute equals the parameter *skills.*

The parameters are specified when the parametric role is assigned, as shown in Figure 7-5.

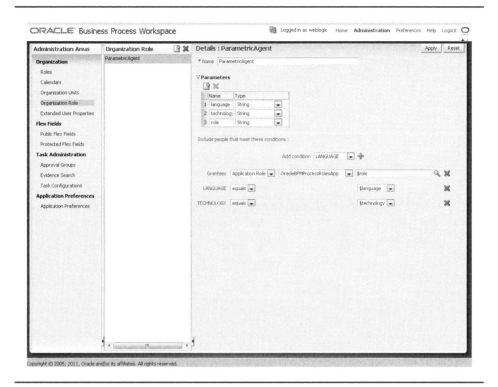

FIGURE 7-4.   *Creating and managing parametric roles*

NOTE
At the time of writing of this chapter, parametric roles were called Organization Roles, *and that name is used in Figure 7-4 and Figure 7-5.*

Organization Units

A related concept to users, groups, and roles is that of an *organization unit*. Users can be associated with organization units in a many-to-many relationship. If a process or a human task is assigned to an organization unit, then only those users who are associated with the organization unit will have access. For example, a bank may have many branches and in each branch a task needs to be done by an *Agent,* but only the agent who belongs

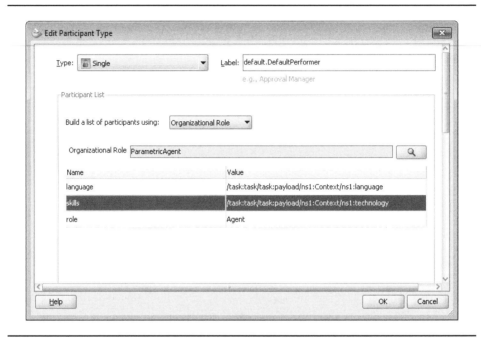

FIGURE 7-5. *Assigning to parametric roles*

to the branch's organizational unit will be able to act on tasks for that branch. This can be achieved by granting the appropriate people the *Agent* role, assigning the task to this role, creating organization units for every branch, organizing users within branches, and then associating the process with the branch's organization unit. The association of a process with an organization unit is done by assigning to the predefined BPMN variable *organizationalUnit*. This association is inherited by the tasks, but can be overridden by assigning to its *execData/systemAttributes/organizationalUnitName.*

Notifications and Deadlines

An important aspect of using process management to orchestrate human activities is to use notifications and deadlines to ensure that things get done on time, and if they don't happen on time, appropriate corrective action is taken. Oracle BPM 11*g* enables the declarative specification of notifications and deadlines to enable this, as discussed in this section.

Deadlines

Oracle BPM 11*g* has three types of deadlines:

- **Duration Deadline**   This is the amount of time allocated to the task. When the duration deadline expires, the task is either escalated, expired, or renewed based on the specified setting. The duration deadline is specified within the Deadlines tab of the human task editor by configuring the Task Duration Settings, as shown in Figure 7-6. In addition to a fixed duration, an expression value can be specified. The choices for the Task Duration Settings pick-list include *Never Expire, Expire After, Renew After,* and *Escalate After.*

- **Due Date Deadline**   This is a soft deadline and is used only for indicating to a user that a task is about to expire or to draw their attention to overdue tasks. When a duration deadline is specified, the due date deadline should be set to be less than that. The due date deadline is specified by setting a value for the Action Requested Before field in the Deadlines tab, as seen in Figure 7-6.

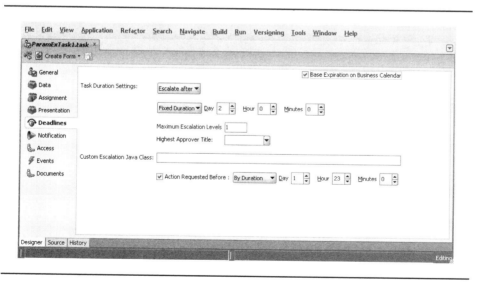

FIGURE 7-6.   *Duration and due date deadlines*

■ **Reminders**   Reminders are defined within the Advanced subtab of the Notification tab of the human task editor and can be set up relative to task assignment, duration deadline, or the due date deadline, as shown in Figure 7-7. Also, multiple reminders can be defined.

Participant-Specific Duration Deadline   As will be discussed later in this chapter, a human task may be worked on by multiple participants. The deadline setting specified at the task level applies to the whole task—that is, from the time the task is created to when it is completed by the last participant. Deadlines can be specified for individual participants as well, within the advanced section of the participant editor, as shown in Figure 7-8. The participant editor can be launched by selecting a participant in the Assignment tab and then clicking the Edit icon.

   If the participant does not act within the specified deadline, then the deadline handling policy, specified at the task level, is applied. For example, if the task is set up to be escalated after three days, but if a participant is allocated only one day and that participant does not act within one day, then the task will be escalated.

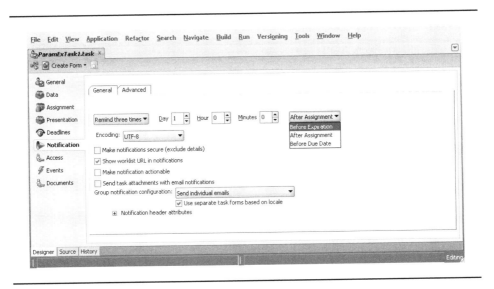

FIGURE 7-7.   *Reminders*

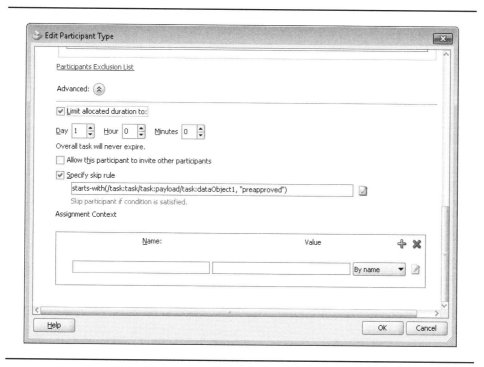

FIGURE 7-8.   *The advanced section in the participant editor*

Escalation

When the *Escalate After* option is selected for the duration deadline, the task is escalated. By default, escalation is based on the management chain hierarchy and the task is escalated from the user to their manager and upward based on the number of levels. If a value is specified for the highest approver title attribute, the task is never escalated beyond a user with the specified title.

Instead of the management chain hierarchy, a functional hierarchy can be used by specifying the *Role Escalation* attribute for the swim-lane role within the Organization editor. For example, tasks can be escalated from *Tier 2 Support* to *Tier 1 Support* by specifying *Tier 1 Support* as the value for the *Role Escalation* attribute of the *Tier 2 Support* role. Custom escalation can also be provided by implementing the *oracle.bpel.services .workflow.assignment.dynamic.IDynamicTaskEscalationFunction* interface and registering it as a function under *Workflow Task Service Properties* under *SOA Administration* using Fusion Middleware Control. The details can be found in the section *28.3.9.6 Specifying Escalation Rules* of the *Oracle Fusion Middleware Developer's Guide for Oracle SOA Suite.* However, the author recommends that most use cases should be addressed with role escalation hierarchy instead of using custom code.

Notifications

The Notification tab of the human task editor allows definition of multiple notifications using a combination of when (task status), who (recipient), and what (notification header) as shown in Figure 7-9 (the options shown in the figure are not exhaustive).

The task status attribute specifies when the notification is triggered. Choices include assign, complete, error, expire, request info, resume, suspend, update, update outcome, withdraw, and alerted. Assign includes assignment, reassignment, renewal, and delegation. Update includes an

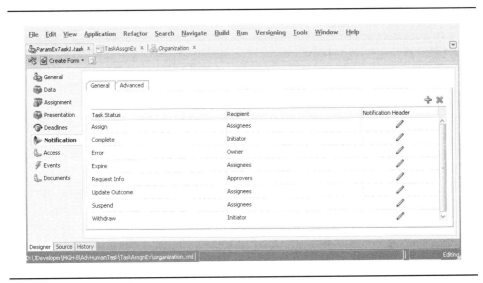

FIGURE 7-9. *The notification editor*

update to a task's data, as well as changes to tasks and attachments and enables notifying interested parties on task data, comments, and attachment changes even while the task is being worked by the assignee. A common-use case would be to notify reviewers. Other choices are self-explanatory.

The recipient may be assignees, the initiator, owner, or approvers— please see the earlier discussion on *Task Stakeholders* for a definition.

The notification header contains the text of the notification that is included in all channels and can be a combination of static text and expressions.

E-mail Notifications   By default, e-mail notifications include a non-editable HTML version of the task form, unless the Make Notifications Secure option is chosen in the Advanced subtab, shown in Figure 7-7. (In Chapter 8, we will discuss how to create forms tailored for e-mail notifications.) E-mail notifications can be made actionable by checking the Make Notification Actionable box in the window shown in Figure 7-7. Actionable e-mails include links for the task's outcome. Clicking an outcome link composes a reply e-mail, which when received by the BPM server, progresses the task with the selected outcome. Attachments added to the reply e-mail get added to a task as task attachments, and any comments in the body of the e-mail within the designated area get added as comments. This provides casual users with the capability to complete their tasks from e-mail clients without connecting to the workspace or BPM server.

Notification Delivery   The notification settings discussed earlier did not include any specification of how to deliver the notification. This is because in BPM 11*g* the channel to receive notifications is a user preference. From within the Preferences pages of the Workspace application, users can define their preferences using business rules—they can specify various conditions or filters and how to deliver notifications matching the conditions, as shown in Figure 7-10.

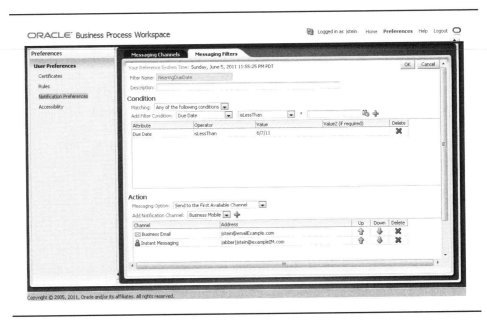

FIGURE 7-10. *Notification preferences*

Data

The data that is available to a task is specified within the Data tab of the task editor. When a human task is created from a BPMN process, the wizard sets up the data definition inside the task as well as maps it to the process data objects. Two types of data elements can be used within human tasks:

- **Variable**   This is the typical usage. In this case, the data element in the task file is specified by an XML schema or is a simple type (simple types are built-in XML types such as String). An example variable data element definition is shown in Figure 7-11.

- **Entity**   This is the option used when working with ADF-BC business components and services. Usage of the ADF-BC entity data type enables advanced patterns, including repeating approvals in parallel for each item in a collection (described later). An example entity data element definition is shown in Figure 7-12.

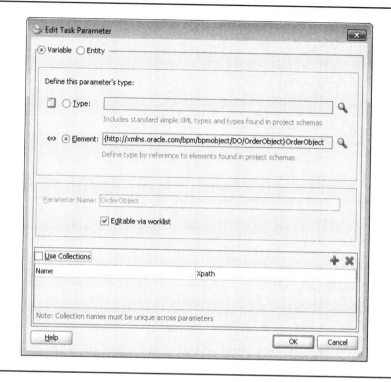

FIGURE 7-11. *A task data definition of Type variable*

To add either type of data element, launch the editor shown in Figure 7-11 by clicking the green plus icon at the top-right corner of the Data section within the Data tab (Data tab not shown in the figure).

Flex-fields

Often it is desired to let process participants use process- (or task-) specific data to search and/or organize their work. To enable this in a high-performance fashion, Oracle BPM 11*g* uses a concept called *flex-fields*. Flex-fields consist of three elements:

- **Reserved Columns** The underlying schema for the human task component contains reserved columns that are designated for mapping to custom attributes of type text, number, date, URL, and Form.

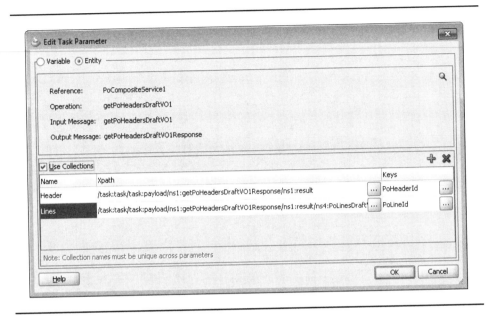

FIGURE 7-12. *A task data definition of Type entity*

■ **Labels** Before a reserved column (or attribute) can be used, it must be associated with a label. The intent is to avoid mapping disparate information to the same column, as that may lead to a confusing presentation when the column is included as a visible column in a view.

■ **Mapping** An element of a task's payload needs to be mapped to the label.

There are two types of flex-fields: public and protected. The difference between the two is that for public flex-fields the mapping needs to be specified within the administration pages of the workspace, whereas for protected flex-fields the mapping is part of the task's definition. For both, first a label needs to be created from within the administration pages of the workspace by clicking the green plus icon next to the Show pick-list, as shown in Figure 7-13.

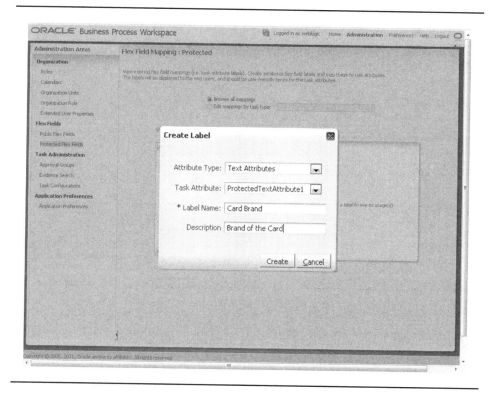

FIGURE 7-13.   *Creating a new label for a flex-field*

Public flex-field mappings are created from the same window as Figure 7-13 by selecting the Edit Mappings By Task Type radio button, choosing the task, and then specifying the mapping as shown in Figure 7-14.

NOTE
Only payload elements of the simple type can be used for public flex-field mapping.

Protected flex-field mappings are defined within the Data tab of the human task editor by clicking the green plus icon at the top-right corner of the Mapped Attributes section and specifying the mapping, as shown in Figure 7-15.

Flex-fields of both types become available in search specifications, as well as custom columns, as shown in Figure 7-16.

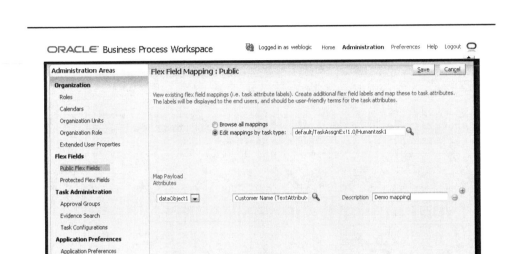

FIGURE 7-14. *Mapping public flex-fields*

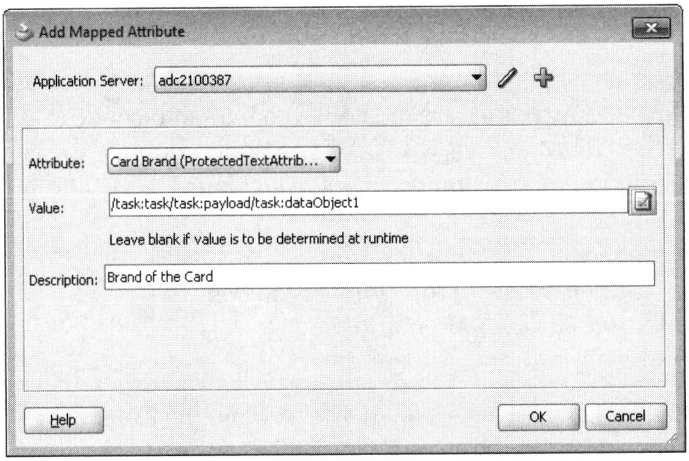

FIGURE 7-15. *Mapping protected flex-fields*

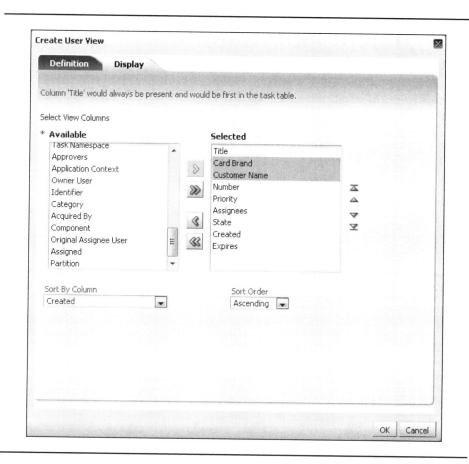

FIGURE 7-16. *The flex-field columns in the view definition*

TIP
Labels for both types of flex-fields, as well as mappings for public flex-fields, can be moved from one environment to another using the ant scripts provided for test-to-production migration, as documented in section 23.6 Moving Human Workflow Data from a Test to a Production Environment of *the* Oracle Fusion Middleware Administrator's Guide for Oracle SOA Suite and Oracle Business Process Management Suite.

Assignment and Routing

The human task component of Oracle BPM 11g includes the ability to route tasks among multiple participants leveraging declarative patterns and business rules. In addition to routing and assignment defined as part of task definition, users can reroute or reassign at runtime.

Modeled Routing

The routing is defined in the task definition within the *Assignment* tab using a combination of participants and stages (these concepts are explained later in this section), organizing them in parallel and sequential participant and stage blocks. An example of a routing slip is shown in Figure 7-17 to

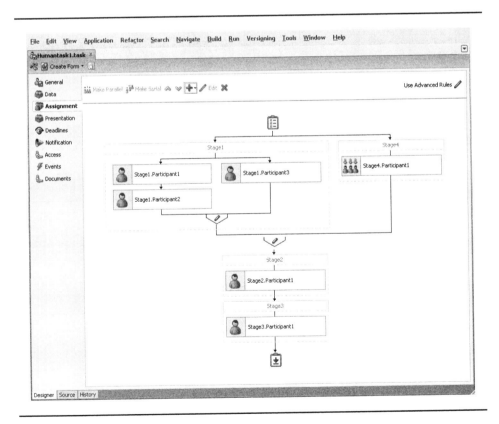

FIGURE 7-17. *An example routing slip*

illustrate what is possible. In this example, the routing slip has four stages named *Stage1* thru *Stage4*; *Stage1* and *Stage4* execute in parallel and are followed by *Stage2* and *Stage3* in sequence. Stage1 is composed of multiple participants—*Stage1.Participant1* and *Stage1.Participant2* execute in sequence, while *Stage1.Participant3* executes in parallel to them. Also, a participant itself can define routing among multiple users. For example, it can be seen in Figure 7-17 that the *Stage4.Participant1* has a different icon—one with three users, indicating that it represents multiple users working in parallel.

NOTE
For a simple BPMN user task, the routing slip consists of a single stage and a single participant; the participant is set to the swim-lane role.

Modeling Routing in Task vs. in BPMN

Readers may note that the routing capability within a human task introduces a design choice of whether to model such routing within the BPMN process or within a human task. Some considerations in choosing the right option follow.

The benefits of modeling routing within the BPMN process are:

- **Business Visibility**   Having routing in the BPMN process communicates it explicitly both as part of a process model and as part of a process audit trail.

- **Process Constructs**   The full palette of process constructs including events and exception handling and conditional branching can be used. Essentially, the task routing can be thought of as a process fragment.

(*continued*)

The benefits of modeling routing within a human task are:

- **Abstraction**   In certain scenarios, the task routing is a detail that should be abstracted from the process model. For example, from the perspective of a process analyst, the process may be that a purchase order needs to get approved; how many people need to approve and under what conditions may be a detail within the approval step.

- **Routing Patterns**   Support for routing patterns such as management chain and group vote significantly simplifies many common scenarios. Trying to model many of these scenarios in BPMN would yield a difficult-to-comprehend and impossible-to-maintain "spaghetti" process.

- **Variability**   When there is significant variability in routing, modeling it inside a task is useful. In approval scenarios, it is common to vary the approvals based on the characteristics of the document being approved, the requestor, and the prevailing business conditions. Specifically, scenarios requiring rule-based rerouting, early-completion, or skipping of participants are ideal for being modeled within tasks.

Stage

A stage organizes a set of participants in a logical grouping for visualization and other purposes.

When working with ADF-BC data, a stage can be associated with a collection (discussed earlier in the section "Data") and made to repeat in parallel for each item in the collection. This is achieved by selecting a stage, clicking edit, and then configuring it to repeat in parallel based on a collection, as shown in Figure 7-18. Use cases for this include scenarios such as purchase order approvals, where line items may need to be approved by different approvers.

A stage also divides a complex task into smaller scopes. For example, the task aggregation feature enables the aggregation of tasks at the stage level or task level. (Task aggregation is discussed later in the section "Task Aggregation").

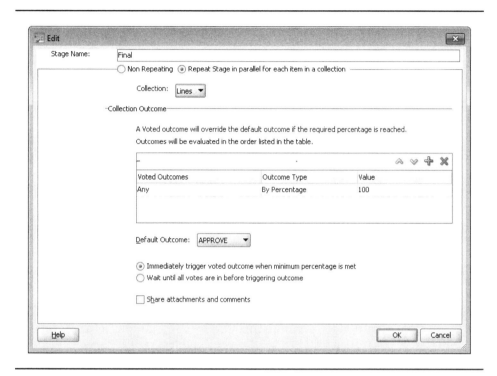

FIGURE 7-18. *Repeating a stage for each item in a collection*

Participant

As explained earlier, a *participant* is the finest granularity of specification in a routing slip, but can potentially specify multiple users. A *participant* is specified using a combination of *participant type* and *participant list* builder. The list builder specifies a collection of people, while the participant type specifies the behavior, such as if anyone needs to act or everyone needs to act.

The following participant types are supported:

■ **Single** As the name indicates only one person needs to act. If the list builder specifies multiple people, including management or a supervisory chain, any one person in the list can claim and act on the task. Once one person claims or acts on the task, others cannot.

- **Parallel** Everyone in the specified list gets the task in parallel and can work on it. The voting pattern described later in the chapter can specify whether the *participant* can be completed with partial responses.

- **Serial** Everyone in the specified list gets the task in sequence and must act on it for the *participant* to be complete. Early completion conditions described later in this section can be used to complete the *participant* under the specified conditions.

- **FYI** Everyone in the specified list gets the task as an FYI—that is, while they receive the task for informational purposes, they need not, and cannot, act on it. The *participant* is completed after sending the tasks—in other words, the current step in the task routing is completed and so the task moves to the next participant in the routing slip.

In addition to specifying the list of participants and the behavior, a *participant* also has a label attribute that can be used to refer to it from the business rules, and so on. Also, the advanced section of the participant editor can be used to specify deadlines for the participant (described earlier) and skip conditions (described later in this section).

Participant List Builders
The available list builders can be divided into three categories: simple list builders, hierarchy-based list builders, and rule-driven list builders.

Simple List Builders This category has four list builders—their difference being the type of user/role supported. Please refer to the earlier discussion on *Users and Roles* for definitions of the various role types.

- **Lane Participant** Specifies the participant based on the swim-lane that the user task sits in within the BPMN process. It's comprised of two options: include everyone in the swim-lane role or only the previous performer of a task in the same swim-lane role (also known as a sticky assignment).

- **Names and Expression** Specifies a list of *users, groups,* and *application roles.*

- **Approval Group** Specifies a list using *approval groups.*

- **Parametric Role** Specifies a list using *parametric roles.*

Hierarchy-based List Builders These list builders create lists based on an organizational or role hierarchy. The four list builders in this category include:

- **Management Chain** Creates a list based on a management chain hierarchy. A management chain list is specified with a starting participant and one or both of the number of levels, and/or the title of the top participant. The number of levels is computed from the starting participant—thus, if only one approval is sufficient, the number of levels will be 0. Management hierarchy is always based on the user directory used (LDAP, Active Directory, and others).

- **Supervisory Chain** Similar in concept to the management chain with a couple of differences. First, the supervisory chain can be based on a custom hierarchy provider. If one is not specified, the same hierarchy as the management chain is used. Second, the top participant in the case of a supervisory chain is a user or principal instead of the title.

- **Job Level** Similar to the supervisory chain but with few differences. First, it traverses the job level hierarchy instead of the supervisory hierarchy; however, if a custom hierarchy provider is not specified, both use the management chain hierarchy. Second, the level specification can be an absolute value representing a specific job level in the organization such as Executive Vice President (whereas in the supervisory and management chain it is only relative). Also, this list builder allows choices to include only the last level, as well as the first and last level, in addition to including everyone in the chain.

- **Position** Similar to the job level, but with a few differences. First, it traverses the position hierarchy. Next, this list builder requires a custom hierarchy provider.

As mentioned previously, the supervisory chain, job level, and position list builders work with custom hierarchy providers that can leverage this information from the human resources application or other existing source. A custom hierarchy provider class needs to implement the *oracle.bpel.services .identity.hierarchy.IHierarchyProvider* interface and be available in a location that is on the class path of the BPM/SOA server. An excerpt of a Java class implementing hierarchy provider is shown next:

```
public class SampleHierarchyProvider implements IHierarchyProvider
{
  public SampleHierarchyProvider()
  {
  }
   //Initializes crawler.
  public void init(Map properties)
  {
    //...
  }
  public HierarchyPrincipal fetchJobLevel(HierarchyPrincipal principal)
    throws HierarchyProviderException
  {
    //...
    principal.setJobLevel(level);
    return principal;
  }
  public HierarchyPrincipal fetchManager(HierarchyPrincipal principal)
    throws HierarchyProviderException
  {
    //...
    HierarchyPrincipal mgrPrincipal = new HierarchyPrincipal();
    mgrPrincipal.setId(mgrId);
    mgrPrincipal.setJobLevel(level);
    mgrPrincipal.setEffectiveDate(effectiveDate);
    return mgrPrincipal;
  }
  public List<HierarchyPrincipal> fetchManagers(HierarchyPrincipal
principal,
                                                int numOfLevel)
    throws HierarchyProviderException
  {
    List<HierarchyPrincipal> pList = new ArrayList<HierarchyPrincipal>();
    //...
```

```
    for (int i = 0; i <  numOfLevel; i++) {
      p = fetchManager(p);
      pList.add(p);
    }
    return pList;
  }
  /**
   * Returns a list of names of additional properties that the
IHierarchyProvider
   * implementation requires for identifying a HierarchyPrincipal, and for
traversing
   * the hierarchy. These properties will be passed in the
HierarchyPrincipal's
   * propertyBag. The ApprovalManagement framework will look up the values
for these
   * properties' approval policy attributes first. If not found in the
approval
   * policy attributes, the values will be looked up from the Task payload
attributes.
   */
  public List<String> getPropertyNames()
  {
    List<String> propNames = null;
    //...
    return propNames;
  }
}
```

The custom hierarchy provider class is registered by adding the following configuration to the *workflow-identity-config.xml* file:

```
<serviceExtensions>
        <serviceExtension name="SampleIdentityServiceExtension">
        <serviceProvider type="supervisoryHierarchyProvider" classname=
"custHierarchyProvider"/>
        <serviceProvider type="jobLevelHierarchyProvider" classname="
custHierarchyProvider "/>
        <serviceProvider type="positionHierarchyProvider" classname="
custHierarchyProvider ">
                  <initializationParameter name="someParam" value="value" />

        </serviceProvider>
    </serviceExtension>
 </serviceExtensions>
```

The *workflow-identity-config.xml* can be found at the location */soa/ configuration/default/* within the *soa-infra* partition of the MDS; WLST can be used to export the file from the MDS and then reimport the modified file. The appropriate WLST commands are shown next (values in italics need to be changed based on the environment):

```
cd $SOA_HOME/common/bin
./wlst

wls:/offline> connect ('weblogic', 'welcome1', 't3://
localhost:7001')
wls:/domain1/serverConfig> exportMetadata(application='soa-
infra',server='soa_server1',toLocation='/tmp',docs='/soa/
configuration/default/workflow-identity-config.xml')

#Make changes to the file as described above

wls:/domain1/serverConfig> importMetadata(application='soa-
infra',server='soa_server1',toLocation='/tmp',docs='/soa/
configuration/default/workflow-identity-config.xml')

wls:/domain1/serverConfig>exit()
```

Rule-based List Builders   Rule-based list builders enable the creation of other types of lists using business rules. Rule-based list builders can be specified by selecting the *Rule-based* option for the list builder and specifying a ruleset name.

NOTE
Most of the other list builders also include an option to use business rules. Using the rule-based list builder versus using rules inside a different type of list builder are essentially the same, with the only difference being that in the second case the rule action is constrained to comply with the type of list builder. The author recommends using the rule-based list builder and not rules within other list builders. Reasons include the simplicity of the conceptual model, as well as that the constraint limiting the action to a specific list builder is enforced only at runtime.

The rules for building the participant lists (as well as for routing, discussed later) are stored in dictionaries named *<Task Name>Rules* and *<Task Name>RulesBase,* referred from here on as *custom* and *base dictionary.* Since task rules can be changed at runtime, to separate runtime changes from developer changes, the custom dictionary should be used for runtime rules and the base dictionary for developer rules. The task attributes and its payload are set up as facts (in the base dictionary) and can be used in the business rules.

NOTE
In the composite editor, only the custom dictionary will be shown. The base dictionary can be found from the Dictionary Links *of the custom dictionary.*

The business rules actions must create participant lists using one or more of the following seeded functions:

- **CreateResourceList**   Corresponds to the Names and Expressions list builder

- **CreateApprovalGroupList**   Corresponds to the Approval Groups list builder

- **CreateManagementChainList**   Corresponds to the Management Chain list builder

- **CreateSupervisoryList**   Corresponds to the Supervisory list builder

- **CreateJobLevelList**   Corresponds to the Job Level list builder

- **CreatePositionList**   Corresponds to the Position list builder

The parameters of the preceding functions mirror the options available in the corresponding list builders. The following additional parameters are available:

- **Lists**   Must set to the fact *Lists.*

- **Rule name**   Used to create a reason statement for assignment. *<Rule Set Name>_<value of this parameter>* is used as a key to look up the resource bundle for a translatable reason for assignment.

- **Required**   Setting it to *false* causes the participant to be treated as an FYI participant (as discussed in the FYI type earlier).

- **Auto Action Enabled and Auto Action**   If *auto action enabled* is set to *true,* the specified action will be automatically taken, and in the task history, the associated reason will get added. The reason for using this versus skipping the participant is that this allows for the reason behind the decision to skip the participant and be available in the audit trail. This option is available only in the CreateSupervisoryList, CreateJobLevelList, and CreatePositionList functions.

Post-processing Rulesets

In addition to the specified ruleset, two additional rulesets—Substitution Rules and Modification Rules—are always created.

The substitution rules allow substituting users, groups, and roles in the created lists with different users, groups, and roles using the seeded *Substitute* function. The *substitutionRules* parameter of this function must be set to the seeded fact *SubstitutionRules.*

The modification rules apply only to job level and position-based lists and allow for extending or truncating the lists using the seeded functions *Extend* and *Truncate.*

Routing Overrides

The routing specified using the features described in the previous sections can be overridden in multiple ways. Participants can be skipped or the task can be completed early based on conditions. Also, business rules or a custom Java class that implements the *oracle.bpel.services.workflow.task .IAssignmentService* interface can be used to override the routing. If the external Java class option is used, the participant list configured in the task is ignored and the class is completely responsible for both assignment and routing.

Skipping Participants

A participant can be conditionally skipped by specifying a skip condition within the advanced section of the participant editor, as shown in Figure 7-8.

A common scenario for skipping a participant is that under certain threshold values self-approval may be sufficient. Also, it may be used to skip participants who may have already been approved. However, as discussed in the next section, the task aggregation feature provides built-in support for it.

Early Completion

It is a common scenario that if one user rejects the requested approval (or selects other similar task action), then further routing makes no sense. This can be modeled by specifying an early completion condition, which is specified by checkmarking the option "Complete task when a participant chooses" and selecting the early-completion outcome within the Routing tab of the Configure Assignment window, which can be launched by clicking the pencil icon next to "Task will go from starting to final participant" at the top-right corner of the Assignment tab, as shown in Figure 7-19.

Instead of a simple outcome, an expression can also be specified as the early completion condition. As discussed earlier in this section, within a task, participants can be working in parallel. To complete a task that could

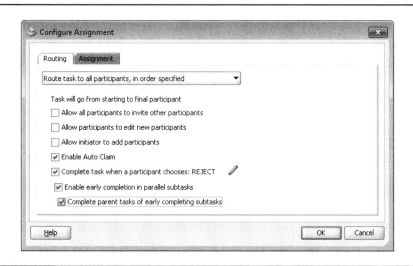

FIGURE 7-19. *Configuring an Assignment—the Routing window*

be accomplished with multiple parallel participants, the options "Enable early completion in parallel subtasks" and "Complete parent tasks of early completing subtasks" should be enabled. (The usage of the term *parent task* in this context is confusing. It simply refers to the task being configured; parallel participants are considered to be subtasks of the task.)

Voting Pattern　　When the routing slip has multiple people in parallel, a voting pattern can be used to specify that a certain consensus is sufficient to complete the parallel tasks without waiting for every participant's action. Readers may note that this implements workflow *Pattern 30— Structured Partial Join,* discussed in Chapter 5. The voting pattern is specified as shown in Figure 7-20.

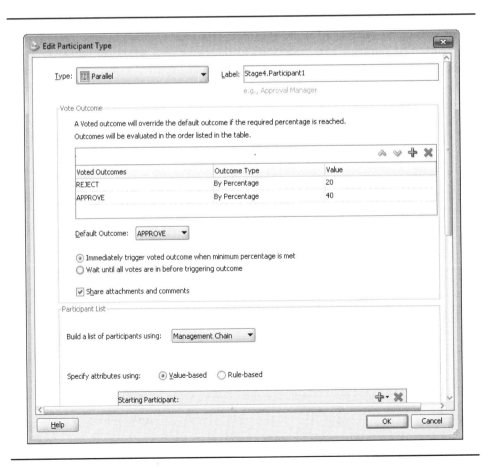

FIGURE 7-20.　*Voting pattern*

The voting pattern allows specification of outcomes to override the default outcome and the associated consensus percentage. The outcomes are evaluated in order. For example, Figure 7-20 specifies that if 20 percent of participants have selected the outcome REJECT, then it is the consensus outcome; otherwise, if 40 percent of participants have selected the outcome APPROVE, then it is the consensus outcome. The first consensus to happen will win—that is, if 40 percent of the people approve, the consensus will be to approve it, even though it is possible that 20 percent of the people intended to reject it.

Parallel routing can be specified in multiple ways. The same voting pattern is supported in all, but the way to access the voting pattern specification differs as described next:

- **Parallel Participant Type**   As shown in Figure 7-20 the voting pattern is specified within the participant editor.

- **Parallel Participant or Stage Blocks**   As can be seen in Figure 7-17, at every join of a parallel block there is a block arrow with a pencil icon within. Clicking this icon launches a window to specify the voting pattern.

- **Repeating Stages**   In the case of a stage repeating in parallel for every item in a collection, the voting pattern is specified within the stage editor, as can be seen in Figure 7-18.

Task Aggregation   In scenarios with a complex routing slip, a user may get assigned a task in multiple steps (that is, resolved as a participant for multiple *participants*). In such scenarios, the task aggregation feature enables the user to act only once—if the task aggregation is enabled, the user is presented with the task, including a collection of all the subitems that need their approval. The approval action is then recorded and played back at each future step in which the user's approval is needed for the task. Task aggregation can be specified at the stage level or task level within the Configure Assignment window, as shown in Figure 7-21. The Configure Assignment window can be launched by clicking the pencil icon next to "Task will go from starting to final participant" at the top-right corner of the Assignment tab.

Rule-Driven Routing   Rule-driven routing is enabled by selecting the option "Use Advanced Rules" in the Routing tab of the Configure Assignment

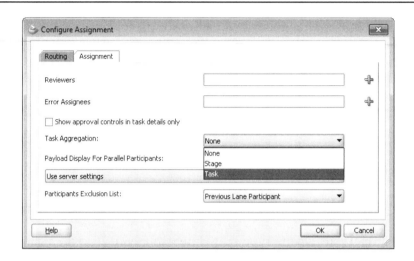

FIGURE 7-21. *Specifying task aggregation*

window, as shown in Figure 7-22. If specified, routing rules are invoked every time a participant completes the task and/or task is assigned to next participant. The routing rules have an opportunity to complete the task or to route it differently.

The same base and custom dictionaries as in the rule-driven participant list builder (discussed earlier) are used for routing rules. A ruleset with the name *RoutingRules* is created in the base and custom dictionaries are used. In addition to the task and its payload, routing rules have access to an additional fact, *Previous Outcome,* that has the following attributes:

- ■ **actualParticipant**   Name of the previous performer; for example, *jstein.*

- ■ **logicalParticipant**   Label for the participant in the routing configuration; for example, *Stage1.Participant1.*

- ■ **level**   If the previous performer was part of a hierarchy-based participant, such as management chain, this is the level of the previous performer. The first participant in the management chain will be level 1 and so on.

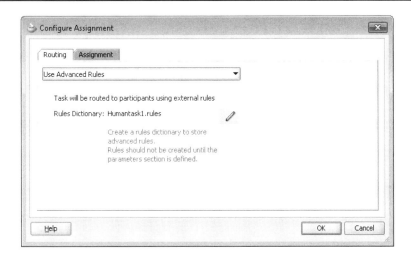

FIGURE 7-22. *Using rule-driven routing*

- *totalNumberOfApprovals* The total number of people who have acted on this task so far.

Routing rules must call one of the following functions as its action:

- **Go Forward** Proceed normally as specified by the routing slip in the Assignment tab. This is the default action.
- **Pushback** Go back to the performer before the current performer.
- **Go To** Go to the participant corresponding to the label specified; for example, *Stage1.Participant1.*
- **Complete** Complete the task.
- **Escalate** Escalate the task as per the escalation policy specified in the task.

An example routing rule is shown in Figure 7-23.

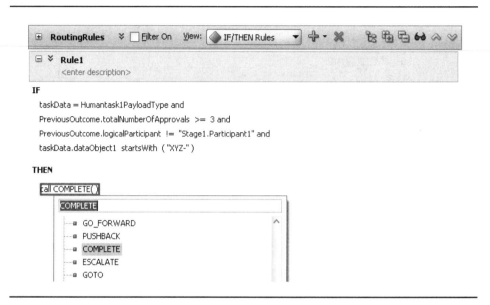

FIGURE 7-23. *An example routing rule*

Runtime Reassignment and Rerouting

While the earlier section discussed sophisticated routing that can be declaratively modeled as part of a task's definition, many scenarios, particularly those dealing with knowledge workers, require that participants have the necessary flexibility to make changes as needed to best accomplish the task. Oracle BPM 11g has some rich functionality in this regard, as discussed in this section.

Adhoc Routing

In addition to performing their approval or action on the task, task participants can add more participants at runtime using the action *Adhoc Route,* if they have been granted this privilege. There are two aspects to granting this privilege:

■ Adhoc routing needs to be enabled for this step of the task. This is enabled in the advanced section of the participant editor (shown in Figure 7-8) by selecting the "Allow this Participant to invite other

Participants" option. This can also be enabled for the whole task by selecting the "Allow all participants to invite other participants" option in the Configure Assignment window, which is shown in Figure 7-19. As mentioned earlier, this window is launched by clicking the pencil icon next to "Task will go from starting to final participant" at the top-right corner of the Assignment tab.

■ The participant's role is granted access to the Adhoc Route action in the Access tab (shown in Figure 7-2). By default, the Assignee and the Owner are granted this access.

If the participant has access to adhoc route action, they can select it from the Actions dropdown which launches the Route Task window, as shown in Figure 7-24. Within this window, the participant can specify the action or outcome, add one or more people to route the task to, and select the pattern used for routing.

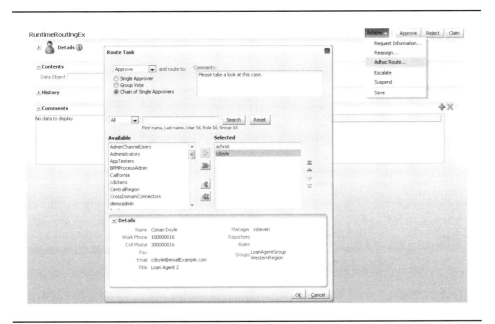

FIGURE 7-24. *Adhoc route tasks*

Request Information

A variant of adhoc route is "request information," where a participant can request some information from a previous participant or another user, as shown in Figure 7-25. As can be seen in Figure 7-25, the user can specify whether the task should come back directly to them after information is submitted or if it should be rerouted through all intermediate participants as per the routing slip.

The user from whom information is requested sees the task in the tasklist and needs to provide the information as a comment and then use the action *Submit Information,* as shown in Figure 7-26. As presented in Figure 7-26, the task has a special state *Info Requested,* which is also visually indicated using a special icon (one with a question mark) next to the task title.

TIP
While previous participants in the request information are limited to the participants within the scope of the task, participants from previous tasks (as well as the initiator) can be included using the reinitiate *option and the* initiator *parameter, respectively, in the human task activity in BPMN.*

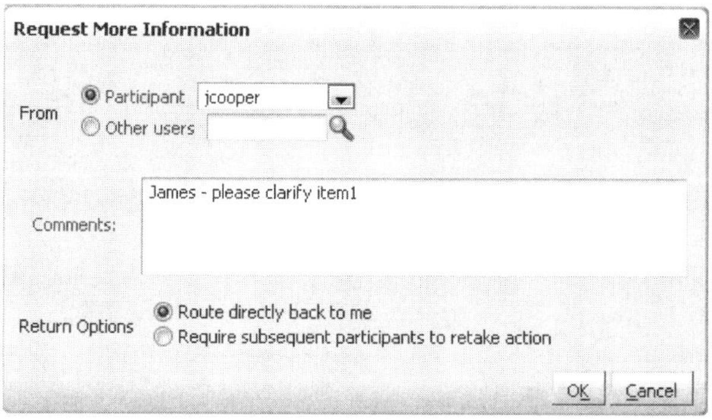

Request More Information

From ◉ Participant jcooper ▾
      ○ Other users 🔍

Comments: James - please clarify item1

Return Options ◉ Route directly back to me
                ○ Require subsequent participants to retake action

OK   Cancel

FIGURE 7-25. *Request information*

FIGURE 7-26. *Submit information*

Inserting Future Participants

As discussed in the earlier section, a task can have a routing slip with multiple participants. Whereas the options discussed so far apply only at the current point in the task's routing (that is, the routing happens immediately after the user doing the routing action), it is also possible to insert additional participants at a future point in the task's routing. To enable such insertion, the option "Allow participants to edit new participants" must be enabled in the window shown in Figure 7-19 (the same place where adhoc routing is enabled). If the option is enabled, the user can use the *History* region within the task form's details to add additional users at the desired point in the task's routing, as shown in Figure 7-27.

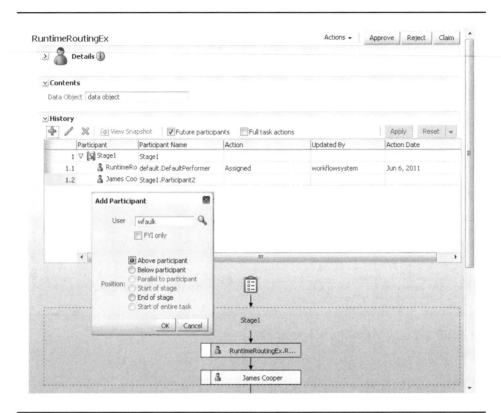

FIGURE 7-27. *Inserting future participants*

Reassignment and Delegation

While adhoc route routes to additional participants after the participant has provided their approval or outcome, reassignment and delegation enable a participant to have others do their task instead. The difference between reassignment and delegation is that in reassignment the assignment is changed and the new assignee works on the task as if it was assigned to him or her, whereas in the case of a delegation the user, who the task is delegated to, acts on behalf of the original assignee. By default, the assignee, the owner, and the admin stakeholders have reassign access, whereas only the assignee has delegate access.

As can be seen in Figure 7-24, *Reassign* is an action available within the *Actions* dropdown. Selecting it launches the Reassign Task window shown in Figure 7-28, which allows the user to reassign or delegate the task to a different user, group, or role.

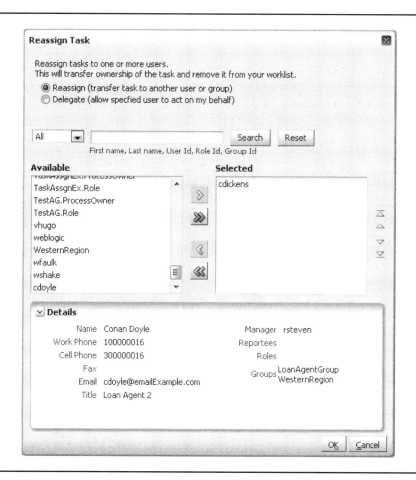

FIGURE 7-28. *Reassigning a task via user action*

Rule-based Reassignment and Delegation   In addition to reassigning or delegating task on a task by task basis, reassignment and delegation can be done automatically based on rules. Reassignment rules are specified within the Rules tab of the Preferences page, which can be launched by clicking the Preferences link within the Workspace application, as shown in Figure 7-29 and Figure 7-30.

Two types of rules can be specified:

■ **Personal Rule**   Every user can specify rules related to tasks assigned to them. Personal rules can reassign, delegate, or even automatically act upon tasks assigned to the user matching the specified conditions and within the specified time period, as shown in Figure 7-29.

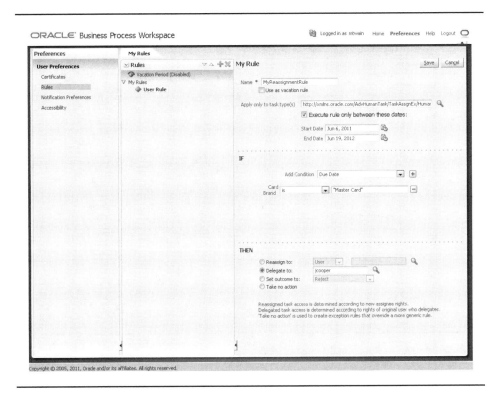

FIGURE 7-29.   *Reassign or delegate a task via personal rules*

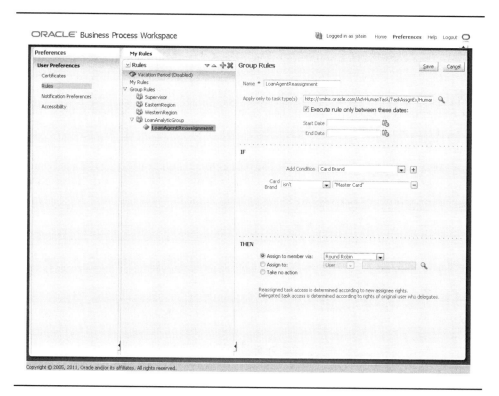

FIGURE 7-30. *Reassigning via group rules*

- **Group Rules** Group rules can be specified by administrators of the group for the tasks assigned to the group. Group rules can reassign tasks either to a specific user, group, or role or using a load-balancing algorithm, as shown in Figure 7-30.

NOTE
At the time of writing of this book, Oracle BPM 11g executes rules only at the time when tasks are assigned.

View-based Delegation   Another way to delegate tasks is to do a view-based delegation. The author recommends this option because it is the most flexible—as soon as delegate access is granted, the delegated user sees all tasks, regardless of when they were assigned to the assignee; the delegated access can also be revoked at any time. For the same reasons, the author recommends this option instead of vacation rules—all outstanding tasks at the start of the vacation can be delegated and at the end of vacation can be "claimed" back.

To use view-based delegation, the *Data radio* button for *Share View* must be selected, and users or groups that would be the target of delegation must be specified, as shown in Figure 7-31.

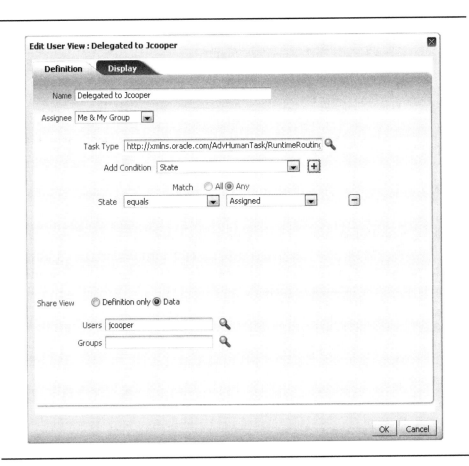

FIGURE 7-31.   *Define view to delegate*

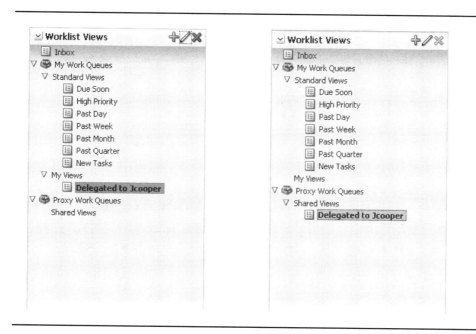

FIGURE 7-32.   *Delegated view in the user's Workspace*

Both the assignee and the delegated user see the view as shown in Figure 7-32; the window on the left shows the view as seen by the assignee, and on the right the one as seen by the delegated user.

Restricting Reassignment Candidates

The list of candidate assignees for reassignment, delegation, adhoc routing, and insert future participant actions, discussed earlier, can be restricted by providing a custom Java class implementing the *oracle.bpel.services.workflow .task.IRestrictedAssignmentCallback interface*, as shown in the following excerpt.

```
public class RestrictedAssignmentCallback implements
   oracle.bpel.services.workflow.task.IRestrictedAssignmentCallback {
   public IRestrictedAssignees getPermittedAssignees(Task task,Map
propertyMap,
         String currentUser, String identityContext, String operation) {
```

```
    if(operation ==
        IRestrictedAssignmentCallback.OperationType.REASSIG.toString()) {
            //Candidate list for Reassign Action
            return new RestrictedAssignees(createReassignTaskAssigneeList(),
true);
        } else if(operation ==
IRestrictedAssignmentCallback.OperationType.ROUTE.toString()) {
            //Candidates for Adhoc Route
            return new RestrictedAssignees(createAdhocRouteTaskAssigneeList(),
true);
        }
        return null;
  }
  public List getRestrictedOperations(Task task, Map propertyMap,
                String currentUser, String identityContext) {
        List retList = new ArrayList();
        retList.add(RestrictedAssignmentCallback.OperationType.REASSIGN);
        retList.add(RestrictedAssignmentCallback.OperationType.ROUTE);
        //Other options are DELEGATE and EDIT_APPROVERS
        return retList;
  }
  private List createReassignTaskAssigneeList() {
   List retList = new ArrayList();
   //add users this way
   retList.add(new TaskAssignee("jstein", IWorkflowConstants.IDENTITY_TYPE_
USER));
   //add groups this way
   retList.add(new TaskAssignee("group1", IWorkflowConstants.IDENTITY_TYPE_
GROUP));
   //add swim-lane roles and application roles this way
   retList.add(new TaskAssignee("Project1.Role1",
                      IWorkflowConstants.IDENTITY_TYPE_APPLICATION_ROLE));
   return retList;
   }
}
```

The Java class implementing the restrictions can be registered with a human task by clicking the Configure Restricted Assignments within the Access tab of the human task editor.

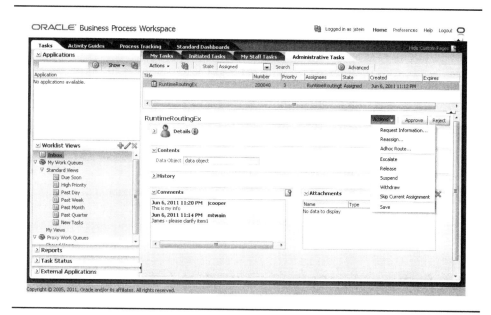

FIGURE 7-33. *Admin actions Including "Skip Current Assignment"*

Admin Actions

The owner and the admin participants have access to additional actions including the ability to skip the current assignment, as shown in Figure 7-33. "Skip Current Assignment" skips the current *participant* in the task's routing slip and moves it to the next step.

Activity Guide

In many scenarios, a user must participate in multiple activities in a process, and they need some sort of help navigating through the process to let the user know what has happened and what they need to do next. The traditional solution to this has been to present an audit trail view of the process diagram. However, there are two limitations to this solution:

- The process diagram may be too overwhelming for some users.

- The process may have sections that should not be shared with all users.

Oracle BPM 11*g* introduces an innovative approach to this requirement called Activity Guide. An activity guide allows the layering of additional metadata on user activities in BPMN processes, organizing them by milestones, as shown in Figure 7-34

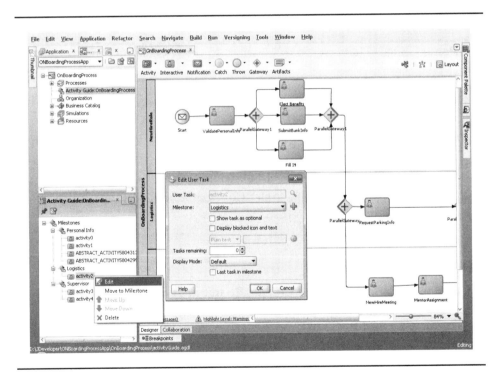

FIGURE 7-34. *Activity Guide metadata*

If an activity guide is configured, in addition to process instances, activity guide instances are created at runtime. These activity guide instances can be found within the Activity Guide tabs of the Workspace application, as shown in Figure 7-35. As can be seen in Figure 7-35, the activity guide user interface provides users with easy-to-understand navigation and a status view of the process with their activities organized by milestones. Also, in addition to tasks assigned to the user, they have review access to other users' tasks based on their access to the task.

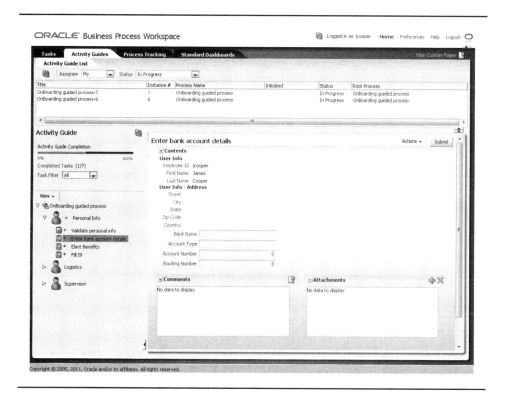

FIGURE 7-35. *The Activity Guide user interface*

Summary

This chapter provides a comprehensive overview of the capabilities offered by the human task component of Oracle BPM 11g. However, in some cases, especially advanced-use cases requiring custom Java plug-ins, additional detail may be needed. At the time of writing of this book, the documentation for human tasks was split between two books: the *Oracle Fusion Middleware Developer's Guide for Oracle SOA Suite* and the *Oracle Fusion Middleware Modeling and Implementation Guide for Oracle Business Process Management*. *Part V—Using the Human Workflow Service Component* of the former provides a good coverage of the basic human workflow concepts and capabilities. Some more powerful aspects of the human task component, including rule-based list builders, swim-lane roles, parametric roles, and activity guides are available only as part of the BPM product and are covered in the second book mentioned. In the next chapter, we will cover building user interfaces for human tasks.

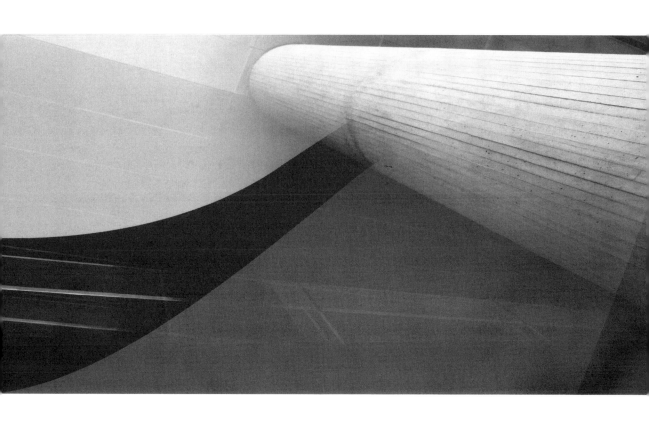

CHAPTER
8

Developing Rich
User Interfaces for
BPM with ADF

ost business processes have a human interaction aspect to them. It is important to provide intuitive and easy-to-use user interfaces to the people interacting with Human Tasks to facilitate adoption, lower learning costs, and improve productivity. Oracle BPM 11*g* sits on top of Oracle Application Development Framework, which is a very powerful and capable development framework that includes rich user interface capabilities. Correct usage of its capabilities leads to significant benefits, while requiring little incremental investment in learning and development. Since this chapter covers some topics in significant detail, readers may prefer to skim some sections (specifically the code snippets), and return to them later as needed. At the same time, this chapter cannot claim to do justice to the breadth and depth of capabilities offered by ADF; interested readers may pursue the pointers provided at the end of this chapter for further learning.

Overview of Oracle ADF

Oracle Application Development Framework (ADF) is an end-to-end application development framework and is built on the principles of model-view-controller (MVC) architecture. It sits on top of the standard Java Platform, Enterprise Edition (Java EE), and leverages this standard. Oracle ADF is pre-integrated with Oracle BPM Suite 11*g* for the generation and development of task forms, which are the user interfaces leveraged by process participants to start a process or perform their activity in a process. However, Oracle ADF is a very capable and deep framework and is used to build all of Oracle's middleware products, including BPM Suite 11*g*, and Fusion Applications. ADF can also be used by customers to build their own custom applications.

Because Oracle ADF is used extensively and exclusively within Oracle for building Fusion Applications and Middleware, it implements the best practices and patterns encountered in building applications. The repository of scenarios, use cases, and requirements it draws upon, and provides built-in support for, is very broad and deep. For example, it not only simplifies data access but also provides out-of-the-box behavior such as master-detail synchronization (automatically changing displayed records for child or detail elements when parent or master record selection is changed), query-by-example (QBE) (querying for records by providing patterns for one or more fields), and transaction management.

The main building blocks of Oracle ADF are shown in Figure 8-1.

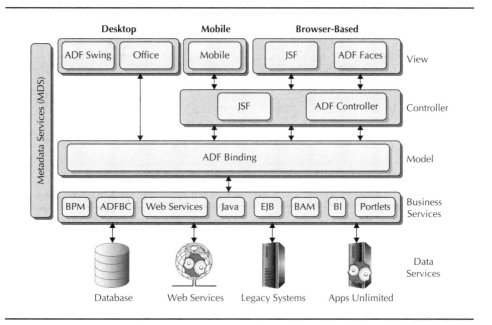

FIGURE 8-1. *ADF building blocks*

ADF Faces Rich Client Framework (View)

ADF Faces Rich Client (ADF Faces for short) is the default view layer for ADF. It comprises more than 150 rich JSF (Java Server Faces) components with built-in AJAX (Asynchronous Java Script and XML) functionality. Components include hierarchical tables, trees, menus, dialogs, accordions, tabs, and dividers. ADF Faces also includes ADF Data Visualization components for rendering dynamic charts, graphs, gauges, Gantt charts, and other graphics.

In addition to a rich set of visual components, ADF Faces provides built-in advanced functionality including drag-and-drop framework, dialog and pop-up framework, and active-data push to automatically push updated data to user dashboards as it becomes available on the server. ADF Faces also promotes reuse with features including templates and declarative components. Plus, it supports customization and skinning, along with internationalization and accessibility and rendering on multiple devices. In addition to ADF Faces, Oracle ADF also supports Apache MyFaces Trinidad, Swing, ADF Mobile, and MS Excel (via Desktop Integration) as view layer technologies.

ADF Mobile

The ADF Mobile framework enables extension of an ADF application to mobile devices, reusing all the business services and other concepts.

The ADF Mobile Browser delivers a mobile-optimized native look-and-feel user interface to mobile browsers. It adjusts to the device's browser capabilities, leveraging advanced capabilities of the smartphone browsers, optimizing UI with browser-specific CSS, and degrading gracefully to support HTML browsers.

ADF Desktop Integration

ADF Desktop integration enables the creation of spreadsheets that are bound to the bindings exposed by the ADF model layer. This allows a user to create spreadsheets that can access and update data from, and invoke operations on, back-end services including BPM, all without writing a single line of code.

ADF Task Flows (ADF Controller)

ADF Task Flows are the controller layer for ADF applications providing an enhanced navigation and state management model on top of JSF page flow. Task Flows, unlike the basic JSF navigation mechanism, can not only handle navigation between pages, but can also include method invocations and case statements. ADF Task Flows are discussed in the section "ADF Task Flows" later in this chapter.

ADF Data Control and Bindings (Model)

ADF model provides a service abstraction called data control, which provides a consistent service and data interface on top of a variety of back-end technologies; the data control is bound to user interface elements via a binding layer, typically as part of an EL (Expression Language) expression. A number of data controls are built-in and developers can add their own. Data controls and bindings are discussed in the section "The ADF Model Layer—Data Control and Bindings" later in this chapter.

ADF Business Components (Business Services)

ADF Business Components (BC) provides a declarative fourth-generation language (4GL) for building database-centric business services. It includes support for entity objects that represent tables in the underlying database and view objects that represent query specifications and that return collection of entities in response to a query. ADF-BC supports declarative specification of properties for attribute, validation logic, list-of-values (LOV), and calculated fields. While ADF-BC enables most common requirements in a declarative fashion, it also provides hooks for developers to extend or customize the functionality with Java. ADF Business Components are discussed in the section "ADF Business Components" later in this chapter.

Some Basics

Before diving further into ADF, it is useful to review a couple of basic JSF concepts that are fundamental to further discussion.

Expression Language

In this chapter, expressions of the form *#{...}* will be frequently encountered. These are JSF Expression Language (EL) expressions. Here are a few examples to illustrate JSF EL:

- **#{myBean.myVar}**   *myVar* property (could have been a method as well) of *myBean*

- **#{bindings}**   The ADF bindings object

- **#{bindings.title.inputValue}**   The *inputValue* attribute of a binding named *title*

- **#{!bindings.Delete3.enabled}**   If *enabled* attribute of a binding *Delete3* is *false*

- **#{a.b != "test"}**   If *a.b* is not equal to *test*

- **#{a.b == "test" ? val1 : val2}**   If *a.b* is equal to *test*, then *val1*, else *val2*

NOTE
In addition to #{} JSF EL also continues to support the JSP syntax of ${}; the former uses deferred evaluation (that is, the JSF controller evaluates the expression at the appropriate stage in the page's life cycle) and the latter uses immediate evaluation (that is, the JSP engine immediately parses and evaluates the expression), and should be used only for read-only access.

More details on JSF EL can be found at http://developers.sun.com/docs/jscreator/help/jsp-jsfel/jsf_expression_language_intro.html.

Managed Beans

Throughout this chapter, Java code snippets will be provided and the term managed bean will be used. ADF and JSF applications support the concept of managed beans—beans whose life cycle is managed by ADF/JSF. The bean is a Java class that allows access to its persistent state through setters and getters. A managed bean is registered with ADF as part of either the bounded task flow definition or the adfc-config.xml file from the *Managed Beans* vertical tab within the *Overview* horizontal tab within JDeveloper's task flow editor.

A scope needs to be specified for the managed bean that governs its life cycle; scopes help control the amount of objects kept in the memory. The rule of thumb is to use the smallest possible scope for managed beans. A bean that does not hold any state or that does not need to persist its state across requests should be set to *requestScope,* which is a standard servlet scope. However, in ADF Faces partial requests (for AJAX behavior; discussed later in this chapter within section "ADF and JSF Life Cycle") spawn a request cycle, and if the bean's state is to be persisted across partial requests *viewScope* should be used. For beans that should save state across the task flow *pageFlow* scope is appropriate. Other scopes with broader scope including *application* and *session* are rarely needed when using ADF for BPM task forms and should be avoided.

Properties exposed by a bean can be initialized in the managed bean by adding managed properties corresponding to the bean properties. For more information on the object scopes, please see section "4.6 Object Scope Lifecycles" within the "Fusion Developer's Guide."

BPM Task Forms

BPM task forms are the user interfaces that end users use to initiate processes as well as perform activities in the process. A BPM task form typically has a form for viewing and editing data. It usually includes the ability to add comments and attachments. Most importantly, it gives end users the ability to take actions (e.g., approve, reject, escalate, and so on) on their work items. By default, Oracle BPM 11*g* leverages ADF for task forms. BPM 11*g* includes form-generation capabilities that can generate fully deployment-ready forms that can be used without any further edits. These generated forms can also be further edited or extended to meet even the most sophisticated requirements.

Task Form Generation

Oracle BPM 11*g* has three flavors of form generation.

- **One Click**   A ready-to-deploy task form is automatically generated in a new project; no options are offered.

- **Wizard Driven**   Offers more options, including the choice of a template and multi-row-column layout; a ready-to-deploy task form is generated in a new project.

- **Task Flow Based on Human Task**   Only a task flow and task data control are generated; the page needs to be created using ADF designer's drag-and-drop form creation capabilities leveraging the generated Human Task data control and possibly other data controls. This option generates the artifacts inside an existing project.

In all three options, a task data control and a bounded task flow are generated. In the first two options, a complete page corresponding to the view activity in the task flow is also generated. In the third option, a page is not generated; however, the Human Task drop handler (as described in the next section and shown in Figure 8-3, Human Task drop handler is the Human Task specific menu presented when the *Task* element is dragged and dropped on the page from a Human Task data control) can be used to create a complete page. Therefore, even the third option is not much extra work. While the first two options are great for those who would be comfortable with the auto-generated form and do not want to get inside ADF, the third option is better for anyone with even minimal comfort with ADF as it provides more flexibility on the structuring of projects and so on.

BPM Data Control

The most important artifact generated as part of any of the form generation options is the Human Task data control. The generated Human Task data control is named *<ui project name>.<task name>*. A sample Human Task data control displayed inside JDeveloper's *Application Navigator* window is shown in Figure 8-2.

As can be seen in Figure 8-2, the *TableExUI_EnterDocTask* task data control has an element **Task** that is a child node of *Data Control* ≫*getTaskDetails* ≪*Return*; this is the effective root node for working with task data controls. Some of the interesting elements contained within *Task* are:

- **Payload** As can be seen in Figure 8-2, *Task* has a child element *Payload*; each parameter of the task is a child of the *Payload* element. The *DocElement* and the *Section* elements seen within the *Payload* node in Figure 8-2 are based on the schema used to define the variables in the payload (the concept of payload variables is discussed within the previous chapter on *Advanced Human Tasks*); the schema used in this example is shown in Figure 8-23.

- **Task Attributes** Attributes of the *Task* element contain task summary information such as task title, due date, priority, and others. These attributes, as well as the system attributes discussed next, are the same for every task.

- **System Attributes** Detailed information about the task; has child elements for assignee (that is, the users, groups, or roles that the task is assigned to), task history, and other information.

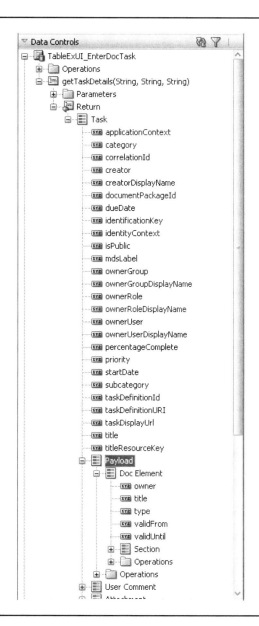

FIGURE 8-2.   *Human Task data control*

Human Task Drop Handlers

In addition to standard ADF drop handlers, when the *Task* element is dragged and dropped on to the page canvas, Human Task specific drop handlers are available that offer options of creating task headers, task actions, comments, and so on, as shown in Figure 8-3.

NOTE
The parameters that are prompted for when the Task *element of a task data control is dropped onto a view can be left unspecified.*

Refreshing Task Data Control

If the task definition changes within the BPM application, the task data control can be refreshed to reflect the new changes. If the changes are

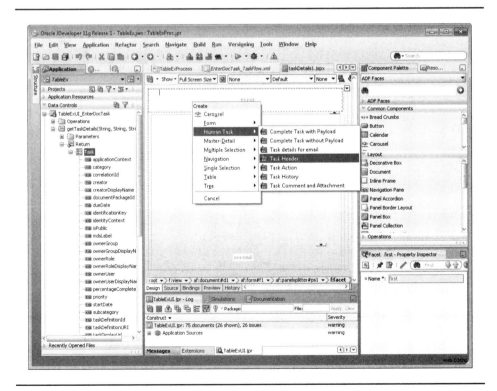

FIGURE 8-3. *Human Task drop handlers*

additive, existing bindings are not impacted and new elements can be added by dragging and dropping them. If a bound element is deleted, then the binding of the UI elements will need to be updated or the UI elements need to be deleted.

Unlike ADF-BC and other data controls, the Human Task data control is not refreshed by the refresh icon in the data controls panel. Instead, to refresh Human Task data control, right-click the data control and select *Edit Definition,* as shown in Figure 8-4.

Data Control Element Definitions

Under *Application Sources* inside a package with the same name as the data control, XML files containing the definitions of task data control elements are generated. In particular, for each parameter type, a *typeName.xml* file is

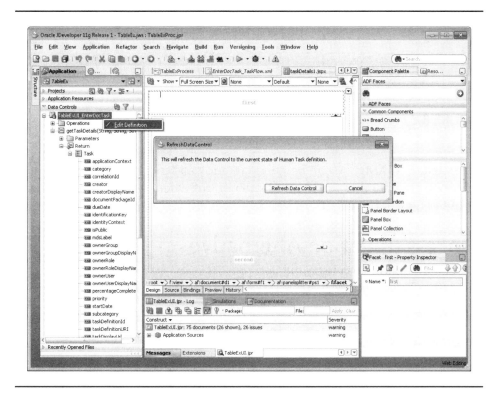

FIGURE 8-4.   *Refreshing task data control*

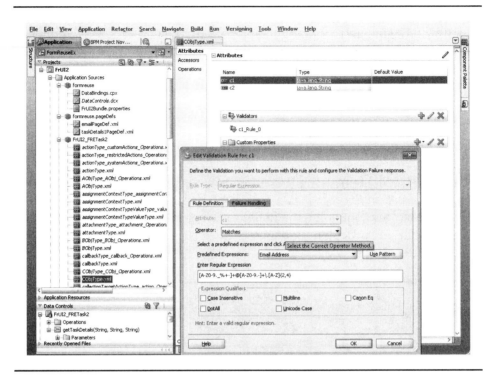

FIGURE 8-5. *Validation rules on task data control elements*

generated. This XML file can be edited to add validation rules as shown in Figure 8-5; the additions made here are not lost when the data control is refreshed (as discussed in the preceding paragraph).

Process Initiation Alternative

The default option for a user-initiated process is to use an initiator task and generate a Task Form for it, as discussed earlier. The benefits of this approach are:

■ BPM takes care of exposing the initiation link only to authorized users.

■ The process can have initialization logic to personalize the form or populate it with appropriate data.

An alternative option is to separate the initiation UI from the process and have the initiation UI launch the process either via a service invocation or via an event (events are discussed later in this chapter in the section "ADF Business Components"). In this approach, a custom mechanism for exposing the initiation link to authorized users needs to be provided because swim-lane roles are not available outside the process. The benefits of this approach are:

■ The initiation UI can be built into a page, which may provide easier access.

■ If the initiation is abandoned, no process is created.

Tips and Recommendations

This section presents a few tips and suggestions to improve the productivity and overall experience of working with ADF, especially in the context of BPM.

Working with ADF Page Editor

While the ADF page editor is a visually intuitive development environment, a couple of tips provided here can improve the overall experience.

Design This Container

Ancillary information on BPM Task forms, such as task header, comments, and attachments, can be distracting when working with the main form content. The design canvas can be focused on the form content by selecting the appropriate element in the structure window (*af:showDetailHeader: #{resource.CONTENTS}* if using the auto-generated form), using right-clicking it, and then selecting *Design this Container*. This causes the design canvas to display only the selected element and its descendents; the normal view can be restored by clicking either the small blue box with two left arrows or anywhere in the canvas outside of the element's design area (the tooltip will show *Click to edit main page* in both cases).

Leveraging the Structure Window

It is sometimes tricky to find the correct drag-and-drop insertion point inside nested layout elements in the design window. The *Structure* window offers a much more precise mechanism for dragging and dropping content into the form as well as for repositioning elements in the form. When adding from the component palette, drag and drop is not even needed; just selecting a node in the *structure* window and clicking the component palette item adds it inside the selected node. Also, right-clicking a structure window node offers insertion choices including *Insert Inside, Insert Before,* and *Insert After.* Cut-copy-paste is also available in the structure window and can be used to add similar items very easily.

Debugging and Running in Integrated Server

Although BPM and SOA 11g cannot be run inside the Integrated WebLogic Server (the one running inside JDeveloper), BPM forms can be debugged and run inside the Integrated Server because BPM tasklists and task forms can be deployed on non-BPM domains using foreign JNDIs (and other mechanisms).

To enable this feature, set up the JDeveloper integrated server with the required foreign JNDIs and libraries (a script to do this, along with instructions, can be downloaded from this book's web site). To debug or run a form inside the integrated server, right-click the bounded task form XML file in the application navigator window and select *Debug* or *Run.* The page that is launched should be ignored; instead, if the environment has been set up correctly, the URL for the form on the BPM server is updated to point to the integrated server. Thus, opening a task from the BPM Workspace will use the integrated server. In addition to debug features such as setting up break points and stepping through code, debugging or running in the integrated server environment provides another powerful benefit—any changes to the page's metadata are picked up on form reload, without needing any compilation or deployment. The automatic reload works only for page metadata changes. Any change in bindings or managed beans requires compilation and deployment (that is, executing the *debug* or *run* command again). Once the debug/run session is over, deploying the form to the BPM server will update the form URL to point to the form deployed on the BPM server.

JDeveloper also allows remote debugging—that is, debugging the form running on the BPM server. However, whenever possible, the integrated server option is recommended as the alternative requires running the whole of BPM server in debug mode and this may degrade performance.

Form Reuse

Although the primary unit of reuse in Oracle BPM is a task file, in some situations there are multiple task files with the same payload data. Different task files may exist due to differences in assignment and other policies. In such cases, the same form can be reused for the different tasks. To automatically register the same task flow for multiple tasks, add additional *hwTaskFlow* entries to the *hwTaskFlow.xml* file in the *Application Sources* folder, as shown in the following snippet (three tasks are pointing to same task flow):

```
<hwTaskFlow>
  <WorkflowName>FRETask1</WorkflowName>
  <TaskDefinitionNamespace>.../FormResuseEx/FRETask1</
TaskDefinitionNamespace>
  <TaskFlowId>FRETask2_TaskFlow</TaskFlowId>
  <TaskFlowFileName>WEB-INF/FRETask2_TaskFlow.xml</
TaskFlowFileName>
</hwTaskFlow>
<hwTaskFlow>
  <WorkflowName>FRETask2</WorkflowName>
  <TaskDefinitionNamespace>.../FormResuseEx/FRETask2</
TaskDefinitionNamespace>
  <TaskFlowId>FRETask2_TaskFlow</TaskFlowId>
  <TaskFlowFileName>WEB-INF/FRETask2_TaskFlow.xml</
TaskFlowFileName>
</hwTaskFlow>
<hwTaskFlow>
  <WorkflowName>FRETask3</WorkflowName>
  <TaskDefinitionNamespace>.../FormResuseEx/FRETask3</
TaskDefinitionNamespace>
  <TaskFlowId>FRETask2_TaskFlow</TaskFlowId>
  <TaskFlowFileName>WEB-INF/FRETask2_TaskFlow.xml</
TaskFlowFileName>
</hwTaskFlow>
```

Differences in actions can also be handled, if needed, by defining the union of actions across all tasks for which, the form is to be reused as the set of actions for the task from which the data control is generated, and then configuring the *Access* settings for this task to disable the extra actions.

Parallel Development of the BPM Process and Task Form

In many cases, different developers work on the BPM process and its related forms. In such cases, development can be parallelized by the BPM developer providing the UI developer with a proxy process application. This application should have a task corresponding to each task in the real process application, with the same payload and actions, along with processes that just create tasks (that is, have no real process flow), initializing data, if needed. The UI developer(s) can then develop and work against these proxy tasks—not only isolated from changes in the process, but also with an easy path to getting to the task (that is, with no need to play the whole scenario). If the payload or action for the actual task changes, the process developer should make the changes to the corresponding task in the proxy task, and the UI developer can update the task data control. The same form that the UI developer develops against the proxy task can be used for the real task as well by just adding an additional entry in the *hwtaskflow.xml* file as described in the subsection on *Form Reuse*.

Another benefit of the preceding approach is that the UI developers don't necessarily need to have a BPM server instance of their own; they can use the integrated server, as mentioned in the subsection on *Debugging and Running in Integrated Server,* and access the proxy tasks on the BPM developer's BPM server instance.

The placeholder data control (described later in this chapter within the section *Data Control*) also has a useful role to play in the early phase of development before the data shape has been defined. However, shift to the task data control as early as possible to avoid surprises—the capabilities of the task data control are sometimes different from the placeholder's.

Deployment

BPM deployment offers the option of deploying the forms (in a separate application) along with the BPM application. The author recommends only using this option when auto-generated forms will be used as is. The UI and the process go through separate life cycles, and typically the UI may iterate a lot more than the process. Also, as recommended earlier, the integrated server should be used for the UI during development. Tying the process application and UI application together is therefore not advisable.

Forms should be deployed instead by right-clicking the application node in the *Application Navigator* (not the project node but the application node), selecting deploy, and then selecting a deployment profile. Deployment profiles for the application can be created, updated, and deleted by right-clicking the application node in the *Application Navigator,* selecting *Application Properties,* and then choosing *Deployment* in the properties window.

For application management reasons, all forms for a process application are usually deployed as one application. However, for iterative development, it is much better to deploy one form at a time. When using the integrated server during iterations, this is not an issue because the debug or run command will deploy and run only one project, so the deployment profile (that deploys to the BPM server) can be configured to deploy a single application. If using BPM server during UI iterations, it may be useful to have multiple deployment profiles: one with all forms in one application, and one each for every project by itself. If doing so, *Web Context Root* conflicts should be avoided by using different project deployment profiles with different web context root settings (just as for application deployment profiles, this is available from the project properties). At the end of iterations, the end-state deployment profile (one with all forms in one) should be deployed and tested to avoid surprises (such as class path conflicts).

NOTE
If deploying multiple projects in one application, each project should have a different view prefix *to ensure that files with common names are in unique packages.*

Forms for E-mail

BPM e-mail notifications include (by default, but can be turned off if needed) a static HTML version of the form. However, since e-mail clients have different HTML and CSS capabilities, it is advisable to provide a form tailored for e-mail instead of relying on the web form to be rendered in e-mail as well. This is even more important if the web form is a multipage task flow.

To provide a different form for e-mail, a router activity can be used to route to an e-mail–specific view based on the test: *#{pageFlowScope .bpmClientType == 'notificationClient'}*, as shown in Figure 8-6. The router activity should be made the default activity for the task flow. Within the e-mail specific page the *Human Task* drop handler, *Task Details for Email*, may be used to generate a form targeted at e-mail clients.

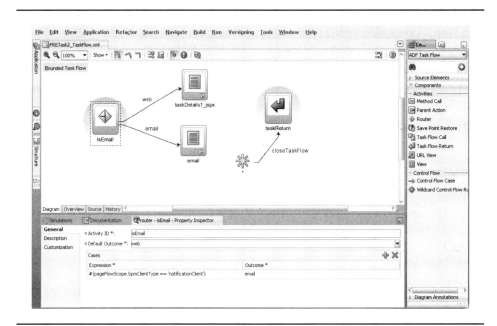

FIGURE 8-6. *An e-mail-specific form in task flow*

Task Forms in Non-ADF Technology

While ADF is the default technology choice for developing BPM forms with many benefits, both from the perspective of ADF's features as well as the integration between BPM and ADF, customers may have standardized on a different framework. BPM provides APIs to support worklists and task forms to be built on a different framework. Chapter 31, "Building a Custom Worklist Client" and Chapter 32, "Introduction to Human Workflow Services" of the "Oracle Fusion Middleware Developer's Guide for Oracle SOA Suite," which is part of Oracle's product documentation, provide good information in this regard. Also, you can find samples and links to samples for this at the BPM's site at the Oracle Technology Network.

The ADF Model Layer—Data Controls and Bindings

Bindings were one of the most powerful new features in JSF. They enabled separation of code from the view definition, allowing access to values from backing bean properties or resource bundles via simple expressions of the form: #{myBean.myAttr}.

Oracle ADF takes the concept further, and using a combination of Data Control and Bindings provides a unified access to data and methods exposed by underlying business services. As shown in Figure 8-7, the Data Controls are framework adapters working with the specifics of different business service technologies. The Bindings layer sits on top of the Data Controls and provides the interfaces needed by the view layer in the application.

Data Control

A data control consists of two pieces: the Java classes implementing the business service adapter, and the metadata, which includes its graphical presentation, describing the business service attributes, collections, and

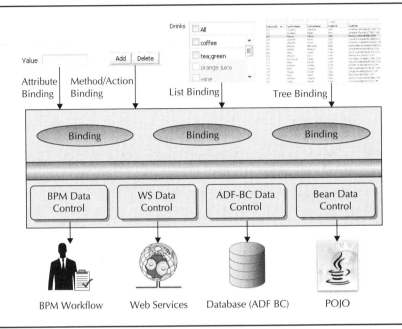

FIGURE 8-7. *The ADF model framework—unified access to business services*

methods. While it's possible for developers to write their own data control implementation, in this chapter we will limit our discussion to the built-in data controls and focus on the metadata aspect. The following are some of the built-in data controls:

- **Task Data Control** The task data control works with Human Tasks in BPM (and is sometimes referred to as the BPM Data Control). This data control is discussed in detail earlier in this chapter in the section "BPM Task Forms."

- **BAM Data Control** The BAM Data Control lets ADF interface with queries on top of BAM data objects. While Oracle BAM provides dashboards that can be designed by business users in web-based BAM studio, the BAM Data Control enables the integration of BAM events and dashboards embedded in ADF pages.

- **ADF-BC Data Control**   The ADF-BC Data Control provides access to ADF-BC views exposed through an ADF-BC module. Unlike other data controls, this data control does not need to be explicitly created and there is no additional XML file used for this data control's metadata. An ADF-BC data control is automatically available for every ADF-BC module in the application. As discussed later in this chapter, ADF-BC is useful in many BPM scenarios. Therefore, for BPM developers, this is usually the second most used data control after the task data control.

- **Placeholder Data Control**   As the name indicates, a placeholder data control is a stand-in data control that works without any backing business service layer and is useful for prototyping. Placeholder data controls can be used to create page layouts and page flows, including all view behavior such as validations and drag-and-drop without using a business service–bound data control. Placeholder data controls can also include sample data that makes it easy to visualize the page, especially when data-visualization components like charts and graphs are used.

A placeholder data control can be created using the *New* gallery, which can be launched by using the File / New menu. In the *New* gallery, *Place Holder Data Control* is available as an *Item* when in the *Categories* tree the *Data Controls* child node of the *Business Tier* node is selected. Once the data control is created, its type is defined by right-clicking the data control node in the *Data Controls* accordion panel in the *Application Navigator* window and selecting *Create Placeholder Data Type,* which launches the placeholder data type editor shown in Figure 8-8.

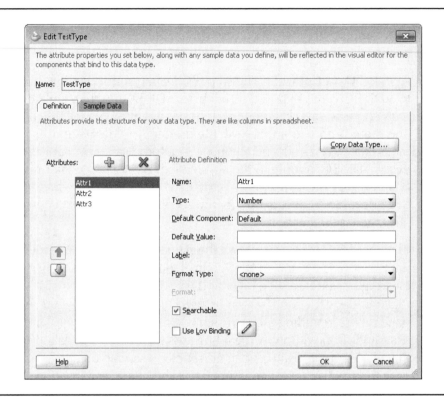

FIGURE 8-8.   *The placeholder data type editor*

The placeholder data control supports String, Boolean, Date, and Number types for attributes. The *Sample Data* tab of the placeholder data type editor allows entering or importing sample data as a CSV file. Instead of creating the type definition manually, the attributes can be created based on an imported CSV file—attributes of type *String* are created based on the first row in the CSV file.

The placeholder data control supports hierarchical types. To create a child element, right-click a placeholder type node in the *Data Controls* accordion panel and select *Create Placeholder Data Type* (as in the preceding paragraph). The parent–child relationship is maintained using the first attribute of the parent as the foreign key in the child. This means that more than two levels of parent–child can be created but cannot be seeded with sample data correctly (this limitation is planned to be addressed in future releases).

- **Web Service Data Control**   A web-service data control provides a quick and zero-code option for invoking web services. It is created from the *New* gallery (the same location as the placeholder) based on a WSDL. However, for more robust usage, using WS Proxy and creating a bean data control from it is a better option because it provides more flexibility in exception handling and service invocation.

- **Bean Data Control**   Data control based on a Java bean can be created by right-clicking the Java file in the *Application Navigator* window and selecting *Create Data Control.*

- **EJB Data Control**   Works with an EJB session bean.

- **URL Data Control**   URL Data Control allows the accessing of CSV and XML files from a URL. This is useful when working with servlets and other providers that return simple text content such as an RSS feed. This type of data control is read-only.

- **JMX Data Control**   Works with JMX MBeans from an MBean server.

Bindings

As shown in Figure 8-7, *Bindings* work in conjunction with data controls, gluing UI components to the underlying data controls and using standard Expression Language (EL), independent of the type of data control.

When UI components are created either using drag-and-drop from a data control or using BPM form generation wizards, the appropriate bindings are automatically created and wired to the component's properties. Therefore, the only thing about bindings that many developers need to know is how to use them in expressions—for example, when making one input field conditionally dependent on another. Bindings are accessed via expression language using the form: #{bindings.*bindingAttribute.property*}—for example #{bindings.title.inputValue}, #{bindings.title.hints.label}—where *title* is the name of a bound attribute. Expression Builder can be used to edit expressions using bindings; bindings are available within the *bindings* child node of the *ADF Bindings* node, as shown in Figure 8-9. The expression builder can be launched from within the *Property Inspector* window by clicking the down-arrow button on the right side of the property-value field for most properties and then selecting *Expression Builder* from the pop-up menu.

The bindings for a page can be accessed from the *Bindings* subtab of the page editor, as shown in Figure 8-10. While JDeveloper automatically adds and deletes bindings, this *Bindings* subtab can be used to manually add, delete, or edit bindings.

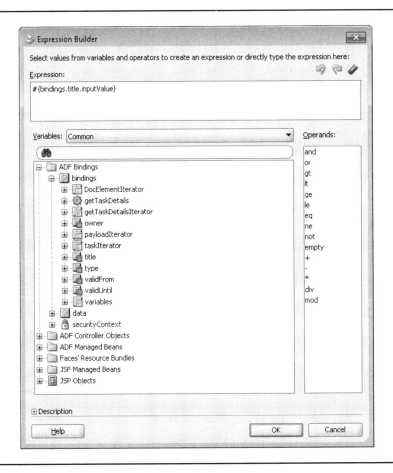

FIGURE 8-9. *Bindings in expression builder*

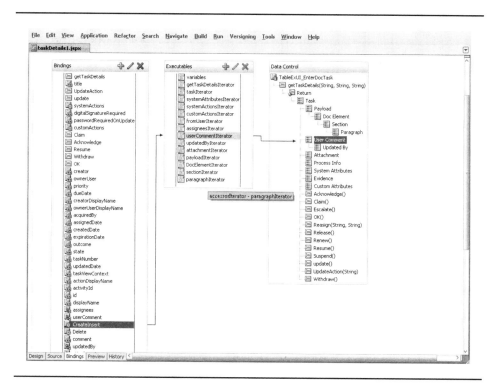

FIGURE 8-10. *Page data bindings*

In Figure 8-10, in addition to the Data Control, we see *Bindings* and *Executables*; the bindings are linked to the data controls via executables. The other thing we see in Figure 8-10 is that different bindings have different icons, indicating that they are of different types. There are different types of bindings because there are different types of UI components. The different types of bindings are:

- **Attribute Binding**   Binds a single attribute value; typically used in input components or output text fields.

- **Tree Binding**   Binds a collection of data; typically used for tables, trees, tree-tables, and hierarchy viewer components. This is discussed further in the section "Collection Components" later in this chapter.

■ **Action Binding** This binds operations provided by data controls. Human Task data control exposes *Create* and *Delete* operations for collection subelements. ADF-BC data controls expose a variety of operations including *Execute, Find, Create, CreateInsert,* and *Delete* for collection subelements. Typically, such a binding will be bound to a button or a link.

■ **Method Binding** Binds methods exposed by a data control. The Human Task data control exposes methods including *Update, UpdateAction, Reassign, Escalate,* and *Claim,* as well as methods for actions such as *OK, APPROVE,* and *REJECT.* Just as in the case of action binding, typically these will be bound to a button or a link.

■ **List Binding** Used for defining the contents of data-bound list components, such as radio groups and drop-down lists. This is discussed further in the section "Select Components" later in this chapter.

■ **ListOfValues Binding** Binds data to list-of-values (LOV) components. This works primarily with ADF-BC components that have model-driven LOVs. For more information on this option, please see the discussion on List of Values in the section "View Objects" later in this chapter.

Executables
The other element seen in Figure 8-10 is *Executables.* The different flavors of executables are:

■ **Iterators** In most scenarios, the executable used will be an iterator, which links other bindings to a data control via attributes and collections. Iterators enable working with collections. For example, if a Human Task has a *Section* child of a *DocElement*, the iterator for *Section* is:

```
    <accessorIterator MasterBinding="DocElementIterator"
Binds="section"
                    RangeSize="25" DataControl="TableExUI_
EnterDocTask"
                    BeanClass="TableExUI_
```

```
EnterDocTask.SectionType"
                        id="sectionIterator"/>
```

As can be seen in the preceding snippet, the iterator points to the parent's iterator. The attributes for the *Section* element are exposed through the iterator defined in the preceding snippet as illustrated in the following underlying XML snippet:

```
<tree IterBinding="sectionIterator" id="section">
   <nodeDefinition DefName="TableExUI_
EnterDocTask.SectionType"                         Name=
"section0">
      <AttrNames>
        <Item Value="title"/>
        <Item Value="type"/>
        <Item Value="subtype"/>
      </AttrNames>
   </nodeDefinition>
</tree>
```

■ **Variables**   Enables local variables defined as part of bindings; typically used for arguments to a method call.

■ **Invoke Action**   Enables invoking an action on another executable. For example, if an ADF-BC component exposes the *ExecuteWithParams* operation, the operation can be invoked using an invoke action executable. This will be used later in this chapter to implement dependent lists in the section "Selection Components."

Accessing Bindings from Java

While the declarative bindings enable a wide variety of scenarios in a zero-code manner, there are scenarios where some logic needs to be programmed in backing Java beans. Scenarios include handling collection drag-and-drops, copying values from one data control to another, and advanced custom behavior. The bindings can be accessed from Java code. Some of the important classes to be aware of are:

■ **DCBindingContainer and BindingContainer**   The *oracle.adf.model .binding.DCBindingContainer* class corresponds to the *bindings* element in the declarative bindings and provides access to bindings contained in a page. It implements the interface *oracle.binding .BindingContainer*. The binding container can be accessed in the backing bean, as shown in the following code snippet:

```
import oracle.adf.model.BindingContext;
import oracle.binding.BindingContainer;
import oracle.adf.model.binding.DCBindingContainer;
...
BindingContext bctx = BindingContext.getCurrent();
BindingContainer bindings = bctx.getCurrentBindingsEntry();
DCBindingContainer bindingsImpl = (DCBindingContainer)
bindings;
```

The binding container may also be injected into the backing bean by having a property *bindings* in the bean of the type *BindingContainer*, having getters and setters for it, and then passing *#{bindings}* as a managed property for the backing bean, as shown in Figure 8-11.

■ **DCIteratorBinding** The *oracle.adf.model.binding.DCIteratorBinding* is used to access the iterator binding. Typical scenarios include accessing the iterator binding to get or select the current row.

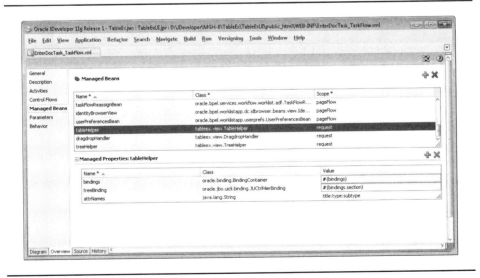

FIGURE 8-11. *Injecting bindings to managed bean*

In this chapter, we will see usage of iterator binding in programmatically selecting a row in a table and in handling collection drag-and-drop. The following snippet shows how an iterator binding can be accessed from a binding container by name.

```
import oracle.adf.model.binding.DCIteratorBinding;
import oracle.jbo.Row;
...
DCIteratorBinding iterBinding =
bindingsImpl.findIteratorBinding("sectionIterator")
```

As with bindings, the iterator binding can also be injected into the managed bean via managed properties, instead of being accessed by name. Also, the iterator binding can be retrieved from a control binding (*DCControlBinding* and its subclasses).

■ **DCControlBinding**   The *oracle.adf.model.binding.DCControlBinding* class is the base class for all component binding classes. It provides methods including *getRowIterator* and *getCurrentRow* to get the current *RowIterator* and *Row,* and *getDCIteratorBinding* to get the iterator binding. The subclasses for different flavors of bindings are:

  ■ **Attribute Binding**   *oracle.jbo.uicli.binding.JUCtrlAttrsBinding,* which implements the interface *oracle.binding.AttributeBinding.*

  ■ **Tree**   *oracle.jbo.uicli.binding.JUCtrlHierBinding;* nodes within the tree are of subclass *oracle.jbo.uicli.binding .JUCtrlHierNodeBinding.*

  ■ **Action** and **Method**   *oracle.jbo.uicli.binding.JUCtrlActionBinding,* which implements the interface *oracle.binding.OperationBinding.* If parameters need to be passed to the method from Java, they can be passed by putting *<param-name, param-value>* pair to the hash map returned by the *getParamsMap* method.

  ■ **List**   *oracle.jbo.uicli.binding.JUCtrlListBinding.*

ADF Faces

As mentioned in the introduction, ADF Faces is the view layer of the ADF stack and provides a large number of AJAX-ready components, browser-safe layouts, drag-and-drop functionality, and other behavior. While we start this section with a discussion on layout, readers who wish to simply extend generated forms may prefer to jump to the section "Data Forms."

Layout Components

In older UI technologies, developers would position elements on a page. However, such positioned page layouts are not ideal for today's web-based UIs, where not only different users have different screen sizes, but they can also access the page from different devices. Therefore, the new generation UI technologies such as ADF and JSF provide page designs based on relative positioning through the nesting of layout containers that adjust nicely to different devices and screen sizes.

ADF has a very rich set of layout components (containers), but the choice and power available, along with the accompanying rules and constraints, may seem intimidating at first. Readers should note that ADF is a full UI development framework and many of the capabilities included are more targeted toward stand-alone UI pages. For BPM forms, which don't typically need to include application facets such as the navigation bar and so on, many developers can get away with simply understanding and using a single layout component: the Panel Group Layout. However, some BPM form developers may want to make their form layout richer. A few example scenarios include:

- Providing summary information like customer profile or spending report dashboard on the left side of the form, such that this left-content does not scroll with the main-content.

- Using tabs to organize and arrange content (please also see the section "ADF Task Flows" in this chapter because task flows also provide a mechanism for arranging content in multiple pages).

- Ensuring that task header information—including title, due date, and actions—occupies the top of the available view area, and task footer information like comments and attachments occupy the bottom of the available view area, while the rest of the form occupies the remaining center position and scrolls within it.

■ Providing the ability to resize or minimize certain areas to maximize the view area available to the primary content.

In this section, we discuss some of the ADF layout components needed to achieve the scenarios just described. The depth of discussion in this section is intended to provide readers with an overview of the available options. Readers who decide to use rich layouts may refer to the additional material referenced in the section "For More Information" at the end of this chapter. The author strongly recommends that instead of building layouts on their own, developers should use the layout options provided by JDeveloper, as shown in Figure 8-12. Or they can use the templates shipped with BPM, or develop their own (as discussed earlier in the section "BPM Task Forms," BPM form generation wizards include templates and support custom templates).

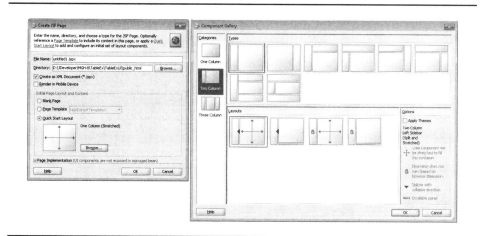

FIGURE 8-12. *Creating a JSF page based on templates and quick start layouts*

Stretching vs. Flowing

An important concept to understand regarding layout in ADF is that of stretching versus flowing. Flowing layout means laying out the child elements of a layout component sequentially, horizontally, or vertically, and wrapping as needed. Child element sizes are determined by their style and other attributes and content. As the name indicates, stretching involves stretching the elements to adjust the view space available.

This concept is best explained with an example. Figure 8-13 shows a flowing page and Figure 8-14 shows its stretched counterpart.

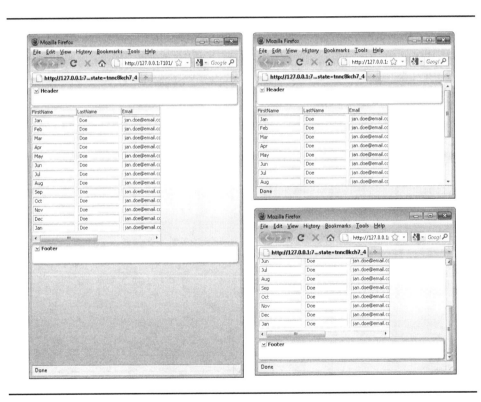

FIGURE 8-13. *Flowing page*

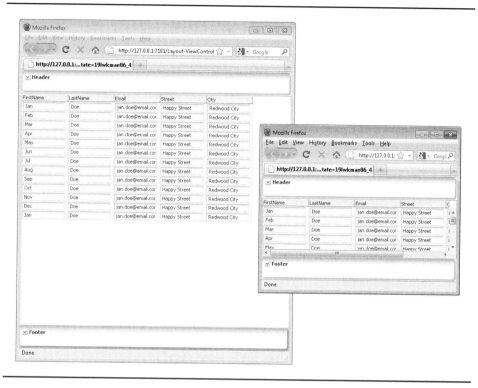

FIGURE 8-14. *Stretched page*

The first browser window in Figure 8-13 highlights the implication of not stretching when more view space is available. Two things can be noticed in this window:

- The *Footer* is placed significantly above the bottom of the browser window. This is because the table in the center has only that many rows and has not been stretched.

- Although horizontal space is available, the table in the center is truncated (as can be seen in Figure 8-14; it has more columns).

NOTE
The table here is simply used as an example of a child element that may need to be stretched. The particular issue of columns being truncated in spite of available horizontal space can be addressed in the preceding example by setting the table's property styleClass *to* AFStretchWidth.

The second and third browser windows in Figure 8-13 highlight the implication of not stretching when view space available is less than needed and scrolling is needed. As can be seen in these windows, scrolling scrolls the whole page and may scroll the *header* and *footer* out of the viewing area.

The first browser window in Figure 8-14 shows how a stretched layout maximizes the use of available view space. The table in the center is stretched—in this case, since there are not enough rows, there is white space—but unlike Figure 8-13, the white space is coming from the component and not the browser. Among other things, this means that the footer is at the bottom of the browser window. The second browser window in Figure 8-14 shows how stretching enables the header and footer to always be within the viewing area even when the table needs to be scrolled.

In ADF, there are two aspects of stretching: whether a component stretches its content or children and whether the component itself can be stretched or not. Table 8-1 summarizes the behavior of some of the components in this regard. Components that cannot be stretched should not be placed inside components that stretch their children; transition components, such as Panel Group Layout with the type set to scroll (or vertical), should be used to nest non-stretching components inside stretching components. As a best practice, when using stretching components, start with stretching components, and within stretching components (which may be hierarchically nested) create islands of flowing content using Panel Group Layout.

Component	Is Stretched?	Stretches Its Children
Panel Group Layout	If: ■ layout="vertical", or ■ layout="scroll"	No; provides transition between stretching and flowing components
Panel Stretch Layout	Yes	Yes
Panel Splitter	Yes	Yes
Decorative Box	Yes	Yes
Panel Tabbed	If: ■ dimensionsFrom = "parent"	If: ■ dimensionsFrom = "parent", and ■ ShowDetailItem contains only one child, or ■ stretchChildren="*first*" for the ShowDetailItem
Panel Box	Stretched if: ■ type="default" and its parent layout component is stretching the panelBox (for example, panelDashboard) ■ type="stretch" Not stretched if: ■ type="default" and its parent layout component is not stretching the panelBox (for example, panelGroupLayout) ■ type="flow"	If: ■ being stretched by its parent, or ■ type="stretch"
Panel Header	No	No
Show Detail Header	No	No
Panel Label and Message	No	No
Panel Window	No	Yes
Dialog	No	Yes

TABLE 8-1. *The stretching behavior of components*

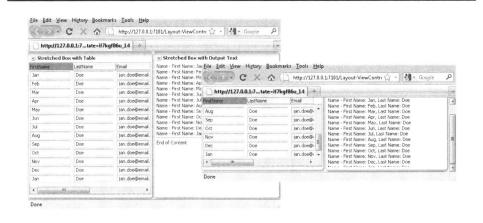

FIGURE 8-15. *Overflowing stretched content*

Stretching and Scrolling

When working with stretched containers, it should be noted that the
browser scroll bar cannot be relied on to scroll the content inside the
container correctly. The first browser window in Figure 8-15 shows an
example where there are two stretched containers (in this case, Panel Box).
One of them encloses a table and the second encloses the table rows
outputted as text (using Iterator and Output Text). The second box includes
an "End of Content" text at the end. The second browser window shows the
same example with the browser resized. As can be seen in Figure 8-15,
even with the browser scroll bar all the way to the bottom, the bottom
content of the second box is truncated. Since the table offers its own scroll
bar, the content inside the first box behaves correctly.

The preceding example highlights that stretched containers should not
contain overflowing content. The issue in this example can be resolved by
using a Panel Group Layout with *type* set to *Scroll*. As shown in Figure 8-16,
the Panel Group Layout offers its own scroll bar that scrolls the content
correctly.

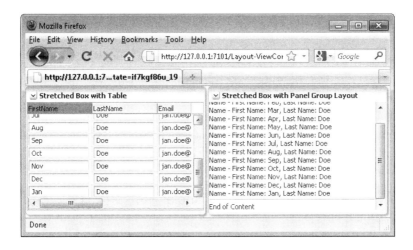

FIGURE 8-16. *Overflowing stretched content wrapped in Panel Group Layout*

NOTE
Multiple scroll bars may lead to distracting pages. Stretched layouts should avoid creating multiple horizontal containers with possibly overflowing content. It may be a good design to primarily use side columns to display content that need not be scrolled and let only the center area scroll.

The Panel Group Layout Component

As mentioned earlier, this is the layout component that every developer needs to know about. This is not only the most commonly needed component, but it is sufficient for many scenarios. This component arranges its children in one of a few simple patterns based on its *layout* attribute. The behavior for different values of *layout* is:

- **default** Consecutive layout as defined by the browser, with wrapping allowed, and following the bidirectional layout algorithm. As a result, in the presence of mixed right-to-left and left-to-right text, contents may not display consecutively.

- **horizontal** Strictly consecutive without wrapping.

- **vertical** Vertically stacked.

- **scroll** Mostly same as vertical; the difference from vertical is that scrollbars are displayed if content overflows (this layout option is only intended for cases where the panelGroupLayout is being stretched as discussed earlier).

TIP
When using horizontal *layout, the* valign *attribute specifies the vertical alignment. Valid values include: middle, top, bottom, and baseline.*

As discussed earlier, this component is the ideal component for transitioning from stretched components to non-stretched components. This component is also useful for creating complex input fields like Name where multiple subfields need to be arranged. This is discussed in the section "Data Forms" in this chapter.

The Panel Stretch Layout Component

This component is probably the most used stretch component. This component stretches the child in the *center* facet to fill all available space. This component also supports *top, bottom, start,* and *end* facets and stretches them as well. A common page design pattern is to have a branding bar on the top along with primary navigational links and some header information about the page, a vertical bar on the left providing utilities such as categories in the context of shopping, a vertical bar on the right offering session and profile information like shopping cart and recent purchases, and a footer with copyright, contact, and other similar information surrounding the main content in the center. The facets of this component directly map to this type of page design.

The sizes of the surrounding facets are controlled by the *topHeight, bottomHeight, startWidth,* and *endWidth* attributes; however, if a facet is empty, it does not render. Instead of specifying absolute pixel values, percentage values may be specified to achieve a multicolumn layout. For example, the page shown in Figure 8-15 and Figure 8-16 has *startWidth* set to *50%.*

The Panel Splitter Component

The Panel Stretch component does not give the end-user any control over the sizing of the different regions. Many times, it is desired that the end-user be able to resize the different regions or even hide them, as needed. This is accomplished with the Panel Splitter, nesting them as needed.

A Panel Splitter divides a region into two parts—the *first* facet and the *second* facet—with a repositionable divider. The splitter tries to stretch the contents of both sections. A panel splitter can split horizontally or vertically based on the *orientation* attribute. Another interesting attribute for this component is *positionedFromEnd* which not only controls which side the initial position of the repositionable divider is measured from, but also which side of the divider can be collapsed—the side from which the position is measured is the side from which it can be collapsed.

The Decorative Box

The decorative box component applies a bordered look (that is, rounded corners) to its children. It also supports changing the rendered theme of its children, so it can act as a visual transition between areas on a page. For example, a page that has a dark background for its template can use the decorative box to transition to a white background for its main area. Otherwise, it is similar to the Panel Stretch component but divides a region into only two sections: a *top* facet and a *center* facet.

The Panel Border Layout

The *panelBorderLayout* component can be considered the flowing counterpart of *Panel Stretch Layout*. This layout element lays out all of its children consecutively in its middle, and supports 12 other facets including top, bottom, left, right, start, and end. For horizontal facets, two flavors—left/right and start/end—are supported. The first is fixed left and right, whereas the second respects bidirectional-text settings and adjusts left and right accordingly.

Tabs and Accordions

The *Panel Tabbed* and *Panel Accordion* layout components can be used to display a group of contents. For each tab or accordion panel, a *Show Detail Item* (common) component must be added to the tabbed or accordion layout component. The content goes inside the *Show Detail Item.*

Headers

Often it is required to group together sections of a form and give it a header. ADF Faces components supporting this include:

- **Panel Box**   Used to place ancillary information on a page, offset by a certain color.

- **Panel Header**   Places a label and optional icon at the top of a section. This can be many levels specified by the size attribute. It can support fancy headers with its facets. It is also used for displaying ADF messages such as errors, warnings, and others.

- **Show Detail Header**   This is just like Panel Header but collapsible.

- **Show Detail**   This is collapsible too but supports a simple header (disclosed and undisclosed text attributes).

Other Layout Components

ADF Faces has many more layout components including:

- **Panel Dashboard**   Arranges fixed-size height children (panel boxes) into rows and columns and supports drag-and-drop reordering. This is useful for displaying a set of fixed-size dashboards, including charts and other visualization elements.

- **Dialog and Popup Window**   *Dialog* control displays its children in a dialog window; it must be a child of *Popup,* an invisible control. *Panel Window* is the same as a dialog except for its buttons.

Some other layout components including Panel Form Layout and Panel Collection are also discussed later in this chapter.

Data Forms

Most BPM UI scenarios involve presenting forms to process participants where they can view and input data elements for the process. Such forms would constitute the content of one or more of the sections created by other layout components in the preceding section. In many cases, the data form is the only element in the UI and, as discussed earlier, can be contained simply within a Panel Group Layout (vertical).

Panel Form Layout

Typically, input and output elements will be surrounded by a Panel Form Layout, which positions its children such that their labels and fields align vertically. A Panel Form Layout is automatically added when using a drop handler to create an *ADF Form* or *ADF Read Only Form.* If needed, it can also be added from the component palette.

NOTE
While Panel Form Layout is technically a layout component, given its importance to data forms, it is covered in this section instead of the preceding section on layout components.

As can be seen in Figure 8-17, Panel Form Layout supports the multicolumnar layout of its children. By default, it lays out its children in a single column because the *rows* attribute is set to a very high number. The *rows* attribute specifies the number of rows after which a new column should be started—for example, a value of 1 means that even if there are only 2 elements, use multiple columns, whereas a value of 5 means that use a second column only if there are 6 or more elements, and a third column only if there are 11 or more elements. The number of columns to

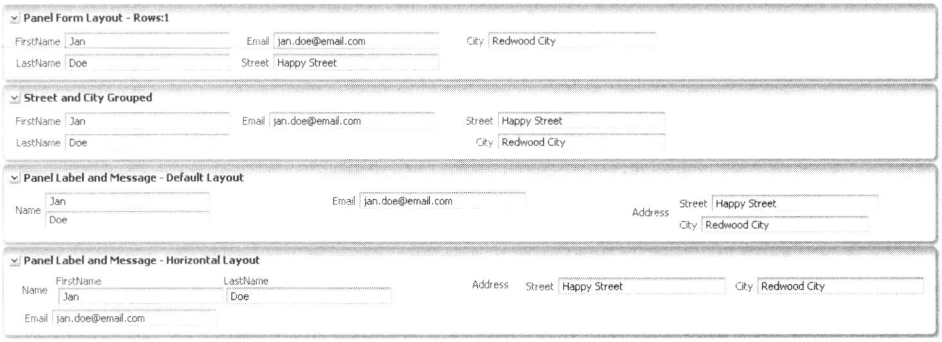

FIGURE 8-17. *Form examples*

use is governed by the *maxColumns* attribute, which defaults to 3 for web and 2 for PDAs; however, if the Panel Form Layout is nested within another, only a single column is used.

The *labelAlignment* attribute specifies where the labels for the child element should be placed: start or top. The Panel Form Layout also has a *footer* facet where buttons and button bars should be placed.

Group

When elements are wrapped in multiple columns, sometimes elements that should be together for ease of understanding can get separated into different columns—for example, in the top-most box of Figure 8-17, Street and City are in different columns. This can be addressed by surrounding the components that should be logically placed together in an *af:group* element. The easiest way to do this is to use right-click one of the elements, select *Surround With*, and then choose *Group* from within the *ADF Faces* category. This adds a group element that the other elements can be dragged and dropped into, preferably within the *structure* window. The second box (from the top) of Figure 8-17 shows the result of grouping Street and City this way.

Within a Panel Form Layout, separators are drawn around the grouped elements if they are adjacent to other form elements.

Panel Label and Message

In some scenarios, it is required to not only group related elements, but also provide a common label. Sometimes this is referred to as compound fields. The Panel Label and Message component can be used for creating such compound fields. In Figure 8-17, the third and the fourth box shows the result of using Panel Label and Message to create *Name* from *First* Name and *Last Name* and *Address* from *Street* and *City*.

Panel Label and Message can be created similar to group by right-clicking one of the elements, selecting *Surround With,* and then choosing *Panel Label and Message* in the *ADF Faces* category, and afterward dragging and dropping the rest of the elements inside the added component.

By default, Panel Label and Message will lay out the children vertically, as seen in the third box in Figure 8-17. Also, the labels for the children can be turned off by setting their attribute *Simple* to true, as has been done for First Name and Last Name in this example. If the labels are not turned off, they will display as per the label display for the enclosing Panel Form Layout; the result can be seen for *Street* and *City* in the third box in Figure 8-17.

Often in compound fields, it is desired to have the subfields laid out horizontally instead of vertically. This can be achieved by nesting a *Panel Group Layout (Horizontal)* in the *Panel Label and Message*. As mentioned in the preceding paragraph, if labels are not turned off, they will be positioned per the setting for the enclosing *Panel Form Layout*. The *Address* field in the fourth box in Figure 8-17 shows the resultant layout. A Panel Form Layout nested inside another panel form layout lays out its labels on top, so if it is desired to lay out the labels for the subfields on top, the subfields should be wrapped in a nested *Panel Form Layout*. The *Name* field in the fourth box in Figure 8-17 shows the resultant layout.

The components used and their nesting is shown in Figure 8-18 for the second, third, and fourth box in Figure 8-17.

Input Components

ADF has a rich collection of input components that allow users to view and edit data. Some of the commonly used input components are shown in Figure 8-19. These components can not only be used in simple forms but also within tables, trees, and others, as discussed in following sections.

FIGURE 8-18. *Structure window for the form examples*

As seen in Figure 8-19, some commonly used input components by data type are:

- **Text (String)** *Input Text* is the component for entering text. If formatted text input is desired, then *Rich Text Editor* can be used. The *Secret* attribute of *Input Text* can be used to hide or mask the input value.

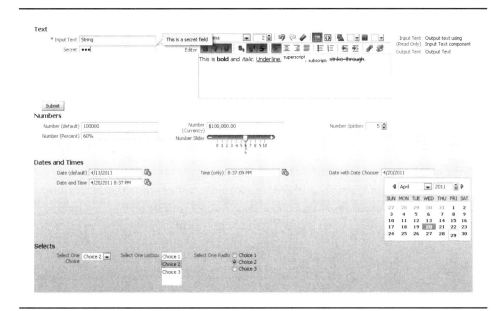

FIGURE 8-19. *Input components*

- **Numbers** *Input Text* is the most commonly used component for entering numbers as well. The built-in converter—*af:convertNumber*— should be used to handle percentages and currencies by setting its *type* attribute to *percent* or *currency,* respectively. The result of using this can be seen in the *Number (Percent)* and *Number (Currency)* elements in Figure 8-19. In addition to *Input Text,* components including *Input Number Slider* and *Input Number Spinbox* are available to input numbers.

- **Date and Times** *Input Date* is the component for entering dates. The attribute *type* of the built-in converter—*af:convertDateTime*— should be used to specify whether the component is used for date, datetime, or time-only input values. The values for the *type* attribute are *date, both,* and *time.* By default, the date and time chooser is a pop-up launched by clicking the calendar icon next to the input area; however, if an inline chooser is desired, a *Choose Date* component can be added to the form and the *ChooseId* attribute of the *Input Date* component should be set to the ID of the *Choose*

Date component (also, as discussed earlier in the section "Group" in this chapter, the two components should be grouped to keep them together). All flavors of the date component discussed here can be seen in the *Dates and Times* section in Figure 8-19.

■ **Boolean**   The *Select Boolean Checkbox* component can be used for displaying Boolean values. If a set of Boolean values are desired to be displayed as radio buttons, the *Select Boolean Radio* component can be used.

In addition to entering values, ADF provides a number of components to select one or more values. These will be discussed later in the section "Select Components." Also, in addition to the components covered here, ADF has a rich set of components including input file selector, color picker, carousels for pictures, and others.

The input components share many attributes in common. Some of the more useful attributes are discussed next:

■ **Value**   The data element that is tied to this component. Typically of the form: *#{bindings.<attr>.inputValue}*. When dragging and dropping from the data control, this is automatically set.

■ **Label**   The label to display. When dragging and dropping from a data control, it is typically bound to *#{bindings.<attr>.hints.label}*. Task data control creates the *hints.label* based on the attribute name—thus, for an attribute named *attributeName*, the label will be "Attribute Name". To use custom labels, as well as use localized strings from resource bundles, the value of the label attribute should be changed accordingly. Some attributes related to a label are:

  ■ **Simple**   If set to *true,* the label is not displayed. This is useful when the input component is nested within a table's column or a Panel Label and Message.

  ■ **Access Key** and **Label and Access Key**   An access key is a mnemonic or key stroke that navigates to the component when the browser-specified modifier (ALT+SHIFT for Mozilla and ALT for Internet Explorer) is used. The Label and Access Key lets a user set the label and access key in one setting, appending "&" to the access key character—for example, a value of *Or&der* will result in a label "Order" and an access key of "d". If needed, the access key can be set separately from the label using the *Access Key* attribute.

■ **ShortDesc**   The value of this attribute is displayed as a tooltip. When bound to a data control, the value of this attribute is typically set to *#{bindings.<attr>.hints.tooltip}*. However, task data control does not provide a value for *hints.tooltip,* so if tooltips are needed, the value for *ShortDesc* should be specified.

■ **ReadOnly**   This indicates whether the component is read-only or editable. Can be an expression based on values of other data elements.

■ **Required**   This indicates whether the component is required. This, similar to read-only and other attributes, can be an expression based on values of other elements; however, dependent validations are somewhat tricky and are discussed in the section "ADF Life Cycle" in this chapter. When bound to a data control, the value of this attribute is typically set to *#{bindings.greeting.hints.mandatory}*. However, task data control always sets *hints.mandatory* to *false,* so if certain elements are required, the value of *Required* should be specified.

■ **RequiredMessageDetail**   The value of this attribute is displayed when a required element is not entered.

■ **Auto Submit**   This indicates whether the value of this component should be automatically pushed when the component loses focus without waiting for a form submit event such as a button click. This is typically needed when there are other components on the page that depend on this component's value. This is discussed in the section "ADF Life Cycle."

While the theme of this section is input components, the same components can be used in read-only mode as discussed earlier. Moreover, the *Output Text* component can be used to display read-only data. The *Output Text* component comes without a label, but can be wrapped in a *Panel Label and Message*. The two options for displaying read-only data are shown in the top-right corner (the third column with *Text*) of Figure 8-19.

Select Components

ADF includes a rich set of select components, some of which are seen in the bottom section of Figure 8-19. The list of choices available in the select components can be configured declaratively for most scenarios.

The easiest way to add a select component is to drag and drop the corresponding element from the data control to the ADF page and choose the select component from the options presented. This launches the List Binding editor shown in Figure 8-20. The *Base Data Source* specifies the data element that is updated with the selection. When dragging and dropping an element from data control, this value is automatically populated to the iterator containing the dragged-and-dropped element. Three options are available for specifying the list of choices:

- **Dynamic List**   The list is obtained dynamically from the specified data source. A common scenario is to obtain the values from a database—in which case, an ADF-BC view object can be used to get the values. In addition to getting the values from a database, they can be retrieved from any other supported data service such as a Web Service, or even passed as part of the same data control as the element to be updated. As seen in Figure 8-20, multiple elements of the list data source can be mapped to elements of the base data source—all mapped elements are updated based on selection. In the example shown in Figure 8-20, selecting a value for *type* will not only update *Attr3* but it will also update *Attr1* to the value of the *Id* corresponding to the selected *Type*.

- **Fixed List**   As the name indicates, a static list of values can be specified. This is useful when the list of choices is not expected to change.

■ **Model Driven List**   This option is available for ADF-BC and other data controls that support the configuration of LOV settings in the model itself. This option is not available for task data control and will not be discussed here. The ADF LOV components require model-driven lists and are therefore not applicable to page elements bound to task data controls.

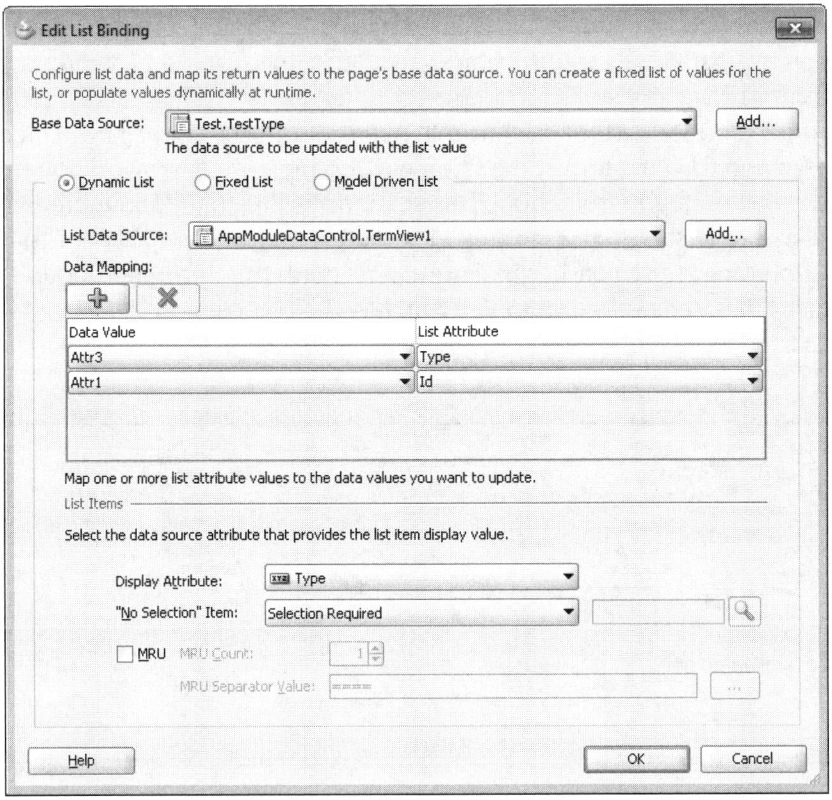

FIGURE 8-20.   *The list binding editor*

NOTE
If instead of dragging and dropping from data control, a select component is added from the component palette, it expects a List binding to be available to bind to the component. If needed, a new list binding can also be created from the Bindings *tab.*

Dependent Lists

As discussed earlier, when using the dynamic list option, the list binding can be configured to select multiple related values in one selection. However, there are scenarios where the choices available in a list are based on a selection in another list. For example, contract terms may be organized in categories, and for ease of selection the UI requires the user to first select a category and then the terms, the choices for which are narrowed down based on the category selection. This scenario is illustrated in Figure 8-21. (In the example shown in Figure 8-21, the *Term* select component is tied to the list binding shown earlier in Figure 8-20, with the *Term* field bound to *Attr3* and the *ID* field bound to *Attr1* of *Test.TestType*.)

Illustrate Pick Lists

Selecting Category determines the choices for Term. Selecting Term automatically sets ID based on the ID of Term.

Dependent Pick Lists

Category PriceHoldOptions

Term FutureProgramPriceHolds

ID 20

Verify Selections

Category - Verify

PriceHoldOptions

Term - Verify

FutureProgramPriceHolds

FIGURE 8-21. *The dependent list scenario*

For the list of choices to filter the data source, the list needs to support filtering. If ADF-BC is used to retrieve the list from a database, as in the earlier example, *View Criteria* can be defined on the ADF-BC view to do the needed filtering. The list data source (iterator) needs to be configured to get the filtered view. This is accomplished by:

■   Defining an *Action* binding to the appropriate operation exposed by the data source. For this example, the action binding binds to the operation *ExecuteWithParams* as shown in Figure 8-22. The parameter *cat* exposed by the ADF-BC view object is bound to the data value for the *Category* field (*Attr2*) via the EL expression *#{bindings.Attr2.inputValue}*.

■   The action binding defined above needs to be invoked by adding an *invokeAction* executable within *Executables*. The settings for this executable are shown in Figure 8-22. The *Refresh* attribute is important in getting this to work properly. If you are not sure, use *ifNeeded* as a safe choice.

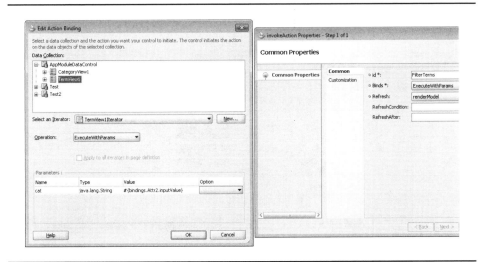

FIGURE 8-22.   *Using action binding and invoke action to get a filtered list*

Finally, the controlling component should be configured for auto-submit and the controlled component should have its partial-trigger set to the controlling component so the choices in the controlled component automatically refresh when a controlled component's value changes. (The concepts of auto-submit and partial-triggers are discussed in the "ADF Life Cycle" section in this chapter.)

Collection Components

BPM scenarios often involve working with collection data elements—that is, data elements that may occur multiple times. Also, these elements may often be nested hierarchically. For example, Figure 8-23 shows a sample

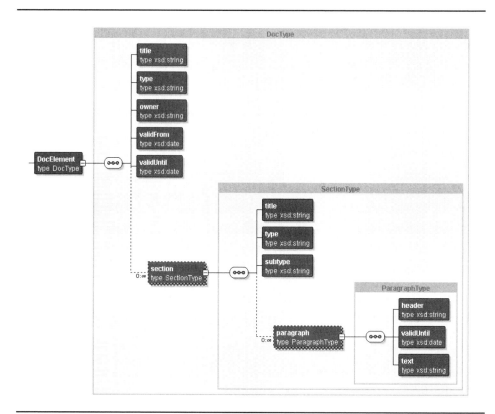

FIGURE 8-23. *Sample data type with hierarchical collection elements*

data type where a document may have one or more sections and each section may have one or more paragraphs. This data type will be used to illustrate the collection components in the following discussion.

Panel Collection

Before diving into collection components, it is useful to mention *Panel Collection,* which is a layout component designed to wrap collection components. In addition to providing a visually appealing rendering of collection components, it offers significant additional built-in functionality related to collections, such as hiding/showing columns. This component provides facets for toolbars, menus, and status bars, and it has a built-in view menu, to which additional menu items can be added using the *viewMenu* facet. Features provided by the panel collection that are not desired can be turned off by setting the value of the attribute *featuresOff* to a space-separated list of features to be turned off—common features include *statusBar, viewMenu, wrap, freeze,* and *detach.*

The panel collection component is stretched by stretching containers. If placed within a flowing container, the *styleClass* property for the component can be set to *AFStretchWidth* to occupy 100 percent of the parent's width.

Tables

The ADF Faces Table component is the most commonly used component for tabular display. The table component provides rich behavior including row and column selection, filtering, sorting, banding, and so on. The columns of a table component can use the input and select components discussed earlier. The table component can be stretched by its parent. Figure 8-24 displays a form for the data type shown in Figure 8-23 designed using the table component. This figure will be used throughout the discussion on tables to illustrate various features. For now, readers may just review the tables and ignore the other details—the relevant details will be called out later.

A table component is typically bound to a *Tree* binding, which is usually created when the table is inserted by dragging and dropping a collection element from a data control to an ADF page. The *value* attribute of the table is typically set to the *collectionModel* property of the tree binding—an

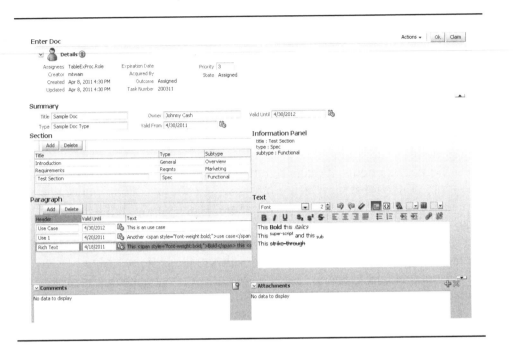

FIGURE 8-24.   *A sample table*

example value is *#{bindings.section.collectionModel}*. The *var* attribute of
the table specifies the name of a variable that would hold the value for
each row of the table; input and other components within the table would
typically access data via this variable—for example, using expression
#{row.bindings.title.inputValue}, where *row* is the value for the *var* attribute
and *title* is an attribute in the collection data element.

Some of the interesting attributes of the Tree component are:

■ **Row Selection and Column Selection**   None, single, or multiple.
(The examples in this section assume the row selection is set to
single.) Row selection is discussed in greater detail later in this
section. Enabling column selection allows the freeze column
behavior.

- **Column Stretching**   Specifies how to fill up empty horizontal space. The default is to do nothing. From a visual perspective, this should be set to either the column that is expected to have the most content or to *empty,* which causes an empty column to be added.

- **Grids and Banding**   *HorizontalGridVisible* and *VerticalGridVisible* specify the visibility of grid lines, and *RowBandingInterval* and *ColumnBandingInterval* specify the banding behavior. (Banding causes groups of rows and columns to be displayed with alternating background colors.)

- **Fetch Size**   ADF tables and trees do on-demand fetching of rows, bringing only enough rows from the server to fill the available view space. The Fetch Size attribute specifies how many rows are fetched in one time; a small value for this setting may result in multiple fetches.

- **Editing Mode**   A close look at Figure 8-24 reveals a subtle difference between the table used for *Section* and the one used for *Paragraph.* In the first, only the selected row (the third row) has input components enabled and the other rows are displaying as read-only, whereas in the second, all rows have input components enabled. This is specified by the *editingMode* attribute; setting it to *clickToEdit* makes only the selected row editable.

TIP
The clickToEdit *mode is recommended due to performance reasons; the author also finds it aesthetically more pleasing.*

Column   A table component wraps one or more column components. The components nested within the column components are displayed within the cells of the table. The header for a column can be specified using the *HeaderText* attribute. If needed, the *header* facet of the column can be used for a richer column header. The *sortable* and *filterable* attributes of the column specify the sorting and filtering behavior.

Columns can nest other columns to create spreadsheet-like grouped columns.

Adding and Deleting Rows   Typically, a data control will provide operations to add and delete rows to a collection. These operations can be bound to buttons on the table. A Human Task data control includes *Create* and *Delete* operations for every collection in the data control. For example, the add and delete button for the sections table in Figure 8-24 have their *action listener* attributes set to #{bindings.CreateInsert3.execute} and #{bindings.Delete3.execute}, respectively, where CreateInsert3 and Delete3 are action bindings bound to the *Create* and *Delete* operation of the *Section* iterator as shown in the following XML fragment:

```
<action IterBinding="sectionIterator" id="CreateInsert3"
RequiresUpdateModel="true" Action="createInsertRow"/>

<action IterBinding="sectionIterator" id="Delete3" RequiresUpdateModel=
"false" Action="removeCurrentRow"/>
```

The partial-trigger for the table should include the buttons, and the buttons should have the *partialSubmit* property set to *true*. If the buttons are added by dragging and dropping the previously mentioned operations from the data control, the drop handler sets up everything correctly including the partial-triggers.

The preceding discussion assumes a single selection table. Deleting multiple rows in a multiselection table can be achieved in backing bean Java code. One possible implementation is to set each selected row as the current row in the iterator and then invoke the *Delete* operation.

Selection   The simplest configuration to handle single selection correctly is to set the *Selection Listener* attribute to an expression of the form #{bindings.section.collectionModel.makeCurrent} and *Selected Row Key* to an expression of the form #{bindings.section.collectionModel.selectedRow}, where *section* is the name of the *tree* binding.

Some scenarios may require some custom processing in the selection listener. If needed, the following code excerpt shows how to handle this in backing Java code:

```
public void onTreeSelect(SelectionEvent selectionEvent) {
    /* custom pre processing goes here */
    // If needed the added rows can be retrieved using
    RowKeySet rks = selectionEvent.getAddedSet();
```

```
    /* Default Make Current */
    RichTree tree1 = (RichTree)selectionEvent.getSource();
    JUCtrlHierBinding treeBinding =
(JUCtrlHierBinding)((CollectionModel)tree1.getValue()).getWrappedData();
    String exp = "#{bindings." + treeBinding.getName() +
".treeModel.makeCurrent}";
    executeExpression (selectionEvent, exp);
}

private void executeExpression (SelectionEvent selectionEvent, String
expr) {
    FacesContext fctx = FacesContext.getCurrentInstance();
    ELContext elctx = fctx.getELContext();
    ExpressionFactory exprFactory = fctx.getApplication()
.getExpressionFactory();
    MethodExpression me = exprFactory.createMethodExpression(elctx,
expr, Object.class, new Class[] { SelectionEvent.class });
     me.invoke(elctx, new Object[] { selectionEvent });
}
```

Also, some scenarios may require working with the table's selected row data outside of the table. For example, the *Information Panel* in Figure 8-24 displays information about the selected row. The selected row of a table can be worked with in backing bean Java, as shown in the following example code fragment:

```
private JUCtrlHierBinding treeBinding;
private String[] _attrNames = null;

public String getSelectedRow() {
  Row row = treeBinding.getCurrentRow();
  String ret = "";
  for (int i = 0; i < _attrNames.length; i++) {
    ret += _attrNames[i] + " : " + row.getAttribute(_attrNames[i]) + "\
n";
  }
  return ret;
}
```

Master-detail The master-detail pattern is commonly used when dealing with hierarchically nested collections. For example, in the page shown in Figure 8-24, the *Section* table and *Paragraph* table, as well as the *Paragraph* table and the *Text* rich-text-editor have a master-detail relationship. What that means is that selecting a row in the *Section* table filters the rows in the *Paragraph* table to only those paragraphs that belong to the selected section, and selecting a row in the *Section* table changes the text in *Text* to the text element of the selected section.

A master-detail pair can be easily added by dragging and dropping the detail element from the data control palette and selecting the appropriate master-detail option from the drop handler choices. Otherwise, it is trivial to establish a master-detail relationship between components bound to hierarchically related data source elements. It requires:

- Ensuring that the master table is configured to invoke the *collectionModel.makeCurrent* on selection as discussed earlier.

- Ensuring that the detail component (table or otherwise) has the master in its partial-trigger, so that it automatically refreshes on selection change in the master.

Tree

While master-detail tables can be used to render hierarchical data, the approach starts getting cumbersome if the depth of hierarchy is more than two levels. ADF Faces also includes a tree component that is ideally suited for displaying hierarchical data in a tree form. The example shown in Figure 8-24 was redone using the ADF Faces Tree component as shown in Figure 8-25.

The .jspx fragment for the tree in Figure 8-25 is shown next, and in the following subsections we will discuss its elements, including the node stamp and path stamp. In the following .jspx fragment, note that, similar to tables, the value for a tree is bound to a tree model (collection model for tables), there is a property *var* to define a variable that will hold the data specific to each node in the tree (row in table), and that the selection listener is set to *#{bindings.elem.treeModel.makeCurrent}*.

```
<af:tree value="#{bindings.DocElement.treeModel}" var="node"
    id="t4" partialTriggers="::cb3 ::cb4 ::cb5 ::cb6"
    rowSelection="single"
    selectionListener="#{bindings.DocElement.treeModel.makeCurrent}">
```

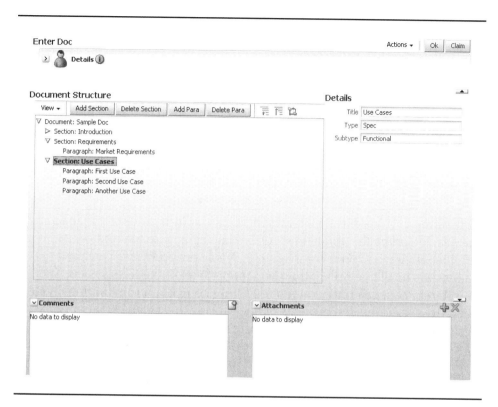

FIGURE 8-25. *A tree example*

```
<f:facet name="nodeStamp">
  <af:outputText
value='#{node.hierType.viewDefName == "TableExUI_EnterDocTask
.ParagraphType" ? "Paragraph" : node.hierType.viewDefName ==
"TableExUI_EnterDocTask.SectionType" ? "Section" : "Document"}:
#{node.hierType.viewDefName == "TableExUI_EnterDocTask.ParagraphType" ?
node.header : node.title}' id="ot16"/>
  </f:facet>
  <f:facet name="pathStamp">
    ...same as nodeStamp...
  </f:facet>
</af:tree>
```

Node Stamp The components defined inside the *Node Stamp* facet of the tree are stamped (that is, rendered) for each element in the tree. Only certain types of components are supported, including all components with no behavior and most components that implement the *EditableValueHolder* or *ActionSource* interfaces—that is, input components and command components. The *af:switcher* component can be used to render different node levels with different UI components (in the preceding code fragment, the value is switched inside the expression for *outputText*). The use of the *af:switcher* component is illustrated in the following section "Detail Form" for this example.

Path Stamp The ADF Tree component has built-in hierarchy management features, including the ability to focus by making a node the root or otherwise simplifying the view on a complex tree. These hierarchy management features are available only if the *Path Stamp* facet of the tree is used. The path stamp facet can only contain read-only components, including images and output text. The components defined inside this facet are stamped (again, rendered) for each node in the path within a pop-up hierarchy browser, which is shown in Figure 8-26 for the example shown in Figure 8-25.

The *Panel Collection* component has built-in toolbar buttons for hierarchy management. For example, the three buttons seen in the top-right corner of the *Document Structure* panel in Figure 8-25 are built-in panel collection buttons (these buttons are *Go Up, Go to Top,* and *Show as Top*). These are enabled only if the *Path Stamp* facet is used and a component in it is bound to the node.

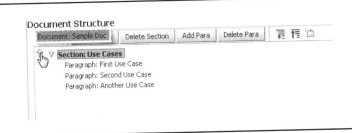

FIGURE 8-26. *The hierarchy browser for a tree*

Determining the Node Type   Since nodes in a tree can have different data definitions, it is important to be able to figure out what is the node type. The *hierType.viewDefName* property of the node can be used to determine the type. The values for each level in the tree can be determined from the bindings file, which would have entries such as the following snippet:

```
<tree IterBinding="DocElementIterator" id="DocElement">
  <nodeDefinition DefName="TableExUI_EnterDocTask.DocType"
                  Name="DocElement0">
    ...
  </nodeDefinition>
  <nodeDefinition DefName="TableExUI_EnterDocTask.SectionType"
                  Name="DocElement1"
                  TargetIterator="${bindings.sectionIterator}">
    ...
  <nodeDefinition DefName="TableExUI_EnterDocTask.ParagraphType"
                  Name="DocElement2"
                  TargetIterator="${bindings.paragraphIterator}">
```

The value of the *DefName* attribute of the *nodeDefinition* attribute is the value that needs to be compared with *hierType.viewDefName,* for example, as in the following snippet:

```
#{node.hierType.viewDefName == "TableExUI_EnterDocTask
.ParagraphType" ? node.header : node.title}
```

Tree Binding   Similar to table, the easiest way to add a tree is to drag and drop an element from a data control to a page. This launches the same tree binding editor as in the case of the tables; however, in the case of trees the hierarchy needs to be configured in the tree binding editor by using the add button on the *Tree Level Rules,* as shown in Figure 8-27. The attributes at each level selected as display attributes will be the only attributes available through the stamped node variable.

In the case of achieving master-detail with separate tables, each table was tied to its own iterator. However, in the case of tree, one tree iterator for the root element handles the whole hierarchy. The individual levels may also have their own iterators—for example, if a detail form is bound to the individual level. To keep the tree iterator and the individual iterator in sync, use the

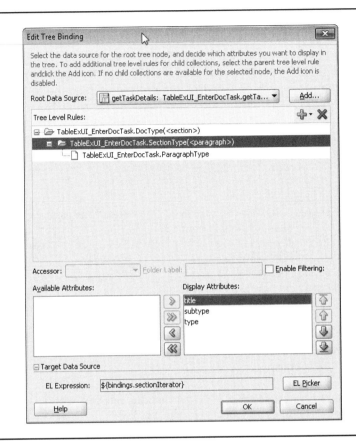

FIGURE 8-27. *The tree binding editor*

Target Data Source specification. For example, in Figure 8-27, for the tree level *sectionType,* the *Target Data Source* is set as *${bindings.sectionIterator}.* This will make sure that when the current *section* is changed from the tree, all components bound to *section* (through *sectionIterator*) will automatically switch to the new current *section.*

Detail Forms   When using a tree to display the hierarchy, it is typically desired to provide a detail form where the selected element in the tree can be edited. A *Switcher* component can be used to switch between different forms based on the selection in the tree. Assuming that there is a property *selectedNode* exposed by a managed bean *treeHelper* (that refers to the selected node in the tree), the switcher's *facetName* attribute needs to be set to #{treeHelper.selectedNode.hierTypeBinding.viewDefName}. Within the switcher, a facet needs to be added for each node type; the facet's *name* attribute needs to be set to the *viewDefName* value for the node type, which can be determined from the bindings file as discussed earlier. Within the facets, the forms for each node type can be added by dragging and dropping the corresponding element from the data control. The .jspx snippet for the *Details* panel in Figure 8-25 is shown next:

```
<af:switcher id="s9" facetName="#{treeHelper.selectedNode
.hierTypeBinding.viewDefName}" defaultFacet="none">
  <f:facet name="none">
    <af:outputText value="Select a node in the tree." id="ot17"/>
  </f:facet>
  <f:facet name="TableExUI_EnterDocTask.ParagraphType">
    <af:panelFormLayout id="pfl5">
      . . .
    </af:panelFormLayout>
  </f:facet>
  <f:facet name="TableExUI_EnterDocTask.SectionType">
    <af:panelFormLayout id="pfl6">
      . . .
    </af:panelFormLayout>
  </f:facet>
  <f:facet name="TableExUI_EnterDocTask.DocType">
    <af:panelFormLayout id="pfl7">
      . . .
    </af:panelFormLayout>
  </f:facet>
</af:switcher>
```

To programmatically find the selected node in a tree, the selected row keys need to be determined using the *getSelectedRowKeys* method of the *RichTree* component and then the corresponding nodes must be found using *findNodeByKeyPath* on the tree binding. The code to expose the *selectedNode* property used earlier is shown below:

```
public JUCtrlHierNodeBinding getSelectedNode() {
    //return _selectedNode;
    JUCtrlHierNodeBinding sel = null;
    if (_treeBinding == null) return sel;

    RowKeySet rks = _richTree.getSelectedRowKeys();
    if (rks == null) return sel;
    //iterate over the contained keys. Though for a single selection
use case we only expect one entry in here
    Iterator rksIterator = rks.iterator();
    if (rksIterator.hasNext()) {
      //get the tree node key, which is a List of path entries
describing the location of the node in the tree including its parents
nodes
      List key = (List)rksIterator.next();
      sel = _treeBinding.findNodeByKeyPath(key);
    }
    return sel;
}
```

As discussed earlier, if the tree binding's *Target Data Source* is set correctly and if the tree's selection listener is set to make the selected element current (as in the selection listener setting used earlier), the synchronization of the selection in the tree and the form element happens automatically. Of course the detail section must have its partial trigger set to the tree.

Add and Delete   Just as in the case of tables, adding or deleting new nodes is as simple as dragging and dropping the appropriate operation from the data control to create a command button. However, a few considerations may improve the user's experience:

- By default, the delete command button's *disabled* attribute is set to *#{!bindings.Delete3.enabled}*. The logic of this method provided by the data control is that *enabled* is true if a node of the appropriate node type is available up and down the hierarchy. In the example shown in Figure 8-25, if a user selects the document node, then delete paragraph will be enabled if there are any paragraphs, and trying to delete a paragraph will delete the paragraph that is current in its iterator. Since what is current will not be obvious to the user, the behavior will be confusing. It may be better to enable the delete buttons only if a selected node type is of the appropriate type. For example, the delete paragraph button's disabled property will be as shown in the following .jspx fragment:

```
<af:commandButton actionListener="#{bindings.Delete3.execute}"
    text="Delete Section "
    disabled='#{treeHelper.selectedNode.hierTypeBinding
.viewDefName != "TableExUI_EnterDocTask.SectionType"}'
    id="cb4" partialTriggers="t4"/>
```

- By default, adding a node does not select it but makes it current. In the example shown in Figure 8-25, if the user has a section or a paragraph selected, then adds a section, and then adds a paragraph, the new paragraph gets added to the new section, while the old selection continues. This can be confusing to the user. It can be resolved by making the selection change on add. The way to accomplish this is described next.

To automatically select the newly added node, the operation exposed by data control to add a node should be wrapped in Java, and the Java code should force the selection of the newly added node. The newly added node can be determined from the underlying iterator binding as it is its current row. The Java code snippet to accomplish this is shown next:

```
public void addNewSection(ActionEvent actionEvent) {
    // Add event code here...
    _addSection.execute();
    setNodeSelected (getNewSectionNode ());
}
private void setNodeSelected (JUCtrlHierNodeBinding node) {
    if (node == null) return;
    RowKeySet selected = _richTree.getSelectedRowKeys();
    selected.clear();
    selected.add (node.getKeyPath());
    _richTree.setSelectedRowKeys(selected);

}
private JUCtrlHierNodeBinding getNewSectionNode () {
    JUCtrlHierNodeBinding ret = null;
    if (_docIter == null || _sectionIter == null) {
        System.out.println ("an iter is null");
        return ret;
    }
    Key docKey = _docIter.getCurrentRow().getKey();
    Key sectionKey = _sectionIter.getCurrentRow().getKey();
    List<Key> keyPath = new ArrayList<Key> ();
    keyPath.add (docKey);
    keyPath.add(sectionKey);
    ret = _treeBinding.findNodeByKeyPath(keyPath);
    return ret;
}
```

NOTE
The preceding code fragment is hard-coded to work only for the section nodes, which are the second level of hierarchy. This can be easily generalized.

In the code, _addSection_ is exposed as a property from the managed Java bean using the code snippet below:

```
public void setAddSection(OperationBinding _addSection) {
    this._addSection = _addSection;
}
public OperationBinding getAddSection() {
    return _addSection;
}
```

The value of _addSection_ is passed to the managed bean by adding a managed property with the name _addSection_, property-class _oracle.binding .OperationBinding_, and value _#{bindings.CreateInsert3}_ (the name of the binding is indicative and may vary).

Selection   As seen earlier, just like in the case of tables, handling selections correctly is a matter of using _#{bindings.elem.treeModel.makeCurrent}_ as the selection listener, and if needed the selected node can be found using Java the code shown earlier. In some scenarios, custom selection handling may be needed. The following code snippet shows how selection can be handled correctly in Java code:

```
public void onTreeSelect(SelectionEvent selectionEvent) {
  /* custom pre processing goes here */

  /* Execute default make current */
  RichTree tree1 = (RichTree)selectionEvent.getSource();
  JUCtrlHierBinding treeBinding = null;
  treeBinding =
(JUCtrlHierBinding)((CollectionModel)tree1.getValue()).getWrappedData();

  String exp = "#{bindings." + treeBinding.getName() +
".treeModel.makeCurrent}";
  executeExpression(selectionEvent, exp);

  /* Sample snippet to show how to retrieve selected node */
  RowKeySet rks2 = selectionEvent.getAddedSet();
  Iterator rksIterator = rks2.iterator();
  if (rksIterator.hasNext()) {
      List key = (List)rksIterator.next();
      _selectedNode = treeBinding.findNodeByKeyPath(key);
  }
}
```

NOTE
The preceding code snippet works only with single-node selection trees as the addedSet *only for those nodes that have been newly selected and not for the existing selected nodes.*

```
private void executeExpression (SelectionEvent selectionEvent,
String expr) {
  FacesContext fctx = FacesContext.getCurrentInstance();
  ELContext elctx = fctx.getELContext();
  ExpressionFactory exprFactory = fctx.getApplication()
.getExpressionFactory();
  MethodExpression me = exprFactory.createMethodExpression(elctx,
expr, Object.class, new Class[] { SelectionEvent.class });
  me.invoke(elctx, new Object[] { selectionEvent });
}
```

Tree Table

ADF Faces also has a tree-table component that displays hierarchical data in the form of a table. The first column of this component is the tree. This component can display additional columns of data for each tree node in the hierarchy. The tree-table component can be understood as a combination of tree and table, and therefore is not covered in detail here; earlier discussions should apply. Some key aspects of the tree-table component are:

- **Node Stamp**   Similar to tree component, tree-table must have a node-stamp facet. However, in the case of tree-table, the node-stamp facet must contain a column. This column is rendered as the first column and as a tree inside the column. The stamping behavior of tree-table is the same as trees.

- **Path Stamp**   Same as tree component.

- **Columns**   Same as table components. However, in the case of tree-table, different levels of hierarchy may have different data definitions, so care should be taken in displaying the column data. Similar to the tree component discussion earlier, the *hierType* can be used to conditionally display elements or switch components to display.

Data Visualization Components

ADF Data Visualization components provide significant graphical and tabular capabilities for displaying and analyzing data. Like any other ADF Faces components, they can be created and bound to data sources via dragging and dropping from data control elements and their behavior is controlled by properties and facets. ADF Data Visualization components also provide the design time preview of live data. ADF Data visualization components include:

- **Graphs**   More than 50 types of graphs are supported, including a variety of area, bar, bubble, combination, funnel, line, Pareto, pie, radar, scatter, spark-chart, and stock graphs.

- **Gauges**   Typically, gauges identify problems in data by plotting one data point with an indication of whether that point falls in an acceptable or an unacceptable range. The types of gauges supported include dial, status meter (horizontal and vertical), and LED (bulbs, arrows, and others).

- **Pivot Table**   The ADF pivot table component displays a grid of data with rows and columns similar to spreadsheets and provides the option of automatically generating subtotals and totals for grid data. A pivot table allows pivoting—that is, moving data labels and the associated data layer from one row or column edge to another to obtain different views of the underlying data, supporting interactive analysis.

- **Geographic Map**   The ADF geographic map component supports representing business data on a geographic map and superimposing multiple layers of information (known as themes) on a single map, leveraging Oracle MapViewer and potentially the Spatial option of the Oracle database.

- **Gantt Chart**   The ADF Gantt chart component supports Gantt charts, a type of horizontal bar graph in conjunction with a table, typically used for project tracking. Types of Gantt charts supported include project Gantt chart, resource utilization Gantt chart, and scheduling Gantt chart.

■ **Hierarchy Viewer** The ADF hierarchy viewer component visually displays hierarchical data, typically with master-detail relationships. The most common use of hierarchy viewer may be to display an organization chart, but it can be used to visualize relationships between any other data—for example, the BPM Composer uses the hierarchy viewer to display the catalog of projects available in Composer.

Page Templates

ADF page templates provide a mechanism to ensure that pages are always consistent in structure and layout across an application. Page templates are reusable ADF Faces pages that define the page layout and common components and page fragments. Page templates contain placeholders called *facets* for authors of pages using the template to insert content specific to the page. When a page is based on a page template, content can only be inserted in the facets defined in the template. Page templates are created in JDeveloper from the *New Gallery* by selecting the *JSF Page Template* within the *JSF* subcategory of *Web Tier* category. Page templates are edited pretty much the same as ADF pages. In addition to facets, a page template can accept parameters from the page using the template. A page template can also have its own bindings in a file.

Page templates are interpreted, allowing the template to change the layout of a page without changing the page or the application itself.

BPM Form Templates

The BPM wizard-driven form generation leverages page templates. Templates included out-of-box are available inside *JDEV_HOME\soa\modules\oracle .soa.worklist_11.1.1\adflibWorklistComponents.jar*. Customers can use their own templates too; any custom template must expose the following:

■ **Facets** *Action, header, body, comment, attachment, history*; the names of the facets are clearly indicative of the content that will be generated within them.

■ **Attribute** *Title* of type *java.lang.String*; the title of the Task will be mapped to this attribute.

Custom templates should be added to an ADF Library JAR, which is created by adding a deployment profile of type *ADF Library Jar File* to the project containing the templates. The jar file containing the templates should be added to the consuming project's libraries, and then the jar file and the template can be chosen when using the wizard.

Drag and Drop

ADF Faces includes a rich drag-and-drop framework. Some drag-and-drop scenarios can be achieved without requiring any code—for example, an attribute of one component can be dragged and dropped on another component simply by adding *Attribute Drag* and *Attribute Drop Target* tags on the source and target component (assuming both attributes are of the same type).

To do something other than copy attributes from one component to another, the *Drop Target* tag needs to be added to the target. Additionally, *Data Flavor* needs to be added to the *Drop Target* to specify the type of object being dropped and the drop handling logic must be implemented in Java as a *Drop Listener.* The object of the drop event is called the *transferable,* which contains the payload of the drop. A drop listener must access the transferable object, and from there use the DataFlavor object to verify that the object can be dropped. It can then use the drop event to get the target component and update the property with the dropped object.

To drag things other than attribute values, the *Drag Source* tag may be used on the source. *Discriminant* property on *Drag Source* and *Drop Target* may be used to pair a drag and a drop.

NOTE
ADF supports additional drag-and-drop tags including Collection Drop Target, Component Drag Source, *and* Calendar Drop Target, *which are not discussed here. Interested readers can refer to Chapter 32— "Adding Drag and Drop Functionality" in the "Oracle Fusion Middleware Web User Interface Developer's Guide for Oracle Application Development Framework."*

The drag-and-drop framework supports three drag-and-drop actions based on the keyboard modifiers used:

- **Copy**   No modifier or CTRL

- **Move**   SHIFT

- **Link**   CTRL+SHIFT

To illustrate drag-and-drop handling, we will modify the example seen in Figure 8-24 to use drag and drop. As shown in Figure 8-28, we will add:

- Drag and drop from the *Section* table to the *Information* panel. On drop, we display the drag-and-drop action as well as the attributes and attribute values for the row dragged and dropped.

- Drag and drop from the *Information* panel to the *Section* table. A new row in the *Section* table is added based on the values in the input text box in the *Information* panel. (This is the scenario shown in Figure 8-28).

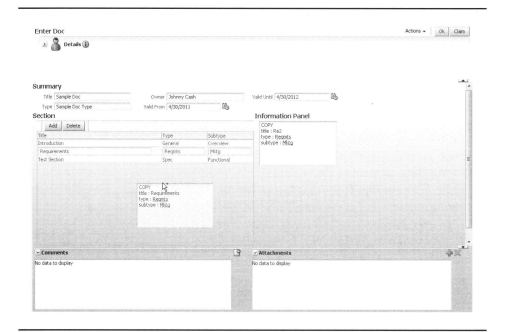

FIGURE 8-28. *A drag-and-drop sample*

Drag-and-Drop Sample: From Table to Input Text

As mentioned earlier, in this scenario we drag and drop a row from *Section* table to the input text within the *Information* panel.

First, we need to specify that the section table is a drag source. Since we are not dragging a simple attribute, we need to use *Drag Source*. This can be accomplished by selecting the table in the *structure* window, right-clicking, selecting *Insert Inside,* and then within *ADF Faces* selecting *Drag Source.* Afterward, select the *Drag* Source in the *structure* window and using the *Property Inspector* window specify *Actions* as *Copy Move, Default Action* as *COPY*, and *Discriminant* as *section.* The resultant .jspx snippet is shown next:

```
<af:dragSource defaultAction="COPY" actions="COPY MOVE"
discriminant="section"/>
```

Next, we need to specify that the input text is a drop target. First, a managed bean to hold the drop handler code should be added, if needed. The *Drop Target* can be added similar to *Drag Source* described earlier. In the dialog prompting for *Drop Listener,* use *edit* and specify a method name in the managed bean (in this case, *dropHandler* in *dragdropHandler*). In the dialog prompting for *Data Flavor, org.apache.myfaces.trinidad.model .RowKeySet* should be specified. This is the data type that the ADF drag-and-drop framework will use to drop one or more rows. Next, a discriminant should be specified on the *Data Flavor* to match the *discriminant* in the drag source. The resultant .jspx snippet is shown next:

```
<af:dropTarget dropListener="#{dragdropHandler.dropHandler}"
actions="COPY MOVE">
  <af:dataFlavor flavorClass="org.apache.myfaces.trinidad.model
.RowKeySet" discriminant="section"/>
</af:dropTarget>
```

In the code for the drop handler, first the *RowKeySet* object is retrieved from the *transferable.* Next, the collection model for the table is retrieved from the *transferable* and from the collection model the tree binding; the row corresponding to the key-path in the row-key-set is found using *findNodeByKeyPath* method of the tree binding. In case of the move drag-and-drop action, the row is removed and the table is programmatically added as a partial target so it refreshes to reflect the deletion of row. The code is shown next:

```
public DnDAction dropHandler(DropEvent dropEvent) {
    DnDAction ret = DnDAction.NONE;
    String discriminant = "section";
    Transferable transferable = dropEvent.getTransferable();
    // The data in the transferable is the row key for the dragged
component.
    DataFlavor<RowKeySet> rowKeySetFlavor =
DataFlavor.getDataFlavor(RowKeySet.class, discriminant);
    RowKeySet rowKeySet = transferable.getData(rowKeySetFlavor);
    if (rowKeySet != null) {
        // Get the model for the dragged component.
        CollectionModel dragModel = transferable.getData
(CollectionModel.class);
        if (dragModel != null) {
            JUCtrlHierBinding treeBinding =
(JUCtrlHierBinding)dragModel.getWrappedData();
            // For simplicity assuming single row drop; for multi-row
iterate over iterator
            List currKey = (List)rowKeySet.iterator().next();
            JUCtrlHierNodeBinding treeNode =
treeBinding.findNodeByKeyPath(currKey);
            Row row = treeNode.getRow();
            info = dropEvent.getProposedAction().name() + "\n" +
getRowData(row);
            RichInputText dropTarget =
(RichInputText)dropEvent.getDropComponent();
            dropTarget.setValue(info);
            if (dropEvent.getProposedAction() == DnDAction.MOVE) {
                row.remove();
AdfFacesContext.getCurrentInstance().addPartialTarget(dropEvent
.getDragComponent());
            }
            ret = dropEvent.getProposedAction();
        }
    }
    return ret;
}
```

Drag-and-Drop Sample: From Input Text to Table

In this scenario, as mentioned earlier, we drag and drop values from the input text to the table and add new rows populated with the dropped data. We expect the dropped data to be a set of *attribute name:attribute value* separated by newlines. While the earlier scenario showed how to retrieve rows from a drop, this scenario shows how to add rows on a drop.

Since we are simply dragging the *value* attribute for the input text, we can just use *Attribute Drag Source,* which can be added similar to *Drag Source* as described earlier. The resultant .jsp snippet is:

```
<af:attributeDragSource attribute="value"/>
```

Next, we need to add *drop target* on the tree, which can be added as described earlier. The data flavor should be *java.lang.String,* and no *discriminant* is needed. The resultant .jspx snippet is:

```
<af:dropTarget dropListener="#{dragdropHandler.drop2TableHandler}">
  <af:dataFlavor flavorClass="java.lang.String"/>
</af:dropTarget>
```

In the code for the drop handler, the table component is retrieved from the drop event and from the table the tree binding is retrieved via the collection model. The row-set-iterator is retrieved from the tree binding and is used to create a new row. This new row is then populated with the dropped value, which is a plain string. The code is shown next:

```
public DnDAction drop2TableHandler(DropEvent dropEvent) {
    // *** Create a new row
    RichTable table = (RichTable)dropEvent.getDropComponent();
    //the Collection Model is the object that provides the structured
data for the table to render
    CollectionModel tableModel = (CollectionModel)table.getValue();
    //the ADF object that implements the CollectionModel is
JUCtrlHierBinding. It is wrapped by the CollectionModel API
    JUCtrlHierBinding tableBinding =
(JUCtrlHierBinding)tableModel.getWrappedData();
    //Access the ADF iterator binding that is used with ADF table
binding
    DCIteratorBinding tableIteratorBinding = tableBinding
.getDCIteratorBinding();
    RowSetIterator rowIter = tableIteratorBinding.getRowSetIterator();
    Row row = rowIter.createRow();
    rowIter.insertRow(row);
```

```
    // *** Now get the data being dropped and add to just created row
    Transferable transferable = dropEvent.getTransferable();
    String data = transferable.getData(String.class);
    ArrayList parsedAttrs = parseStringForAttrs(data);
    addRowData(row, parsedAttrs);
    return dropEvent.getProposedAction();
}

private void addRowData(Row row, ArrayList data) {
    for (int i = 0; i < data.size(); i++) {
        String[] pair = (String[])data.get(i);
        String attrName = pair[0];
        String attrVal = pair[1];
        try {
            row.setAttribute(attrName, attrVal);
        } catch (Exception ex) {
            System.err.println(ex.getMessage());
        }
    }
}

private ArrayList parseStringForAttrs(String str) {
    ArrayList ret = new ArrayList();
    String[] tokens = str.split("[\\s]*[,\n;][\\s]*");
    for (int i = 0; i < tokens.length; i++) {
        String[] tokens2 = tokens[i].split("[\\s]*:[\\s]*");
        if (tokens2.length != 2) {
            continue;
        }
        ret.add(tokens2);
    }
    return ret;
}
```

ADF Life Cycle

In this section, we will discuss concepts related to the life cycle management of ADF applications, including built-in AJAX behavior, implications of the life cycle on validations, and some other ADF optimizations.

Partial Page Refreshes (AJAX)

AJAX (Asynchronous JavaScript and XML) is a popular web development technique where only portions of a page are re-rendered. This enables highly interactive and responsive web interfaces by minimizing the amount of data being exchanged with the server, as well as providing a better visual appeal by avoiding unnecessary redrawing.

AJAX is built into the ADF Faces framework and is exposed as a feature called partial page rendering (PPR), which enables certain components to re-render without re-rendering the whole page. PPR manifests itself in the following two flavors.

Single Component

Many ADF Faces components include built-in partial refresh functionality. For example, a Table component allows scrolling, sorting, column reordering, and so on, without refreshing components outside of the table. These components are recognized as event boundaries and any events happening within them don't refresh other components outside of them. Another example of such a component is the pop-up dialog component—any events triggered inside a dialog do not refresh components outside the dialog.

Also, certain events like disclosure and sort events indicate a component as a root. In response to such events, only the identified root component and components contained within it are refreshed.

NOTE
We have simplified the discussion here by using "refreshed." To be more accurate, the life cycle is run only for those components. (The concept of the life cycle is discussed in the section "ADF and JSF Life Cycle.")

Cross Component—Partial Triggers

While the preceding flavor is built in, this flavor is interesting to understand because it needs to be specified as part of the page design. It can be specified that a component, referred to as the target component, refresh (including all components contained within it) when any event occurs on another component, referred to as the trigger component.

A trigger component can initiate a cross-component partial page event to be triggered if its *autoSubmit* (for input components) or *partialSubmit* (for command components) is set to *true*.

A component is specified as a target for a trigger component by including the relative ID of the trigger component in its *partialTrigger* attribute. Since some components are naming containers and others are not, getting the ID right may be tricky and so the partial trigger editor shown in Figure 8-29 should be used.

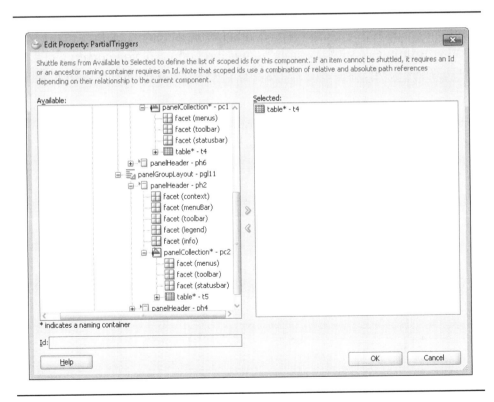

FIGURE 8-29. *The partial trigger editor*

PPR behavior can also be programmatically specified from backing Java code using code like the following snippet:

```
AdfFacesContext adfFacesContext = AdfFacesContext.getCurrentInstance();
adfFacesContext.addPartialTargets(comp);
```

ADF and JSF Life Cycle

While it is possible to write ADF applications, especially in the context of BPM UI forms, without understanding the details of the underlying technology, having some understanding of the underlying life cycle will help developers. Particularly when designing forms with validations, including required fields, an understanding of the life cycle and its impact on validations will eliminate unnecessary frustration.

The stages in the JSF life cycle are:

- **Restore View**   The component tree is established; this phase is not interesting from the perspective of the web UI developer.

- **Apply Request Value**   A component's values are retrieved from the request parameters and stored locally (the model is not updated yet). If the *immediate* attribute is set for the component, then conversions, validations, and events associated with the component are processed in this phase.

- **Process Validations**   First, the local values are converted from the input type to the underlying data type. If conversion succeeds, required test is performed on the component—that is, if the required attribute is set on it, then testing that it has a value. If the required check succeeds and the value is not empty, all associated validation rules for the component are run (even if some fail).

    If any of those just listed—conversion, required-check, *validations*—fail, the component is marked as invalid *and an e*rror message is added. However, this phase runs to completion—that is, all components are tested. At completion, if any component is found to be invalid, the life cycle jumps to the *Render Response* phase.

At the end of this phase, converted versions of the local values are set (no updates are made to the model yet), any validation or conversion error messages and events are queued on the FacesContext object, and any value change events are delivered.

■ **Update Model Values**   It is only in this phase that the model is updated with the new (local) values.

■ **Invoke Application**   The application is invoked—that is, all actions and listeners such as action listeners and disclosure listeners are executed. If an action has a navigation associated with it and if the *immediate* property for it is not set to *true*, the navigation is performed in this phase.

■ **Render Response**   The page (or view) is rendered.

Some aspects that web developers must understand about the life cycle are:

■ Model values are updated only during the update model, whereas validations are run before. This means that if validation rules for a component depend on values of other components, by default the updated values are not available during validation.

■ If any component fails validation, model values are not updated for all.

■ The default behavior can be overridden using the *immediate* attribute, which is discussed in more detail later.

The ADF Optimized Life Cycle
ADF improves upon the JSF life cycle in the following ways:

■ **Partial Page Refreshes**   As discussed earlier.

■ **Client-side Life Cycle**   Built-in and custom Javascript-based conversion and validation that runs on the client without requiring a roundtrip to a server.

■ **Subform Component** A subform component submits a group of form entries without impacting others, enabling parts of a page to be validated and submitted independently, while maintaining a single page state.

Immediate

As noted earlier, the *immediate* attribute can be used to change the JSF Life Cycle. There is a difference in behavior of this attribute between command components (such as buttons) and input components (such as input text).

The *Immediate* attribute on command components cause application events, such as action listener, to be delivered in the *Apply Request Value* phase instead of the *Invoke Application* phase; essentially all other phases are skipped. Therefore, this is useful in scenarios, such as cancel, where the validation or updating of other values is not needed. This can also lead to better performance by avoiding unnecessary validations, such as when a command component would navigate to another page. A command action that is only meant to navigate to another view also benefits from *immediate=true* because validation is omitted (as is the full life cycle). Only when navigation should occur after a model update, then immediate=false makes sense for such command components

An *immediate* attribute on input components causes only the component event handling and validation to move up to the *Apply Request Value* phase instead of the *Process Validation* phase, so that they execute before components that don't have *immediate* set to *true*. Unless *renderResponse* is called explicitly (from an event handler), the life cycle continues normally. *Immediate* on input components is needed in scenarios where some components need to process ahead of validation running on others, including where the validation of the other components depend on this component. Such a scenario is discussed in the next section.

If an *immediate* action needs values from an input component, the input component should also be made *immediate*; however, since actions are processed before the model is updated, either the value should be retrieved from the component or the component's event handler should update the model (as in the example in the next section). While *immediate* input components process before *immediate* actions, validation failures do not prevent the action from firing.

NOTE
Setting immediate=true *on a component does not mean that it is processed alone; if no errors are detected in its processing all other components follow their normal life cycle. To avoid processing of life cycle for other components, for example when dependent list boxes need to be set without validating other form fields, the* FacesContext.getCurrentInstance() .renderResponse() *method needs to be called from the value change listener.*

Validation Example

To illustrate the preceding concepts, consider an example where there is a *comment* field that is required only if the *required* checkbox field is checked, as shown in Figure 8-30.

To start with, *autoSubmit* needs to be set on the *required* checkbox, and the *required* checkbox's ID must be added to the *partialTrigger* attribute of the *comment* field to ensure that as the checkbox is changed, the *comment* field is updated. Also, the *required* attribute on the *comment* field is set to #{bindings.required.inputValue} (*required* is the binding for the checkbox).

At this point, the behavior will be that, once the *required* checkbox is checked, it cannot be unchecked without specifying some value in the

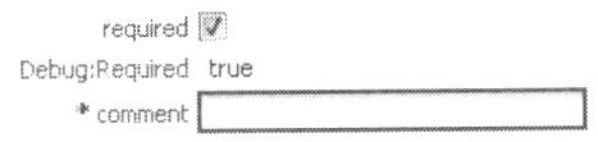

required ☑
Debug:Required true
* comment [   ]

FIGURE 8-30. *Validation example scenario*

comment field. This happens because the validation for the comment field happens in the *Process Validation Phase* ahead of the value for *required* getting updated, and once validation fails, model updates are skipped.

To get this scenario working correctly, two things are needed:

■   Since the model update for *required* cannot wait for the *Update Model Values* phase, a value change event listener is needed and within that listener the model value needs to be updated explicitly, as shown in the following code snippet:

```
public void reqChanged(ValueChangeEvent valueChangeEvent) {
   BindingContainer bc = BindingContext.getCurrent()
.getCurrentBindingsEntry();
AttributeBinding cb = (AttributeBinding) bc.getControlBinding
("required");
   cb.setInputValue(valueChangeEvent.getNewValue());
}
```

■   The event listener needs to be run ahead of the *Process Validation Phase.* This is achieved by setting *immediate* on the *required* checkbox to *true.*

ADF Task Flows

ADF Task Flows define flows of pages and methods. Typically, task flows are interesting to application developers because any application involves navigation between pages. In the context of BPM forms, while many scenarios may have traditionally been addressed by a single page form, the ability to break down a page into multiple pages and provide some guided navigation has the potential of simplifying the user experience, especially when dealing with complex forms.

ADF has two flavors of task flows: unbounded task flows and bounded task flows. An unbounded task flow is useful for building application navigation and does not apply to BPM forms; therefore, we will not cover unbounded task flows in this section.

Bounded Task Flows

A bounded task flow has a well-defined entry point and can be invoked with parameters. A BPM ADF UI is always wrapped in a bounded task flow, even when the UI is a single page; therefore, BPM UI elements are typically referred to as BPM Task Flows (although in this chapter we have been loosely referring to them as BPM forms). In addition to being used for BPM UI, some other use cases for bounded task flows are:

- Creating regions that are contained within other pages
- Encapsulating reusable page flow logic that is invoked as a subtask flow
- Creating regions to be included in Web Center

An example bounded task flow is shown in Figure 8-31. The activity with a shaded circle around it is the entry point for the task flow. The rest of the elements in the task flow are discussed in the following sections.

Transitions or Control Flow

Control Flows (similar to transitions in BPMN) define navigation between activities in a task flow. The attributes *From Action* and *From Outcome,* if specified, limit the applicability of the control flow to only when the navigation is caused by the specified action or outcome. In bounded task flows, the *From Outcome* is the more commonly used option.

Wildcard Control Flow

In Figure 8-31, a big star, which is the source of transition labeled *closeTaskFlow* can be seen. This is a wildcard control flow, which means that regardless of the source, if the outcome from the navigation is *closeTaskFlow,* follow the transition (assuming that there is not an overriding local definition on the source activity). In addition to a pure wildcard, a trailing wildcard such as *pre** can be specified, in which case the control flow is limited to navigations whose source has an *activity-id* starting with *pre.* This is useful for grouping together pages with similar control flow requirements and simplifying the specification of control flows.

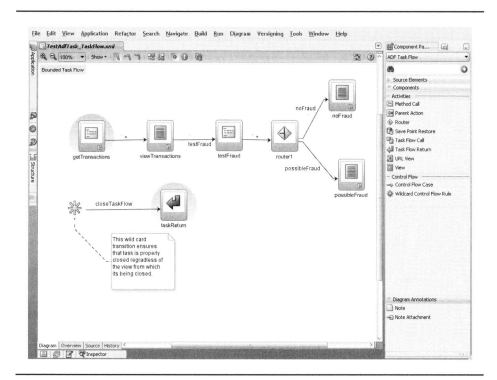

FIGURE 8-31.   *A sample bounded task flow*

View Activity

The view activity, the most commonly used activity in a task flow, represents a page or a page fragment within a task flow. A new page for a view activity can be created by double-clicking the activity, or it can be associated with an existing page by specifying the *page* attribute accordingly. Also, an existing page can be dragged and dropped into the task flow to add a new view activity representing the page.

Router Activity

The conditional navigation provided by control flow is limited to *actions* and *outcomes* and doesn't support BPMN like data-based expressions. The router activity addresses this limitation by mapping data-based conditional expressions to outcomes that can then be used in control flows. In the example shown in Figure 8-31, a router activity is used to determine which page to navigate to, depending on the return value of the previous activity. An example of router activity was also discussed earlier in the section "Forms for E-mail."

Method Activity

A method activity allows invocation of a method or a service between page navigations. A method activity may be useful to fetch the data needed to populate a page, do processing between page navigations, and to evaluate rules on what page to show next. A method activity can be bound to a method or operation exposed by a data control as well as to backing bean methods.

Task Flow Entry Point—Default Activity

As noted earlier, every bounded task flow must have a well-defined entry point. The *default* activity in a task flow is the entry point. An activity can be marked as default by right-clicking it and then selecting *Default Activity* within *Mark Activity.*

Task Flow Return Activity

A bounded task flow should end with a task flow return activity to ensure that resources are appropriately released. Also, the *outcome* property of the task flow is returned to the calling task flow.

NOTE
To ensure that the task flow return activity is always invoked on task close, BPM-generated task flows include a wildcard transition to a task flow return activity.

Task Flow Trains

As mentioned earlier, a big value-add of providing multipage task flows as BPM UI is to navigate the user through bite-sized pieces of information. A common metaphor to facilitate such navigation is to provide the user with a navigational tool that shows them where they are in the context of the overall task, as well as to navigate easily between pages. ADF Trains provide a built-in framework for adding such navigational context to bounded task flows. Figure 8-32 shows a BPM ADF Task Flow using a train to navigate a sales representative through the various steps in creating a quote: enter header, select products, request discounts, request terms, and review (and submit).

A train can be added to a bounded task flow by right-clicking the task flow canvas and then selecting the *Create Train* submenu item within the *Train* menu item. The ordering of activities within a train can be changed by right-clicking the activity, selecting the *Train* menu item and then selecting the appropriate ordering option (such as move forward).

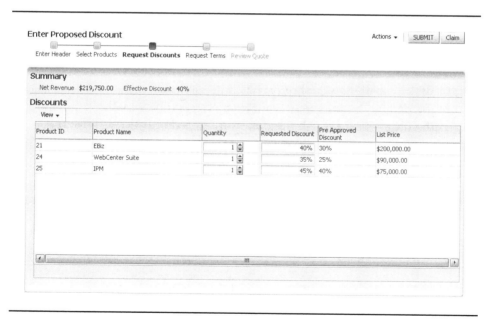

FIGURE 8-32. *A sample task flow train*

While the default navigation for task flow trains is that each train stop is visited in sequence, it can be modified using the following attributes on the activity:

- **Sequential**   If the sequential attribute evaluates to false, the activity can be performed in any order; otherwise, it can be visited only after the preceding stop.

- **Skip**   If the *skip* attribute evaluates to true, the train-stop is skipped.

The label and tooltip to display for a train stop can be specified by selecting the *train-stop* child of the activity in the *structure* window and adding *Display Name* and *Description* to it. For the navigation bar to be included in a page, the ADF Faces *Train* or *Train Button Bar* component should be added on the page.

ADF Business Components

In many BPM scenarios, data stored in a database needs to be accessed. Some use cases include:

- BPM is working with entity data and, since the process does not own the data and others may want to access and modify the data while the process is in flight, the data is mastered outside of BPM in a database and BPM accesses it.

- Supporting data is needed for users to perform their tasks intelligently—for example, a list of products for a user creating a quote, or credit card transactions for a user approving a credit change request.

- A list of values used for fields in a task form is stored in a database to facilitate easy changes to the list.

Oracle ADF includes a business services framework—ADF Business Components (BC) —that not only enables the development of database-backed applications but is also very useful in the context of BPM for the scenarios mentioned earlier. The ADF-BC framework provides Object-Relational (O/R) mapping, the definition of application-specific views possibly with custom validation rules and other business logic, default operations including CRUD (create, read, update, delete), the caching of data, management of transactions, and the coordination of master-detail behavior.

ADF-BC components can be added to the model project in a Fusion Web Application (essentially a project that has ADF Business Components in its technology scope) by using the *New Gallery* and selecting the *Business Components from Table* option from the *ADF Business Components* subcategory of the *Business Tier* category. ADF-BC is a declarative framework and metadata for all components is stored in XML files. While most use cases, especially in the context of BPM, can be addressed with just the declarative framework, ADF-BC provides hooks to add Java classes to extend or modify the behavior of the framework.

If the database schema is set up correctly with the right foreign key and other constraints, creating ADF-BC components is a matter of walking through the wizard. The wizard creates the ADF-BC components with the right relationships based on the foreign keys, as shown in a sample ADF-BC diagram in Figure 8-33 (this diagram is generated by JDeveloper). Most users will need to make very few changes. Although more advanced usage such as employing Groovy for business logic or using Java extension classes is possible, it is out of the scope of this book. Since the simple usage of ADF-BC is trivial and advanced usage is out of our scope, this section only gives a high-level overview of ADF-BC.

Entity Objects

The entity object provides O/R mapping, exposing columns in the underlying database table as entity object attributes. The entity object holds the data retrieved from the database and is responsible for manipulating it. Business and validation logic is implemented in the entity object. An entity object can be created against a database table, view, or synonym, as well as against a Web Service data source.

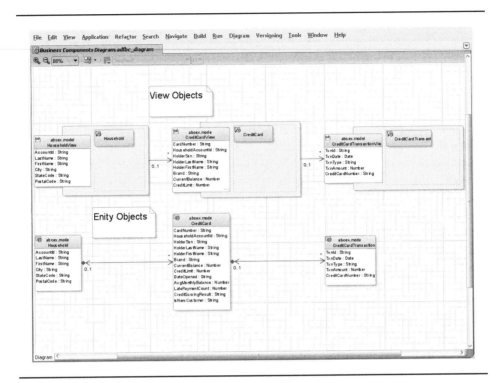

FIGURE 8-33. *A sample ADF-BC diagram*

Associations

As can be seen in Figure 8-33, entity objects can have relationships among themselves. These relationships are defined by associations. As mentioned earlier, default associations are generated by the wizard based on foreign key relationships. The default associations should suffice in most scenarios.

Attributes

Attributes represent columns in the underlying table. They define the column data type, primary key, unique key settings, and more. Optionally, entity attributes can be created as transient, in which case they don't have a related database column and are based on calculations. Also, display hints can be specified. While the hints can be overridden by the view objects or within the page, providing hints at the entity level leads to consistency and less work when the entity is used by multiple views.

Validations

One of the benefits of using ADF-BC is the ability to define business logic in a declarative way. Validations can be specified on the entity object attributes as well as the entity object itself. Validations on the entity object attributes are triggered when the attribute value is changed, while those on the entity object are triggered when rows are changed or during commit.

The following types of validations are supported:

- **Compare**   Compare the attribute against a literal value, a Groovy expression, or another attribute value. *View Accessors* can be used to get a value from a view definition.

- **List**   Test if the attribute value is in a list. The list can be a static list of values, values from a view object, or specified by a SQL query.

- **Key Exists**   Test if the value already exists as a key.

- **Length**   Test the value's length either in characters or bytes for a specified condition.

- **Range**   Test if the value is within or outside the specified range.

- **Regular Expression**   Test if the value matches a regular expression pattern. Regular expression patterns for U.S. phone numbers and some other common scenarios are built in.

- **Script** and **Method**   Execute a Groovy script or a Java method returning *true* or *false* to indicate success or failure.

In addition to the preceding validations that are available for attributes, the following validations are available at the entity object level:

- **Collection**   Test against aggregated value—sum, average, min, max—of an attribute across all records.

- **Unique Key**   Test if the primary key or an alternate key is unique across all records.

Validations can be conditional—that is, only when the specified condition is true the validation is executed. Also, validations allow for the specification of failure messages, which can be internationalized.

Java Extension

JDeveloper provides an option to generate an implementation class for the entity object. The getters and setters for the attributes can be modified to add desired behavior. Also, this class allows for extending the logic when creating and removing rows, as well as executing data operations.

Events

From within the *Business Events* tab of the entity object editor, business events and their publication can be defined; the editors to create business event definition and to set up a business event publication are shown in Figure 8-34. The event definition consists of an event name and a list of attributes; attributes may be either always included in the event or only if the attribute value changes. For example, in Figure 8-34 we see an event named *CardEvent* that includes two attributes *CardNumber* and *AvgMonthlyBalance*; *AvgMonthlyBalance* is included in the event only if its value is changed. Events can be set up to be published on the entity object create, update,

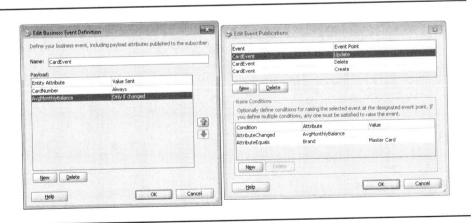

FIGURE 8-34.   *Business event editors*

or delete; also, publication can be filtered on conditions that test for an attribute value change or an attribute value. For example, in Figure 8-34 we see that the *CardEvent* is published whenever the underlying entity object is updated and either attribute *AvgMonthlyBalance* is changed or the attribute *Brand* equals *Master Card.*

These business events are published to the Event Delivery Network (EDN) and can be consumed by BPM processes via signals.

View Objects

The view object is the heart of ADF-BC for UI developers. It defines what the end-user sees in the application. The view object defines the SQL statement that selects and orders the required data into the underlying entity object, and at runtime the view object is a collection of entity objects that represents the result set of the specified SQL query. Although typically a view object will be based on one entity object, it can be based on multiple entity objects (via joins), as well as none (read only view objects).

Query

The view object is essentially a select statement. *Group By* directives can be specified or the SQL can be tweaked as needed.

View Criteria

The query can be further filtered by defining view-criteria. These filters can use bind variables, in which case an *Exec with Params* operation is exposed (something we have already encountered in this chapter.) View-criteria can also be associated with a view instance in an application module to expose a filtered version of the view. Another use of view-criteria is that it is available to use in query panels to provide search behavior.

Attributes

Attributes in the view object map to attributes in the underlying entity objects. Similar to entity objects, transient attributes can be defined. Transient attributes are attributes that don't match an entity attribute and are not persisted on a transaction commit. Also, display hints for attributes can be specified. Display hints specified on view objects override those specified on the underlying entity objects.

View Links

As can be seen in Figure 8-33, views can be related to one another. Such relationships are defined by view links. Default view links are generated based on the associations in the underlying entity objects. Additional view links can be added to create custom relationships—for example, an *active address* link from a *customer* to filter only those addresses marked as active.

List of Values

Earlier, within the discussion on selection components, we saw how selection components can be bound to a static and dynamic list of values. ADF-BC allows specifying the list of values as part of the view object definition itself. A list of values can be added for a view object attribute by clicking the plus icon in the *List of Values* section in the Attributes tab. This launches the *Create List of Values* window where another view object can be selected as the list data source, as shown in Figure 8-35. When the list of

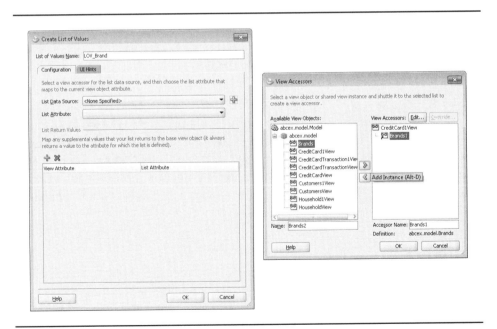

FIGURE 8-35.   *Creating a list of values*

values is specified on the view object attribute, when using select components, the *Model Driven List of Values* option must be selected.

In the section on "Selection Components," we also discussed the dependent lists scenario. For ADF-BC objects, dependent lists can be configured as part of the model definition—view-criteria needs to be associated with the view accessor added as part of the LOV definition. This automatically achieves the desired behavior.

Custom Methods and Other Java Extensions

The view object implementation class for a view object can be generated. This is useful for adding custom methods to the view object beyond the standard operations, as well as to introduce custom behavior such as programmatically managing query and view-criteria. Custom methods exposed on a client interface are available as part of the data control and can be dragged and dropped as a command component onto a view.

A custom method can be added to the view object by implementing the method in the implementation class and then editing the *Client Interface* within the *Java* tab to add the method to the interface.

Application Modules

An application module packages a collection of view objects and defines the data model available for client users. A data control is automatically available for every application module and exposes the view objects included in the application module as immediate children of the data control node. If a view object is not added to an application module, it will not be accessible from the data control. In addition to view objects, methods can be added to an application module.

The configuration tab of the application module specifies how the connection to the database is made. By default, a JDBC URL of the form *jdbc:oracle:thin:bpmserver:1521:XE* is used. Before deployment, the configuration should be changed to use a JDBC data-source of the form *jdbc/dataSource*, so that the deployed application can leverage JDBC data-sources defined in the application server.

Service Interface

An ADF-BC application module can be exposed as a service by adding a service interface from the *Service Interface* tab. Operations, methods, and view-criteria of view instances in the application module, as well as methods on the application module, can be selected for inclusion in the service interface, as can be seen in Figure 8-36. Also shown in Figure 8-36 are two Java files in addition to the WSDL and XSD files. The first defines the interface of the service, and the second Java file is the remote server class, which is an EJB 3.0 stateless session bean that implements the interface.

A BPMN process can consume the service exposed using the ADF-BC Service adapter component.

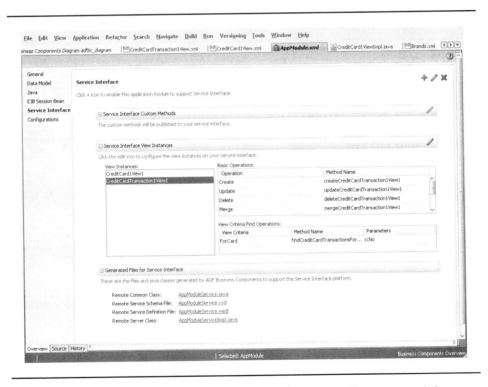

FIGURE 8-36. *A Service interface exposed by an application module*

BPM and ADF-BC

In addition to being used in BPM UI either to get supplementary data or for a list-of-values, ADF-BC and BPM work together in the following ways:

- **Document-based Routing**   The human workflow component of BPM can provide rich document-based routing when working in conjunction with ADF-BC data. This was discussed in detail in chapter 7.

- **ADF-BC Service**   Services exposed by ADF-BC application modules can be consumed by BPM using the *ADF-BC Service* adapter.

- **Events**   Events published by ADF-BC entities can be subscribed through BPM processes.

ADF-BC vs. Database Adapters

BPM also includes a database adapter that can be used to retrieve data from a database into a process. In the context of getting data for displaying as part of a task form or for using as a list-of-values, using ADF-BC is recommended because it provides the following benefits:

- **Data Currency**   If a database adapter is used, then the process will need to retrieve the data. This can result in a time lag between when a user interacts with the data and when the process retrieves it. However, when using ADF-BC, the data can be fetched by the UI itself, ensuring it is current.

- **Business Logic**   ADF-BC is much more than object-to-relational mapping. As discussed earlier, it supports business logic like validations, as well as provides hooks for the inclusion of custom business logic.

   In the context of a process accessing data from a database for processing (and not for a user interface), working with a database adapter is simpler. However, using ADF-BC means that business logic is shared between BPM and user interface layers. Therefore, if ADF-BC already exists, or there is a possibility of building user interfaces on top of the data, or there are business logic and validation requirements, ADF-BC should be used. Otherwise, a database adapter should be used.

For More Information

ADF documentation is available under the category "Development Tools" within the Fusion Middleware documentation library.

Anyone working with ADF Faces is recommended to leverage the "ADF Faces Cheat Sheets" within ADF documentation. A runtime demo showcasing these components is also hosted at http://jdevadf.oracle.com/adf-richclient-demo, which is a great way to learn by seeing different components in action. The source code for this demo can also be downloaded from www.oracle.com/technetwork/developer-tools/adf/downloads/index.html by selecting the Oracle ADF Faces Components Demo. The ADF page at Oracle Technology Network (OTN) at www.oracle.com/technetwork/developer-tools/adf/overview/index.html has a wealth of information including articles and step-by-step tutorials.

Two other books available in the documentation library that are particularly useful are "Web User Interface Developer's Guide" and the "Fusion Developers Guide." The former is focused on ADF Faces and topics such as working with trees, tables, pop-ups, drag and drop, and so on, while the latter is focused on the full application stack, including ADF-BC, Task Flows, and others.

In addition to the Oracle documentation library, the "Oracle Fusion Developer Guide" by Frank Nimphius and Lynn Munsinger (Oracle Press, McGraw-Hill Professional, 2009) is an excellent resource for readers seeking to go deep into ADF. The Oracle ADF Code Corner (www.oracle.com/technetwork/developer-tools/adf/learnmore/index-101235.html) is a great collection of how-tos and code snippets.

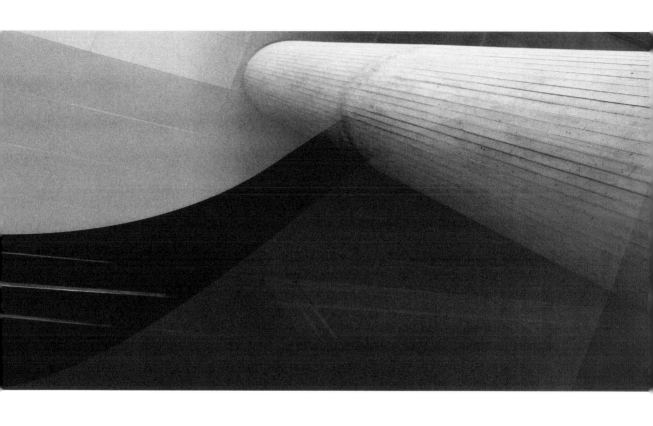

PART
III

Essentials of Oracle
BPM Methodology

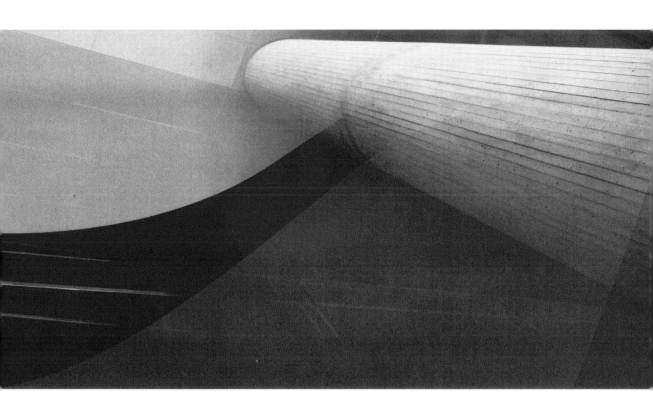

CHAPTER
9

Planning BPM
Adoption

art III of the book explains how to address the broader issues associated with adopting and expanding BPM within an organization. Chapter 9 starts with the broadest view of enterprise BPM adoption and planning. This chapter looks at all aspects of BPM in an organization, discusses the importance of assessing the organization's readiness, and shows how to create a roadmap. Along the way, a set of important frameworks and methods are identified. Of these, business process selection and BPM project delivery strategies are described in detail in the chapters that follow.

Chapters 9 through 11 of this part of the book encompass strategic planning, business analysis, and the IT perspective of process automation projects, respectively. For a rapid start in a BPM initiative, in which time constraints may preclude strategic planning, it is reasonable to start with business analysis (Chapter 10) since this includes a detailed approach for process identification and selection. In this way, the more involved strategic approach can be revisited as the BPM program gathers momentum. However, it is never appropriate to skip both chapters and start with IT implementation since this clearly suggests an absence of coordination between business and IT.

Introduction

The much referenced quote from Lewis Carroll's *Alice's Adventures in Wonderland* is commonly paraphrased along the lines of, "if you don't know where you are going, any road will get you there." In order to make a plan for BPM, however, it is not only necessary to know where you are going, but also where you are starting from. This may seem obvious, but in a complex business environment, typically neither the current state nor the readiness for change are well understood. This is one of the great strengths of the Oracle approach to BPM, since it provides, among other things, an assessment of your organization's readiness to successfully adopt BPM. Based on an extensive maturity model spanning all aspects of enterprise BPM adoption, the BPM Capability Maturity Assessment can be used to create a roadmap to ensure that all the elements necessary for successful BPM adoption are addressed in a single coherent plan. Ideally, the assessment should be performed at regular intervals to validate that planned activities are on track, take measurements to present quantifiable improvements, incorporate changes arising in the business environment, and adjust the plan as needed.

Many factors can influence the success of BPM adoption. If all concerns are not viewed holistically, or even if one aspect is neglected, the project or program as a whole will be adversely affected and may even fail altogether. The Oracle BPM Maturity Model (which forms the basis for the maturity assessment) provides comprehensive coverage for the concerns of a BPM program from all the potential BPM stakeholder viewpoints. In this way, we can establish a quantitative understanding of the current state of readiness, as well as a consistent measurement approach for future comparison.

Another common problem arising when adopting BPM is whether to take a strategic or tactical approach (top-down versus bottom-up). Projects grounded in technology are often tackled tactically. This often occurs out of necessity due to constraints such as time, budget, scope, or, in particular, a lack of executive sponsorship. As such, these tactical projects often serve a purpose to prove a concept or establish a new approach. The risk, unfortunately, is that a strategic approach is never applied because the tactical approach appeared to work and so there seems to be no need to go to the trouble of changing it. Commonly in this case poor practices become the norm and very soon people are left wondering why the success of the original project can't be repeated and the new technology falls by the wayside.

Does this mean a tactical proof of concept is the wrong approach? Should all projects wait for a full-scale business case, full support, and budget before getting started? In this case, it may be years before the new idea is accepted, and without the experience of having tried it, it may seem like an impossible task to prove the value on paper.

So how do we overcome this dilemma of tactical versus strategic? The answer is to take a pragmatic approach by considering all the dimensions of the problem, understanding the organization's strengths and weaknesses, developing a long-term plan to fill the gaps, and developing new capabilities while executing business process automation projects at the same time. This is essentially roadmap planning.

In summary, the elements of planning a successful BPM adoption are as follows:

- Assess the current level of BPM maturity and the ability to make changes across all dimensions of the problem space and all levels of the organization.

- Develop a roadmap to reach the maturity level necessary to meet the goals of the program.

- Coordinate business process projects.

- Continuously measure improvements and adherence to the plan and make course corrections as needed.

Another important consideration for BPM adoption is the scope: Are we looking at a departmental effort or an enterprisewide approach? In some ways, this question is similar to that of tactical versus strategic and it is highlighted in the assessment through the adoption dimension of the maturity model. The maturity model is covered in more detail in the following sections, but for now it is important to understand that in order to realize the full benefits of BPM, its adoption must ultimately be enterprisewide. Business processes by their very nature span organizational boundaries. Therefore, any process viewed within the boundaries of a single department is unlikely to represent an end-to-end business process supporting a significant value chain of a company (value chains are explained in Chapter 10). While such a narrowly scoped orchestration is still important to BPM, some of the key benefits of BPM are not available until it is viewed in the context of the complete process. In fact, without a broader evaluation of the suitability of a business process (of which the narrower orchestration or activity is a part) there is no concrete justification for its automation. A procedure for evaluating the suitability of a process for automation is covered in Chapter 10 in the section "Business Process Selection."

A common pitfall for BPM includes the infamous gap between IT and the business: When either of these groups attempts to do BPM without the full cooperation of the other, the effort will be much less successful. BPM must be a well-orchestrated collaboration between IT and the business. By using the Oracle BPM Maturity Model, we can measure the strengths and weaknesses across these two groups, and by predicting where problems might occur we can apply remediation in advance.

The following sections of this chapter describe the Oracle approach to BPM adoption, which includes a comprehensive guide to BPM Roadmap Planning and an outline of supporting frameworks and methods.

The Oracle Approach to BPM Adoption

The Oracle approach to BPM adoption is made up of three major parts. At the program level there is an extensive assessment and process selection activity leading to roadmap planning. This is supported by a variety of methods and frameworks, all of which come together to support a Program

Management Office (PMO) or Center of Excellence (COE). Not neglecting the all-important implementation of business process automation at the project level, the Oracle approach describes the BPM project, distinguishing the unique characteristics of a BPM project from the traditional facets of project management.

The diagram in Figure 9-1 summarizes these elements showing both the program-level and project-level activities.

A BPM Roadmap provides guidance to the BPM initiative, allowing multiple projects to progress in parallel and yet remain coordinated, ultimately resulting in a common end goal that provides value greater than

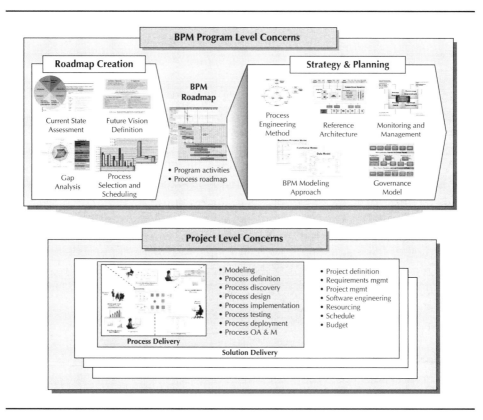

FIGURE 9-1. *Elements of the Oracle approach to BPM adoption*

the sum of the individual projects. While the roadmap is comprised of program-level and project-level activities, the program-level concerns are particularly broad and include the following:

■ An assessment of current state versus future vision

■ Process selection and scheduling

■ A set of frameworks and models to guide business process engineering

The assessment uses simple-to-use spreadsheet-based tools and workshop scenarios to measure the current state and establish relevant statements of future goals. Program-level efforts create the assets that are leveraged across all the individual projects such as the BPM Reference Architecture, governance policies and processes, standards, metrics, training and mentoring, business process engineering method, and others.

In addition, a portfolio of business application functions and shared services is an important input to roadmap planning since it supports the assessment of the integration effort to be associated with the projects in the roadmap.

The approach to roadmap creation, including Gap Analysis and use of the BPM Maturity Model, are covered in the following sections of this chapter. While business process scheduling is included in the roadmap creation section, a detailed approach for business process selection can be found in the next chapter. Although the broad set of frameworks and models required to set up a BPM Program Management Office or Center of Excellence are outlined in this chapter as part of roadmap creation, the business process engineering method will be covered in greater detail in Chapter 11.

The roadmap follows the classic IT approach of identifying "as-is," "to-be," performing Gap Analysis, and assessing the effort to close the gap.

Frameworks and Methods

The frameworks and methods represented in the diagram in Figure 9-1 are made up of a collection of guides, templates, spreadsheet tools, and training materials designed to be tailored to any given organization's needs and to provide support for the management of a BPM program. These frameworks and methods are outlined in the following sections simply to indicate the scope of the Oracle BPM approach; however, they are not the primary focus of this chapter. The first in our list, business process engineering methodology, is possibly the most important in our set of frameworks and methods, and for this reason it gets a chapter of its own later in the book. The other subjects here are beyond the scope of this book and some in fact might justify a full book of their own.

The Business Process Engineering Methodology

The Oracle Business Process Engineering Methodology is an agile strategy that defines an iterative approach to Business Process Engineering highly suited to the rapidly changing business environment (driven by market demands, mergers and acquisition, and others) and continuous incremental business process improvement. It is an adaptable strategy that complements existing software engineering practices and is compatible with common integration approaches. The Oracle Business Process Engineering Methodology and its relationship to iterative methods are described in more detail in Chapter 11.

By using the pragmatic and incremental approach described by the Oracle BPM Methodology, organizations can expect to accelerate their business process automation while reducing the risks associated with the development of any business application. Using the Oracle BPM Methodology ensures that the automated business processes meet the needs of the business and eliminates unforeseen outcomes.

While a number of mature and robust software engineering methodologies are available today, BPM demands some additional considerations that must be addressed to ensure the success of business process engineering projects. In general, these extra steps can be integrated into any existing agile-like software engineering practice. As will be seen in the business process engineering chapter of this book, the approach we have taken focuses on these BPM-specific engineering activities while describing them in an agile-like framework ready for integration into existing methods.

Reference Architecture

A reference architecture is a communication vehicle intended to present the technological approach to supporting business needs (in this case, BPM) to ensure consistency and understanding across the full range of stakeholders. Since different stakeholders tend to speak different languages, the greatest challenge of a reference architecture is to present a consistent solution description in a variety of different forms. These different representations are generally formalized into *architectural views* with a minimum set of views spanning conceptual, logical, and implementation descriptions.

A conceptual architecture is a representation of the capabilities of a "system" relevant to the business problem being addressed. This conceptual view identifies the aspects of the system that are critical to the operation of a particular business capability.[1]

The BPM conceptual architecture should highlight the core capabilities of a BPM system, identify the major intersecting systems, and outline their relationships. As much as possible, the BPM system should be described in business terms, without the supporting IT functions and without regard for technical constraints. The conceptual architecture represents what the business needs from a BPM system. An example of a conceptual architecture model for BPM is shown in the diagram in Figure 9-2.

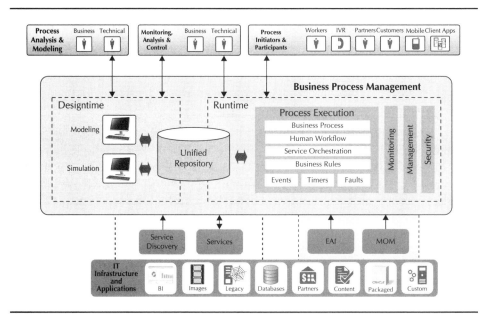

FIGURE 9-2. *The BPM conceptual architecture*

---

[1] The word "system" is used here for its broader meaning of any cohesive group of related elements, technical and non-technical.

At this conceptual level of abstraction, the BPM architecture can be seen to be comprised of modeling capabilities in the designtime portion, with definitions of various types of process orchestrations and business rules conveyed via some form of repository to the BPM runtime. The details of how the various forms of process orchestration are stored and transferred, and whether they require transformation to their executable state, are implementation details that can be found in the logical architecture.

In order to achieve an effective deployment and adoption of BPM, it is necessary to identify the infrastructure capabilities required for alignment with business goals. Infrastructure capabilities should be realized through the implementation and deployment of the components of the logical architecture, while others may involve operational, organizational, and other aspects not directly related to infrastructure.

The logical architecture identifies the components of a system needed to achieve the capabilities described by the conceptual architecture. Unlike the conceptual view of the architecture, the logical view is concerned with understanding the functions required from the IT environment. The components of the logical view commonly manifest as features of products or potentially custom subsystems. The physical constraints of the IT environment, such as capacities of networks and servers, and nonfunctional requirements, such as redundancy for high availability, are not considered in the logical architecture because they belong to the implementation or deployment architectural description.

In addition to conveying a consistent solution to a variety of audiences, the reference architecture also serves a number of other purposes. The reference architecture also defines architectural principles and guidelines which serve as the core tenets that ensure consistency across multiple implementations. Similarly a set of standards are identified (for example, BPMN) for all BPM implementations.

Management and Monitoring

While management and monitoring are core concerns for any IT implementation, BPM demands a much broader treatment of this topic. The mantra of today's BPM is "monitor, manage, and optimize." Key differences between BPM and traditional software engineering include the empowerment of business users and the continuous improvement of the business processes. These benefits are achieved largely through monitoring providing both real-time visibility and data to support effective post-implementation analysis.

The purpose and benefits of monitoring in BPM are:

- **Conformance** The ability to operate consistently within predefined values

- **Performance** The ability to measure performance and gather the information necessary to improve

- **Better Understanding of Business Process Effectiveness and an Enabler for Root Cause Analysis**

- **Competitive Advantage** The right information collected for the business, allowing management to make better business, IT, and operational decisions

- **Understanding Business Value and Providing Justification for Strategic Changes**

- **A Basis for Automated Responses to Anticipated Operational Issues**

The intrinsic role of monitoring in BPM presents four major opportunities to improve support to the business which must be carefully considered when defining the method for business process engineering. These four opportunities are:

- Continuous Business Process Improvement

- Business Process Operational Administration and Management (OA&M)

- Technical Optimization

- Process Analytics Providing Supporting Information for Enterprise Performance Management (in addition to supporting all of the earlier entries)

The diagram in Figure 9-3 shows these elements of management and monitoring along with their associated activities.

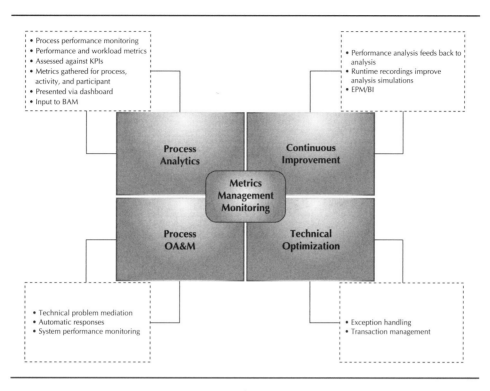

- Process performance monitoring
- Performance and workload metrics
- Assessed against KPIs
- Metrics gathered for process, activity, and participant
- Presented via dashboard
- Input to BAM

- Performance analysis feeds back to analysis
- Runtime recordings improve analysis simulations
- EPM/BI

Process Analytics

Continuous Improvement

Metrics Management Monitoring

Process OA&M

Technical Optimization

- Technical problem mediation
- Automatic responses
- System performance monitoring

- Exception handling
- Transaction management

FIGURE 9-3. *BPM management and monitoring*

The Governance Model

Governance is about creating and maintaining an environment for success; it is fundamentally concerned with making sure effective policies and procedures are established and enforced. When it comes to BPM, ensuring success involves a broad spectrum of factors around the enterprise. It is about having a single source of guidelines tailored to the scope of the BPM program with clearly defined metrics with which to measure success against established objectives. This approach ensures consistency and accountability, supports ongoing business justification, and establishes a feedback loop for continuous improvement and growth of the BPM strategy.

The governance model shown in Figure 9-4 conforms to a unified approach developed by Oracle that incorporates all the concepts of designtime and operational governance, in addition to vitality (ensuring methods, standards, and other items are always current), portfolio (all

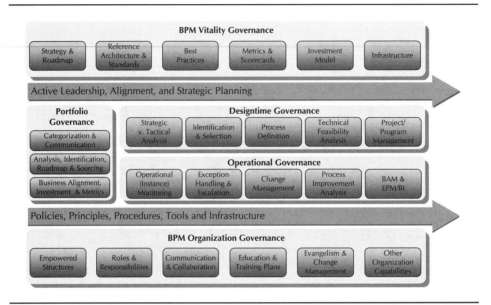

FIGURE 9-4. *The BPM governance model*

related assets), and organization (supporting the methods as well as the impact arising from process change). This unified approach enables rapid integration with other related governance frameworks such as SOA governance, thus avoiding duplication and conflicts. The Oracle BPM Governance Framework also identifies and supports relationships with other IT, EA, and corporate governance approaches.

Roadmap Creation

The program-level aspects of roadmap creation revolve around the assets that are used across all the individual BPM projects. Examples include the BPM reference architecture, governance policies and procedures, standards, metrics, training and mentoring, the business process engineering method, and so on. These program-level efforts enforce the necessary consistency required for BPM adoption to succeed.

For most companies, it is advantageous to separate the business process infrastructure deployment and configuration into a separate project from the business solution projects. This separate project can focus on creating a sound business process infrastructure that meets the needs of multiple business solution projects. Each phase of the BPM Roadmap should have its own dedicated project to incrementally deploy the process infrastructure. In addition to offering greater efficiency and coordination, this centralized infrastructure deployment approach enables the simplified management of architectural requirements.

Under normal circumstances the business process to be managed by the BPM system already exists (creation of an entirely new process is much less common), so the activities, both human and system, are already known in some form. The challenge for a process automation project is how to streamline, optimize, and integrate these activities. In many cases, application functions (and human workflows within them) will be found in vertical applications, and information will be found in data silos, with human tasks tying them together. In an ideal scenario, a repository of SOA services will be available for rapid and flexible integration. In cases of other integration strategies (for example, Enterprise Application Integration [EAI]) more effort will be needed to identify and integrate application functions. Human worklists can be managed with portal interfaces and potentially integrated directly with the applications.

The initial procedure for placing a business process under the control of a BPM system, however, need not involve significant development of new functions or system replacement of human tasks. Instead, the effort should focus on identifying the human and system functions that make up the steps of the business process and assessing their integration needs. This assessment of the integration effort should be performed at the earliest possible stage of planning in order to (1) assess the suitability and the degree of process automation that can be achieved and (2) avoid scope creep when software/ process engineers discover integration challenges later in the engineering process.

Generally, the most effective planning horizon for a BPM Roadmap is two to three years. This could be longer or shorter depending on the planning cycles for any given organization. A strategic roadmap of this kind can and should be integrated with the tactical and pragmatic delivery of BPM projects with relatively short timeframes. In the initial development, the early phases (for example, the first six months) will typically contain much greater detail than the later phases. It is unrealistic to expect to plan in any great detail so far ahead, and the BPM program should be seen as a journey of discovery, incremental improvement, and regular course corrections. The BPM Roadmap should be regularly reviewed and updated to take account of changes in business conditions and technological evolutions.

The Oracle BPM Maturity Model

Since the roadmap creation process relies heavily on the Oracle BPM Maturity Model, it is necessary to spend a little time describing the model, its purpose, and how it is used in an assessment of the readiness of an organization to adopt BPM.

The Oracle BPM Maturity Model defines a number of key concepts, namely, capabilities, domains, maturity, and adoption.

Capabilities

We use the term *capabilities* to refer to the skills, experience, culture, and other attributes that can influence the success of a BPM program. The BPM Maturity Model includes over 60 capabilities that capture the best practices that Oracle has collected over many years working with a wide variety of companies. There is still considerable debate over what constitutes BPM best practices and, while standards and products change from time to time, the BPM Maturity Model remains technology, standards, and product agnostic in order to capture the key elements of a complete BPM strategy.

Additional capabilities can still be added to the BPM Maturity Model as additional best practices emerge. Thus, the details of the BPM Maturity Model will continue to evolve as more experience with BPM is gained.

An example of a capability from the maturity model is shown in Figure 9-5.

As we can see from this illustration, for each capability included in the model a description for each level of maturity, and each level of adoption is provided. (The maturity and adoption levels are defined in the following section.) Although there is always some level of subjectivity when measuring capabilities, these descriptions help provide an objective measure of both maturity and adoption.

Topic	Business Process Analysis (BPA)		
Description	A conceptual map of how the business operates today and could operate in the future. Use of business process modeling tools. The migration from system-led development to business-led development.		

Maturity		Adoption	
Optimized	Ongoing analysis of business opportunities enabled by BPM & SOA approach. Direct linkage process performance to key org performance measures.	**Enterprise Wide**	Business process modeling across all lines of business within the enterprise.
Managed	BPM tools map existing processes and link them to key services. Business analysts are modeling and deploying limited changes through the tools.	**Cross Divisional**	Business process modeling of business processes that span multiple divisions.
Systematic	Conceptual and modeled understanding of how work flows between systems. A target state, at the process level, has been developed.	**Division Level**	Business process modeling of business process contained within a single division.
Opportunistic	In development of overall conceptual business process models, selective modeling of BPs.	**Program Level**	Business process modeling applied across all projects within a program.
Ad Hoc	Investigating tools and approaches for process modeling and execution.	**Project Level**	BPM being applied to one or few isolated projects in a department.
No BPM	Limited/no process understanding or deployment. Process changes require heavy code changes.	**None**	Limited/no process understanding or deployment. Process changes require heavy code changes.

FIGURE 9-5. *Business process analysis capability*

Domains

The BPM Maturity Model uses the concept of domains to classify and organize related capabilities. Figure 9-6 shows the eight domains in the maturity model:

- **Business and Strategy**   Contains capabilities that provide the high-level constructs that allow the BPM initiative to proceed. This includes such things as business motivation, expected benefits, guiding principles, expected costs, funding models, and so on.

- **Architecture**   Contains capabilities concerning the definitions of the overall architecture and guidelines for various practitioners to ensure adherence to the architecture.

- **Infrastructure**   Contains capabilities concerning the process infrastructure and tools that provide the technical foundation for the BPM initiative.

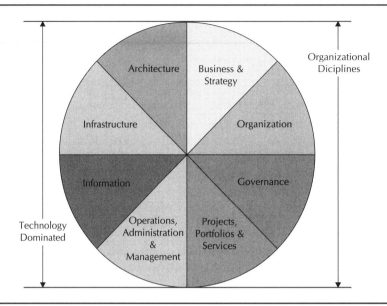

FIGURE 9-6. *BPM capability domains*

- **Information**   Contains capabilities concerning the information aspects of BPM. These include shared data models, message formats and schemas, model management, content management, and others.

- **Projects, Portfolios, and Services**   Contains capabilities concerning the planning and building of processes and the process usage guidelines of process consumers.

- **Operations, Administration, and Management**   Contains capabilities concerning the post deployment aspects of solutions based on a process-oriented architecture.

- **Organization**   Contains capabilities concerning the development of corporate competency around BPM, including the organizational structure and skills development.

- **Governance**   Contains capabilities concerning the governance structures and processes that support and guide the BPM efforts. Maturity and adoption of an adequate amount of governance is a leading indicator of the overall BPM success.

Individual capabilities are categorized within the preceding eight domains. Although inevitably overlapping and interrelated, these eight domains are sufficiently distinct for the purpose of a maturity assessment. To succeed at BPM adoption, an organization must achieve the appropriate levels of maturity in all domains sufficient to meet its BPM objectives. Typically, an organization will be more advanced in some domains (and in some of the capabilities within a domain) than others. Lagging or neglected domains will invariably prevent the organization from realizing the true value of BPM or, in some cases, cause it to fail altogether. It is important, therefore, to be able to measure the relative maturity within each domain (and the capabilities within them) and to identify areas that are lagging. Once the lagging areas have been identified, it is possible to formulate remedies and improve the success of the overall BPM initiative.

Maturity

Within the software industry, maturity is frequently related to the Capability Maturity Model (CMM) and the CMM successor, the Capability Maturity Model Integration (CMMI).[1] The BPM Maturity Model parallels this understanding and measures BPM capability against defined maturity levels. The levels of maturity used in the BPM Maturity Model (from lowest to highest) are:

- **No BPM**   There is no BPM approach being taken—BPM is not underway.

- **Ad Hoc**   Awareness of BPM exists and some groups are embarking on process automation. There is no BPM plan being followed.

- **Opportunistic**   An approach has been decided upon and is being opportunistically applied. The approach has not been widely accepted nor adopted. It may be informally defined, or if documented, may exist primarily as "shelf ware."

- **Systematic**   The approach has been reviewed and accepted by affected parties. There has been buy-in to the documented approach and the approach is always (or nearly always) followed.

---

[1] CMMI is a registered trademark of the Carnegie Mellon University.

- **Managed** The capability is being measured and quantitatively managed via some type of governance structure. Appropriate metrics are being gathered and reported.

- **Optimized** Metrics are being consistently gathered and used to incrementally improve the capability. Assets are proactively maintained to ensure relevancy and correctness.

The maturity levels progress from "No BPM" up to "Optimized." These levels define the path an organization usually takes moving toward BPM maturity. BPM by its very nature requires coordination, cooperation, and a common vision to be successful. Therefore, it is necessary to define the strategy before it is possible to be truly successful at repeating it and then ultimately optimizing it.

Adoption

Adoption measures how widely BPM is being accepted, embraced, and applied within the enterprise. For smaller organizations within a single line of business, maturity and adoption are usually tightly related since there is a single approach to BPM being followed by the entire organization.

Within large companies with multiple divisions or lines of business, however, this is not usually the case. It is common to have one or more divisions that are relatively mature in BPM while other divisions are not even attempting BPM. The BPM Maturity Model handles these situations by providing a separate measure for adoption level. This allows a single division to be effectively evaluated for BPM maturity while still capturing the lack of widespread adoption as a separate measure.

The levels of adoption used in the BPM Maturity Model are:

- **No Implementation** There is no current implementation anywhere in the organization of the capability being measured.

- **Project Level** Individual projects implement the capability as appropriate for that specific project. There may be informal and unregulated sharing across projects.

- **Program Level**   A relatively small group of projects (program) share an implementation of the capability. The program is under a single management structure below the VP level and encompasses less than an entire division or business unit.

- **Division Wide**   The capability is implemented consistently across a division or business unit. A division or business unit is typically led by an executive at the VP level or higher.

- **Cross Division**   The capability is implemented by multiple divisions using a common approach—in other words, the approach is being shared or is spreading to multiple divisions.

- **Enterprise Level**   The capability is implemented consistently across the enterprise—meaning, all divisions or business units are applying the same approach.

Maturity Assessment

For small organizations, it may be desirable to ignore the adoption dimension altogether and simply measure maturity. Conversely, for very large organizations with a goal of achieving enterprisewide BPM adoption, it may be desirable to measure the maturity for each division or line of business separately and then provide a single measure of adoption across the enterprise. It should be noted, however, that for the realization of many of the key BPM benefits, a level of adoption across the organization is critical. For example, it is possible to have two divisions with mature but incompatible capabilities, in such cases the adoption is lower (divisionwide) and that will inhibit an enterprisewide BPM initiative. Therefore, to properly measure the overall progress of a BPM initiative in a large organization, the maturity of the individual capabilities and the degree of adoption of such capabilities across the organization is vital.

An assessment of BPM maturity can be performed in various ways through workshops, interviews, web-based survey applications, or some combination of these. In any case, questions are constructed around the capability descriptions and the domain categories may be used to target various stakeholders' segments. The responses are captured in a spreadsheet that enables the scoring of both maturity and adoption across the full set of capabilities. An example of the analysis of the maturity assessment scores will be seen in the following sections as part of the roadmap creation process.

The Roadmap Creation Process

As you have seen already, four main phases comprise the core of the roadmap creation process: Current State Assessment, Future Vision Definition, Gap Analysis, and Activity Selection and Scheduling. These phases are shown in the diagram in Figure 9-7, along with some of the key artifacts that are exchanged between them.

The current state is measured using the Oracle BPM Maturity Model. By using an established maturity model, a consistent measurement scale is applied while maintaining focus on capabilities that are important to BPM success and thus avoiding the scope creep that frequently undermines current state evaluation efforts.

The Future Vision Definition phase is used to establish the high-level goal and reason for the BPM program. While a fully developed future vision is needed eventually, the initial roadmap creation only requires the high-level vision, while development of the detailed vision can be incorporated into the BPM Roadmap itself. Of course, if the current state of the BPM initiative includes a more detailed future vision, that vision can be leveraged when creating the roadmap.

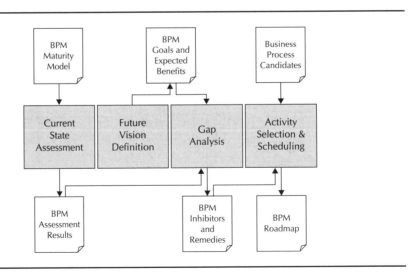

FIGURE 9-7. *The roadmap creation process*

The Gap Analysis phase evaluates the gap between the current state and the future vision for each of the capabilities. Generally, the capabilities exhibiting the largest gap are given highest priority during the roadmap creation phase. However, part of the Gap Analysis also includes an evaluation of the relative importance of each of the capabilities for your particular organization. Size, organizational structure, existing assets, funding priorities, even organizational politics can significantly impact the relative importance of capabilities.

The final phase is the Activity Selection and Scheduling phase. This phase uses the output from the Gap Analysis phase to create a logical ordering of work to be done. Emphasis is placed on the program-level efforts for the initial phases to establish the assets and processes used across projects. Candidate business processes are evaluated for their suitability for automation and are then prioritized based on that evaluation. The project portfolio is derived from the needs of the business processes selected for automation.

Current State Assessment

Attempting to capture a fully detailed description of the current state of an IT environment of a large company can lead to analysis paralysis. To avoid this problem, the method described here uses a focused scope and a pragmatic, time-boxed approach. The underlying goal is not to fully capture an IT environment current state; rather it is to evaluate the current state relative to the capabilities that are required to successfully adopt BPM.

The current state assessment is based on the Oracle BPM Maturity Model described in the previous section. The BPM Maturity Model includes an extensive set of capabilities that provide the detail necessary to accurately measure and guide the progress of a BPM initiative. Grounding the current state analysis on these specific capabilities ensures a focused scope for the assessment.

The current state assessment should be tightly time-boxed to ensure timely completion of this phase. The size and complexity of an organization determines the actual amount of time that must be allocated to the assessment. In general, two weeks is a good guideline for the time required for a current state assessment.

An overview of the current state assessment process is illustrated in the flow diagram in Figure 9-8.

The first step is to establish the scope of the assessment. For example, the scope may be limited to a single division or line of business within a larger

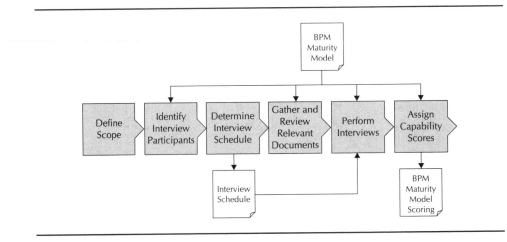

FIGURE 9-8. *The current state assessment process*

enterprise or it may be confined to a single geographic location. The scope defines both the scope of the assessment and, ultimately, the scope of the roadmap.

Once the scope has been determined, the participants in the assessment can be identified. The participants are chosen to ensure that all capabilities within the BPM Maturity Model can be accurately scored. Table 9-1 describes the typical areas of interest and interview participants.

Once the interview participants have been identified, the next step is to create a schedule for when each participant will be interviewed. The goal is to limit the length of the Assessment phase by creating a compacted schedule. It may be necessary to delay the start of the assessment to get times on the participants' schedules that fit into a two-week (or so) period. Time before or between interviews can be productive time spent reviewing documentation and deciding the next steps.

Before beginning the interview process, the assessment team should gather and review all the existing documents that describe various aspects of the current IT environment and BPM initiative. This allows the assessment team to ask more focused questions in the interviews and also provides the opportunity to ask questions about the written material for clarification or to resolve conflicting information. Table 9-2 is an example checklist of the types of documents that should be gathered and reviewed.

Area of Interest	Typical Participant
Business Objectives	VP of Business Unit(s)
	LOB IT
IT Objectives	CIO
	VP of Application Development
	VP of IT Infrastructure
Enterprise Architecture	VP of Enterprise Architecture
	Enterprise Architect(s)
	Business Specialists and Process Owners
Program Management	Program Management Office (PMO) Manager
	Project Manager(s)
Development Process	Application Architect(s)
	Business Analyst(s)
	Business Process Engineer(s)
	Methodologist
	Build Manager
	Configuration Management (CM) Manger
	QA Manager
Operations	Director of Operations
	Administrator(s)
Security	Chief Security Architect

TABLE 9-1. *Typical Interview Participants*

Typical Documents to Review

Balanced Score Card, Strategy Map (or similar business strategy/goals document)

Enterprise Architecture Document(s)

Project Management Handbook(s)

Business Process Model(s)

Application Functional Breakdown

Application Portfolio

Integration Architecture Document(s)

Operational Process and Procedures Document(s)

Corporate Security Policies

Organizational Structure Document (org chart)

BPM Program Document(s)

TABLE 9-2. *Typical Relevant Documents*

Before each interview, the assessment team should review the BPM Maturity Model to identify capabilities that are particularly relevant for the person being interviewed. It is not recommended that the assessment team simply ask a question for each of the capabilities. Rather, the interview team should ask open-ended questions that allow the interviewee to describe how things are currently done and to identify any problems that currently exist. Remember, the interviewees are the experts on what goes on within the organization being evaluated, so encourage them to explain the current situation.

Once the interviews have been completed and the documents have been reviewed, each of the capabilities in the BPM Maturity Matrix should be scored for both maturity and adoption. These scores provide the raw data that can then be analyzed in the Gap Analysis phase of the roadmap creation process.

When scoring a capability, the scores selected should be the scores where the descriptions of maturity level and adoption level most accurately match the current situation based on the information collected in interviews and from the documents reviewed. Although there is always some level of subjectivity when measuring capability, the goal is to provide an objective measure. This allows future measurements to be performed by a different assessment team, yet still provide results that can be used to accurately measure progress.

Frequently, when the assessment results are presented, there are questions and even disagreements about the score that was assigned. Therefore, it is also important that in addition to the score, the assessment team also record the rationale for assigning the maturity and adoption scores. This rationale could include quotes from interviews or specific sections from the documents that were reviewed.

The output of the current state assessment is the maturity and adoption score for each of the capabilities in the BPM Maturity Matrix. Additionally, the assessment team will have an understanding of the current state and should have collected known issues and problems that were identified and discussed during the interview process.

Future Vision Definition

For the BPM Roadmap creation process, the Future Vision Definition phase focuses solely on the high-level goals and principles that will be used to guide the entire BPM initiative. This phase does not attempt to create a detailed future state vision. While a more detailed future vision is required to achieve successful BPM adoption, it is not something that must be created prior to creating the initial BPM Roadmap. Other activities in the initial phases of the BPM Roadmap may focus on creating the detailed BPM future vision.

The BPM vision definition answers the following questions:

- What are the goals of the BPM initiative?

- What is the organizational scope of the BPM initiative?

- What are the benefits that BPM is expected to deliver to the organization?

- What are the guiding principles for the BPM initiative?

These questions must be answered by the executive(s) leading the BPM initiative. This is accomplished in a facilitated workshop. Nominally, the workshop should take about two hours, but may take longer if there is no preexisting understanding of BPM or there is substantial disagreement on why BPM is being pursued.

The focus should be to clearly define the goals for the BPM initiative by the end of the roadmap. The recommended roadmap planning horizon is two to three years. Therefore, these should be the goals of the BPM initiative two to three years from now. Table 9-3 contains suggested goal statements and scoring (5 being highest) that may be used as a starting point and adapted for a particular organization's needs.

The goal statements in Table 9-3 are used to gauge the extent and complexity of the entire BPM initiative and are listed in reverse order of difficulty. It should be obvious that accomplishing the first goal statement is far more difficult than accomplishing the fifth goal statement. Greater organizational maturity is required to achieve the more difficult goals for BPM. Of course, the benefits provided by BPM are correspondingly greater as well. The Score column in the table is used and will be explained further in the Gap Analysis phase.

Goal Statement	Score
Enable rapid response to changing business conditions (for example, competition, market forces, acquisition, and so on)	5
Develop a cycle of continuous improvement of business processes	5
Monitor business process efficiency and the effectiveness of change based on Key Performance Indicators (KPIs)	4
Improve business process transparency and visibility for improved control and consistency	3
Facilitate streamlining of human tasks through automation.	2
Apply BPM to a limited set of projects to demonstrate the benefits of BPM and build credibility with the business owners.	1
Improve business/IT alignment through common business process language and shared repositories	1

TABLE 9-3. *BPM Goal Statements*

The organizational scope defines which departments, divisions, lines of business, and so on are included in the BPM initiative. The most common scopes are either division or enterprise, but other options are possible depending on the company's organizational structure. Table 9-4 provides example levels of scope for the BPM initiative.

Defining the scope of the BPM initiative is essential to determining a roadmap. With greater scope, the number of organizational boundaries that must be crossed increases. This in turn increases the complexity of the effort, and therefore requires greater organizational maturity. The Score column in the table is used and will be explained further in the Gap analysis phase.

An organization can realize many different benefits by successfully adopting BPM. However, not all benefits can be realized in parallel. When creating a BPM Roadmap, emphasis should be placed on the benefits that are of highest priority, while the lower priority benefits should be left for later phases. Table 9-5 lists a few possible benefits of BPM adoption.

The items in Table 9-5 can be used as a starting place to identify the benefits that an organization hopes to achieve via BPM adoption. Every organization is different. Table 9-5 is only an overview of the possible benefits and is by no

BPM Initiative Scope	Score
A small number of projects will be applying process-orientation.	1
One or more business units will use BPM to address all of their projects.	2
The BPM initiative will span all business units within a single division.	3
The BPM initiative will span multiple divisions within the enterprise.	4
The BPM initiative will span the entire enterprise.	5

TABLE 9-4.   *BPM Initiative Scope*

Continuous improvement of business processes	Rapid deployment of business processes
Rapid/flexible process business change	Flexible architecture that enables business and IT agility
Ability to support cross-functional and cross-divisional processes	Effective use of external service providers
Single implementation and enterprise-view of business processes	Operational improvements
Process granularity recognized by a business user	Skill-set portability
Standardize process and technologies	Standards-based integration
Quicker re-composition of business processes	Integration with business partners
Extending value of legacy applications	Better visibility into business processes
Efficiency and/or consistency through automation	Business process standardization
Decoupling of applications	Productivity gains

TABLE 9-5.   *Example BPM Benefits*

means a comprehensive list. Part of the vision definition is in fact to create a list of possible BPM benefits and prioritize the list.

Once a list has been created, the benefits should be prioritized based on the business and IT objectives of the organization. The easiest way to prioritize the benefits is to assign a high, medium, or low prioritization to each possible benefit. Roughly one third of the possible benefits should be in each prioritization—in other words, it does no good to list all the possible benefits as high priority.

■ Every core business process must be documented following company standards.

■ Apply a consistent and controlled automation candidate identification process.

■ Utilize standards-based process automation infrastructure.

■ Business process is owned by the enterprise.

■ Reuse existing/legacy application functionality wherever possible.

TABLE 9-6.   *Example BPM Guiding Principles*

The guiding principles are derived from the top priority benefits and provide enforceable guidance to the BPM initiative. Table 9-6 provides some example guiding principles.

The guiding principles should be sufficiently clear and detailed that the principles can be enforced across the entire scope of the BPM initiative and on specific projects that fall under the purview of the initiative. The principles should also serve as a foundation to make more specific decisions in the future.

The output from the Vision Definition phase is the overall goal of the initiative, the scope of the initiative, the expected benefits, and the guiding principles to achieve the goal and the benefits. This vision for the BPM initiative can be captured in a single summary slide and used to educate and align the organization with the BPM initiative. An example of this summary slide is shown in Figure 9-9.

This clearly shows the goal and scope of the BPM initiative. It also shows that the BPM principles will be enforced across the entire BPM initiative and that the BPM initiative is expected to deliver the prioritized benefits.

Gap Analysis
The Gap Analysis phase compares the current state of the BPM initiative (as measured in the Assessment phase) with the goal for the initiative (defined in the vision phase). The gap between these two is then analyzed to determine the causes and remediation approaches are identified.

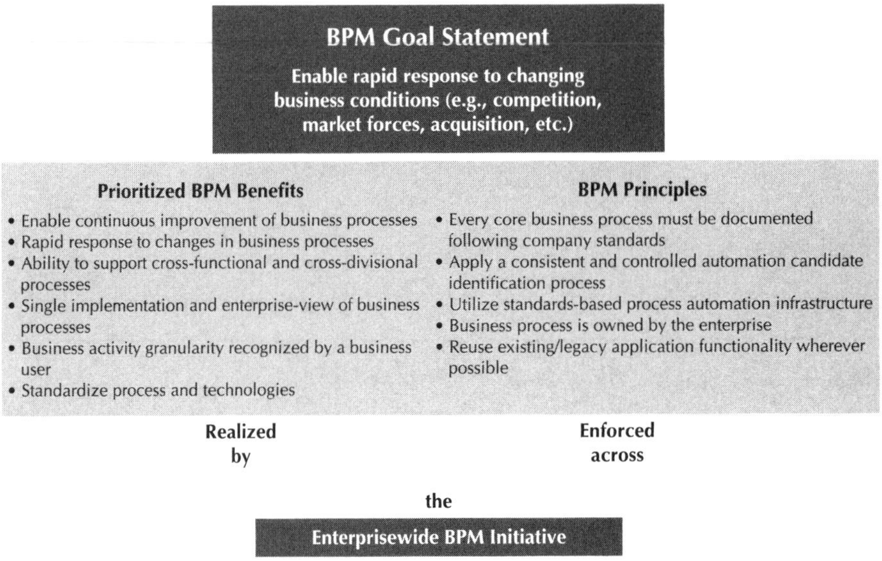

FIGURE 9-9. *An example BPM vision summary*

The maturity and adoption scores from the Current State Assessment phase measure the progress of a BPM initiative and, more importantly, identify specific capabilities that are lacking or lagging and are therefore inhibiting the BPM initiative. The gap between where the organization is currently and where they need to be to achieve their goal is broken down by capability domain from the BPM Maturity Model to identify lagging domains. It is further broken down by individual capability to identify specific capabilities that are lacking or lagging. The diagram in Figure 9-10 illustrates the process.

Once the lagging capabilities have been identified, a remediation approach for each of the identified inhibitors is determined from industry best practices.

The first step in the Gap Analysis phase is to identify the domains that exhibit the largest gap between current maturity and the maturity needed to achieve the BPM goal. The gap for the domains can be visually represented by a spider graph, as shown Figure 9-11.

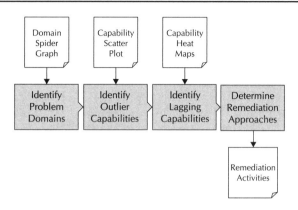

FIGURE 9-10. *The Gap Analysis process*

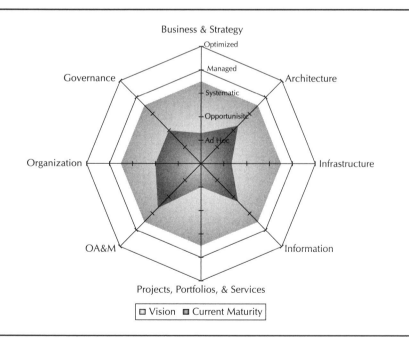

FIGURE 9-11. *Vision vs. current maturity*

For the example spider graph shown in Figure 9-11, the Vision level was derived using a spreadsheet formula and the following statements:

■ **Goal Statement**   Improve business process transparency and visibility for improved control and consistency.

■ **Scope Statement**   The BPM initiative will span multiple divisions within the enterprise.

The Current Maturity level for each domain is calculated by simply averaging the maturity score for each capability within the domain. This provides an average maturity for each of the eight domains that is then plotted in the spider graph.

Plotting the Current Maturity relative to the Vision (as shown in Figure 9-12) provides a visual representation of the gap between where the organization

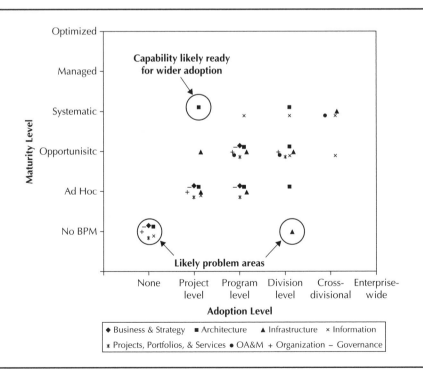

FIGURE 9-12.   *A capabilities scatter plot*

is with respect to BPM and where it needs to be to meet the goal of the BPM initiative. In this example, the graph clearly shows that the Projects, Portfolios, and Services domain is the area requiring the most attention, followed closely by the Business and Strategy and Infrastructure domains.

This analysis is fed into the roadmap creation phase. In this example, initial activities in the roadmap should include remediation for the lagging capabilities in the Projects, Portfolios, and Services; Business and Strategy; and Infrastructure domains.

Outlier capabilities are capabilities where the maturity and the adoption are significantly out of sync. This usually indicates a capability that should receive attention early in the roadmap. The outlier capabilities can be easily detected by plotting the maturity and adoption score for each capability in a scatter plot, as shown in Figure 9-12.

As shown in the figure chart, the maturity and adoption scores for capabilities usually fall along the diagonal when plotted against each other. In the preceding example, two scores are significantly off the diagonal, one well above the diagonal and one well below the diagonal. The capability well above the diagonal is a capability from the Architecture domain. The capability well below the diagonal is a capability from the Infrastructure domain. A cluster of capabilities is also highlighted as a likely problem area; although these are on the diagonal, they are at the bottom of the maturity scale. The analyst will need to review the actual capability scores to identify exactly which capabilities yielded the outlier points on the graph.

A capability that falls well above the diagonal indicates a capability that is done very well within a relatively small area of the organization. In this example, there is a capability at a Systematic level of maturity done within a single project. Fostering greater adoption of this capability provides an easy win for the BPM initiative—in other words, there is no need to develop greater competency for this capability within the organization since it already exists within the organization. Some training or mentoring can spread the ability more broadly within the organization.

A capability well below the diagonal indicates a capability that is done poorly (or in a non-BPM-compliant fashion). In this example, there is a capability being done at a No BPM level of maturity across the entire division. Corrective action needs to be taken for this capability, because if left uncorrected, it will inhibit (and probably already has inhibited) the BPM initiative.

Capabilities that plot nearer the lower left corner are capabilities that are either nonexistent or are lagging behind the other capabilities. These capabilities will be addressed in the next step of the Gap Analysis process.

The capabilities that plot toward the upper right corner are capabilities that are currently being done well. No remediation is required and the organization should continue business as usual for those capabilities.

The capabilities that plot nearer the lower left corner in the scatter plot are capabilities that require attention in early phases of the roadmap. Capability heat maps can be used to visually identify these low maturity capabilities, as shown in Figure 9-13.

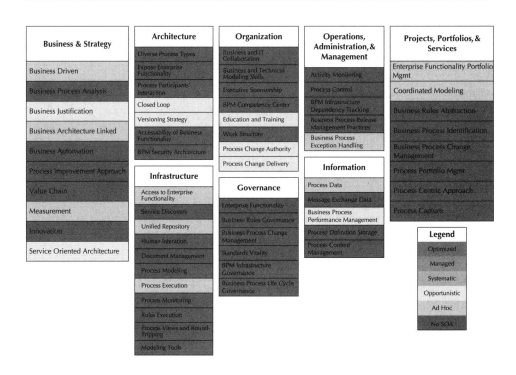

FIGURE 9-13. *Capabilities heat map*

The capabilities heat map colors each of the capabilities by maturity levels based on the maturity score recorded for that capability. The diagram in Figure 9-13 shows the color coding legend as well as each capability with color coding applied. The capabilities are organized by the domains used in the BPM Maturity Model.

The heat maps draw immediate attention to the capabilities that require attention. In the preceding example, there are five capabilities in the Business and Strategy domain (Business Process Analysis, Business Automation, Process Improvement Approach, Value Chain, and Innovation) that scored at the No BPM level of maturity. These capabilities should be addressed in early phases of the BPM Roadmap. Likewise, there are six capabilities in the Projects, Portfolios, and Services domain that scored at the No BPM level of maturity. All of the capabilities in the Governance domain were scored at the "No BPM" level of maturity, an obvious indicator that BPM is very immature for this organization.

It is important to point out that not all capabilities are of equal importance for a particular organization. In fact, there may be capabilities that are deemed unimportant or even not applicable for a particular organization. Thus, it is necessary to review each capability with a low score and determine whether it is a top priority, a low priority, or unimportant from a roadmap creation perspective.

If a capability is deemed unimportant for a particular organization, it should be removed from the maturity model and the graphics should be regenerated. This should be done with caution. A capability should only be removed if it is clearly not appropriate for the BPM initiative at this organization.

At this point in the Gap Analysis process, the problem domains have been identified and the problem capabilities within each domain have also been identified. The next step is to identify remedies for each problem domain and capability. The remedies clearly depend on the problem being addressed and also frequently have some aspect that is organization specific. It is not practical to provide a prescriptive approach to determining remediation activities for all 60+ capabilities; however, Table 9-7 offers a summary at the domain level.

Domain	Remediation Comments
Business and Strategy	Remediation for this domain and the capabilities within this domain usually require executive management decisions and directives. A common remediation activity is a facilitated workshop with appropriate executives to define the necessary strategies, make decisions, and formulate directives.
Architecture	Low scores in this domain usually indicate the lack of a reference architecture for the BPM initiative, or if the reference architecture exists, it lacks completeness and details. Remediation usually entails workshops with Enterprise Architects to specify a complete and detailed reference architecture.
Infrastructure	Low scores in this domain usually indicate that the process infrastructure is lacking significant elements. Infrastructure installation and configuration type projects are common remediation activities.
Information	Low scores in this domain usually indicate issues with the information architecture, data quality approach, and/or information stewardship. Common remediation activities are workshops to address the causes for the low scores.
Operations, Administration, and Management	Remediation activities for low scores in this domain usually entail definition, documentation, and enforcement of BPM-compatible OA&M procedures. Low scores could be due to lacking BPM knowledge/ skills or could be due to a low maturity of OA&M in general.

TABLE 9-7.   *Remediation per Domain*

Domain	Remediation Comments
Projects, Portfolios, and Services	Low scores in this domain usually indicate a lack of BPM compatible management and delivery processes. Common remediation activities entail workshops to modify existing management and delivery processes to inject BPM best practices.
Organization	Low scores in this domain usually indicate that roles and responsibilities appropriate for BPM have not been instituted within the organization. There may also be a lack of BPM knowledge/skills. Common remediation activities include developing training plans and workshops to define the necessary roles and responsibilities. Remediation may also require organization restructuring.
Governance	Most organizations have existing IT governance in place, so low scores in this domain usually indicate that governance has not been extended to cover BPM. Remediation usually requires a workshop to define and institute the governance extensions required for BPM.

TABLE 9-7. *Remediation per Domain* (Continued)

The output from the Gap Analysis phase is an understanding of which domains and which individual capabilities are inhibiting the successful achievement of the goal of the BPM initiative. Additionally, remediation activities have been identified to address the lagging domains and capabilities. These remediation activities provide the primary input into the roadmap creation process.

Activity Selection and Scheduling

The remedies identified in the Gap Analysis phase are prioritized and used to create a plan, called the BPM Roadmap. Business processes are then evaluated to select the business processes that are most appropriate for the application of BPM technology. This should not be equated to evaluating the value of the business process itself; rather, it measures the benefits (versus the risks) of the application of BPM technology.

Four steps comprise this final phase in creating a BPM Roadmap, and are illustrated in Figure 9-14.

As shown in the diagram, the main inputs to this phase are the remediation activities identified in the Gap Analysis phase, the identification of the integration requirements, and the business process selection framework. The final step is to determine timelines and dependencies and organize all the activities into a schedule.

The program-level activities are determined by prioritizing the remediation activities identified in the Gap Analysis phase. Top priority is usually given to remediation activities that focus on the domain with the lowest current maturity score. Top-priority remediation activities are usually the first activities in the roadmap since the results from these activities are leveraged across the solution and process delivery efforts.

Program-level activities frequently entail changes with wide-ranging impacts. For example, changing the software development process (to inject process-oriented best practices) impacts all development teams within the scope of the BPM initiative. Organizational changes can be even more taxing. Therefore, it is usually necessary to undertake these changes in a series of iterations. These iterations become the phases of the overall BPM Roadmap. At a high level, this can be shown graphically as illustrated by Figure 9-15.

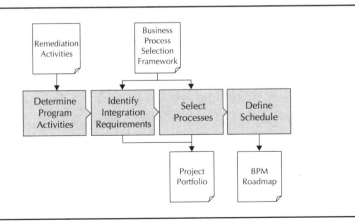

FIGURE 9-14.   *The roadmap scheduling process*

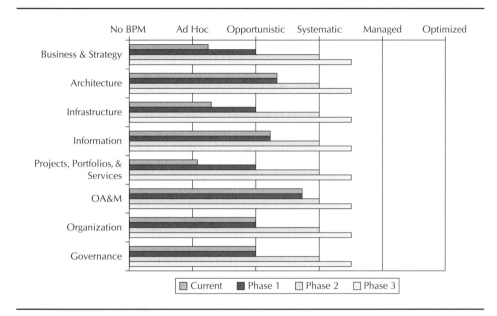

FIGURE 9-15. *Increasing maturity over time*

The graph illustrates three iterations, each increasing the maturity of one or more domains until the desired vision level of maturity is achieved. Notice that the first phase focuses on bringing all domains up to the Opportunistic level of maturity. This means that the first phase will include remedial activities for the Business and Strategy; Infrastructure; and Projects, Portfolios, and Services domains. Once near parity is achieved across domains, follow-on phases address the eight domains more uniformly to keep the BPM initiative progressing smoothly.

The amount of change introduced by an iteration must not exceed the organization's ability to absorb that change; therefore, the scope of each iteration must be carefully planned. Likewise, the duration of each iteration must be long enough to accomplish some meaningful progress, yet remain short enough to minimize risk and maintain a continuous pace of incremental progress.

Having selected the program-level activities, the next step is to identify processes that should be included in the roadmap. One of the selection criteria used for the process candidates is the accessibility of functionality from existing applications. It may be necessary to make modifications to these applications to support the new project. Two main types of changes exist:

- Application integration efforts

- Implement functional enhancements to existing applications and SOA services

The most likely case is that the existing application or SOA service needs extensions to support the integration in the process automation. These changes should be factored in to the process selection and the effort and integration approach clearly established in advance of project start. Ideally, the changes can be done in a backward-compatible manner, thereby allowing existing consumers of the SOA services to move to the new version deployed to support the new process.

Typically, integration requirements are best satisfied through a SOA approach; however, since a new SOA project is likely to provide additional benefits, such projects should be justified separately using the SOA roadmap planning and engineering strategies.

It is possible that the required business application functions do not currently exist anywhere in the organization. In this case, the process candidate may support justification for the development of application or service capabilities in a separate engineering project.

Any of the preceding types of change to existing application functionality or SOA services needs to be reflected in the BPM Roadmap regardless of whether or not they are handed off to a separate project. Obviously, the processes that use the SOA services have a dependency on the external change activities, so these dependencies must be captured in the roadmap.

Process Selection

A full description of business process selection is covered in a separate chapter of this book. However, an overview is provided here for the purposes of roadmap planning.

Three primary areas (shown in Figure 9-16) should be analyzed to identify process automation candidates:

■ Alignment with strategic goals

■ Value of benefits, such as frequency of process change, opportunities for optimization, and so on

■ Availability and accessibility of required business application functions

The level of difficulty is also usually factored-in during process selection. This helps with prioritization and enables a relatively quick and simple implementation on the first few projects.

This example shows six business process candidates. A positive "Decision Basis Score" indicates a process candidate that should be realized into an automated process. Thus, process candidates 1, 2, 3, 5, and 6 should be included in the BPM Roadmap with process candidates 5 and 6 tacked into

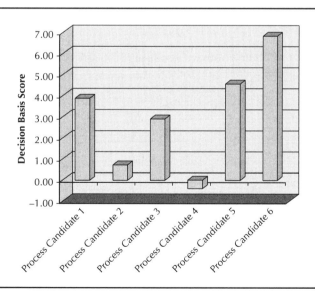

FIGURE 9-16. *Process candidate analysis*

the earliest phase of the roadmap. Process candidate 4 should not be realized (at this time).

The process candidates that are selected are included in the BPM Roadmap. Process candidates that are not selected should be recorded for future iterations of the roadmap. Although the process candidate did not make the cut for this iteration of the roadmap, it might very well make the cut in a future iteration.

Define Schedule

The schedule defined in this step is the schedule for the entire BPM initiative. Thus, it is the high-level schedule that illustrates the ordering and dependency relationships between program-level activities, the selected projects, service modifications, and the selected process candidates.

The high-level process for the BPM Roadmap development was shown in Figure 9-14, but actual timelines could not be determined until the projects, integrations, and process candidates had been identified. The final steps needed to assemble the complete schedule are:

1. Create the program-level activities schedule.

2. Create a high-level project schedule.

3. Determine delivery dates for application integrations and service modifications.

4. Determine delivery dates for process candidates.

The first activity of defining the schedule is to determine the start date and duration for the program-level activities. These are the initial activities put into the BPM Roadmap.

The next step is to determine the start dates for the selected projects. Projects that are expected to leverage the outcomes of the program-level activities (usually all projects) should not begin in earnest until the program-level activities complete. Some overlap is allowed since the earliest phases of a project (for example, the inception phase in the Unified Process methodology) can usually commence before the program-level activities are completed. The end date for the project is determined by effort, complexity, and resource availability. Sometimes the end date is mandated by business needs. In either case, the end date for the project is put into the schedule.

The delivery dates for the application integrations and SOA service modifications are determined by the needs of the project requiring the changes. Generally, the integrations and SOA service modifications must be available in time for project integration testing. Of course, an earlier delivery date is certainly acceptable and is, in fact, preferable.

Most of the projects included in the BPM Roadmap will have business process management automation as the primary delivery of the project. Exceptions include the infrastructure projects that deliver the shared BPM infrastructure used by multiple process management automation projects. The delivery dates for the selected business processes are determined and are incorporated into the schedule. The delivery dates for the selected business processes lie within the enclosing project delivery time line.

At this point, any resource constraints need to be incorporated into the schedule. This may require that start dates are delayed or durations increased. Once these constraints have been included, a schedule can be created and might look something like the schedule shown in Figure 9-17.

The schedule in Figure 9-17 begins with three program-level activities to address the three domains (Business and Strategy; Projects, Portfolios, and Services; and Infrastructure) that scored below the "Opportunistic" maturity level. The results from the program-level activities are then disseminated to all the projects and the process candidate realization activities are shown in the bottom half of the figure. The Infrastructure Project in the roadmap delivers the BPM infrastructure used by the other two projects shown. The Infrastructure Planning (that was part of the program-level activities) defines which technologies and products are deployed by the Infrastructure Project.

Project 1 and Project 2 both deliver the automation of business processes (Process Candidate 5 and Process Candidate 6). These two process candidates were selected via the Business Process Selection Framework as described earlier and shown in Figure 9-17. Finally, the graphic shows the application and SOA Service modifications that are required to support the projects. This is to expose the necessary functionality that is required by the tasks in the business processes.

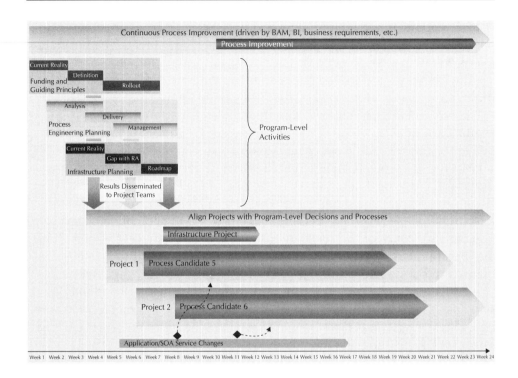

FIGURE 9-17. *The roadmap phase 1 schedule*

As discussed earlier, the detail in the initial phase of the BPM Roadmap will be much greater than the detail provided for the later phases. The later phases likely include additional program-level activities and more projects, as well as the process candidates on which they are dependent, but will contain less detail. An example of such a schedule is shown in Figure 9-18.

The first phase schedule was broken down into weeks but only covered two quarters. This schedule covers the entire planning horizon (three years) but with significantly less detail. The projects chosen for the first phase were relatively short in duration and effort. This is to help ensure early wins for the BPM initiative. Subsequent phases can then afford to undertake more complex efforts (for example, integrate fulfillment systems and warehouses) that could take years to complete.

BPM Roadmap	2010	2011				2012				2013			
	Q4	Q1	Q2	Q3	Q4	Q1	Q2	Q3	Q4	Q1	Q2	Q3	Q4
Phase 1 (see detailed schedule)													
Program Activities													
Funding and guiding principles	▓												
Process engineering planning	▓												
Infrastructure planning	▓												
Projects													
BPM infrastructure project	▓	▓											
Project 1		▓											
Project 2		▓											
Processs													
Process candidate 1		▓											
Process candidate 2		▓											
Application modification		▓											
Service construction		▓											
Phase 2													
Program Activities													
Adopt industry standard process models			▓										
Define a BPM reference architecture			▓										
Establish a core set of modeling tools				▓									
Establish modeling standards enforcement				▓									
Evangelize benefits realized from BPM					▓								
Projects													
Process portal infrastructure project					▓								
Integrated, process portal–based interface for CRM					▓								
Retrofit fresh digital to leverage BPM						▓							
Decouple UIs from back-end technology						▓							
Phase 3													
Program Activities													
Define procedures for process model updates							▓						
Establish procedures for process optimation								▓					
Establish test procedures for process updates								▓					
Implement security auditing practices									▓				
Foster BPM tool usage to define business reqmts									▓				
Create charge-back models									▓				
Projects													
BPM infrastructure project										▓	▓	▓	▓
Integrate fullfillment systems and warehouses										▓	▓	▓	▓

FIGURE 9-18. *The BPM roadmap's subsequent phases*

Subsequent phases will also likely have additional infrastructure projects that continue to build out the reference architecture. The capabilities of the reference architecture built out in each phase depend on the needs of the processes that are included in the phase.

The output from the roadmap creation phase is the BPM Roadmap that includes a detailed initial phase and less detailed subsequent phases. The BPM Roadmap provides guidance for achieving the goal of the BPM initiative via a series of much smaller transitions. Ideally, each of the smaller transitions has its own individual business benefit, but it is frequently necessary to invest a little up front to reap larger benefits down the line.

It is worth noting that projects, in the context of the roadmap, include projects for remediation activities identified in the assessment (infrastructure improvements, the SOA service portfolio, organizational changes, and so on) in addition to business process automation projects (which will be explained in more detail in Chapter 11).

Summary

Using the roadmap approach, program-level improvements, infrastructure deployments, and process improvement projects are prioritized and coordinated to maximize the benefits and minimize the conflicts and complexity of a BPM initiative.

It is important to keep the end goal in mind when applying a roadmap approach—that is, achieving the objectives of the BPM initiative—it is NOT just to arrive at a particular score in the BPM Maturity Model. The success of the BPM initiative is measured by the realization of the prioritized BPM benefits identified in the Future Vision phase. The BPM Maturity Model and the various frameworks are merely tools to help build a plan to achieve these goals and benefits.

Finally, and perhaps most importantly, this is an incremental approach. The process described in this document to create a BPM Roadmap should be regularly reapplied and the roadmap should be updated to reflect the changing reality. This allows each iteration to focus on the most pressing needs. Areas not of immediate concern can be relegated to future iterations, thereby reducing the size and complexity of the current iteration.

CHAPTER
10

Strategic Analysis,
Process Selection,
and Design

his chapter focuses on a key part of the business process engineering method necessary to get started on a path to successful implementation of composite business process applications. We'll leave the full definition of the project strategies, participants, and implementation details to the next chapter.

Following the enterprise-level planning activities described in the last chapter, we need to get down to the implementation of business process automation. But before we do that and move into the IT realm of technical analysis, design, and implementation, we must be sure we have selected the appropriate processes and performed an adequate business analysis.

Let's start by getting the terminology straight. We've called this chapter *Strategic Analysis, Process Selection, and Design* because these are the aspects of the engineering methodology that we are focusing on to get the executable process implementation started. Process selection is really part of the analysis activity, so it may be considered part of the more general category of business analysis or it may be part of higher-level strategic analysis depending on the approach and use of terminology. This chapter is also going to cover the initial stages of "process design," although *design* is such an overloaded term we prefer to use the words *definition* and *refinement* to describe this part of the implementation. Definition is where we are finally applying the necessary details of the process in order to make it a process model (in the sense of a BPMN model at least). Once defined, the current "*as-is*" business process model is ready to enter the cycle of continuous process improvement, starting with an initial round of changes, which we call *refinement,* to create the "*to-be*" model.

The Object Management Group (OMG) defines three stages of model development, starting with *descriptive,* through *analytical,* and finally *executable.* It is important to understand these distinctions and to ensure that the approach accommodates these stages and the various stakeholders involved in the process model development throughout its life cycle.

In the next chapter, we will describe the technical aspects of process design and ultimately, of course, business process application composition. This will take us to the last stage of modeling, the executable stage. In this chapter, the focus is purely on the descriptive thru analytical model development. Sometimes it's very hard to draw the line between the levels of detail we can put into a business process model versus a technical one.

As an example, it might be tempting for a business analyst to describe the business data objects that flow between the activities in a process. A technical definition of this type in this stage could potentially lead the business analyst down an unnecessarily detailed path, missing an opportunity to describe the process in more appropriate business terms.

Regardless of the motivation for business process automation (for example, process redesign, continuous improvement in a process-centric organization, or just plain visibility and control in response to regulatory requirements), we must first understand what our business processes are and prioritize them for computerized management under a BPMS.

Business process selection is the most critical step in BPM. It is about picking the *right* processes for automaton. Getting this step wrong can mean spending a lot of effort for no measurable benefit. If this is the first attempt at automation, the resulting disillusionment can stall an entire BPM program.

Not all processes are suitable for automation and, indeed, not all processes are even business processes, so we must start by determining just what our business processes are. We can simply refer to this as business process *identification.* Another term in common use at this stage in the BPM life cycle is *discovery*—unfortunately, there seems to be little agreement on the scope and meaning of this term (see the "Business Process Discovery" section later in this chapter), which commonly entails some degree of automation in the mechanism for identifying processes. To avoid the ambiguity in the use of the term, we prefer to describe *discovery* as the straightforward sequence of identification, selection, and definition for the first steps in business process engineering. Realistically, as with all the collaborative elements of the BPM Approach, these activities are iterative and incremental and so it is equally valid to think of them as the focus of the *inception* and *elaboration* phases in a Unified Process (UP) or other Iterative and Incremental Development (IID) project. You can find information about project strategies for BPM in Chapter 11.

Business process identification is the primary input to process selection. Here we identify potential candidates to become automated processes. Identification and selection make up the core of business analysis where we may choose to take either a strategic or tactical approach depending on whether we have access to business architecture and associated commitment from executive management. The bottom line is that effective process selection need not be sacrificed even in the absence of business planning information from the executive team. This will be explained further in the following sections.

Business process design is about expanding the detail of the process sufficiently before passing it to the next stage for technical implementation. Design (specifically *definition*) is the point at which BPMN process modeling begins. All too often, business process projects start by immediately modeling processes. This usually means that any realistic measure of business analysis has been skipped, leading to unpredictable results.

The Business Process Life Cycle

Now is a good time to introduce the Oracle Business Process Engineering Life Cycle. However, since we are only focusing on process analysis and design at this stage we will only introduce the life cycle here for context. We'll describe the engineering life cycle in much more detail in Chapter 11.

Most engineering methodologies follow similar sequences of activities spanning analysis, design, implementation, and deployment. In modern software engineering methods, these activities are applied iteratively while making incremental changes. The life cycle of an executable business process is, in many ways, similar to traditional methodologies, but with a particular emphasis on in-built monitoring and with analysis driving the iterative cycles of continuous (incremental) improvement. The diagram in Figure 10-1 shows the business process life cycle covering the complete set of activities in the cycle of continuous business process improvement.

In the case of business process engineering, analysis occurs in two separate activities, shown here with the labels *Identify* and *Select*. These are separated because of the different activities involved in getting started with process automation. In order to enter the continuous improvement cycle, an analysis activity is required to *identify* business processes and *select* those most appropriate for automation. Identification involves describing the process only at the highest level in order to understand its current ("as-is") state, while process selection applies analytical techniques to evaluate the

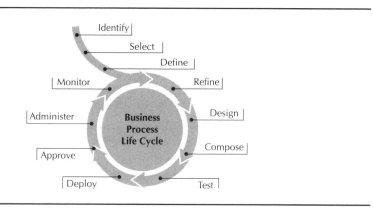

FIGURE 10-1.   *The business process engineering life cycle*

suitability of the process for automation. The details of business process identification and selection are described in this chapter.

Before entering the cycle for the first time, the business process goes through the first stage of process design (*define* stage) to describe it at the next level of detail and prepare it for the first iteration of improvements (*refine* stage). Subsequent iterations through the cycle only need to be concerned with further refinement because the definition will have already been developed and future cycles are only concerned with incremental improvements. The first iteration of the life cycle takes business analysis as input, so changes to the business process should be limited to minimize the impact and risk in the initial automation project; however, subsequent iterations of the life cycle benefit greatly from the analytical information provided by the new *monitor* stage activity and changes in subsequent iterations can be supported by more quantitative information.

Technical Design explores the capabilities of IT and determines the feasibility of the implementation of the process model as an executable process. Where possible, existing services are identified for use in subsequent implementation activities. If gaps exist, they must either be filled through traditional software (or service) engineering or the process specification is returned to the previous step for rework. This is an example of various loops that can occur within the main business process life cycle.

Traditional implementation is replaced with business application *composition* (*compose* stage) and associated testing (*test* stage). Unlike implementation in software engineering, composition involves only declarative coding (for example, business rules) and graphical construction (such as process flows) and wiring (for instance, messages between service components).

Business process administration and monitoring are closely linked in the traditional sense of Operations, Administration, and Management (OA&M) since the *monitor stage* provides information for process control dashboards; however, monitoring plays another important role in the business process life cycle since it also drives the analysis needed as part of the next iteration of process improvement.

As we shall describe later in the book, the Oracle Business Process Engineering Methodology elaborates on this outline while providing a business-focused approach that is intended to augment, rather than replace, existing software engineering practices.

Business Process Discovery (BPD)

We mentioned Business Process Discovery earlier in this section, so it is worth taking a moment to define it and put it into context with our life cycle.

BPD is a set of techniques that *automatically* construct or extend a model of an organization's current business processes. Classically, these techniques use artifacts found in the existing application systems, such as log files, that run the organization's business processes. This is a *bottom-up* analysis of process paths and exceptions through an application that typically leads to a highly detailed process flow model. In many ways, BPD is similar to the reverse-engineering of code to produce a UML (Unified Modeling Language) model. These efforts help in the exploration of undocumented code, for example, but rarely serve as a useful starting point for business analysis due to their overwhelming detail.

The term "discovery" is also used for the generation of first-cut process flows from a set of manually defined activity descriptions. This involves a simpler approach to model generation, typically only using process information entered by business users in the initial life cycle stages of *identification* and *definition*.

Business Process Identification and Selection

There are various ways in which a business process project or program can be initiated. In some cases, a business process project might be requested by a business sponsor with a predetermined requirement to automate a process. In these cases, there is an understandable tendency to leap over the complexity of process candidate selection and justification. After all, isn't a business requirement justification enough? Unfortunately, there are two major risks in oversimplifying this entry into process automation. The first risk is that BPM benefits will not be realized because the process may not be suited to automation or its automation may be beyond the capabilities of the organization to deliver it (IT infrastructure, modeling and analysis skills, and so on—described in Chapter 11). The second risk is that the process may not be a business process at all: It may be simply a subprocess or an individual activity that should be handled as a technical orchestration in a different layer of the architecture. Already we can see three important things we need to be aware of when selecting a business process candidate for automation: suitability of the process to realize BPM benefits, capabilities and maturity, and distinguishing the right kind of process for automation. Since capabilities and maturity were covered in the previous chapter, our focus in this chapter will be on identifying measurable benefits for automation and making the right architectural choices to handle different types of processes.

Clearly, complexity of the business process is a factor in selection, and we have seen an assessment of maturity and capabilities handled in the Oracle Approach to BPM. An objective definition of a business process, distinguishing it from other types of processes, will be elaborated on in the following sections. Numerous other considerations should be taken into account before embarking on business process automation, and these will be covered in the following section on business process selection.

The diagram in Figure 10-2 shows a high-level process flow for business process identification and selection. The two distinct paths into process selection highlight strategic and tactical approaches. These two approaches commonly arise from either strategy-driven (with executive sponsorship in a process-centric organization) or operational (arising from a specific business problem) initiatives. Either approach feeds into a scoring system, requiring no more sophistication than a spreadsheet, which leads to process selection and prioritization.

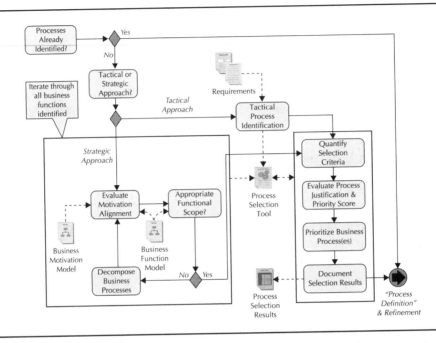

FIGURE 10-2. *High-level flow for business process identification and selection*

The strategic approach focuses on business process identification and selection using a variety of tools and techniques discussed in the following sections. The tactical approach, on the other hand, assumes the business process automation candidates have been identified by some other means and need only to be justified and prioritized for business process automation projects. In this case, *tactical* simply means processes have been identified without an enterprisewide analysis using strategic business planning artifacts; this does not mean, however, that we cannot proceed with the selection procedure. As we will show in the section on process selection, numerous criteria can be evaluated even in the absence of known strategic objectives.

The following sections focus on the strategic approach and include an introduction to business functional modeling and decomposition, as well as business motivation artifacts.

Strategic Approach to Process Identification

Business architecture is the formal link between business strategy and operational BPM projects. The business architecture captures the enterprise's goal, strategy, and the business practices of the enterprise as the primary set of requirements that other initiatives like business process improvement projects must satisfy.

Strategic analysis, using the business architecture assets, provides the greatest benefits to process selection by identifying processes that are most in alignment with business goals and objectives. Strategic process identification may be the result of adjacent efforts focused on business strategy planning, business architecture, business process redesign or other business process improvement efforts (such as Six Sigma). The assets discovered during strategic analysis enable a direct linkage to business value.

While it is not our intention to provide instruction in the techniques of business architecture, we will introduce some common strategic business planning concepts to illustrate how to extract the information needed for business process identification and selection.

Functional Models

Function modeling has played many roles throughout the history of IT and software engineering approaches. It has been applied at the project level as a tool to organize requirements against functional concerns and assist the development of application architectures. Function modeling has also been applied at the management level to assist enterprises in understanding current IT capabilities, where they are used to plan and justify additional IT projects. For our purposes, function modeling is especially useful in organizing concerns and establishing consistent leveling throughout process identification, analysis, and design.

Across these various uses of functional modeling, all share the same hierarchical structure, which makes them easily recognizable and therefore useful to a wide range of stakeholders. The broad adoption of this concept also fosters a common approach (although not a standard) between tools and there are many different tools available that support non-cyclic tree structures.

A functional model is a means of representing business functions and processes in a hierarchy. Before we jump into the use of function models, we need to establish a convention for the number and naming of levels in a functional tree structure. There is no standard or even much consistency in the use of functional hierarchies, so we'll use the Oracle leveling definitions shown in Figure 10-3. You can feel free to use any naming or even number of levels; however, the Oracle convention is supported by many years of practical experience implementing BPM and is used consistently in other Oracle technology strategies (this is particularly beneficial when communicating SOA service requirements in the implementation stages of process automation). Furthermore, in a functional decomposition activity, which we will outline later in this section, it is important to define the bottom of the pyramid as a point at which further decomposition is no longer useful.

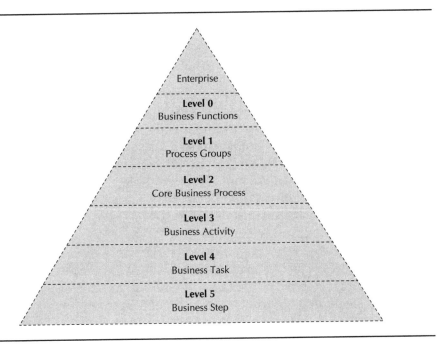

FIGURE 10-3. *Functional hierarchy*

At the top of the pyramid is the enterprise definition. In some cases, this may be represented simply by the company name, but for our purposes we imagine this is a broader definition including business plans, motivation models, strategy, and various other business architecture assets. Once again, it is important to note that BPM practitioners are not typically expected to create business architecture assets at this level; however, some understanding is required in order to make use of them in the strategic analysis activities.

The following is a summary of the levels of the functional hierarchy that are important, not only to strategic analysis, but also in process design as we move down the pyramid. These functional hierarchy level definitions will be used through the remainder of this chapter to anchor our systematic progress through business process analysis and design.

- **Level 0 – Business Functions**   This level defines the top-level business functions of the enterprise, which might include topics such as Manage IT, Manage Financial Services, Manage Customer Service, and so on. Typically, very little detail is required, other than high-level descriptions for the function performed by each child node defined in this level.

- **Level 1 – Process Groups**   This level decomposes the parent high-level business functions into groups defining similar processes performed by the high-level business function. For example, Manage Enterprise Information, Manage IT Knowledge, and Develop and Maintain IT Solutions are all examples of children of the Manage IT from Level 0. Again, descriptive information defining the family of processes should be sufficient at this level for detailing nodes.

- **Level 2 – Core Business Processes**   This level defines individual core business processes within the parent business process group. Following the theme of the previous example in level 1, a core business process within Develop and Maintain IT Solutions might be Business Process Engineering. Other examples of core business processes (better suited for automation) include Product Development, Customer Acquisition (Sales), and Product Delivery and Servicing. Core process definition includes identifying the roles and high-level functions performed by the process. Understand that it is not always necessary to have more than one child for each parent. High-level use cases can be introduced to begin detailing the processes identified in this level and potentially high-level business process models (or *process maps*) can be established.

- **Level 3 – Business Activity**   This level breaks down a business process into corresponding Business Activities. Business Activities are the activities performed as part of a business process that may yet be broken down across several tasks. It is often useful to think in terms of a transaction, rather than a single method here, where the transaction may be executed, as a unit, over several actors. Again, use case analysis is a great way to represent nodes in this level when taking a purely functional approach.

- **Level 4 – Business Task**   This level breaks down Business Activities into finer-grained Business Tasks. Tasks are typically performed by a single actor (system or manual), but may involve many steps. Again, use cases are a valid way to represent nodes of this level, although at this level, they are more likely to also involve other descriptive documents and diagrams to supplement their definition.

- **Level 5 – Business Step**   This level breaks down a business task into finer-grained steps. This is the lowest level of detail necessary for functional modeling. Typically, detailed requirements are all that is necessary at the step level.

The strategic analysis phase of business process engineering focuses only on the functional hierarchy from level 0 to level 2 based on the Oracle definitions mentioned earlier. The practitioner can use the descriptions above to align function and process descriptions and, if necessary, decompose to the next level until a set of core business processes has been identified.

In order to identify business processes, as our first step toward automation, we must first understand the organization's business functions. The Functional Decomposition Diagram (FDD) is a business planning tool that represents the hierarchy of business functions, processes, and subprocesses within an organization that are later described in detail using process models.

The exercise of breaking down or decomposing the business functions into processes makes complex systems easier to understand and analyze, provides consistency when talking about processes at the different levels, ensures the correct starting point for BPMN modeling, and encourages the use of appropriate modeling techniques at every level. An example of a simple FDD, alongside the functional hierarchy pyramid to illustrate its alignment, is shown in the diagram in Figure 10-4.

A FDD or simply "function model" (also called an activity model), is a graphical representation of an enterprise's function within a defined scope. The purposes of the function model are to describe the functions and processes, assist with the discovery of information needs, help identify opportunities, and establish a basis for determining product and service costs.

Functional decomposition refers broadly to the process of resolving a functional relationship into its constituent parts in such a way that the original function can be reconstructed from those parts by function composition. In general, this process of decomposition is undertaken either for the purpose of gaining insight into the identity of the constituent components, or for the purpose of obtaining a compressed representation of the global function,

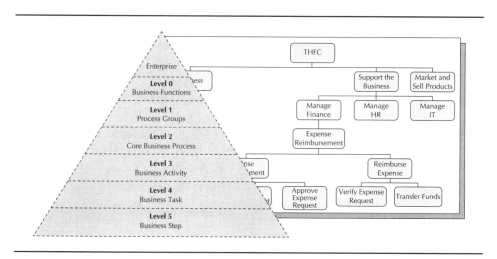

FIGURE 10-4. *A simple function model aligned with the functional hierarchy*

a task that is feasible only when the constituent processes possess a certain level of modularity.

Further information about functional decomposition can be found later in this chapter in the section "Business Process Design."

Business Strategy Modeling

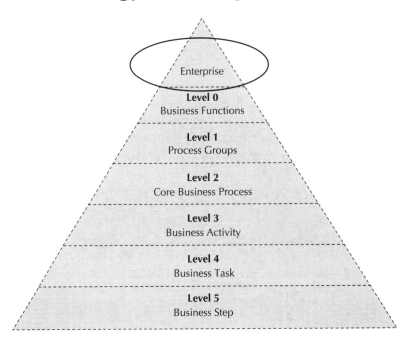

As with many aspects of business management, even de facto standards are rare and any degree of consistency between organizations is uncommon. In some cases, a recognizable approach to business strategy is entirely absent and some consider business management more of an art than a science. With that in mind, we still have to identify a clear path from business strategy to process identification (described at a certain level of detail and decomposition) and through process selection before we can embark on a well-founded implementation. Since we clearly cannot describe all the approaches, proprietary or otherwise, we shall instead highlight some of the more common techniques that have emerged from Harvard Business School, or that have been standardized by the OMG and others.

Remembering this is not intended to provide instruction on how to create a business strategy, but rather how to identify and use it, the following paragraphs provide a brief introduction to business architecture in order to identify some of the established structures and strategies.

Business Strategy Overview

Business strategy modeling provides the ability to prioritize efforts, justify decisions, trace automation decisions and other activities of the IT organization, and align them with the strategic goals of the business. This adds tremendous value to many initiatives such as IT Optimization, SOA, and BPM in particular, since it enables a clear understanding of which projects to undertake, which business processes are currently most important to the company, and which processes are most aligned with business strategy. Hence, activities related to initiatives such as SOA, BPM, and IT optimization can directly lead back to business goals and financial objectives. When the process projects associated with a strategic roadmap are implemented, the results provide a measurable competitive advantage and improved stakeholder value. This association not only aids process identification of strategic processes at the right level of granularity, but also supports selection and justification of projects.

Strategic planning is the responsibility of senior management and is usually carried out by a corporate planning department reporting to executive management. The diagram in Figure 10-5 shows the relationship between business strategy and the associated architecture that drives actionable, strategic projects.

These strategic projects can be many and varied and should include the capabilities improvement projects identified in the maturity assessment described in Chapter 9, in addition to initial process automation, ongoing optimization, and redesign.

In order to drill-down a little further into the business architecture, it is useful to understand the meta-model and terminology for *business motivation* development by the OMG before we look at various forms of business motivation models.

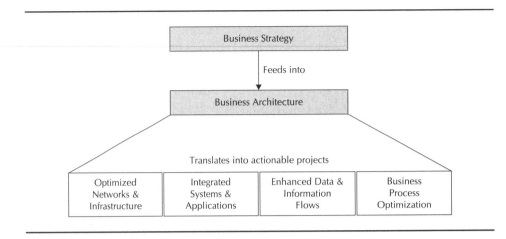

FIGURE 10-5. *Strategy—architecture relationship*

The OMG Business Motivation Model (BMM)

The OMG BMM establishes the semantics for describing the *business motivation*. From its name alone, we can see immediately that it is a model—that is to say, a description of the motivation and not a process for modeling motivation (we will provide specific examples of motivation modeling approaches in the next section). This semantic model is equally relevant to *business planning* for IT and may be used to formalize the structure of an IT business plan.

Spanning such topics as mission, goal, objective, strategy, and tactic (the *ends and means*), conforming Business Motivation Models provide semantic definitions for the capture, retention, traceability, and reasoning behind business decisions.

The OMG Business Motivation Model (or more accurately meta-model) is a formal means of expressing the semantics of motivation for business desires and actions. It is not intended that the business architects create diagrammatic representations of business motivation, but rather the BMM definitions convey the relationships of the language elements.

In defining a language in support of modeling business motivation, the BMM is similar to the approach taken by the IEEE 1471 standard that specifies semantics for Enterprise Architecture. In both cases, terms are defined and their relationships modeled to enable both consistency in practitioner usage and the foundation for the specification of repository tooling. The IEEE 1471 and OMG BMM documents both use UML diagrams to describe their semantic models.

Scope of the BMM Standard

The BMM does not define Business Processes, Rules, Policies, and others, but instead focuses exclusively on capturing the motivation for an action (such as execution of an engineering project, creation of an SOA service, and so on) and defining the language for the consistent expression of business motivation. Although often relevant in assessment and other aspects of motivation, organization structure is also beyond the scope of standard BMM.

BMM describes the *means and ends* (the strategies and tactics) of business plans and captures assessments about various types of influencers that may have the potential to impact the means and ends.

The BMM and associated standards are also intended to provide the basis for repository tooling and the exchange of models using mechanisms like XMI. However, the BMM does not specify a methodology, process, or an approach for business planning.

The Outline of the BMM

The OMG BMM is a meta-model for the standardization of descriptions of motivations for the elements of a business plan. An enterprise might use the BMM meta-model approach to establish the factors that motivate the creation of a business plan and identify and define the elements of such a plan.

The BMM is made up of four major areas of concern, which are in turn broken into other elements, each with very specific meanings. The four high-level elements of the meta-model—*Means, Ends, Influencer*, and *Assessment*—are shown in the simplified representation of the BMM in Figure 10-6.

Fundamentally, *means* and *ends* refer to the *strategies, tactics,* and *business policies and rules* that the business might employ to achieve a *desired result* (the *ends*). Along the way, these are supported by *assessments* of things, such as risk/reward or Strengths, Weaknesses, Opportunities, and Threats (SWOT analysis).

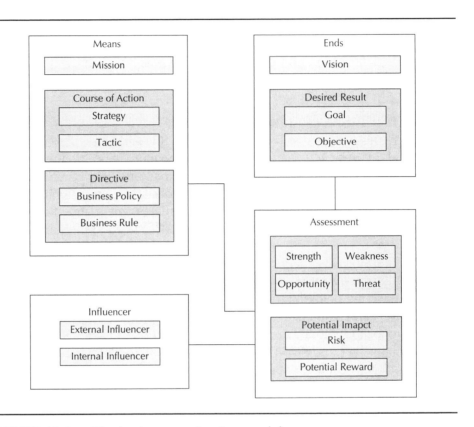

FIGURE 10-6. *The business motivation model*

So if a business plan is used to specify what an enterprise wants to achieve, the elements of the business plan lay out the *means* necessary to achieve the *ends* (*desired result,* and so on). Motivation refers to the influencers that underlie the choices of *means* to serve the *ends* of each element of a business plan.

The BMM is not intended to be used as a business plan by itself. A business plan requires the support of numerous other factors that are external to the BMM, such as organization models, business rules, business process models, and others. Other referenced elements of business models that might support the Business Motivation Model include a common business vocabulary (for example, OMG's Semantics of Business Vocabulary and Business Rules [SBVR]). Boundaries between the various aspects of a complete business plan are not hard and fast. There is the potential for considerable overlap, and every organization is free to choose to make distinctions appropriate to its own needs.

Here are definitions to some common terms appearing in Figure 10-6, along with some additional related terms, are outlined in Table 10-1.

Term	Definition
Vision	Every company has a *Vision* of where the business is trying to get to in the long term, and takes into account the needs of the market and stakeholder expectations. A Vision describes the future state of the enterprise without regard to how it is achieved. Where do you want to be in five years? It should be lofty but attainable (#1 player, best supplier, and so on). It should resonate with all members of the organization and help them feel proud, excited, and part of something much bigger than themselves. The vision has to be succinct and simple to communicate.
Goal	A *Goal* amplifies a Vision. It points out what must be satisfied on a continuing basis to effectively attain the Vision. It is qualitative in nature and long term.
Objectives	*Objectives* are short term and quantitative in nature. It is a statement of an attainable, time-constrained, and measurable target that needs to be fulfilled in order to achieve the Goals.
Mission	A *Mission* encapsulates the actions a business might take in order to achieve its Vision. The Mission is a precise description of what an organization does. It is a definition of *why* the organization currently exists. Like the Vision, a Mission is high-level and takes a long-term perspective—it makes a Vision operative. The detailed parts of the Mission are courses of action and directives.

TABLE 10-1.   *Definition of Terms in Business Motivation and Planning*

Term	Definition
Business Strategy	A *Business Strategy* involves the development of policies and plans (often in terms of projects and programs), which are designed to achieve corporate objectives. It then shows the allocation of resources to implement the policies and plans, projects and programs. Strategies get funded. Strategies can be realized and resourced. Business Strategy consists of plans at the corporate as well as the business unit level. Corporate strategic plans are enterprise-level plans—overarching plans that might span 3 to 10 years. They are fundamental to the survival and growth of the organization. They are also heavily influenced by investors in the business and act to guide strategic decision-making throughout the business. Plans at the business unit level—also referred to as Business Plans—are used to implement corporate strategic plans. Corporate strategic plans are linked to Goals, while Business Plans are related to Objectives.
Critical Success Factors (CSFs)	A *Critical Success Factor* (*CSF*) cites certain key measures that, when attained, will ensure the success of an organization and the achievement of its business goals. The identification of Critical Success Factors helps the organization focus its efforts and build capabilities around selected areas. Organizations evaluate the feasibility of the CSFs, which are used to set the right perspective and reevaluate the business strategy if required.
Key Performance Indicators (KPIs)	Once a strategy is defined to achieve a goal or objective, its implementation will need to be measured. This is achieved by *Key Performance Indicators* (*KPIs*) defined for each strategy. KPIs are measures that quantify objectives and enable the measurement of strategic performance.

TABLE 10-1. *Definition of Terms in Business Motivation and Planning (continued)*

Term	Definition
Risks & Controls	*Risks & Controls* are designed to comply with regulations, to limit losses, and preserve value. Risk analysis is an important part of strategic decision making. Should the organization merge or acquire a competitor? What risks are presented by new product development? Will an agreement with a new supplier compromise brand integrity?
Products/ Services	The main purpose of doing business is creating value producing products and services for internal and external customers. *Products and Services* are business outcomes that are produced by business processes. From an architectural viewpoint, we are concerned with products and services because these are often exactly what the underlying IT architecture is built to support. Furthermore, the analysis of the performance and revenue of these business outcomes identifies business transformation opportunities.

TABLE 10-1.   *Definition of Terms in Business Motivation and Planning (continued)*

The Mission and Vision descriptions should be part of the business model that is created when the company begins doing business. They may persist for the entire life of the business, or evolve over time as markets change.

The diagram in Figure 10-7 shows how the elements of the business motivation model relate—in particular where strategic plans can be found in the hierarchy and how they drive business projects. Also of interest here is the emergence of Key Performance Indicators (KPIs) from objectives (the quantifiable manifestation of goals). Establishing good KPIs is critical to effective measurement and analysis of business process performance in a composite business application.

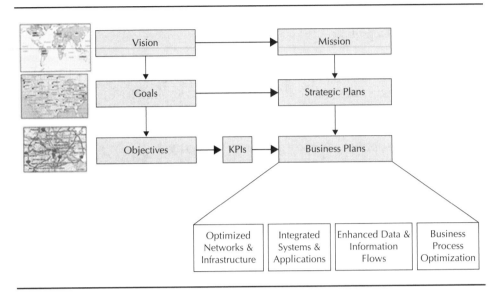

FIGURE 10-7.   *Relating the elements of business motivation to business process projects*

Although many techniques are employed for business planning, and although in our experience many are unique to an organization (or even individual business executives), it is best to use the well-recognized methods of the Harvard Business School Kaplan and Norton's Balanced Scorecard and associated Strategy Maps.[1]

Typically, there is a gap between the level at which the corporate strategic plans are defined and what the lines of business do on a day-to-day basis. This is where Strategy Maps can be used to help in propagating the goals (corporate objectives) from the enterprise level all the way down to business and IT objectives that in turn lead to actionable business process transformation and IT projects. It is a means to organize business strategy into actionable perspectives that promote the vision and goals of the organization. Strategy maps are developed by businesses to create an

---

[1] *The Balanced Scorecard* (Harvard Business Press, 1996) and *Strategy Maps* (Harvard Business Press, 2004), both by Robert Steven Kaplan and David P. Norton.

understanding of how financial goals are supported by nonfinancial aspects of the business. The nonfinancial aspects drive financial results, therefore mapping and alignment between the two must be captured.

The Strategy Map is a common tool used to articulate and visualize an organization's business strategy. It is based on the Balanced Scorecard, which promotes the idea of looking at strategy in a balanced way—for example, across multiple perspectives. In a strategy map, the financial goals influence customer goals, which influence business processes, which in turn influence company assets. The goals across perspectives are linked and support each other.

The diagram in Figure 10-8 shows the categories used as a starting point for the development of a strategy map. Kaplan and Norton developed the approach of categorizing lagging versus leading indicators of business health in their seminal work known as the Balanced Scorecard approach to measurement. These indicators can be seen in the horizontal categories in

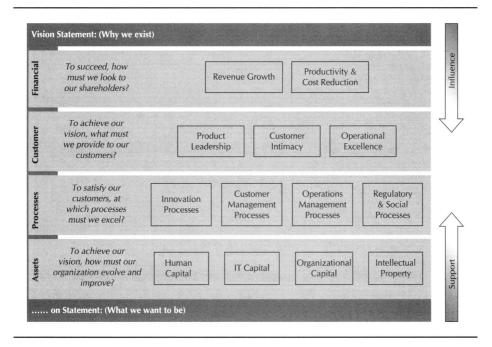

FIGURE 10-8. *A Balanced Scorecard outline*

the diagram (with lagging indicators at the top progressing to leading indicators at the bottom). Strategy maps are used in conjunction with Balanced Score Cards to represent business strategy categories and their relationships to represent the effect of change.

An example of a strategy map consistent with the Balanced Score Card approach is shown in Figure 10-9.

By identifying linkages between candidate business processes and key business strategies in the strategy map, we can evaluate the significance of the processes to the business. This technique is referred to as value alignment, which appears later in our process selection procedure.

The development of strategy maps and other motivation models is beyond the scope of business process engineering, but they are described here as a guide to help the BPM practitioner identify important sources of information as input to the process.

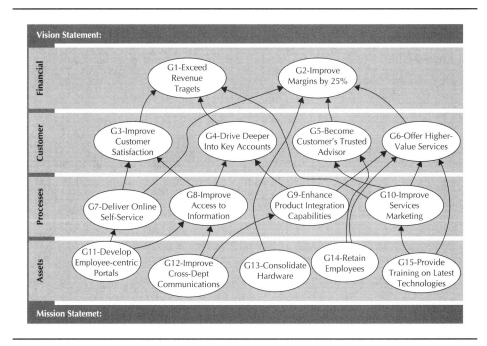

FIGURE 10-9. *An example strategy map*

Motivation models, such as the strategy map, are not only a useful starting point for process identification, but they are also used in the strategic approach to process selection (later in this chapter) by establishing a business value alignment.

Business Analysis

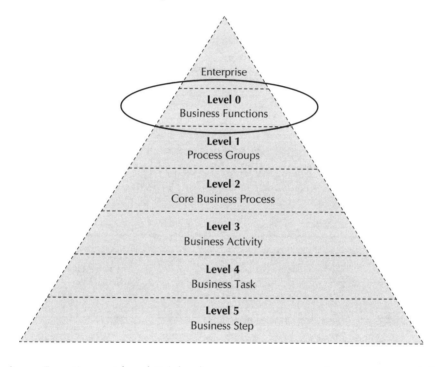

Business Functions at level 0 (also known as an enterprise process model) initially assist in framing discussions and are used to get an overview of the business functions across the enterprise or within the domain scoped for the BPM program.

This starts the process of business analysis (also called requirements analysis) where groups of requirements can be attached at level 2 and below. Requirements encountered at a parent node cascade through the hierarchy and implicitly apply at the child levels (and grandchild, and so on).

This is an especially useful method for scoping or establishing a hierarchy of requirements ensuring complete coverage all the way down to the detail level. It is also a useful way to broadcast nonfunctional requirements rather than repeating them at every node in every child level. For the purposes of strategic analysis, this approach can be used to document more granular requirements prior to breaking them down into finer-grained requirements.

A well-established approach to developing and communicating this high-level enterprise process model was developed by Michael Porter, known as the Porter value chain. Porter's model is intended to represent a series of functions that create value for the organization, referred to as the "money pipe," and that have a number of supporting functions. See the diagram in Figure 10-10 for the typical graphical representation of Porter's model.

Porter Value Chains

The value chain is a concept from business management that was first described and popularized by Michael Porter in his 1985 book, *Competitive Advantage: Creating and Sustaining Superior Performance* (Free Press).

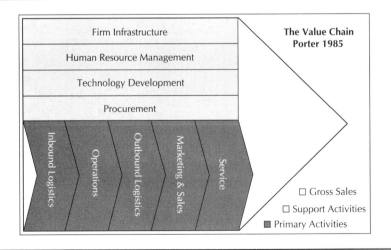

FIGURE 10-10. *An example Porter value chain*

In addition to the generic value chain discussed earlier, industry-specific models are available with activities relevant to vertical industry groups. The business unit is the appropriate level for construction of a value chain—not the divisional level or corporate level. Products pass through all activities of the chain in order, and at each activity the product gains some value. The chain of activities gives the products more added value than the sum of added values of all activities. It is important not to mix the concept of the value chain with the costs occurring throughout the activities. Typically, the described value chain and the documentation of processes, assessment, and auditing of adherence to the process routines are at the core of the quality certifications for businesses, such as ISO 9001.

A more recent refinement of the Porter value chain is described by the American Productivity & Quality Center (APQC). Figure 10-11 offers a representation of the highest-level generic business functions using the APQC approach.

FIGURE 10-11. *Generic business functions*

The APQC model defines a Process Classification Framework (PCF) with 12 highest-level business functions that are common to all businesses (industry-specific versions of the PCF are also available). These 12 functions correspond to our level 0, categorizing the key business activities. Five *core* business processes are shown across the top while *supporting* processes are listed horizontally below them.

The APQC is a member-based nonprofit research and education organization whose mission is to work with organizations worldwide to improve productivity and quality. Their belief is that a common language to describe organizational processes is necessary to perform measurement and improvement of business processes. In the absence of existing standards, the APQC created the Process Classification Framework (PCF), claiming:

> Today, the PCF is the world's most widely used process framework and allows organizations to speak a common language about functions, processes, and activities independent of structure. Updated annually the PCF is organized into 12 distinct categories, including five categories of operating areas and seven of support areas. Each category contains groups of processes and activities that, when considered as a whole, represent the operations of an organization. The frameworks are available in cross-industry and select industry-specific formats.[2]

The purpose of the PCF is slightly different from the Porter value chain in that it classifies business processes in a first step toward benchmarking, or the measurement of their effectiveness using a database of objective metrics. While the objectives of the PCF and the Porter value chain are slightly different, they both present the level 0 business functions in a similar fashion (despite the reversal of horizontal and vertical aspects in the presentation).

The PCF uses the Open Standards Benchmarking Collaborative (OSBC) database of measures for business process benchmarking. The OSBC is a global initiative to develop a common standard framework for process

---

[2] http://www.apqc.org

definitions, measures, and benchmarks that are available to participating organizations worldwide to improve performance. The OSBC Research Database has over 1000 individual metrics and performance drivers, covering approximately 65 processes and functions.

The APQC PCF decomposes the 12 business functions to level 1 process groups in our function hierarchy. An organization can begin functional modeling by developing its own model down to this level or simply by using the PCF (or one of its industry-specific versions) as a starting point.

Process Groups

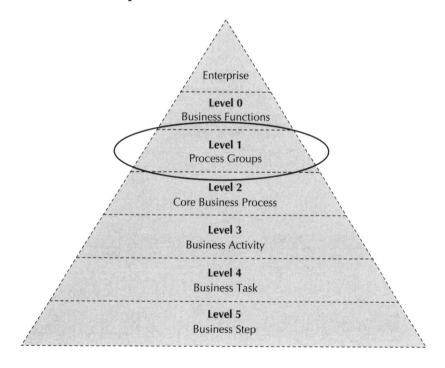

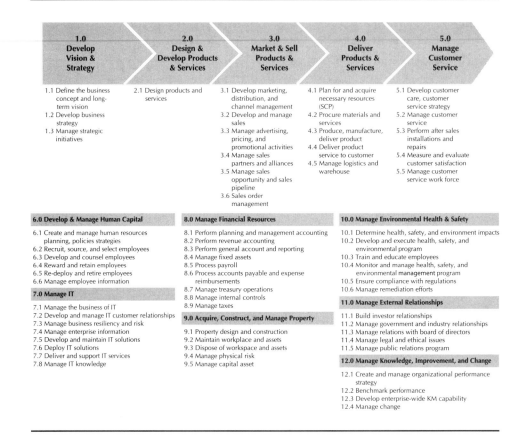

FIGURE 10-12. *Process groups*

Once the Business Function(s) have been identified, the next step is to narrow down the focus to the Process Group(s), which have been categorized as a level 1 in the example levels of the enterprise group. See Figure 10-12 for some sample process groups.

Core Processes

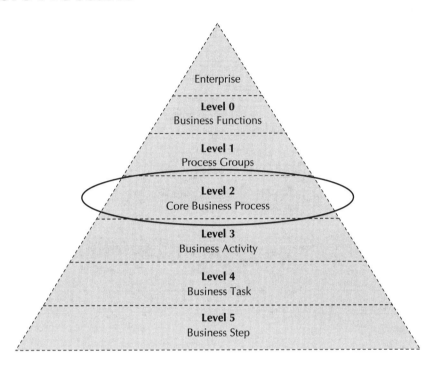

While business processes are often categorized as being "Core," "Supporting," or "Strategic," we are only concerned here with the level of decomposition, so the word "Core" is used here within the context of the function hierarchy.

Once the Business Process Group(s) have been identified, the next step is to decompose these into Core Business Processes. Figure 10-13 shows a useful representation for this step and the following section outlines the functional decomposition approach.

At this point, these core business processes should represent high-level, cross-business-unit activities where each activity in a corresponding process flow is functionally independent. The diagram in Figure 10-14 shows an example of a process flow at this level.

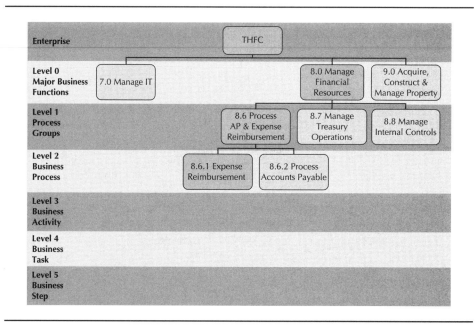

FIGURE 10-13. *Defining core business processes*

Each of the steps in a core process will ultimately become a high-level subprocess in a BPMN model. However, at this point the flow representation must be very simple since the details of swim-lanes, exceptions, and so on are not relevant to the process description at this stage.

Finally, we have arrived at the definition of individual core business processes that can now be used in the process selection procedure that will be described in the following sections. Once selected for automation, high-level use cases can then be used to begin to provide the details behind the processes identified in this level.

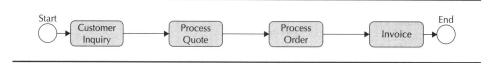

FIGURE 10-14. *Example core business process activities*

A Tactical Approach to Process Identification

In the absence of strategic business inputs, such as top-level functional models and business motivation, it is still possible to document process selection criteria and to evaluate candidates without the assessment of value alignment.

A tactical approach is often taken when getting started with BPM to raise visibility and to gain senior management commitment for future project work. In the early stages of a BPM program, it is fairly straightforward to identify core business processes and *low-hanging fruit* for process improvement. In such cases, we focus on existing processes that are causing the organization the most pain—for instance, high cost, inefficient, taking too long to complete, inconsistent behavior, low satisfaction, and so on.

Business processes identified in this way can now proceed as process candidates to be used in the next step of process selection.

Business Process Selection

The Oracle Business Process Selection Framework is used to select which potential business processes should be realized through automation. Candidate process scoring is not used to decide if a new process or functionality should be created, rather it is simply used to decide if the business process should be realized as an automated process. If a process candidate fails selection for automation, it does not reflect on the value of the business process. Instead, it merely indicates that the business process is not a suitable candidate for employing BPM technologies, at least under the prevailing conditions.

Now that a number of processes have been identified, they can be prioritized based on a scoring mechanism.

The right-hand side of the diagram in Figure 10-15 is the core of the selection process used to determine which business processes are most appropriate for automation. Business processes can be evaluated regardless of whether they were identified taking the tactical approach (driven simply by requirements), or by employing the strategic approach using top-level functional decomposition and business motivation inputs.

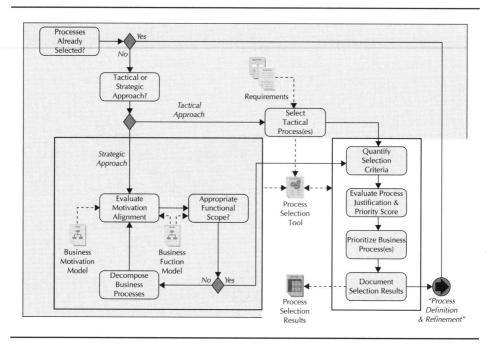

FIGURE 10-15. *Process selection*

Process Candidates Evaluation Criteria

The Oracle Business Process Selection Framework is a spreadsheet tool that can be used to evaluate the suitability of business processes for automation and determine which are most suitable for execution in a BPM system. The tool also prioritizes business processes as engineering projects. The tool evaluates the business value alignment (in the case of strategic analysis) along with various other benefits expected from automation. Inhibitors to automation are also considered, and in some cases a process may be determined unsuitable. For example, if a process is too complex (high risk), or is well optimized and doesn't change, there may be no value in automating it.

The following section describes the parameters used for evaluating business process candidates.

Business Process Information

For tracking purposes, the following information should be captured to identify business processes throughout the engineering life cycle:

Name   A unique name identifying the business process candidate.

Owner   This information is used to indicate who owns an organization or project. The name and title of specific individual(s) responsible for the overall goals, objectives, and decision making should be captured.

Status   The status represents the current state of the process candidate within its life cycle. The set of available statuses can be customized for a particular business, but the defaults include:

- **Proposed**   Represents a candidate that has been proposed but not yet justified for decomposition.

- **Justified**   The candidate has been justified for decomposition.

- **Not Justified**   The candidate failed justification and will remain inactive.

- **Assigned**   The candidate has been assigned to an owner, but process analysis work has not yet commenced. A process candidate becomes assigned when justification has determined that the process candidate should be decomposed into service candidates and assigned to an analysis team.

- **In Progress**   The process candidate has been assigned and decomposition work has commenced.

Version   The version field comes into play when an extension to an implemented or in-progress process candidate is required. In this scenario, a new version of the process candidate is created. A new version of a process candidate has its own life cycle, and when created, it starts out with a status of "Proposed," which must be justified before it will become scheduled for computerization.

Benefit Parameters

The following lists the benefits parameters for the business process candidate evaluation. Classifications for evaluation are provided where scoring is not simply applied on a range of high to low. Scores are assigned to these parameters, and weightings can be applied as needed.

Value Alignment Score   The value alignment score weighs the alignment of the business process to the enterprise's business and BPM goals. This score is evaluated in the Process Value Alignment worksheet using inputs from strategic analysis.

Process Category Score   The category score weighs the process based on how the process contributes to the business. Evaluation of this score has the following options (high values indicate positively towards justification):

■ **Core Process**   Indicates that the process represents the main business activities of the enterprise. They represent the core competencies that can differentiate the organization in its market. Examples of core processes include:
  – Order Management
  – Account Management
  – Claim Processing

■ **Strategic Process**   This signifies that the process represents the enterprise's strategic activities by ensuring that the enterprise's meets its specified objectives.

■ **Supporting**   This signifies that the process represents the non-core activities that support the core and strategic activities. Support processes guide, control, plan, enable, or provide resources for the core processes of an organization. Just because a process is a support process does not mean it should be worked on last. Core process problems are sometimes caused by ineffective support processes. Examples of support processes are:
  – HR on-boarding
  – Maintenance
  – Procurement
  – Scheduling

Executive Interest Score   The executive interest score weighs executive interest and support. A higher score value indicates positively towards justification. Proposed values include:

- Senior executives have a strong interest in the results and output from this process and are willing to sponsor and support this initiative.

- An appropriate executive has a strong interest in the results and output from this process and are willing to sponsor and support this initiative.

- Senior executives have a strong interest in the results and output from this process but no clear indication of support or sponsorship is known.

- An appropriate executive has a strong interest in the results and output from this process but no clear indication of support or sponsorship is known.

- There is no clear interest in the results and output from this process from any executive.

BPM Project Score   The BPM project impact score weighs to what extent a project has been identified, justified, and scheduled for development. A higher score value indicates positively towards justification.

- BPM Project justified and scheduled for development

- BPM Project justified

- BPM Project identified

- No BPM Project identified

Business Impact Score   The business impact score weighs the impact automating the process would have on the bottom line of the business by either reducing costs or increasing revenue.

Improvement Opportunity Score   The improve opportunity score weighs the opportunity for improving the process once the process is managed and monitored.

Response to Change Score The response to change score weighs the likelihood that the process will require modifications to meet changing business needs.

Inhibitor Parameters

The following list describes the inhibitors that have a negative impact towards process selection.

Lack of Structure Score The lack of structure score weighs the lack of structure in the process. Sample categories for the evaluation of this score are:

- The process is an ad hoc or highly unstructured collaborative process.

- The core process is structured, but frequently cases arise that do not follow the structure and instead require ad hoc processing.

- The process is mostly a structured process with infrequent exception cases requiring ad hoc processing.

Complexity Score The complexity score weighs the scope and complexity of the process. The process should be small enough in scope and simple enough in complexity to be appropriate for this effort.

Organization Impact Score The organization impact score weighs the extent of reorganization and/or the changed organizational policies that are required for this process. The authority to make these changes must be taken into consideration.

Resources Involved Score The resources involved score weighs to what extent resources such as employees are involved in the process.

Integration Complexity Score The integration complexity score weighs the complexity of integrating the applications necessary to support the process.

Knowledge Gap Score The knowledge score weighs the availability of knowledge about this process.

- There is little or no knowledge about the processes available.

- There is minimal access to knowledge about the process, resulting in significant gaps in knowledge about the process.

- Some gaps in knowledge about the process exist, but the gaps are manageable.

- There is plenty of information available about the process.

Decision Basis Score

The Oracle Business Process Selection Framework measures alignment with goals, objectives, and initiatives along with benefits and inhibitors to automation. The framework generates a numeric Decision Basis Score that can be used to select and prioritize business processes for automation.

The collection of benefits and inhibitors make up 13 parameters that are weighted according to their importance in any given customer situation. More parameters can be added or removed as needed, and weightings can be adapted to suit any specific company's needs.

The Business Process Selection Framework generates a graph from the Decision Basis Score. An example of this graph is shown in Figure 10-16.

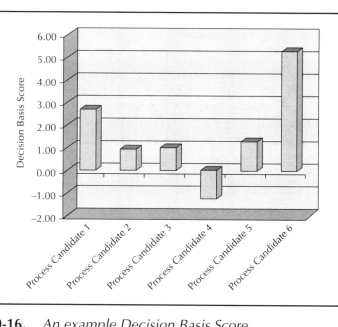

FIGURE 10-16. *An example Decision Basis Score*

Business Process Design

It is important to understand that *Business Process Design* is not the same as technical design (discussed in Chapter 11).

Unlike traditional software engineering, design and implementation are not easily delineated in BPM due to the model-based, zero code approach. In traditional software engineering, modeling is a design activity, while implementation is about producing code that will run within the current infrastructure. In process engineering, the business process model evolves through a series of steps and through stakeholder input until it is finally executable. The last step of making the model executable is called *business application composition* and it is the closest parallel to implementation in software engineering.

The design portion of this phase is comprised of a number of distinct steps. First, in the definition step, there is a one-time activity to define the business process model needed to introduce the selected business process into the continuous improvement cycle. For this and for all subsequent iterations of the continuous improvement cycle, a refinement step is all that is needed to make the business level adjustments to the model that will emerge from business process analysis.

A technical analysis and design step follows either the one-time discovery and definition step or subsequent refinement steps. This determines the feasibility of having the business process model execute using the existing capabilities of the IT application infrastructure. Specifically, this step checks that the supporting application functions and data meet the requirements of the process model step and are suitably exposed so they can be accessed by the process engine. In this case, a complete portfolio of SOA services is a significant asset, providing a service contract to describe the service capabilities and interfaces that enable rapid integration into the model in the final implementation step.

In many cases, however, gaps will be identified in the business specifications of an existing service or in the technical implementation of the application's functionality. Technical analysis and design are needed here, not just to specify how to fill these gaps, but also to determine whether it is feasible to implement the business process in this way. In some cases, a model will be returned to the previous step to be redesigned to operate with the current constraints of IT application infrastructure; in other cases, a service (or software) engineering project is initiated to change or create new services. Technical analysis and design will be covered in more detail in Chapter 11.

Process Definition and Refinement

Process Definition is the elaboration of the business process in which a process flow diagram is introduced using Business Process Modeling Notation (BPMN). The definition represents the as-is (current) state of the business process and it is the first point at which BPMN modeling techniques should be used to describe the process. Initially a *descriptive* model is created (corresponding to the OMG's three levels of model definition), which is then developed into the *analytical* state during this definition activity. The analytical model is then used in the subsequent refinement steps for transition of the model to the desired future to-be state.

The diagram in Figure 10-17 shows both definition and refinement together in order to identify their separate entry points and explain the interplay between the two steps.

Definition and refinement represent the business elaboration and optimization steps of the engineering process. Definition happens the first time through, and refinement happens at each new version or revision. In definition, the as-is details of the business process context, process details, and the process model are captured. This initial capture of "what the business does today" needs to be performed only once prior to first automation. In the refinement procedure, the to-be business process model includes incremental improvements to be carried into the first and all subsequent iterations of the continuous improvement cycle. In subsequent cycles, process activity metrics from the real-world operation of the process should be available to help with refinement. At the completion of either definition or refinement, technical concerns such as technical analysis, test case development, and UI Design are addressed in the next major activity.

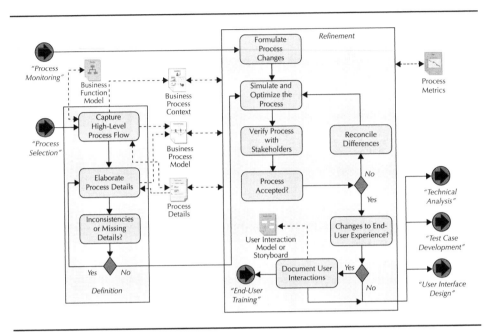

FIGURE 10-17. *Process definition and refinement*

The entry points shown in the diagram are from either:

- Process selection into definition where the high-level process model is elaborated (and documented) until a sufficiently detailed model is ready for input to the main engineering cycle via refinement, or

- Entering from process monitoring when already in the continuous improvement cycle and simply needing to formulate changes as the cycle reenters the refinement activities. Inside refinement, simulation, and verification activities support the assessment of changes to user interaction and associated test cases.

Process Definition

Process definition is the activity in which the details of the core business processes, identified previously in the analysis phase, are expanded in a business process model, which is later to become the executable model.

The diagram in Figure 10-18 separates definition in order to look in more detail at each of the steps, along with inputs and outputs.

In this activity, we need to discover and define details about the as-is process. Inputs include a set of selected processes that are at the core business process level of abstraction (supported by corresponding value chains, and so on). For each of these processes, there should be a corresponding functional model, decomposed at level 2 in our hierarchy, from an earlier business analysis.

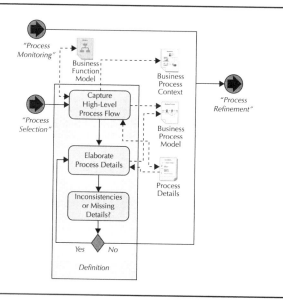

FIGURE 10-18. *Process definition*

Using the functional model as the reference and the business requirements as the input, we will create context maps for each process (a sample context map was shown in Chapter 1 and will be included again later in this chapter). The context map will highlight key information, such as participants in the process, dependencies on applications, requirements being addressed (which likely would be a subset of the business requirements coming in as input, hence the need for a refined to-be model), and so on.

Decomposition of the functional model through levels 4 and 5 and the associated process context map provide the detail necessary to draw the process model depicting the as-is process. Functional decomposition and development of a context map are covered in the following sections.

Oracle BPM Modeling Spaces is an ideal tool for modeling at this stage because it is a web-based modeling tool embedded in WebCenter Spaces, which provides Enterprise 2.0 functionality. This allows business analysts and other stake holders to collaborate on the modeling exercise. Figure 10-19 shows an example of a shared BPM project in WebCenter Modeling Spaces with its various collaboration features (left of the pair of screenshots) and the corresponding launch of the model itself in Oracle Business Process Composer (right).

BPMN process models produced at this stage through the OMG levels 1 and 2 (descriptive and analytical) will be abstract. This means that all activities will be without any implementation details.

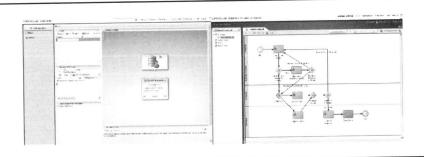

FIGURE 10-19. *An Oracle BPM Modeling Spaces screenshot*

Once the model is ready, it is subjected to a series of simulation models that represent the resources and constraints of the current business environment. In cases where either the processes are not managed by a BPM engine or no such performance data exists, look for traditional sources for this information such as BI, ERP reporting, and others. It is important that the simulation model represents current conditions as much as possible. This will be important when we refine the model to address requirement gaps and process performance issues.

In the following sections, we will describe the steps in process definition and refinement in more detail. As we have mentioned already, a functional decomposition will be used in these next steps of process definition, so for those readers who are unfamiliar with decomposition, the next section should demystify this relatively simple technique.

Functional Decomposition

Function models (described earlier in this chapter) are used for a variety of purposes in both business and technical analysis situations. The following are some common scenarios in which functional modeling can be applied:

- At the management level to assist enterprises in capturing and understanding business functionality

- At the process level as a tool to organize process specifications against functional concerns

- At the application level as a tool to decompose and categorize functional capabilities

- At the service level to aid in service identification and discovery

Functional decomposition is a technique for developing an understanding of business processes and their level of granularity in an enterprise. The focus for business process selection should be Core Business Processes (level 2). For example, Expense Reimbursement is a core business process in the earlier example in Figure 10-13.

It is important to note that a functional decomposition is NOT an organizational chart. Simply mapping the activities that people perform in their organizational roles will not lead to an effective functional model since many functions and processes have variations occurring in other parts of the organization. This approach requires a top-down decomposition without regard for organizational boundaries in order to get a clear picture of the core processes that span the enterprise.

A true business process model (as opposed to technical orchestration) can now be recognized as representing a Core Business Process. These business process models, also known as process maps at this level, identify the primary Business Activities at the highest level of the business process flow. Further business and technical analysis, in later phases of the engineering process, continue this decomposition into the lower levels of the functional model.

The levels in a functional model follow a broadly used approach; however, there is no standard for leveling or naming, but any variation on this theme should help facilitate consistent communications, as long as it is widely adopted across the enterprise.

The functional modeling is commonly used in business and IT for a number of different purposes. Some example uses are listed here.

- At the management level to assist enterprises in capturing, understanding, and communicating business functionality

- At the process level as a tool to organize process specifications against functional concerns

- At the application level as a tool to decompose and categorize functional capabilities

- In SOA Service engineering as an aid to service identification and discovery

Capturing High-Level Process Flow

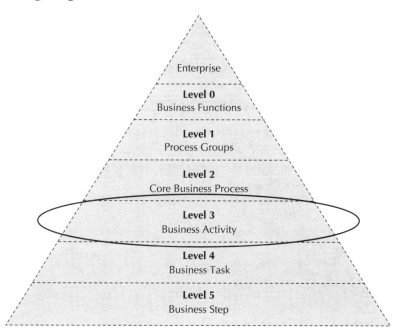

In the first step of process definition, the Process Analyst meets with the Process Owner and process participants (the end users who interact with the process and perform process steps) to understand the process from a high level. Typically, not all participants are available, or needed, for this step (we will describe participant roles in detail in Chapter 11). The analyst captures the big picture of what the process is intended to do and as much detail as the audience and time permits.

The first thing to be captured is the business process context, which is as follows:

Performed by: Process Analyst

Actions:

■ Meet with the Process Owner and business leadership—for instance, those familiar with the business context (goals, objectives, rules, and others) and have an understanding of the high-level end-to-end flow of activities.

■ Capture process context and high-level flow.

■ Not concerned with the intricate details of how something is done or why it is done that way. Subject matter experts (SMEs) will be expected to participate in later stages where this greater level of detail will be necessary.

Deliverables:

■ Business process context

■ Initial capture of the process model

The model should be captured in an iterative process as a continuation of the functional decomposition that was started in the earlier business analysis phase in support of business process candidate selection. This is a hierarchical model that is ideally represented by a hierarchical notation (as is the case with BPMN). The benefits of this hierarchical approach are:

■ Entire business process is captured in a single model

■ Model begins with top-level view that depicts the entire end-to-end process on a single page

■ Each activity represents a subprocess that can be expanded to reveal more detail

■ Lowest level includes technical details required for runtime execution

The modeling starts by capturing the highest-level process flow that represents the core business process identified in our earlier analysis.

- Capture the happy path (the paths most commonly taken in the process)

    - Focus on manageable portions

    - Use only basic symbols (activities, decisions, split/join, start, end)

    - Work through the flow in iterations: start shallow, then fill in more details later

    - Use Post-its and/or a whiteboard; capture results afterward in a modeling tool

- Identify:

    - What is commonly done, and what decisions are made?

    - Who performs the activities, or are they automated?

    - Where are they done, and when (according to the business calendar)?

    - Who makes decisions, and what business rules/policies/ regulations are involved?

    - What are the goals, objectives, measurements, and KPIs?

    - What are the initiating events, business objects, and end state?

Use a limited pallet of BPMN symbols to develop this business process flow (start, end, activities, gateways, and flow connectors).

The tools used here can be as simple as a whiteboard or flip chart in a workshop scenario. Tools that are too complex are likely to create unnecessary distractions or put off the business users.

To get started, capture the human and system triggers that unambiguously define the start and end events of the process flow as in Figure 10-20.

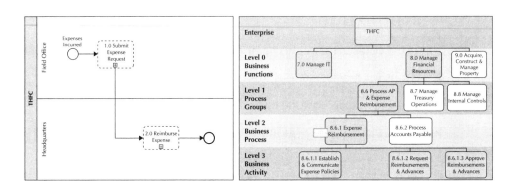

FIGURE 10-20. *Define start and end and the level 3 business activities*

The high-level core business process model can be linked to our function model. Now we can proceed with functional decomposition to the "level 3" business activities.

Drill Down to Business Tasks

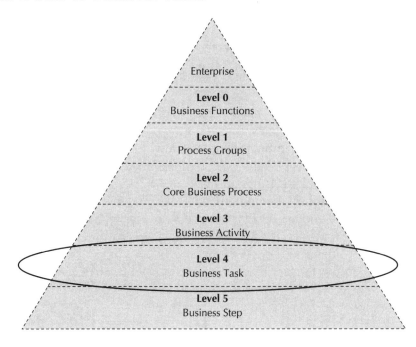

Drilling down a level deeper into our expense processing example, we see the consultant completes an expense request, a coordinator reviews the request, and a manager approves it. The expense report is implicitly transferred between these participants' activities, but the detail of the message flows is not yet developed at this stage in the modeling (see the example in Figure 10-21).

Back at our functional model, we check that our business tasks for this activity are showing up in the process model.

As we move through this process of mapping our increasingly more detailed models to the function model, we can ensure that process models are maintained at the right level of granularity.

Finally, we start to see application functions/services and human tasks (the things that people actually do) appearing in our model along with exception handling and external data relationships.

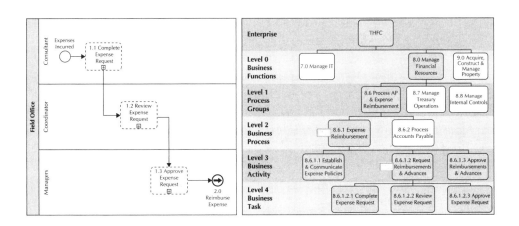

FIGURE 10-21. *Identifying level 4 business tasks*

Drill Down to Business Steps

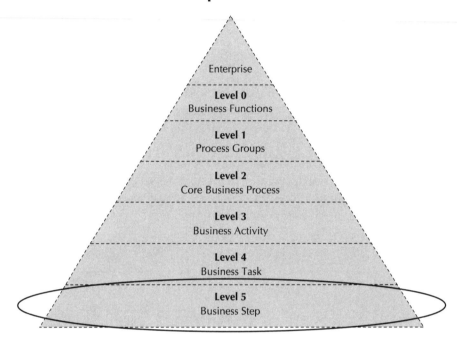

This is the final stage of decomposition corresponding to the OMG level 2 model (analytical), which is now ready for technical preparations before finally becoming an executable model (see the example in Figure 10-22).

Again, we check our function decomposition to make sure we have captured all the necessary business steps and that our model is showing appropriately leveled activities.

Here we see a numbering scheme indicating that our process elements have been decomposed to the last level in the hierarchy (so the diagram encapsulates a *task*). It is also important not to decompose this any further (this becomes apparent when a model describes software programming steps rather than steps in a business process).

Activity diagrams of this type can be used to apply filter criteria (for instance, manual steps) to help us pick appropriate operations. It should also be used in conjunction with functional models for grouping (this will support service boundary analysis in subsequent delivery activities).

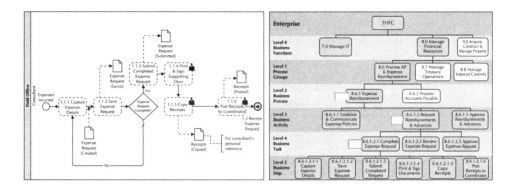

FIGURE 10-22. *An analytical model*

Creating a Business Process Context Model

The business process context identifies all the things associated with our business process that are separate from the concerns of the flow of the process.

Figure 10-23 shows a simple graphical representation of an example process context model.

The process context model identifies the things we hope to capture as we elaborate the process details in the next step of the definition activity.

Key Performance Indicators

In the business process context model, the goals have been transferred from the strategic analysis. The difference is that they appear in this context as *objectives* (quantitative statements of things that must be achieved to meet the goals). These objectives will later support the selection of KPIs for measurement of process performance.

More detail in the KPI definition can be developed later in the process, but it is still important to capture these high-level statements from the business at this stage.

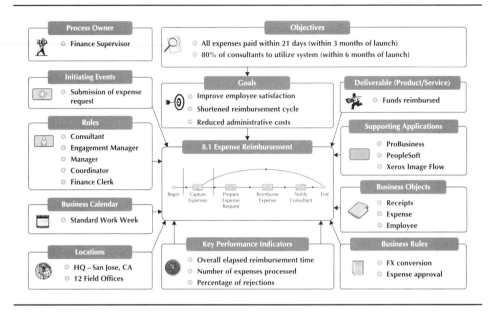

FIGURE 10-23. *An example context model*

Identifying Supporting Applications

The mapping of business functions to applications can be surprisingly complex. The diagram in Figure 10-24 shows a graphical representation of applications mapped to a functional model. This example uses the APQC PCF approach described earlier. This form of diagram will make it easy to determine the application(s) involved in a process, as well as where multiple applications happen to perform the same function.

Another example in the diagram in Figure 10-25 maps applications to the organizations that use them. This model might help ensure that applications that are used in the process are not forgotten during process modeling. Using this model, applications can be checked against the organization unit that uses them and determine if they play a role in the process.

1. Concept to Product	2. Marketing to Sales	3. Demand to Supply	4. Order to Cash
A. Develop ideas and define customer requirements	A. Develop, execute, and review marketing plans	A. Forecast demand	A. Enter orders
B. Design, engineer, and develop new products	B. Conduct market, customer, and competitor research	B. Plan supply requirements	B. Allocate supply to demand
C. Refine existing products	C. Manage product life cycle	C. Source and purchase finished goods	C. Release and pick orders
D. Create, review, and test samples	D. Manage product pricing	D. Purchase expense/ MRO items	D. Ship orders
E. Create and test prototypes	E. Create and maintain catalogs	E. Transfer materials to DCs	E. Invoice orders
F. Develop product literature and packaging	F. Manage promotions	F. Receive product	F. Collect cash
G. Initialize to product	G. Channel management	G. Inspect product	G. Manage receivables
	H. Manage customer relationships	H. Rework product	H. Manage customer returns
	I. Sell products	I. Put away product	I. Manage deductions
	J. Develop product training	J. Authorize and process payments to suppliers	J. Provide post sales support and service
	K. Collect & maintain customer information	K. Manage inventory	K. Pay commissions to sales reps

Support Business Processes

5. Finance to Manage	A. Create financial budget	B. Record financial actions	C. Close financial periods	D. Report on financial results	E. Manage and define cost structure	F. Manage treasury activity	G. Manage fixed assets	H. Pay and file taxes
6. Hire to Retire	A. Attract talent	B. Hire employee	C. Pay Employee	D. Manage employee benefits	E. Manage dev. of employee	F. Manage perf. of employee	G. Terminate employee	
7. Propose to Measure (project mgmt)	A. Create project proposal	B. Validate project proposal	C. Execute project	D. Measure results of project				
8. Develop to Maintain IT Systems	A. Prioritize requests for IT projects	B. Design solutions	C. Develop solutions	D. Test solutions	E. Implement solution	F. Maintain solution		

☐ Finance Systems   ■ CRM   ■ ERP   ■ HRMS   ☐ WMS   ☐ Other

FIGURE 10-24.   *Applications mapped to functional model*

Business Objects

Business objects are the pieces of information that flow between the activities in the business process model. An example of high-level information flow is shown in Figure 10-26. In the later technical design phase, these will become the message flows in the technical representation of the model.

ID	Organization Unit	ProBusiness	PeopleSoft	Oracle Financials	Xerox Image Flow	LearnLinc	EDM	Enterprise Scorecard Manager	TOCS	Regional Trip Planner	Transport Advanced Traveler Info Implementation	ITS High Availability Redundancy Enhancement	Migrate Trns:Port to Client Server	Utility Management System	Right of Way Data Management System	Project Delivery Electronic Bidding	ITS-A TMS Connection to 911 Consortium	Federal SAFETEA-LU Act Unified Registration System	IFTA Electronic Credentialing-CVISN Level 1	Automated Clearing House	Expand Trucking Online
																		Application Portfolio			
HR	Human Resources	●					●		●	●	●				●			●	●	●		●
FI	Finance											●		●		●	●				
OP	Operations																				
DI	Distribution	●											●	●							
PR	Production	●			●									●						●	

FIGURE 10-25. *Applications mapped to organizations*

In the earlier example of the expense approval, the initial focus was identification of the activities in the business process flow. The next step is to identify the business objects that are necessary to perform each activity and that are passed between them as inputs and outputs. These business objects are shown in the lower portion of the diagram and require that details be completed before moving to the next stage.

An important part of identifying business objects is the mapping of entities to applications. This helps to determine which systems are responsible for the information needed in our business process flow.

Figure 10-27 is an example of a "CRUD" (Create, Read, Update, Delete) matrix, showing not only which applications hold the information we need, but also giving us some insight into their level of responsibility for the data and whether they update or merely read it.

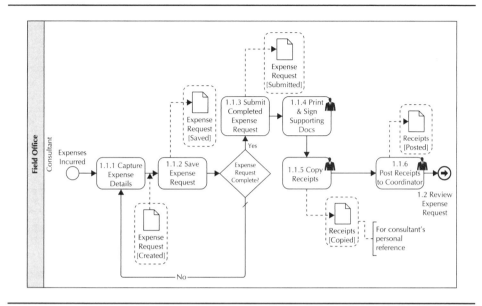

FIGURE 10-26.   *An example of high-level information flow*

Some business objects are easy to identify, having perhaps just one *system of record.* When it is unique and stored in one place it's easy to produce a canonical data model. Unfortunately, most core entities, such as customer, product, and others, are not so easily defined. Stored across a wide variety of applications, these business objects are more difficult to define. For this reason, it is important to start to collect this information early in the business analysis phase, asking the business user directly which systems he/she uses in each activity in the process flow. In this example, we see multiple applications read and updated product information.

- Some business objects are fairly unique and clearly identifiable, typified by:

    - Single source

    - Clearly defined gold source

ID	Entity	ProBusiness	PeopleSoft	Oracle Financials	Xerox Image Flow	LearnLinc	EDM	Enterprise Scorecard Manager	TOCS	Regional Trip Planner	Transport Advanced Traveler Info Implementation	ITS High Availability Redundancy Enhancement	Migrate Trns:Port to Client Server	Utility Management System
EX	Expense	U	CUR	R										
EM	Employee		C											
AC	Accounts		R	CUR										
CU	Customer	R	UR	CUR										
PR	Product					CUR	CUR	R	R	CU				
RO	Roles	U	CUR											
JO	Job		CUR											

FIGURE 10-27. *An example "CRUD" matrix*

- ■ Master data management
- ■ Canonical data model
- ■ Other business objects can be a source of great confusion and frustration:
  - ■ Many unrelated sources
  - ■ Same name, different meaning

- ■ Same meaning, different values

- ■ Similar objects, different attributes

- ■ For each business object, attempt to determine:

  - ■ What is the primary source for the object?

  - ■ Who is the owner of that source?

  - ■ Are there other sources, and how do they relate to each other?

  - ■ How can this object be semantically defined to be unique from other similar objects, and what semantic community does it belong to?

Elaborate Business Process Details

The next step in process definition collects a lot more detail about how the process actually works. This involves interviewing the people that actually perform the process.

Performed by: Process Analyst
Actions:

- ■ Meet with each person or representative of a group that performs a business task or makes a decision as part of the process. Capture the details.

- ■ Watch for issues such as unnecessary risks, delays, challenges, and others.

Deliverables:

- ■ Process (task-level) details
- ■ Enhancements to process model

A practical approach to capturing the as-is business process is to hold a series of collaborative workshops where key stakeholders detail the business process.

The information we collect can be logically divided into three categories: general information, execution of the task itself, and the involvement of IT resources in carrying out the task. This information is gathered for each task.

General task information:

- Description
    - Task name
    - Structured/unstructured
    - Manual/automated
- Background
    - Why the task is performed
    - Why it is performed this way
    - Known issues
    - Suggestions for improvement
- Roles
    - Roles, groups, or persons that perform this activity

Task execution details:

- Initiation and timing
    - What triggers the start of this task
    - When this task is performed
    - What happens if it times out
    - Expected duration of task and when it times out

- Actions performed

  - Step-by-step description of what is done to complete the task

  - Alternate scenarios

  - Basis for decisions made

  - Business exceptions and how they are handled

- Business rules

  - Business logic, company policies, or regulations that govern the execution of this task

- Results

  - Normal and possible alternate outcomes

IT involvement:

- Supporting assets

  - Applications used in the execution of this task

  - Devices or interfaces used to complete the task

- Information needs

  - Inputs

  - Outputs

  - Objects created, read, updated, or deleted (CRUD)

  - Business intelligence required to make decisions

- Locations

  - Physical locations (for example, countries, time zones, buildings, and so on)

  - Network locations (for example, intranet, Internet, VPN, disconnected)

- Internationalization

  - Language support

  - Localization requirements

Correcting Issues and Resolving Inconsistencies

The final step in process definition is to identify and rectify problems and inconsistencies that arise in the detail definition of the business process. Examples of problems arising include the following:

- Differences between the process as stated by LOB owners and what the workers involved were actually doing

- Inconsistencies between business goals, objectives, business rules, regulations, and how the process is being performed

- Contradictory details captured from different participants in the process (for example, person A said use system X, but person B said use system Y)

- Unnecessary steps, churn, risks, delays, duplicate data entries, and so on

- Inconsistencies in the way the overall process is carried out. For example:

  - One group takes time to capture data that no one uses

  - Two groups are doing the same work

  - Decisions are not being made consistently throughout the process

  - Known issues and suggestions (from task detail capture)

If the issues highlighted are minor, they can be corrected and the model republished. If there are major issues raised, however, it may be necessary to reconvene additional workshop sessions to correct them.

Once the documented business process has been agreed upon, a decision must be made about whether another level of detail is required. If this is the case, then another round of interviews/workshops must be scheduled.

Refinement

The original as-is process capture was performed in the definition portion of the engineering cycle. This included high-level capture, elaboration (task detail capture), and rectification of inconsistencies. The next step is refinement, in which we consider improvements and the to-be business process that we will eventually pass into technical design.

The diagram in Figure 10-28 shows the activities in the refinement process.

Based on the process context, simulation results, and business requirements, we can now start modeling the to-be process.

While using Oracle BPM Suite 11*g*, we already have the as-is process defined in the shared MDS so the refinement activity can be performed collaboratively using any or all of the Oracle BPM tools: BPM Studio, Process Composer, or Modeling Spaces.

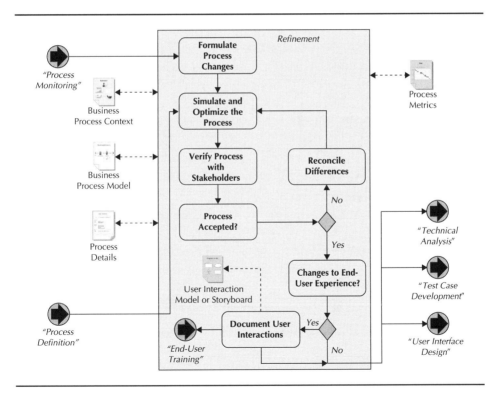

FIGURE 10-28.   *The refinement process*

It is important to version the model in the source control system at this stage so we always have the original as-is state for reference because the process is refined through multiple iterations towards its to-be state. BPM Studio is required to manage the source code versioning.

Business analysts can start with the as-is process in Process Composer and refine the model to address the gaps and the more obvious inefficiencies in the current process.

It is good practice to start consultation with the process architect at this stage so the resulting model(s) make good *executable process* candidates in a way that does not materially change the business flow but makes it technically feasible to implement. Technical feasibility analysis is performed in greater depth in subsequent implementation steps (described in Chapter 11).

As part of the process refinement, it may be necessary to further decompose the process. Availability of a business catalog of services, as in the case of Oracle BPM Suite 11g, can help with part of the exercise. For example, if the business process has a two-step activity that now needs to be automated, it could be modeled as a single activity if a service is found in the catalog that does what is needed by the original two steps.

This can also provide a good opportunity for business analysts to document gaps in available business services in the catalog according to the needs of the process. This will be an input to the service identification and justification steps in an adjacent SOA service engineering project.

The activities in the refinement flow are further elaborated in the following sections.

Formulating Process Changes

This step determines the improvements to be made in the to-be process in the initial automation of the business process and in subsequent iterations of the continuous improvement cycle.

Process model changes may be influenced by many factors, including:

- New or changing business goals and objectives

- Known issues and suggestions (from task detail capture)

- Internal policies and business regulations

- Mergers and acquisitions

- Business process redesign effort

- Analysis of runtime process metrics / optimization (for example, with input from BAM or BI systems)

- Changes triggered by business that affect the IT environment—for example, new applications, cloud/SaaS, automation, and so on

Simulation and Optimization

The screenshots shown in Figure 10-29 offer a brief glimpse of the dynamic operation of a simulation animated within the process model itself, analysis of metrics during the simulation run, and as example of a report that can be expected from follow-up analysis.

Simulation models are supported by the BPM engineering tools and maintained alongside the model itself, potentially taking metrics from the runtime system (in cases where refinement is being applied subsequent to the initial entry into the improvement cycle) to improve the realism of the model. Initially, parameters are defined to try and represent the real-world environment for the process. For human tasks, this includes worker availability, everything from the business calendar to the thinking time for process activities. Similar parameters can be defined for systems. With this information assembled to define the simulation model, the tool executes various scenarios to calculate limits, such as maximum throughput, the identification of bottlenecks, and estimates of exception rates. All of this can be used to improve the flow and predict the process performance and necessary resource capacities in the runtime BPM environment.

With these details in the simulation model, obvious process improvements can be identified, such as:

- Activities that can be performed in parallel

- Activities that no longer need to be performed

- Duplication

- *Dead-end* activities

- Reordering the process to improve efficiency and to eliminate rework

- Activities and decisions that can be automated

- Ways to improve efficiency by creating a better user experience

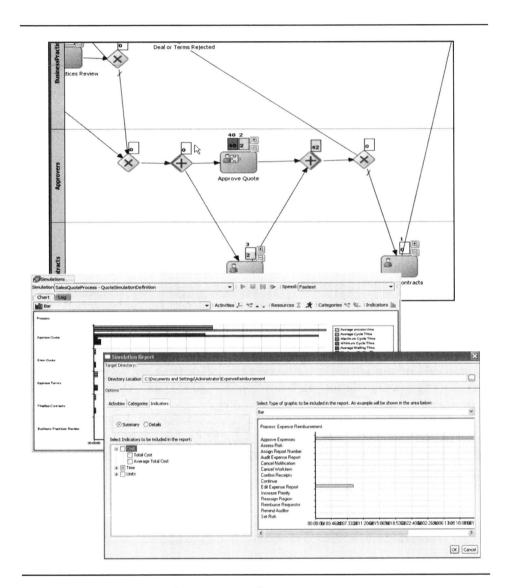

FIGURE 10-29. *A simulation screenshot*

Final Business Verification

Here, the business users review the business process model (ideally using a view within the same modeling tool as the architects and analysts who constructed the model, as is the case with Oracle BPM 11*g*) and its simulations to confirm the model accurately represents their needs.

The review of the process model with all stakeholders should highlight the following:

- Applicable business goals, objectives, rules, and regulations

- Flows, activities, decisions, subprocesses, exceptions, and other items

- Triggering events, inputs, outputs, end state

- Business calendar, timeouts, durations

- Inconsistencies that were rectified

- Proposed changes based on simulation, findings, observations

- Systems, applications, and interfaces

- User interface additions/changes

Documenting User Interactions

Storyboards showing just key attributes and page flow can be used for quick and simple illustrations of user interactions and User Interface (UI) requirements; otherwise, for more detailed definitions, screen mock-ups are used. This is the domain of more traditional software development, so we won't spend much time here, but the interface to the process participants is vital to the success of the BPM implementation.

Summary

In this chapter, we have seen the initial stages of a structured approach to a process automation project, from the high-level strategic activities associated with process identification and selection, to the original definition and refinement (design) of a business process model. This approach has taken us through a critical selection procedure that ensures we are spending our effort on true business processes (at the right level of decomposition) that are most suited to automation regardless of whether we choose to take a strategic or tactical approach. Clearly, the strategic approach is much more involved, but it can not only improve process identification and process selection justification through business value alignment, it can enable long-term business motivation traceability as well. We have shown a variety of techniques to support the full scope of business analysis and establish the first two OMG levels of the process model: descriptive and analytical. In Chapter 11, we will look at the final stages of composite business process application implementation by taking the analytical model to the executable level and beyond, and encompassing the full business process engineering life cycle.

CHAPTER
11

Technical Design and Project Delivery Strategies

o far, we have described the overall approach to BPM in Chapter 9, and then we drilled into the critically important details of business process identification and selection in Chapter 10. In this chapter, we will look at the engineering details required to make the process executable. Here we will identify all the activities in a business process engineering life cycle, the roles required to support it, and finally discuss how to apply these activities using established project methodologies.

Chapter 9 included a high-level description of program-level concerns for BPM and introduced the idea of projects for both the improvement of enterprisewide capabilities (described as remediation resulting from the maturity assessment) and the implementation of business process automation. The latter, automation (and associated business process improvement) projects, is the subject of this chapter.

The previous chapter introduced the business process life cycle states and described in detail the strategic analysis and process design activities that kick-start the cycle of continuous business process improvement. This brought us all the way to an analytical model in its first *to-be* state.

The first section of this chapter focuses on taking the analytical model through technical analysis and design activities to finally create an executable business process model/composite business process application. This section proceeds through the engineering life cycle to outline the additional considerations for BPM in testing, deployment, and production operations to complete the cycle.

The Motivation for Adopting a BPM Methodology

Why do we need an engineering method for the business-driven activity of business process automation? IT organizations have become very adept at delivering reliable software engineering projects, although historically this was not the case. This change is due in part to the emergence and refinement of the project delivery methodologies that exist today. With an increased need for business and IT alignment and the enterprise scope of most BPM programs, the lessons learned in traditional software engineering must be applied to BPM.

The abundance of software engineering methods in common use in IT tend to be inadequate for BPM because they:

- Are code-centric (BPM strives for "zero-code" implementations)

- Are rarely model-driven and process-centric to the extent of BPM

- Lack the steps necessary to effectively capture the business process

- Overlook business Key Performance Indicators (instrumentation is typically an afterthought)

- Do not support continuous improvement (beyond the planned iterations of the project)

- Lack vision beyond the scope of a single project

- They are not adapted to the use of BPM technology and tooling

An effective method for BPM must address these inadequacies and support discovery of existing processes while encouraging the cataloging and linking of related assets, and the separation of business concerns from technical concerns, while fostering business-IT cooperation. Part of that involves establishing a common language and understanding through techniques such as functional decomposition and process leveling. Business automation cannot be specified in a single requirements document (or "thrown over the wall to IT"). Effective cooperation between business and IT is an absolute requirement, and an ongoing cycle of improvement—as the process evolves—mandates a continuous dialogue. All these needs must be addressed by a BPM method.

Ultimately, BPM will put more control in the hands of business leadership and enable IT to focus on exposing application services as we move closer to the idea of the third wave.[1] To do that requires a method, along with the effective use of modern BPM tooling, which unambiguously assigns responsibilities and ensures a consistent, repeatable, and effective approach to business process automation.

---

[1] *Business Process Management: The Third Wave* (Meghan-Kiffer Press, 2003), by Howard Smith and Peter Fingar.

An effective method must address these inadequacies and promote:

- The cataloging and discovery of existing processes and related assets
- The proper separation of business concerns from technical concerns
- The proper process leveling
- Improved coordination between business and IT
- More control by business
- The effective use of modern BPM tools
- Concepts like identifying business KPIs and the abstractions of business rules

Introduction to the Business Process Engineering Life Cycle

We introduced the business process engineering life cycle in Chapter 10 as a sequence of composite application development states. We will now look at the same life cycle as a series of activities to be performed in a loop of continuous business process improvement.

The diagram in Figure 11-1 shows the major activities in the business process engineering life cycle, along with the associated states identified in Chapter 10. This diagram uses only short names for the engineering activities for readability, but these names are expanded using their full names in outline descriptions in the paragraphs following the diagram.

An Outline of Life-Cycle Activities

In terms of naming, there is a tendency to use the overloaded terms "analysis" and "design" to mean different things to different people. For example, a business analyst may equate identification and definition with analysis and design (respectively) These terms, however, are already used by IT in subsequent activities, but worse than this is that the output of definition and refinement is referred to as an "analytical model" (see the upcoming

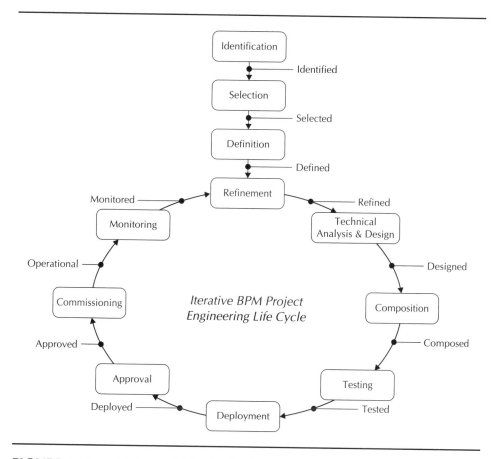

FIGURE 11-1. *Major activities in the business process engineering life cycle*

section "The Relationship to Business Process Modeling Levels"). It is important to establish a common understanding of terms to maintain effective communication between business and IT stakeholders, so for this reason the activity names have been carefully selected. The terms "analysis" and "design" will occur from time to time, but their context and association of our life-cycle activity names should ensure clarity.

The following paragraphs provide a brief description of the 11 activities in the method life cycle, while subsequent sections of this chapter cover the core activities of the loop in more detail.

Business Process Identification, Selection, Definition, and Refinement

These activities were the focus of Chapter 10, so we will only briefly recap them here for context in our engineering life cycle. Identification through refinement makes up the major business analysis activities required to start a business process automation project and the subsequent cycle of continuous improvement.

With the exception of refinement, these steps should not need to be repeated for a given process or project. As we shall see later in this chapter, the refinement activity not only reoccurs for each loop of the cycle, but may be revisited to address the findings of the technical feasibility analysis in the next activity, technical analysis and design.

Successful business process engineering ideally starts by taking business drivers from various potential sources of business motivation descriptions including business plans, strategy maps, associated value chains, and so on. This approach helps identify the core business processes and determines their strategic alignment in the Selection activity. A tactical approach was also shown in the previous chapter that allows selection to proceed when access to these sensitive business documents is not available or in cases where business processes have been identified by some other means.

In Definition (Business Process Definition), the selected business processes are subjected to an analysis process in which many participants collaborate to agree upon a model describing the next level of detail for the business process as it is in its current state—the "as-is" state. The Process Analyst applies further detail to the business process model, elaborating the model and resolving inconsistencies.

In the *defined* state the major elements of the process have been captured using BPMN in a business process modeling tool that enforces modeling disciplines. The model includes the flow, its start and end events, business exception paths, the process participants and their interactions, the exchange of data between the process activities, and the interaction with external information sources and application functions.

Business Process Refinement (the Refinement activity in Figure 11-1) refers to the improved version of the business process, also known as the "to-be" state. This is the point at which the process enters the cycle of continuous business process improvement. On entering the loop for the first time (that is, from the Definition activity) changes should be limited, avoiding the risk of over-ambitious change while still demonstrating value through early wins. It is better to separate the initial automation from significant process change for two important reasons: (1) risk is reduced by limiting the scope of incremental changes and avoiding process change problems being confused with automation itself, and (2) process changes can be better managed once automation is established.

In this activity, the model is enhanced with details of business rules, Key Performance Indicators (KPIs), business requirements, and underlying application and information services that are expected to support the business process model.

Subsequent iterations through the continuous improvement cycle bring greater intelligence about the business process along with augmented simulation data from monitoring and analysis. New or changed business drivers may also be introduced in this activity to accommodate changes in the business environment.

Technical Analysis and Business Process Design

This next major activity in the engineering life cycle includes a feasibility analysis to ensure that the IT applications and systems are capable of supporting the model in its *refined* to-be state. A Gap Analysis is performed to specify requirements for extensions to existing IT capabilities needed to support the business process model. Approved IT changes initiate parallel software and service engineering projects separate from the business process engineering project since these engineering activities require different skills, methods, and project disciplines.

The business process design describes the details of User Interfaces (UIs), the messages that flow between process activities, transactions and transaction boundaries, security constraints, and exception paths for system error events.

On completion of this IT-focused activity, the business process is said to be in the *designed* state.

Business Process Application Composition

The Business Process Application Composition activity completes the technical steps necessary to make the business process model executable.

Implementation of the technical aspects of the business process includes configuring business rules, human task definitions, and wiring Service

Component Architecture (SCA) components to support integration and service orchestration requirements; UI applications may also be constructed.

In this activity, the business process advances its state from designed to *composed.*

Integration Testing

This activity takes a white-box testing approach (that is, initial development-level testing in which testers are fully aware of the operation of underlying code) to ensure the technical integration between the process engine and the underlying application functions, information services, and various other external data and systems performs appropriately.

After successful integration testing and any necessary problem resolution, the business process enters the state of *tested.*

Deployment Planning

Deployment planning packages the composite business application and all its supporting software components and describes the procedures necessary to transfer it out of the development environment. The deployment plan also includes operational procedures and end-user documentation and training. The first target for the deployment package, prior to production deployment, is user acceptance and, potentially, performance testing environments.

Once a complete deployment package has been transferred out of development it is said to be *deployed,* or at least, deployment-ready.

Approval

Next we enter the approval process. Here the Quality Assurance (QA) team plans and manages the end-user and performance testing. This step is commonly called user acceptance testing (UAT).

Commissioning

Once approved by QA the composite business process application moves into commissioning. This is where the business process transitions into full production operation and hence, the state changes to *operational.* The process is no longer undergoing testing, but is live in production. This live production state may, at first, be limited to a small set of end users (say, a pilot or limited production release), during which aspects of the business process other than its technical implementation may be examined.

Monitoring and Analysis

Monitoring and Analysis support both Operational Administration and Management (OA&M) of the business process in the production environment and business process improvement. The analysis of data gathered from predefined KPIs provides critical information to the business analyst to support continuous improvement and continue the engineering life cycle by reentering the *refinement* step.

The final state of the composite business process application, before restarting the continuous improvement cycle, is *monitored.*

Incremental and Iterative

One of the primary reasons for putting a business process under the control of a BPM system is to enable ongoing continuous improvement of the business process. The Oracle BPM Methodology focuses on getting this life cycle of continuous improvement started by injecting a degree of business architecture to support the identification and selection of business processes best suited to computerized BPM treatment. Once the business process has been automated, the engineering cycle is *iterated* to produce *incremental* improvements throughout the life cycle of the business process.

By employing the BPM Methodology in every iteration of continuous, incremental improvement, successful implementation is ensured. This is achieved, for example, by early identification of IT application changes, simulation with the support of actual runtime data, effective testing, recording change justification for traceability, and so on.

Further details of the use of Iterative and Incremental Development (IID) approaches can be found in the later sections of this chapter.

Related Software Engineering Activities

The business process engineering project (abbreviated to "BPM project" here) is defined (or identified) by the selection of a process (or processes) suitable for automation.

During the analysis phase of the BPM project, deficiencies in the supporting application capabilities may be identified. These gaps spin off separate engineering activities that are subject to other practices, such as service engineering, traditional software integration, and others. The interaction with these additional engineering efforts is indicated by the dotted lines in Figure 11-2.

Development work can be performed external to the process method, as we will discuss later. It may require the instantiation of a new project. These associated engineering projects are shown in Figure 11-2 in which requirements from the Technical Analysis and Design activity drive development of assets that are consumed by the Business Process Project in the Composition activity. Methods for such software and service engineering projects are well known and distinct from process engineering and are therefore not described here other than to explain the exchange of information and the identification of project dependencies.

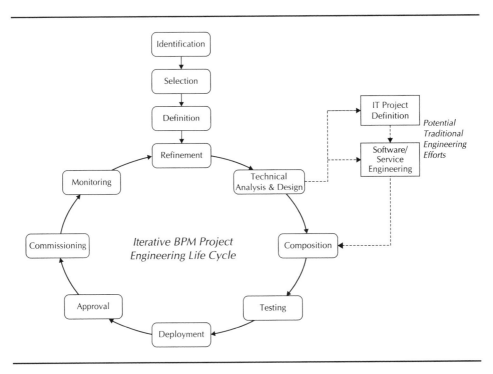

FIGURE 11-2. *Related software engineering activities*

The Relationship to Business Process Modeling Levels

Many "levels" and categorizations are used throughout the Oracle BPM Methodology and it is important to apply them in their appropriate context to avoid confusion. One such set of levels used in this document refers to the degree of detail in a business process model as it transitions from an early analysis communication vehicle to its ultimate executable state. A hierarchy of three levels is typically described as follows:

- **Level 1** Documentation of the "happy path," used to describe how the Business Process flows to achieve the desired result. Level 1 is intended for use by the business stakeholders, it should be constrained to a limited palette of notational elements suitable for untrained users.

- **Level 2** Bridges the gap between business and IT by filling in the details of the exception handling, answers difficult questions like how to handle compensating transactions, and so on. Level 2 makes extensive use of the modeling notation and is intended for Business Analysts and Process Architects.

- **Level 3** Completes the technical activity of associating (wiring) "services" together, defining message flows and data mapping and transformation, and others, in order to make it executable. Level 3 is intended for use by IT, generally the process developer and architect.

This outline is similar to the three levels of modeling commonly used by the Object Management Group (OMG). The OMG names the three stages of business process model evolution "descriptive," "analytical," and "executable."

The development of the business process model through these states is closely is closely aligned with a sequence of activities in the business process engineering life cycle. The diagram in Figure 11-3 illustrates this alignment with the life cycle. Here we have included business models, such as value chains, and while these are not process models themselves, it is important to recognize them as inputs to the life cycle.

The relatively simple descriptive model may or may not be considered a formal deliverable from the process identification activity, but may be a useful aid during the associated interviews and workshops. Descriptive modeling

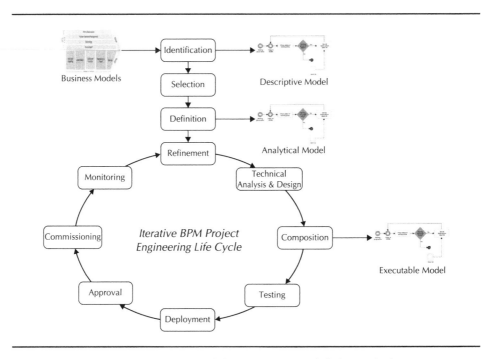

FIGURE 11-3. *The evolution of the process model through the engineering life cycle*

may be nothing more than a free-form whiteboard or flipchart exercise or it may be captured in a simple drawing tool for the benefit of presentations and discussions at this stage in the life cycle. The use of sophisticated BPMN modeling tools should be avoided at this stage, however, because the constraints and complexities of formal modeling are likely to be a distraction for the participants engaged in this high-level analysis activity.

The use of formal tooling for business process modeling starts with the detailed definition of the as-is business process state. Here the model is developed to the analytical stage where simulation and other formal analysis activities can be applied as part of the following refinement activity. The model does not become executable however until the composition step, as indicated in Figure 11-3.

Many other kinds of levels appear throughout this document, such as the levels in a functional model, and it is important not to clarify their usage to avoid confusion.

Business Process Engineering Roles and Responsibilities

The following section outlines the core organizational participants required for a successful BPM project. A number of new roles have been identified by best practices emerging from BPM experience in the field. While role names and the distribution of skills vary between organizations, it is important to ensure that the responsibilities identified here are mapped appropriately to any given organization structure.

The long list of roles may appear overwhelming at first sight if it is assumed that the number of roles equates to the number of people needed to run a BPM project. Realistically, however, several of these roles are often combined, particularly when first starting with BPM. The main goal of staffing a BPM project should be to ensure that all necessary responsibilities can be assigned. Depending on the size of the organization and the BPM project, some roles may be filled by more than one person, while others may always be combined. And, of course, during the project's life cycle, participants will be required in different degrees. A number of business and technical participants are involved in the Oracle BPM Methodology, and it is important to ensure coordination between these two major groups. The Process Analyst and Process Architect, in particular, represent an important point of convergence between business and IT. The core set of participant roles is shown in the diagram in Figure 11-4, which shows the Process Analyst and Process Architect at the center of the process engineering life-cycle loop.

Business Participants

The following sections outline the responsibilities of the business participant roles shown in the top portion of Figure 11-4.

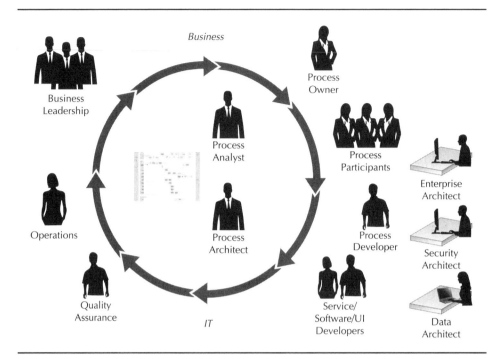

FIGURE 11-4. *BPM method participants*

Business Leadership

Drives requirements by setting business goals, objectives, and priorities. The business leadership provides initial inputs, such as business motivation definitions including high-level vision and mission statements. The business leadership provides funding for the BPM initiative and typically expects a measurable return on investment.

Business leadership might include the following more specific role names:

- Executive (C-level) Management
- Line-of-Business (LOB) Management
- Business Process Manager
- Unit/Division/Departmental/Branch Manager

■ Business Service Owner

■ Quality Manager

■ Compliance Manager

The business leadership uses BPM analytics in a broader Business/ Enterprise Performance Management (EPM) context and determines the need for major business process change.

A significantly large BPM initiative may identify a new executive role, perhaps called "Chief Process Officer," which will be responsible for fostering a process-centric business culture, influencing the development of skills, systems, and behaviors, and championing an enterprise "process architecture."

The Process Owner

Managing process flow, task assignments, policies, rules, objectives, and performance measurement, the Process Owner is responsible and accountable for the performance of end-to-end business processes. The Process Owner owns a specific process or processes, and is the primary authority for making decisions necessary to resolve conflict or overlap between processes.

Process Owner is the subject matter expert (SME) for the business process(es). He is the primary business contact for the Business Process Analyst. People in this role, however, specialize in a small number of processes and don't have the broader perspective of other business leadership across the enterprise.

Establishing the Process Owner role has emerged as a best practice for BPM since the key business processes cross organizational boundaries and typically have no single point of responsibility. Commonly, gaps (known as the white spaces) exist between the departmental silos of business process activity where ownership is undetermined and knowledge is sparse. The creation of the Process Owner role solves these problems by identifying individuals to be the experts responsible for the end-to-end flow of key business processes. While authority for departmental or divisional business process activities remains with respective managers, the Process Owner is able to take a holistic view and make better recommendations for enterprisewide process improvement.

Business process administration during runtime also requires considerable business knowledge, and the Process Owner should be expected to support this key operational activity.

Process Participants

The participants (also known as "process performers" or "end users") in a business process perform the human aspects of the business process task. These participants provide task execution details to the Process Analyst and may be involved in acceptance testing. During analysis for process automation, it is important to interview the end users and watch them work to see what they actually do (human activities are commonly more diverse than expected).

Some more specific role names for users of the business process might be:

- Administrator

- Supervisor

- Worker

- Call Center Agent/Customer-Service Representative (CSR)

- Clerks (Back-office processing)

- Business Partner

- Customer

In addition to the end-user performers of the business process work, the automated process commonly requires the support of additional participants categorized here as administrators and supervisors. While supervisors are responsible for overseeing the work performed by the end-user participants at the process instance level, administrators are responsible for more general oversight, such as role assignments, view management, and so on. In addition, supervisors are in charge of making sure the work is processed in a timely manner, managing exceptions, delegation, and the reassignment of work as needed.

The Process Analyst

Also commonly known as Business Analyst (or Business Process Analyst), the Process Analyst is primarily responsible for capturing and managing the graphical business process models. The Process Analyst also captures related business process requirements, drives process optimization, recommends changes, and evaluates change requests from the business. The Process Analyst has business and modeling skills and liaises with the Process Architect for technical coordination.

The Process Analyst is primarily responsible for making incremental process improvements (as opposed to major changes from the business leadership). The Process Analyst also:

- Identifies and codifies business rules

- Uses business objectives as input to determine KPIs

- Provides business specifications for new capabilities

- Directs UAT

IT Participants

The following sections outline the responsibilities of the IT participant roles shown in the bottom portion of Figure 11-4.

The Process Architect   Performs analysis and design of technical aspects of the process, taking the process specification from the Process Analyst for technical analysis. The Process Architect also specifies additional technical software requirements, such as application integration, UI development, and so on, and works with the Process Analyst to design technical specifications for new functional requirements.

The Process Architect may also be responsible for:

- Defining technical integration strategies

- Technical specification for new IT capabilities

- Directing system and integration testing

In an environment where SOA is fully implemented, the discovery of services for functional requirements in the process model can be performed effectively by nontechnical participants (typically the Process Analyst). In cases of less developed integration architectures, however, the Process Architect would be required to identify the most suitable sources of application functionality and business entities.

This is a specialized architecture role similar to "solution architect" in traditional software engineering, but with an emphasis on understanding business process modeling and the details of process implementation in addition to more general software architecture skills.

The Process Developer

Also called the Process Designer, the Process Developer enhances the process model to make it executable in the IT environment by configuring data mapping and the transformation of activity inputs and outputs, and defines external data required by the process and others.

The QA Manager

Directs acceptance testing and validation.

The Operations Manager

The Operations Manager handles deployments and technical OA&M (Operations, Administration, and Management).

Contributors and Advisors

Contributors and advisors are not typically permanent members of the project, but instead provide assistance such as security, data, and enterprise architecture, along with traditional software and service development needs identified by the business process project. The activities performed by these participants commonly follow their own methods and should be handled separately from the core BPM activities.

These supporting roles include:

- **Software/Service/UI Developers**   Develops any required new or extended functional capabilities specified by the Process Architect. Traditional software development requirements may emerge from the BPM project including integration, SOA services, or enhancement to existing application functionality. In the case of human workflow, a task-list UI or existing application UI may need to be developed to support the human interface to business process.

- **The Enterprise Architect**   Provides oversight to ensure IT strategies and standards are applied. The Enterprise Architect works with the Business Leadership to

    - Identify business architecture inputs to BPM (for example, objectives for program, business motivation, strategy maps, and so on)

    - Helps determine the need for major business process change

- **The Security Architect**   Ensures corporate security policies are followed and provides input to the process design for authentication, authorization, and access between potentially siloed applications and departments.

- **The Data Architect**   Provides support for information access in the process design and may be responsible for accepting process analytics feeds from the BPM system to support broader BAM/BI/EPM initiatives.

The preceding list is intended to identify roles specific to BPM (indeed a number of these are entirely new roles identified by best practices emerging from practical experience in the field) so some traditional IT software engineering roles have been omitted for brevity. This is not to suggest that roles such as project manager are not needed. In fact, all BPM projects should follow the highly successful software engineering pattern for the project leadership team, which encompasses stakeholder liaison (Project Manager), technical liaison (Process Architect), and project sponsorship (Process Owner).

The Process Analyst and Process Architect are critical roles in the automation of a business process (and are therefore drawn in the center of the diagram). These roles are categorized separately under business and IT because one has a greater business focus while the other is more technically oriented. In other respects, the skills of the Process Analyst and Process Architect are very similar, and so, in smaller projects, they may be performed by a single person. This is just one example of how the role-to-people relationship is applied in accordance with the size of the project. The value of a complete role list is in ensuring that all the skills and responsibilities needed for successful business process engineering are accommodated by the project, regardless of the way in which they are mapped individual performers.

Participant Responsibilities

In addition to identifying roles for process engineering participants, it is necessary to also determine their responsibilities and level of involvement for a given process project. As an example of this, we'll use a modified Responsibility Assignment Matrix.

The Responsibility Assignment Matrix

A Responsibility Assignment Matrix, also known as a "RACI chart," describes the involvement of the defined roles in completing tasks or deliverables for a project. The matrix is especially useful in clarifying roles and responsibilities in cross-functional/departmental projects and activities.

RACI is an acronym derived from the four key levels of involvement commonly assigned to project participants: Responsible, Accountable, Consulted, and Informed. For the purposes of our extended responsibility assignment example, we use the "RASCI" variation, which includes the participation level "Supporting." These participation levels are explained next:

- **Responsible**   Those who do the work to achieve the task and create associated deliverables. This participant is responsible for the task, ensuring that it is done as per the requirements of the Approver (see Accountable next). A project typically has only one role with a participation type of *Responsible* to avoid misunderstanding, although others can be delegated to assist in the work required (this is why we use the *RASCI* variation to separately identify those who participate in a supporting role).

- **Accountable** (also called Approver or final Approving authority) Those who are ultimately accountable for the correct completion of the deliverable and assignment of the task to the *responsible* participant. The *Accountable* participant must sign off (Approve) the work that *Responsible* produces. There can only be one *Accountable* participant specified for each task or deliverable.

- **Supporting**   Resources allocated to the *Responsible* participant. Unlike *Consulted,* who may provide input to the task, *Supporting* will assist in completing the task.

- **Consulted**   Those whose opinions are requested and engage in communication about the project.

- **Informed**   Those who are kept up to date on progress of the project milestones or just completion of a task or deliverable. Unlike *Consulted,* this involves just one-way communication.

In some situations, the *Accountable* participant may also be *Responsible* for completing the task or deliverable. This situation is indicated in our example chart with both shown in a cell of the matrix (this may also be indicated by showing a role as *Accountable* for the task or deliverable, but no role *Responsible* for its completion, in which case *Accountable* is implicitly *Responsible*). Other than this exception, each role in the project should be assigned just one of the participation types.

The RASCI-style chart in the sample shown in Figure 11-5 also uses pie chart–like icons as utilization indicators providing a five-stage visual estimate for a participant's level of involvement (ranging from occasional, represented as an open circle, to 100 percent utilization being the black-filled circle).

Engineering Life Cycle Phase	Process Engineering Participants											
	Business Participants				IT Participants				Contributors/Advisors			
	Business Leadership	Process Owner	Process Participant	Process Analyst	Process Architect	Process Developer	QA Manager	Ops Manager	Software Developer	Enterprise Architect	Security Architect	Data Architect
Process Identification & Selection	C	A		R						S		
Definition & Refinement	C	A	C	R	S							
Technical Analysis & Design		I			AR		I			S	C	C
Business Process Application Composition		I			A	R			S			
Testing (SIT)		I			A	S	R		S			
Deployment Planning		I			AR	S	I	C	S	C	C	C
Approval (UAT)		R	S	C	I		A	S				
Comissioning		I	I		S	S			RA	S		
Monitoring & Analysis (inc. OA&M)	I	R		C					A			

FIGURE 11-5.   *An example of a RASCI matrix*

Business Process Engineering Life-Cycle Detail

In order to adjust our thinking towards business process projects we're going to group our life-cycle activities to adjust to the idea of "disciplines." Disciplines will be useful to us when we come to map our business process engineering activities to various project methodologies. The diagram in Figure 11-6 shows the mapping of disciplines to our life-cycle activities.

Chapter 10 has already covered the activities grouped here as strategic analysis and business process analysis. We are now going to explore the more technical activities within the disciplines commonly found in the IT department. The architecturally focused technical analysis and design activity, along with developer focused implementation of composite business applications are the

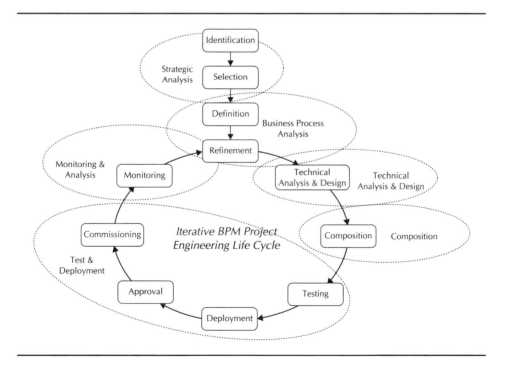

FIGURE 11-6. *A mapping of disciplines to life-cycle activities*

major technical concerns for business process engineering. There is a tendency to think these activities should be combined, however, they are in fact two distinct disciplines requiring separate skill sets.

Technical Analysis and Design

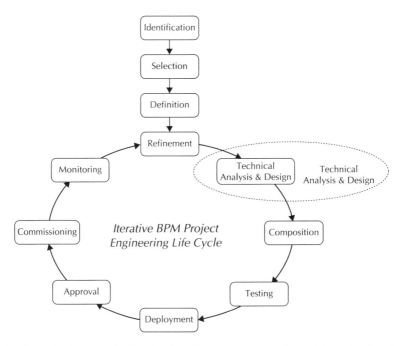

Technical analysis and design is the first step towards making the business process model executable (described previously as "level 3" in the evolution of the process model).

The initial output from the first pass through the refinement activity (described in Chapter 9) is a completed abstract model. In this activity, the abstract model is analyzed from a technical perspective to define the requirements for building the composite application for the business process. Here we determine what technical enhancements should be applied to the model and what technical steps need to be taken to transition the abstract model into a concrete executable form.

Oracle BPM 11*g* clearly delineates process modeling, composition, and user interaction, and thus it is a good practice to create design documents that address elements of design separately:

- Application architecture that defines all the different technology pieces and how they come together.

- Composite Application design that specifies all the components such as BPMN, BPEL, Mediator, Adapters, and Web Services that are required to make the abstract to-be process executable.

- A process design document will also be required that specifies:

  - Technical exception handling

  - Event handling not addressed by the business flow, but required for the executable model

  - Optimization of the flow

  - Measurements and measurement points to support KPIs

- A User-Interface design document that specifies the application design for providing a User Interface for the business process. This would most likely follow a standard Java/J2EE design methodology.

The process for technical analysis and design is shown in the diagram in Figure 11-7.

We start with the process definition from process refinement (the "to-be" model) and collect additional technical details to support the technical analysis in this phase. The Gap Analysis shown here is very different from any Gap Analysis that may have been performed as part of the business analysis: Here we are assessing the ability of the IT applications and systems to support our business process. Supporting software engineering activities follow to ensure the composition in the next phase has all the necessary IT assets needed to make the business process model executable.

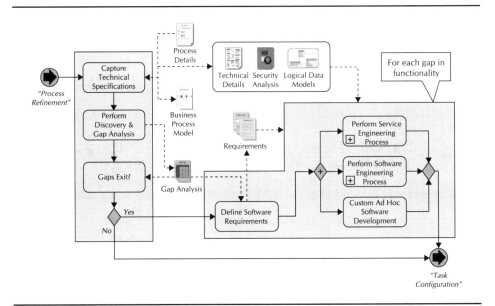

FIGURE 11-7. *The technical analysis and design process*

Capturing Technical Specifications

In this step, we capture the technical details of the business process and its system and human interactions. It is performed by the Process Architect, with support as needed from Enterprise Architect, Data Architects, and Security Architect.

Technical Details   Taking the abstract model as input, this step involves the following actions:

- Map business process activities and decisions to IT assets.

- Capture detailed technical mappings and requirements.

- Enterprise Architect can help ensure proper alignment with technology principles, standards, and application mapping

- Data Architects can help define data models, mappings, and translations

- Security Architect can provide insight on applicable security policies, risks, and architecture specifications

The deliverables from this step are technical specifications and models:

- Process model technology level view

- Technical specifications

- Logical data models

- Security analysis findings

The diagram in Figure 11-8 represents all the potential elements of the technical solution.

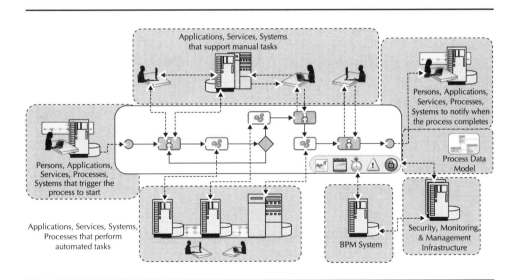

FIGURE 11-8.   *Elements of the technical solution*

To capture the technical specifications, we will need to look at different aspects of the process itself, including the following:

- Triggering events
- Manual tasks
- Automated tasks
- Process completion
- Process management
- Information
- Security

Figure 11-8 offers a technical summary view that can be used to represent the technical considerations for the process. The process model itself appears in the center of the diagram, while all the external systems and human actors it touches are highlighted and linked to the process model.

A business process flow must always be started by a start event (shown on the far left of the diagram in Figure 11-8). This can include human initiators as well as any number of system interactions, from receiving a fax to a complex event analysis system detecting some significant condition. The BPM system itself (bottom right) might also start a process based on the timer for example.

The following checklist provides a set of questions (and example responses) that helps develop the information we need to know about the process:

- What triggers the process to start? Person, application, process, service, and so on.

- What transport mechanisms and protocols are used? SOAP, TCP-IP, FTP, XML, JMS, and others.

- What forms of response need to be supported? Synchronous reply, asynchronous reply, no reply, exceptions.

- What information is supplied? Data model, content type, schema, entities...

- What validation needs to be performed on the data?

- What access control restrictions apply? Roles, groups, devices, locations, times, and others.

- How is authentication and authorization performed? LDAP, IdM system, Identity propagation, and so on.

- How is identity provided? Username and password, certificate, WS-Security token...

- What are the confidentiality and integrity needs? Encryption and digital signature requirements?

At the top of the diagram we have the people the process is interacting with. Three types of interaction are represented here:

- The user on the far left is interacting with a traditional application, which is in turn integrated with the BPM system, saving the additional steps (and potentially not changing the way he interacts with the system).

- A user is prompted to interact with a traditional application, but most likely through a task management interface.

- The user is involved in an entirely manual interaction with the BPM system, such as approving a request.

Regardless of the type of interaction, there are many details to capture, such as:

- Who are the human actors and how are they notified to begin a task? Roles and groups; task list portlet, e-mail, mobile notification, and so on.

- What systems will the process interface with to support manual tasks, and what is the sequence of interactions?

- What systems will the user interact with to perform manual tasks?

- What information needs to be presented to the user, and in what form?

- What timeout behavior must be implemented?

- What metrics must be collected for this task?

- What security requirements apply and how will they be implemented? User authentication, authorization, audit logging, LDAP, IdM...

- What security requirements apply to the information? Encryption, data masking, content protection...

The backend systems (represented in the lower left of the diagram in Figure 11-8) are integrated with service tasks ideally using SOA techniques, but potentially also using legacy integration architectures (EAI/MOM, point-to-point, or custom integration). These back-end systems commonly have their own departmental-level workflows and technical processes. In many cases, it is not necessary (or technically feasible) to decompose these business activities and take control of the flows in the core business process model. This will be an area for discussion of feasibility and requirements between the business and IT.

- What functions need to be performed?

- What information needs to be processed?

- What are the RASP (Reliability, Availability, Scalability, Performance) requirements?

- What are the QoS (Quality of Service) and transactional integrity requirements?

- What SOA services are available to satisfy these requirements?

The BPM system itself is also capable of injecting events into the flow, such as alarms or detection of certain conditions. It also collects performance information about the running processes and may even perform real-time analysis triggering certain events or notifications.

- What key performance indicators need to be captured and reported from the process itself?

- How will they be propagated?

- What measures need to be taken to ensure process integrity? Data quality, transactions, rollback, audit, and others.

- What business calendar will the process follow?

- What task or process timeouts need to be configured?

- How are exceptions handled and reported?

- What security considerations apply to the process itself? Data encryption, administrator auditing, and others.

Information Needs Analysis   Information needs analysis takes the steps discussed below.

For each interaction, determine:

- What data (entities, attributes, content) must be supplied to the actor in order for the activity to be completed or the decision to be made?

- Where will the data come from?

- In what form will it be presented? XML, Object, HTML, DOC, and so on.

- What logical data model(s) should the process adhere to?

- What aggregations, mappings, and transformations are required to produce the desired presentation format?

- What data is returned?

- What state change(s) have occurred?

- What systems need to be updated/notified/synchronized?

- Are there any transactional requirements?

- What mechanism will be used to move data?

Review each of the preceding with Data Architects.

Figure 11-9 shows an example of the logical data models that may be associated at the various different functional levels of the enterprise. Each data source inherently has its own logical model. In some cases, a higher-level model has been defined, perhaps via Master Data Management (MDM) or data integration efforts. If such a model exists, then processes within the scope of that model should use it. If no higher-level models exist, then a logical model should be defined for the process. This is preferred over adopting the source model in that it avoids propagating the source model beyond its intended scope.

In the diagram, each of the logical models shown belongs to an application. In a business process that typically spans applications, it is important to be aware of data dependencies that span applications since this demands specialized data services that may not already exist.

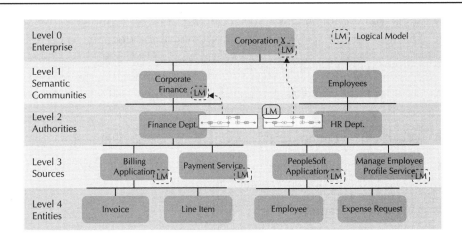

FIGURE 11-9. *Logical data models*

Some organizations have an enterprisewide canonical data model (shown at the top of the model). The enterprise data model is rare, but if available, it should be used as much as possible in defining data needs for the process.

In the case that data models are not already defined, it is often better to start with an industry standard model (for example, HR-XML for HR systems, HL7 for health care, and so on) rather than an application-specific data model.

Oracle's Application Integration Architecture (AIA) for example defines canonical models independent of the applications, but with translations and transformations for interaction with the applications.

At whatever level(s) the logical model exists, our technical solution may need data transformation services to exchange data with the applications.

Security Needs Analysis   One of the problems encountered in business process automation lies in bestowing the authority to initiate the application functions on the BPM system. This authority must be maintained and propagated securely to the applications where credentials are commonly not uniform between systems. Worse still, the authenticating mechanisms may be different.

Use these steps to determine the scope of the security issues and formulate appropriate solutions.

Identity and Access Control:

- Determine mechanisms used to authenticate users that interact with the process.

- Determine mechanisms used to authenticate system interactions.

- Map identified roles/groups/people to identity management system entities.

- Establish access control policies for process triggers (start and resume points).

- Determine authentication and/or identity propagation strategy.

For human interaction, much of this is handled automatically. Authentication is usually handled using the mapping between the swim-lanes in the process diagrams and the Groups created in LDAP.

Integrity and Confidentiality:

- Review security classifications of data and/or content used by the process.

- Determine security risks to information based on network exposure, location, and other items.

- Identify encryption requirements to ensure the required level of confidentiality.

- Identify data masking requirements based on data classifications and user access levels.

- Identify process and data integrity requirements that might necessitate digital signatures and/or nonrepudiation.

- Determine the key management strategy.

- Identify and address risks introduced via process execution such as persisted state, cached data objects, audit logging, and cluster network traffic.

Finally, review the security specifications with Security Architect.

Originally, the "swivel-chair business process" involved a human participant login to multiple back-end application systems. To provide equivalent access to the BPM system, a number of solutions are available. The simplest solution is a centralized single sign-on system that authenticates the BPM system to all back-end applications. However, it is sometimes necessary to provide access based on the status of the human initiators and participants and this may even influence the flow of the process. In these cases, it is necessary to propagate the participant's credentials or security tokens (there is an option in which the BPM process is assumed to be authorized to interface with the back-end systems).

Confidentiality can often be delegated to a Content Management System (CMS), but again it is necessary to appropriately identify the user involved in the activity to enable the CMS to provide the right amount of information.

Gap Analysis and Technical Feasibility

The Gap Analysis is also known as a technical feasibility study since the supporting services, information needs, or application integration may not be available, and the cost or delay to develop them may be sufficient to return the business process back to the previous phase to be reworked (this exception flow is not shown in the diagram in Figure 11-2).

This step is performed by the Process Architect and involves the following actions:

1. Locate existing SOA services, applications, interfaces, and so on that match functional and data needs.

2. Compare nonfunctional requirements versus needs.

3. Determine:

   a. Which existing assets are an exact match for the process

   b. Which assets are a partial match (functional or nonfunctional)

   c. What capabilities are not currently provided

4. Contact SOA service/application owners to discuss usage of existing assets and feasibility of revisions where partial matches are found.

The deliverable from this step is a "discovery and Gap Analysis findings" document. This document reports on what functions need to be built or accessed to support each task in the business process model versus what currently exists.

If we are implementing BPM over a solid SOA foundation, it should be relatively simple to line up the functional models used for service engineering along with service contract descriptions to determine where services meet the requirements of the business process tasks.

SOA service discovery methods include repository searches, an examination of the Functional Model, and the examination of service contracts. Other forms of application functions can be found in an Application Functionality Matrix and a Data Entity Matrix.

The functions required by the process should be scored according to the following criteria:

- Partial Match: Revisions to existing SOA services, application integrations, and so on

- No Match: New functionality to perform automated tasks

- Software to support user interactions and devices

- Means to integrate the process with existing systems, other processes, applications, and others

For each gap identified in the technical application and information support, we define software requirements and perform the necessary software engineering activities to fill these gaps. This method does not define how these other engineering activities should be performed. They may be fulfilled through SOA service engineering, for example, or by any other established method and integration architecture.

Defining Software Requirements

The process architect defines the requirements for the missing functionality and integration needs for each identified gap. These requirements might take the form of use cases, "stories," and so on, according to the software methodologies employed by the IT organization.

The task is performed by the Process Architect and involves the following actions:

- For each gap, create specifications needed to support the development of missing functionality

- Include functional and nonfunctional criteria

■ The form of documentation can be whatever the development team can best work with—for example, use cases, requirements list, storyboard, and others

Deliverables:

■ Software/service requirements documentation

Filling the IT Gaps   The preferred approach to filling the IT gaps is SOA service engineering because it lends itself to optimal integration with the BPM method. SOA service engineering is a capability that appears in the BPM Maturity Model (described in Chapter 8) and is used in the assessment of a BPM maturity.

In some circumstances, SOA may not be an available option, or is simply not sufficiently matured, in which case other legacy strategies, such as EAI, may need to be applied.

A last resort is ad hoc development, although this never results in a long-term sustainable solution and so should be avoided.

In summary, the options for fulfilling the additional software needs are classified as follows:

■ **Service Engineering Option**   All needed functionality is fed into a service engineering process where proper service justification, classification, development, testing, and provisioning are performed.

■ **Software Engineering Option**   A formal software development process is used either when service-enablement is not justified or when the service engineering option does not exist.

■ **Ad Hoc Development Option**   Software is developed by the process team strictly to satisfy requirements of the process.

The resulting software may include:

■ New automated functions not performed by existing applications

■ Enhancements to existing applications to support the process

■ Custom code to integrate the process with existing applications

Composition

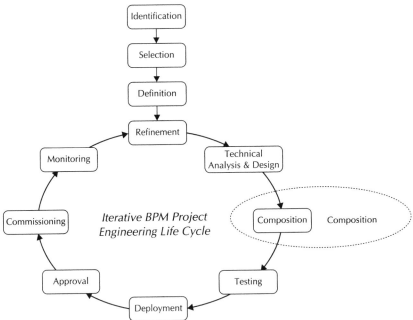

The goal of BPM in any IT environment should be to get to the point where business processes can be composed (and recomposed) by the Process Developer without the need for the intermediate step of software engineering. Although SOA will certainly help in realizing this goal, the current reality is that many business processes require that new SOA components be developed by IT.

Ultimately, this activity should be sufficiently nontechnical that we start to eliminate IT involvement in business process engineering altogether. In any case, business process application composition is the final technical step needed to make the business process executable.

Composition is a graphical and declarative activity (that is, there is no procedural programming) for wiring services to tasks, specifying the attribute level details of the message flows and data mapping between tasks, KPIs, and so on.

The task is performed by the Process Developer and involves the following actions:

- Compose the process in accordance with the technical specifications defined by the Process Architect

Composition may include:

- Importing interfaces to SOA services and other external points of integration

- Importing or configuring data sources and logical data models

- Message mapping, transformation, and validation

- Technical component wiring and exception handling

- Defining transaction boundaries

- Configuring process and task timeouts

- Setting up alerts and notifications

- Declarative encoding of business rules

- KPI instrumentation

- Configuring process security

- User Interface

- Worklist/WorkSpace configuration

- Any remaining task/role assignments and business rules configuration, and so on

- Unit testing

The key deliverable from this step is a composite business process application ready for testing.

These activities are represented in the process model in Figure 11-10.

Some of the technical aspects of the business process application composition are shown using Oracle BPM 11*g* in Figure 11-11.

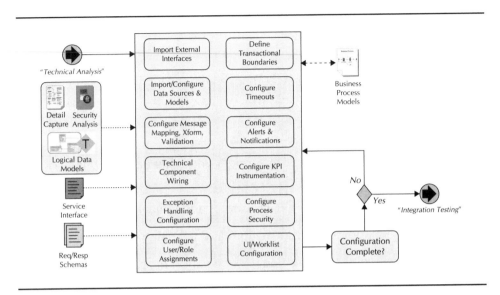

FIGURE 11-10. *Composition activities*

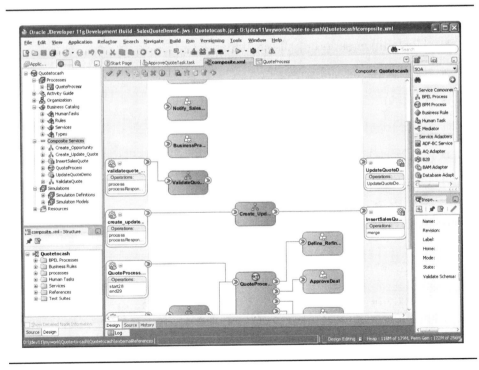

FIGURE 11-11. *Business process application composition in Oracle BPM 11g*

The resulting assembly of the business processes with application services integration, business rules, KPIs, worklist/WorkSpace applications, and so on is now a composite business process application ready for testing and other preparations prior to live operation.

Unit Testing   Unit testing in software engineering refers to testing (usually by the developer) of individual software modules, typically the class level in object-oriented programming. In BPM, this equates to testing at the process step level, or a collection of steps making up an activity, by the Process Developer. This level of testing simply ensures that the individual process steps (or activities) execute, within the constraints of the development environment, as specified by the requirements. It is unlikely that anything but the simplest of business processes can be tested from end to end at this stage in the engineering process. Testing of the complete process can only be effective after all points of integration have been tested (see integration testing later in the chapter) and the complete composite application is deployed to a near-as-possible real-world environment.

Unit tests are usually written by the process developer using full knowledge of the working of the code and its environment (this is known as white-box testing). These tests are constructed to ensure the process step acts appropriately on the possible range of inputs it can receive and produces an appropriate result. This activity focuses heavily on testing the handling of exceptions to ensure corner cases (that is, inputs and other stimuli outside the anticipated boundaries of normal operation) and all available branching paths are executed.

Use of a testing framework, such as JUnit, can provide significant benefits, including repeatable tests leading to more effective regression testing, and the systematic development of a catalog of tests providing opportunities for later system testing and even load simulation for performance and scalability testing. Test Driven Development (TDD) may also be applied in which automated tests are derived from the business and technical requirements (and may even become part of the requirements) prior to any development of the process steps.

Testing and Deployment

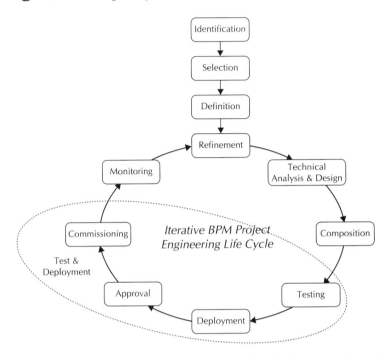

Unlike the earlier phases of BPM engineering, the final stages of testing through commissioning do not deviate significantly from traditional software engineering; therefore, this chapter provides only a brief description of production readiness procedures while highlighting areas of particular interest to BPM.

The procedure for taking an application from development to a live production environment is commonly summarized under the heading of *deployment.* Deployment, however, refers only to the part of the process in which the application is prepared for transfer from the development environment, in a complete integrated package, and made ready for use in a runtime environment. Initial uses for the deployment package and associated runtime environments include various levels of testing and approval prior to the ultimate production go-live. Numerous other activities are required along the way and the complete procedure for production readiness of a composite business application should include the following steps:

1. Integration and system testing

2. Deployment preparation

3. Acceptance testing and approval

4. Commissioning

Many variations exist on these basic software engineering themes, but the sequence is particularly important to maximize the effectiveness of testing and to minimize rework when problems are discovered. For example, integration testing and system testing (also known as requirements testing) should not require a complete end-to-end working composite application and can, therefore, be completed before deployment preparation, eliminating the need to repeat deployment when problems are found in these testing steps. On the other hand, acceptance testing, which may include performance and load testing, requires a complete deployment to a near-as-possible production environment.

Testing clearly does not occur exclusively in the "testing phase," but this is where the majority of the testing effort is focused, and typically a QA team comes together to design and execute these tests. More detailed descriptions of these testing steps appear under the relevant phase sections later in this chapter, but a summary of common test types relevant to BPM is listed by phase in Table 11-1.

Rather confusingly "integration testing" is often called "system integration testing (SIT)," and "system testing" is often referred to as "requirements testing." These may also be combined under the heading of "system and integration testing."

It is also important to note that the cost of testing, in terms of equipment, personnel, and coordination increases as we move through this list and, as with any software engineering project, it should not be necessary to apply every test in its entirety to every change. BPM by its nature is also particularly prone to change due to its strategy of continuous improvement and its core

Phase	Activity
Refinement	Simulation
Composition	Unit Testing Regression Testing
Testing	Integration Testing, System (requirements) Testing Process Collaboration Testing, User Interaction and Usability Testing
Approval	User Acceptance Testing (UAT) Performance and Load/Stress Testing
Commissioning	Operation Testing Availability and Disaster Recovery (Business Continuity) Testing

TABLE 11-1. *Test Activity by Phase*

objective of business agility, so we need to determine the scope of a release, categorize changes, and assess a risk level for every type of change in order to apply testing efficiently.

Some of the key issues for business process engineering arise from the broader involvement of business participants and the ease with which major changes can be made using current BPM tools. Changes to business process flows can now, theoretically, be made by business Process Owners and Process Analysts without support from IT. However, IT must still ensure changes are not allowed to flow into production in an uncontrolled manner. This is largely a concern for BPM governance, but governance first requires a complete and consistent method for BPM engineering, upon which to define its policies and procedures. So, although governance is beyond the scope of this discussion, this business process engineering method is an important part of the foundation for BPM governance.

Business process engineering raises a number of new governance questions that require us to assess the potential impact of changes, specify which roles should be permitted to make changes, and what testing and acceptance criteria should be applied.

One example of a BPM-specific concern is the testing of business rules: Should we test and approve every business rule change, or should we limit the scope of business rules to minimize the potential impact to a running system? In extreme cases, there are modifications (refinements) that will trigger a software change. This is likely to trigger both traditional software testing and, separately, business process testing and approval.

The first step in an approach to production readiness is to identify all the different types of changes that can arise in a BPM system. The question of roles and responsibilities can be deferred to the governance framework. The following list is a suggested starting point for categorization, with some examples of changes with varying potential impact to a production system.

- Roles

    - Addition of end-user participants

    - Addition of new swim-lanes with new flow paths and their mappings to corresponding LDAP groups of Key Performance Indicators

    - Add new indicators, modify indicators, or remove them

- Business rules

    - Add new rules to the existing rule chain

    - Add input or output arguments

    - Change threshold values

- Model and business process flow

    - Further automation of existing business processes

    - Creation of new business process

- Activities
    - Addition of service task using a well-established (SOA) service
    - Call-out to a new or non-SOA service
    - Human task workflow
- Events
    - The addition of timers
    - Business exceptions
        - The addition of exception paths and activities
- System errors
    - Activity and process SLAs
- System interfaces and integration techniques
    - Changes to underlying architecture (for example, the introduction of SOA)
- Underlying application code
    - Additional custom code
    - Updates to the packaged application
    - Packaged application replacement
- Other system considerations
    - Infrastructure upgrades
- Changes in business conditions
    - An anticipated increase in sales volume
    - The introduction of new business partners
    - Mergers and acquisitions

Considering the diversity of this by no means complete list, it is immediately clear that we not only need to form complex rules about how changes flow into production, but we also need a comprehensive impact analysis mechanism. Changes to business process could impact the operation of IT systems, while changes in the IT applications and infrastructure could have significant up-stream effects on business processes (if they are not sufficiently decoupled).

Some of the items in this list seem fairly innocuous. For example, "Addition of end-user participants" is unlikely to have much effect on the business process flow; however, increasing the number of participants (for example, rolling out a pilot automation across the enterprise) is likely to increase the load on the BPM infrastructure and the underlying systems.

KPIs, on the other hand, have no bearing on the infrastructure; however, the addition of new KPIs can have an impact on the process in the form of argument mapping and the addition of measurement marks (and potentially even the way the process is designed). Instead, changes to KPIs affect the measurement of the business process and so the impact to the analytics, particularly trend analysis and long-term performance measurements, must be considered carefully. KPIs may fall outside the scope of testing considered here, but the potential impact to existing analysis and reporting activities must be traceable.

By using a categorization scheme of this type, a matrix can be developed specifying the level of testing required by every change type within a release. The following matrix in Figure 11-12 shows a simple example of such a matrix using the testing types and some sample change candidates from the categories we have discussed here.

Another consideration unique to BPM is the introduction of long-running business processes to the IT environment. Some business processes span days or even weeks, but in traditional non-BPM environments, IT maintenance schedules work around business user needs, and these users manage the flow of the business process between systems outages. In a BPM system, business process states must be carefully maintained between outages and upgrades, and most interestingly between business process changes. In these cases, a policy must be established to ensure consistent handling: Should all

Type of Change	Change detail	Simulation	Unit	Regression	Integration	System	Collaboration	Interaction	UAT	Performance	Operational	Availability
Roles												
	Addition of end-user participants	✓								✓		
	Addition of new swim-lanes	✓	✓	✓	✓	✓	✓					
Business Rules												
	New business rule chain	✓										
	Add new arguments	✓										
	Changing threshold values	✓										
Model and Flow												
	Further automation of existing BP	✓	✓	✓	✓	✓	✓	✓	✓			
	Creation of new BP	✓	✓	✓	✓	✓	✓	✓	✓	✓	✓	✓
Activities												
	Addition of service task	✓	✓	✓	✓	✓	✓	✓	✓			
	Human workflow	✓	✓	✓	✓	✓	✓	✓	✓			
Events												
	Addition of timers	✓	✓	✓	✓	✓		✓				
	Business exceptions	✓	✓	✓	✓	✓		✓	✓			
	System errors	✓	✓	✓	✓	✓		✓				

FIGURE 11-12. *An example of a test-level requirements matrix*

long-running processes be quiesced (that is, allowed to flow to the end activity in the process using its version) to an end state before changes are applied? Should prior versions of a business process be allowed to run to completion after a change? Or should an "upgrade" process flow be necessary to transition in-flight processes from an earlier version? The answers to these questions will ultimately be unique to the organization, so the important thing is to consider them carefully in advance and develop well-communicated policies to ensure the consistent handling of all eventualities.

Oracle BPM 11*g* includes a versioning capability for the process model in both the designtime and runtime forms. The two sample screenshots in

FIGURE 11-13. *Versioning in Oracle BPM 11*g

Figure 11-13 show (left) the deployment of a composite version as the new default process using Oracle JDeveloper Studio and (right) the Oracle Enterprise Manager dashboard for monitoring instance versions.

Deployment of a process requires no interruption to existing processes, allowing a new version to be introduced while existing long-running processes are allowed to complete. A new version of the process may be run selectively (by a subset of users, for example) in order to exercise it thoroughly before making the new version the default.

The following sections explore these major phases of the business process engineering life cycle that contribute to production readiness in more detail.

Testing

This phase encapsulates the most rigorous testing activities and is commonly the responsibility of a separate Quality Assurance (QA) team in collaboration with the developers, architects, and analysts. Here, a test plan is created along with a set of test cases for functional and nonfunctional testing. The various testing types are outlined in the following sections.

Integration Testing

Since a BPM system is fundamentally concerned with managing the process flow between business process activities, both system and human, it necessarily involves significant integration with the systems and applications that provide the underlying functions. These functional assets may be geographically dispersed and technologically disparate. Similarly, the architectural strategies used to perform the integration may also involve multiple approaches. All the integration points arising from various combinations of applications, technologies, and geographies must be tested in the context of our composite business application before proceeding with the next steps of deployment packaging, acceptance testing, and so on.

Integration testing in the context of BPM is required to test all the interfaces between the business process flow and all its touch-points. These touch-points include:

- Business application functions

- Data and content

- User-Interface applications involving human participants

- Other external events

Each of these touch-points may use various integration technologies and architectural strategies, such as SOA, MOM, EAI, or proprietary mechanisms. These combinations must all be tested to ensure consistent operation in the final composite business application.

A best practice in integration testing is to create a separate test plan for each integration. This includes interaction diagrams and test cases that covered the interactions. This approach isolates changes to back-end systems, compartmentalizes the integration testing, and ultimately makes regression testing easier.

System Testing

Also known as "requirements testing," this activity validates the functional capabilities of the BPM composite application against the business and technical requirements specifications.

Process Collaboration Testing

Process Collaboration Testing is an extension of system testing that is unique to BPM. Process Collaboration refers to the interaction, via message flows, between processes both within processes and choreographies between processes—that is to say, the interaction between business processes that execute within the same environment as well as those communicating between separate environments.

The focus of collaboration testing is ensuring messages that flow between business processes are acceptable to all participants in all cases.

User Interaction and Usability Testing

User interaction is primarily concerned with the interaction between the BPM system and the end user. Other user interactions that may be tested at this stage include process monitoring and administration interfaces, as well as KPI analysis when custom solutions have been developed.

User interactions may be handled through the end-user's WorkSpace or a simple web interface integrated with underlying applications.

Deployment Planning

Before proceeding to the various end-to-end tests and final go-live, the composite application must be prepared to be transferred efficiently and completely to real-world environments. The environments we refer to are ultimately live production platforms, but prior to go-live there are various testing environments needed to facilitate stakeholder approvals.

Deployment is comprised of the following activities:

- **Release planning**   Software release planning is usually represented by a document describing a policy for organizing the production of regular software releases. It describes an approach for iterative software releases including a versioning scheme, milestones, release frequency, supporting practices, and tools to be to be used. In the case of BPM, the regularity of business process releases is unlikely to be as predictable as traditional software; however, some aspects still apply. Versioning, in particular, along with its associated practices and tooling, is critical to the BPM release process.

- **Version tracking**   A versioning scheme identifies what is running in the production and testing environments at any given time and supports problem analysis, migration, deprecation, and retirement.

- **Document dependencies**   A full description of the dependencies for the composite application being deployed is necessary to ensure the suitability of the target environment. For example, specific versions of underlying applications and a named list of associated services should be included. A full dependency description not only defines the operating environment but also enables impact analysis when dependent systems are being considered for update, replacement, or retirement.

- **Preparation for use by end users**

  - User documentation

  - Training

- **Packaging**   Packaging is a central concern for deployment. It identifies the constituent parts of a deployable composite along with the mechanisms for building, updating, and unpacking the package.

- **The development and documentation of procedures for:**

  - Installation and activation of the package

  - Installation reversal (in case of problems)

- **Upgrade procedures**

- **Deactivation and decommissioning**

Factors Influencing Process Deployment

A key concern for BPM composite application deployment is cohesiveness of the packaging. BPM 11g has the technical capability to promote certain types of changes to a running environment (including production) while the system is fully operational without any interruption to in-flight processes. These changes may include roles, business rules, KPIs, and even the flow of a business process. Other systems may simply require the deployment package to be broken into separate parts (when deploying to disparate systems, for example). Either case must be carefully managed.

Process Migration

When a new version of a business process is being provisioned, migration procedures must be developed to specify how the transition should be handled. In the simplest case, all in-flight process instances would be allowed to run to completion while all new instances run the new version: perhaps a time limit is determined for the retirement of the previous version and a process administrator is required to intervene to complete or re-run outstanding instances. The ability to concurrently run multiple versions in this way is, however, dependent upon the capabilities of the BPM system (Oracle BPM 11*g* is, however, able to run multiple concurrent process versions).

Another consideration for process migration would be user training in cases where a change to a business process impacts the flow of human tasks or the system's interaction with human participants.

Approval

Approval simply means to get agreement to put the composite business application into a live production environment, which implicitly involves various forms of acceptance testing to verify its readiness.

Various stakeholders have different concerns that result in different types of testing. Tests are categorized into functional and nonfunctional testing and the test types that commonly apply in business process engineering are as follows:

- Nonfunctional testing

    - Security testing

    - Usability testing

    - Performance and scalability testing

- Regression testing

- User Acceptance Testing (UAT)

The performance and scalability testing is also called load testing or stress testing; however, it is important to note that this nonfunctional test at the approval stage is very different from any form of load testing that may have been performed in a designtime simulation tool. Designtime workload simulation typically attempts to predict the workload of nonsystem assets—for example, human workers, delivery trucks, milling machines, and so on. At this final approval stage, with the benefit of a complete functional system, performance testing focuses on the ability of the system assets (in other words, processors, applications, rules engines, and other items) to operate at the workload levels predicted by the business requirements.

Best Practices

A SOA strategy underpinning the BPM architecture provides an isolation layer separating the BPM platform from the source systems that provide application data and functionality. This "loose coupling" can be exploited during testing to simulate application functions and avoid the need for a complete implementation of all enterprise applications for the purpose of functional testing.

Nonfunctional testing—in particular, performance testing—does require as-near-as-possible replication of all production platforms involved in the business process. Some simplification can be achieved by establishing the performance characteristics and load limitations of individual applications and systems and using the data to augment the business process simulation model.

The practice of running test "streams" within a production environment incurs substantial risks and should be avoided. On the other hand, using test data that replicates real production data (without violating client confidentiality) is a best practice.

Commissioning

In software, as with any engineering practice (for instance, building, industrial plant, and so on), commissioning is defined as the process of assuring that all systems and components are installed, tested, operated, and maintained according to the operational requirements from the business owner. Once again, testing and assurance appear outside the scope of the core testing owned by the QA team. In this case, testing is required to ensure that the operational procedures perform according to requirements.

This phase may also involve the installation of additional hardware and infrastructure software based on sizing specifications from the architecture team.

Operational procedures take the form of documents ("the ops manual"), scripts, and an operations management framework (tool suite) capable of incorporating new dashboards and operational information. The standard operational procedures relevant to a BPM system include the following:

- **Start/Stop**   Procedures for cleanly starting and stopping process instances, queues, engines, and hardware platforms for maintenance, upgrades, and so on.

- **Escalation**   Describes how to respond to problems that may arise, such as stalled queues, systems failures, and others.

- **Backup and Restore**   Backup systems must ensure transitional consistency for business processes during data or system recovery.

- **Business Continuity Plans**   Specifies how to recover business services spanning all forms of service disruption from minor hardware failures to full-scale disaster recovery.

The acceptable duration and other parameters (loss of data, business opportunities, and so on) for maintenance cycles, problem resolution, and disaster recovery should all be specified by Service Level Agreements (SLAs).

In this phase, the operations team usually takes responsibility for the deployable software package and works with the process engineering team to execute installation and upgrade procedures. Typically, these procedures are tested during the commissioning of the test systems, which requires careful planning since the test systems are a prerequisite for the testing phase.

Commissioning of the composite business application may also involve setting up support, such as training for both end users and helpdesk personnel.

Ultimately, the purpose of commissioning is to create a secure and effective environment to enable the OA&M (Operations, Administration, and Management) team to maintain continuous operation of the business applications.

Business Process Monitoring

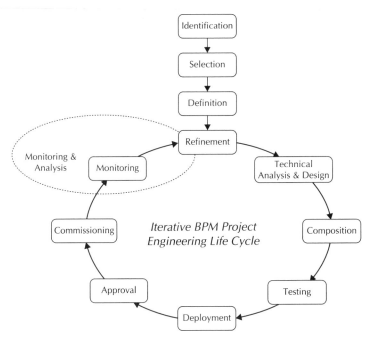

Keep in mind that this chapter is concerned with "methodology," it is not intended to be a recipe for monitoring business processes. Rather, its focus is what we should expect from business process monitoring and what we need to do to achieve those objectives.

Although monitoring finds itself at the end of our cycle (and the end of this document), it is important to recognize that there would be nothing to monitor without the earlier steps of establishing requirements for Key Performance Indicators (Definition Phase) and attaching them to the model (Technical Analysis and Design). Since the activities of selecting and attaching KPIs have been covered previously, they are not revisited here and this chapter focuses instead on what little remains for an engineering team to do to ensure that monitoring (and analysis) provides the fullest benefits to the business community.

Benefits and Opportunities

The mantra of today's BPM is "monitor, manage, and optimize" and key differences between BPM and traditional software engineering include the empowerment of business users and associated enablement of continuous improvement of the business processes. These benefits are achieved largely through monitoring, providing both real-time visibility and data to support effective analysis.

The purpose and broad benefits of monitoring in BPM are summarized in the following list:

- **Conformance**   The ability to operate within predefined values

- **Performance**   The ability to measure performance and gather the information necessary to improve

- **Better Understanding of Business Process Effectiveness and an Enabler for Root Cause Analysis**

- **Competitive Advantage**   The right information collected for the business, allowing management to make better business, IT, and operational decisions

- **Understanding Business Value and Providing Justification for Strategic Changes**

- **Basis for Automated Responses to Anticipated Operational Issues**

- **Reduced Cost**

Figure 11-14 shows an example of the process workload dashboard with drilldown into the workload by activity. The lower section of the screenshot shows details of an actual process instance based on the selection in the chart. Standard dashboards are available from Oracle BPM Workspace, but the user can also define new graphs and assemble them into create custom dashboards.

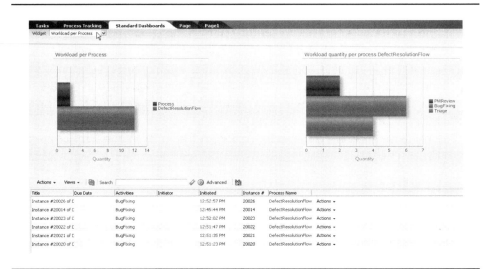

FIGURE 11-14. *The process workload dashboard*

The intrinsic role of monitoring in BPM presents three major opportunities to improve support to the business, which must be carefully considered when defining the method for business process engineering. These three opportunities are described in the following sections.

Business Process Administration   Business Process Administration is a category of operational management related to IT's OA&M; however, it requires specialist business knowledge and should be the responsibility under the business owner. For this reason in particular, the information should not be confused with system information (such as server resource utilization) and must be presented, along with the necessary controls, in an easy-to-use dashboard.

The key objective of process monitoring for administration is to monitor the health of business processes and respond to alerts and exception conditions. The category of exceptions we are primarily concerned with here is unhandled business process exceptions in which the process flow has not accommodated particular business scenarios. This may be by design, leaving rare and complex circumstances to drop out for human intervention, perhaps with the intention of providing further analysis of these situations before designing a computerized flow to handle them. The other category of exceptions, which must be separated from business exceptions, is system errors and exceptions. Examples of system exceptions include server resource exhaustion and software errors. These conditions should be intercepted by IT administration or else immediately escalated by the business process administrator.

Business processes can be better managed during runtime when monitoring supports effective response to alert conditions. Common scenarios in this category are:

- Unhandled exceptions

- Stuck or stalled processes

- Excessive queue length or processing times

Business process exception monitoring enables the business users to proactively detect exceptions and initiate procedures to resolve issues. Administrators can also identify common exceptions, such as a repeated ordering mistake with a particular supplier, and may respond by pausing the affected processes until a resolution is reached.

In addition to defining an approach for responding to alerts, the business process engineering method should also identify the need for escalation procedures. The role associated with process administration, in addition to handling a variety of situations, must also be responsible for triage of issues to other support organizations, such as unhandled business process conditions to customer support or system exceptions to the IT helpdesk.

Another opportunity for monitoring within business process administration should enable the BPM system to dynamically change the behavior of a business process instance, thereby providing an automated response under carefully predefined circumstances. An automated response requires the system to modify the execution of a process instance based on real-time, higher-level analysis, potentially combining other Business Intelligence (BI) gleaned through Business Activity Monitoring (BAM) and/or Complex Event Processing (CEP). This approach may be the ultimate resolution to the rare complex cases where the process flow drops out to the administrator via an unhandled business exception because the information necessary to complete the flow is not directly available to the BPM system or the process model designers. An example of an automated response to an unhandled exception might be an alternative handling of credit card transaction risk assessment when the in-house credit card validation system is unavailable.

The ability to promote process changes at runtime provides greater agility in the business process by enabling the business users to dynamically change process behavior without redeploying the process. Also, business rules are used to decouple decisions from the process flow while BAM allows users to adapt alerts based on real-time analysis of broader business events and influences.

In the case of business process administration, the method must make provisions for both detecting and reporting these conditions, as well as specifying the administrative role that responds to them. The associated administrative duties require access and authority to make appropriate runtime changes to individual process instances.

Continuous Business Process Improvement   This second category aggregates and analyzes data from KPI collectors to monitor the performance of business processes (rather than individual process instances) to identify optimization opportunities. Data collected through monitoring and its offline analysis supports the following activities:

- The enhancement of business process simulation models to ensure more realistic analysis

- The discovery of bottlenecks to improve business process efficiency

- Quantifying of the benefits of incremental improvements

This category of activities supported by monitoring is concerned with analysis of as-is business processes running under BPM and associated incremental improvements. This is distinct from major process change (see the next category) and commonly is the responsibility of the Process Owner. Again, the method must provide for extraction of the necessary data and the chain of activities that deliver it in a usable form to the Process Owner, while also empowering that user to make process improvements.

Supporting Information for Business/Enterprise Performance Management
EPM is a topic that is beyond the scope of business process engineering (although some may group it with Business Process Management); however, it is important that a business process engineering method recognizes and accommodates this valuable category of data collection and its preliminary analysis, which is required to support a major process change. This case requires executive level authority and design, commonly involving Business Activity Monitoring and other Business Intelligence techniques, in which analytical data from BPM is just one source of input.

The collection and analysis of business process performance information may be much the same as that described earlier, but its target users and their analysis (and associated tooling) are quite different.

The process engineering method in this case, having little to do with the use of the data, must merely ensure that the appropriate data to support this activity is collected and transmitted accordingly. This is fundamentally a case of collecting requirements from executive-level management and ensuring that corresponding indicators are applied to the executable process model.

Business Process Engineering Concerns

The primary enabler for business process monitoring lies in establishing KPIs, which has already been covered in earlier steps in this method. Also, much of what is done with the intelligence provided by the monitoring system is beyond the scope of an engineering method, while the challenge of providing it is largely an architectural concern. All that remains for a business process engineering effort at this stage is to identify the roles and their responsibilities to ensure effective implementation of monitoring technologies and ongoing analysis and application of the data it produces.

The participant roles along with their concerns and associated activities are summarized in the following list:

Executive business leadership:

- Identifies business KPIs

- Real-time business insight and Business Activity Monitoring in combination with other Business Intelligence

- Ultimately supporting a broader Enterprise/Business Architecture enabling Business/Enterprise Performance Management

Process owners:

- Identifies process (instance-level) KPIs

- Incremental process improvement, problem resolution, and escalation

- Not requiring a broader Enterprise Architecture (although still desirable), this level of monitoring may be implemented stand-alone or within a departmental BPM initiative

IT operations:

- Augments technical support, service-level monitoring, and Root Cause Analysis

- The runtime monitoring of processes provides data that can be correlated with system resource utilization to support real-time insight into business load characteristics and enable long-term capacity planning

- Requires a coordinated IT architecture strategy to establish the link between business metrics and system resources

Mapping to IID Methodologies

Although the BPM life cycle has been described as an iterative cycle of continuous process improvement, applying the 11 steps of the engineering method sequentially to produce a single automated business process unfortunately still constitutes a waterfall project approach. To make a single pass through the engineering life-cycle activities in one project (or even one iteration of process improvement) is not iterative in the true sense of Iterative and Incremental Development (IID).

IID requires that a complete work product be developed in a number of passes (iterations) through each of the engineering project disciplines, each time producing a testable, tangible increment of the complete deliverable. The weaknesses of the waterfall project approach are well understood: a one-off, up-front requirements specification (followed by sequential application of engineering disciplines) fails because the sponsors cannot be expected to completely foresee all the nuances of the resulting application. Each software project is a new product development so the manufacturing-style production line sequence of treatments doesn't work.

Various methods are ascribed to IID, including numerous variations of the Unified Process (UP) and a number of Agile methods, but they all apply the same fundamental strategy of collecting some requirements, designing and building something, presenting it to the sponsors, making adjustments, and moving on to the next increment. The key benefit to this approach is the ability to incrementally develop an understanding of requirements, all the while with a continuous feedback mechanism to ensure we are on the right path. The downside is either not knowing when you are done or how long it will take to satisfy a particular need.

How does this apply to BPM? First the good news: The typical disadvantages of IID may not be a problem since we are embarking on a cycle of continuous process improvement which, by definition is never done! This may seem rather flippant, but realistically what it means is that some parts of the complete solution (for example, a fully developed rich User Interface) may be of a sufficiently low priority that implementation can be deferred to the next cycle. The bad news, however, is that a typical business process requires a lot of analysis (business and technical) before anything tangible can be executed in a machine environment. Worse than that, in the absence of a fully developed SOA service portfolio and mature SOA environment, application integration efforts may add considerable time to a business process project iteration.

Fortunately, we can overcome these challenges through the disciplined application of an IID method. We can even produce tangible incremental results while ancillary software and service engineering projects are in progress.

One important point to note before we proceed is that we are discussing project methodologies and not broader enterprise methods. This limits our focus to single process projects, and while these are unusually broad in scope (spanning strategic analysis to BAM analytics), compared to traditional software projects, the enterprise concerns discussed in Chapter 8 are not included here. For those readers interested in the broader enterprise scope, we recommend starting with Scott Ambler's Enterprise Unified Process (EUP).[2]

In the following paragraphs, we'll focus on integrating process engineering projects with the Unified Process (UP) because it is the most well known and most adapted generic engineering method, making it likely the best match to integrate with any given organization's preferred project method.

An additional benefit of UP lies in the similarity of its traditional combination with the OMG's Unified Modeling Language (UML, providing an architecture-model driven approach) to BPM using the OMG's BPMN, which itself is very much a model-driven approach.

Alignment with the Unified Process

The Unified Process (UP) is an Iterative and Incremental Development (IID) method requiring short iterations through all engineering stages which leads to the rapid delivery of fully functional increments of a complete business application solution.

Traditional UP defines the following disciplines to a complete cycle (iteration) of an engineering project:

- Business Modeling
- Requirements

---

[2] *The Enterprise Unified Process* (Prentice Hall, 2005), by Scott Ambler et al.

- Analysis and Design

- Implementation

- Test

- Deployment

Change Management, Project Management, and Environment are additional management disciplines described by UP.

The 11 core activities in the business process engineering life cycle have already been mapped to BPM-specific disciplines (refer to Figure 11-6). Activities have been grouped and annotated with common engineering activity names in order to start to show the relationship between the business process engineering life-cycle activities and those of traditional UP.

While we could map the six core disciplines of standard UP, the six disciplines shown in the diagram more closely reflect the relative importance of the activity groups and distribution of project participants and their associated skills. "Implementation" could easily be substituted for "Composition," but the term is so overloaded, while our "Composition" (as with Technical Analysis and Design) is so important to process engineering, that it is a discipline by itself. Others bear some resemblance to it, while strategic analysis and monitoring/analysis significantly extend the scope of business process projects beyond traditional UP software projects.

A UP project is divided into four phases, each containing at least one iteration through the core disciplines (Inception normally has only one):

- Inception

- Elaboration

- Construction

- Transition

These phase names can remain unchanged in the mapping of process engineering, but it must be remembered that it is the intention of BPM to iterate continuously through cycles of the engineering process core activities to repeatedly refine (or even redesign) the business process. Here we start to overuse and confuse the term iterate, so we need to make a choice about the scope of a process project: Is the first production implementation of a composite business process application, the first major refinement or redesign of the process, or does it span process improvements ad infinitum? Usually it is a good idea to limit the scope of a project to a single tangible set of results, although this may be more than simply automating a process.

Theoretically, identification, selection, and definition occur only once before entering the loop of continuous business process improvement, in which refinement is the only business-level analysis task that is ever repeated. This may be true to some extent when the loop is used exclusively for incremental continuous improvement, but even then strategic analysis and corresponding definition are likely to be developed over a small number of initial iterations (in this way individual parts of the process—subprocesses perhaps—can be implemented separately, and the complete value chain established over a series of iterations). Realistically, some more substantial process redesign, perhaps resulting from business strategy changes, is likely to occur at various stages. These effects are reflected in the emphasis of activity disciplines in the diagram in Figure 11-15. Strategic analysis and definition span the inception and elaboration phases, while refinement is minimized in the first iteration. Further strategic analysis occurs in varying amounts in later iterations, although the real extent of this is entirely unpredictable. Note that process selection must only occur once (in inception) for a single process project.

The diagram in Figure 11-15 is a representation of the UP distribution of effort across the adapted disciplines through iterations within each phase.

A common misrepresentation of IID's iterations is to assume this means to execute loops within subsets of the full engineering cycle; however, the intention of IID is for every iteration to pass through each activity of the method's life cycle. Each iteration may focus on an activity to a greater or lesser extent as the product/application develops, but each iteration must produce a tangible work product.

IID requires us to execute every engineering phase and produce a demonstrable result. This ensures that the discipline of the method is not circumvented, but in order to make the first iteration as short as possible, we need to make some assumptions about the environment and reduce the scope of each phase without compromising the method or the result.

Initial Proof-of-Concept

How quickly can we demonstrate results from a BPM project?

UP places significant emphasis on requirements analysis in the first iteration of a project. Unfortunately, business process engineering is already dominated by business process analysis—indeed, this is where the bulk of time and effort will be spent (in fact, later iterations of process improvement might require minimal IT involvement). To do an initial iteration (or even Proof-of-Concept) in the shortest time, the project must be largely IT-driven and business analysis (at least at a strategic level) may be minimized.

The question is how do we minimize normally critical business analysis without introducing significant risk to our project? The answer is to pick the right process for the first automation project. In most cases, a small number of business processes are already well known to IT because they need constant attention from software engineering due to business change requests. In these cases, much knowledge of the business process (or at least its underlying functions) already exists, reducing the need for substantial analysis. This low-hanging fruit already meets the key criteria qualifying it as a candidate for automation—that is, frequent change. So we already have a key qualification and a strong existing business and technical knowledge of the process.

The diagram in Figure 11-15 represents a typical distribution of effort for a business process engineering project; however, this assumes a greater requirement for strategic analysis than we are anticipating in our rapid process project. Here we have identified another variation from classic UP, where the initial analysis and requirements activities will be substantially reduced.

Other practical constraints for the first iteration include the use of a generated UI for worklist and human task interfaces. UI development should be minimalistic in the first iteration, which mandates generated task forms rather than the more sophisticated ADF or even application integration. Initiating events may be constrained initially to a basic human task interface, and monitoring and analytics may be limited to a minimum operational set required to manage process instance health.

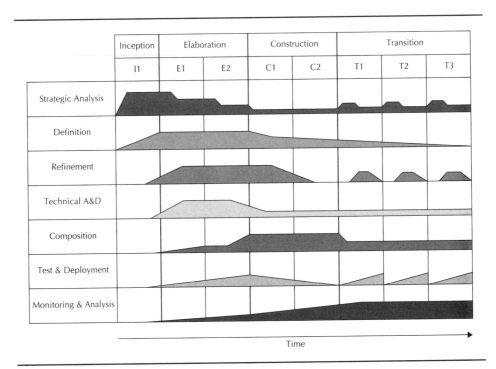

FIGURE 11-15. *The Unified Process distribution of effort across process engineering disciplines*

The following lists summarize the practical constraints that should be applied to the first iteration, separated into business and technical scope.

Business scope constraints:

■ Limit process changes to minimize risk

■ Make only the "obvious" changes

■ Avoid significant organizational impact

■ Restrict initiating events

■ Only implement a subset of the full process functionality in the first iteration

Technical scope constraints:

- Reduce scope if technical integrations are too big
- Enterprise 2.0 process collaboration techniques deferred
- Human task UI is generated
- Only basic KPIs are implemented
- BAM integration is deferred

Correspondingly, the following are deferred to future iterations:

- A more robust Rich Internet Application (RIA) or even deeper integration with existing applications can be the subject of future iterations

- E-mail, web, EDN, and other initiating events may be added in future iterations

- Analytics for process improvement analysis, simulation, and BAM, along with extended process instance monitoring can be deferred

Naturally, in addition to these deferred improvements and extensions to the process implementation, subsequent iterations should be made for each cycle of continuous incremental improvement. All these improvements, however, should be performed in individual project iterations.

Summary

In Chapter 9 we described the broadest scope of BPM concerns with the Oracle BPM Approach. Chapter 10 introduced the process engineering life cycle but focused on the most critical aspects of process automation, that is, picking the right process. In this chapter we described one of the key methodologies from the Oracle Approach for business process engineering. This engineering approach highlights all the elements of an engineering effort that are specific to BPM and in this way may be considered addition to existing (software) engineering practices.

It is important to understand that the series of steps described in the process engineering method should not, in general, be executed as a waterfall project (there may be exceptions to this, for example where the process is well established, the interfaces are already in place, and automation is being applied purely for process monitoring). Ideally, automation projects should not only be incremental in their implementation, but also in continuous process improvement, and they should be closely coordinated with enterprise capability maturity improvement projects.

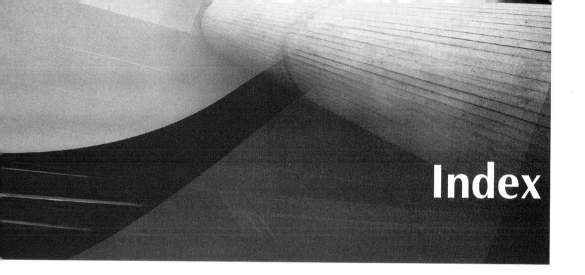

Index

N

GET YOUR FREE SUBSCRIPTION TO *ORACLE MAGAZINE*

Oracle Magazine is essential gear for today's information technology professionals.
Stay informed and increase your productivity with every issue of *Oracle Magazine*.
Inside each free bimonthly issue you'll get:

- Up-to-date information on Oracle Database, Oracle Application Server, Web development, enterprise grid computing, database technology, and business trends
- Third-party news and announcements
- Technical articles on Oracle and partner products, technologies, and operating environments
- Development and administration tips
- Real-world customer stories

If there are other Oracle users at your location who would like to receive their own subscription to *Oracle Magazine*, please photocopy this form and pass it along.

Three easy ways to subscribe:

① Web
Visit our Web site at **oracle.com/oraclemagazine**
You'll find a subscription form there, plus much more

② Fax
Complete the questionnaire on the back of this card and fax the questionnaire side only to **+1.847.763.9638**

③ Mail
Complete the questionnaire on the back of this card and mail it to **P.O. Box 1263, Skokie, IL 60076-8263**

ORACLE®

Want your own FREE subscription?

To receive a free subscription to *Oracle Magazine*, you must fill out the entire card, sign it, and date it (incomplete cards cannot be processed or acknowledged). You can also fax your application to +1.847.763.9638. **Or subscribe at our Web site at oracle.com/oraclemagazine**

○ **Yes, please send me a FREE subscription** *Oracle Magazine*.   ○ No.

○ From time to time, Oracle Publishing allows our partners exclusive access to our e-mail addresses for special promotions and announcements. To be included in this program, please check this circle. If you do not wish to be included, you will only receive notices about your subscription via e-mail.

○ Oracle Publishing allows sharing of our postal mailing list with selected third parties. If you prefer your mailing address not to be included in this program, please check this circle.

If at any time you would like to be removed from either mailing list, please contact Customer Service at +1.847.763.9635 or send an e-mail to oracle@halldata.com. If you opt in to the sharing of information, Oracle may also provide you with e-mail related to Oracle products, services, and events. If you want to completely unsubscribe from any e-mail communication from Oracle, please send an e-mail to: unsubscribe@oracle-mail.com with the following in the subject line: REMOVE [your e-mail address]. For complete information on Oracle Publishing's privacy practices, please visit oracle.com/html/privacy/html

X_____   _____
signature (required)   date

name   title

company   e-mail address

street/p.o. box

city/state/zip or postal code   telephone

country   fax

Would you like to receive your free subscription in digital format instead of print if it becomes available? ○ Yes ○ No

---

YOU MUST ANSWER ALL 10 QUESTIONS BELOW.

① WHAT IS THE PRIMARY BUSINESS ACTIVITY OF YOUR FIRM AT THIS LOCATION? (check one only)

- □ 01 Aerospace and Defense Manufacturing
- □ 02 Application Service Provider
- □ 03 Automotive Manufacturing
- □ 04 Chemicals
- □ 05 Media and Entertainment
- □ 06 Construction/Engineering
- □ 07 Consumer Sector/Consumer Packaged Goods
- □ 08 Education
- □ 09 Financial Services/Insurance
- □ 10 Health Care
- □ 11 High Technology Manufacturing, OEM
- □ 12 Industrial Manufacturing
- □ 13 Independent Software Vendor
- □ 14 Life Sciences (biotech, pharmaceuticals)
- □ 15 Natural Resources
- □ 16 Oil and Gas
- □ 17 Professional Services
- □ 18 Public Sector (government)
- □ 19 Research
- □ 20 Retail/Wholesale/Distribution
- □ 21 Systems Integrator, VAR/VAD
- □ 22 Telecommunications
- □ 23 Travel and Transportation
- □ 24 Utilities (electric, gas, sanitation, water)
- □ 98 Other Business and Services _____

② WHICH OF THE FOLLOWING BEST DESCRIBES YOUR PRIMARY JOB FUNCTION? (check one only)

CORPORATE MANAGEMENT/STAFF
- □ 01 Executive Management (President, Chair, CEO, CFO, Owner, Partner, Principal)
- □ 02 Finance/Administrative Management (VP/Director/ Manager/Controller, Purchasing, Administration)
- □ 03 Sales/Marketing Management (VP/Director/Manager)
- □ 04 Computer Systems/Operations Management (CIO/VP/Director/Manager MIS/IS/IT, Ops)

IS/IT STAFF
- □ 05 Application Development/Programming Management
- □ 06 Application Development/Programming Staff
- □ 07 Consulting
- □ 08 DBA/Systems Administrator
- □ 09 Education/Training
- □ 10 Technical Support Director/Manager
- □ 11 Other Technical Management/Staff
- □ 98 Other

③ WHAT IS YOUR CURRENT PRIMARY OPERATING PLATFORM (check all that apply)

- □ 01 Digital Equipment Corp UNIX/VAX/VMS
- □ 02 HP UNIX
- □ 03 IBM AIX
- □ 04 IBM UNIX
- □ 05 Linux (Red Hat)
- □ 06 Linux (SUSE)
- □ 07 Linux (Oracle Enterprise)
- □ 08 Linux (other)
- □ 09 Macintosh
- □ 10 MVS
- □ 11 Netware
- □ 12 Network Computing
- □ 13 SCO UNIX
- □ 14 Sun Solaris/SunOS
- □ 15 Windows
- □ 16 Other UNIX
- □ 98 Other
- 99 □ None of the Above

④ DO YOU EVALUATE, SPECIFY, RECOMMEND, OR AUTHORIZE THE PURCHASE OF ANY OF THE FOLLOWING? (check all that apply)

- □ 01 Hardware
- □ 02 Business Applications (ERP, CRM, etc.)
- □ 03 Application Development Tools
- □ 04 Database Products
- □ 05 Internet or Intranet Products
- □ 06 Other Software
- □ 07 Middleware Products
- 99 □ None of the Above

⑤ IN YOUR JOB, DO YOU USE OR PLAN TO PURCHASE ANY OF THE FOLLOWING PRODUCTS? (check all that apply)

SOFTWARE
- □ 01 CAD/CAE/CAM
- □ 02 Collaboration Software
- □ 03 Communications
- □ 04 Database Management
- □ 05 File Management
- □ 06 Finance
- □ 07 Java
- □ 08 Multimedia Authoring
- □ 09 Networking
- □ 10 Programming
- □ 11 Project Management
- □ 12 Scientific and Engineering
- □ 13 Systems Management
- □ 14 Workflow

HARDWARE
- □ 15 Macintosh
- □ 16 Mainframe
- □ 17 Massively Parallel Processing
- □ 18 Minicomputer
- □ 19 Intel x86(32)
- □ 20 Intel x86(64)
- □ 21 Network Computer
- □ 22 Symmetric Multiprocessing
- □ 23 Workstation Services

SERVICES
- □ 24 Consulting
- □ 25 Education/Training
- □ 26 Maintenance
- □ 27 Online Database
- □ 28 Support
- □ 29 Technology-Based Training
- □ 30 Other
- 99 □ None of the Above

⑥ WHAT IS YOUR COMPANY'S SIZE? (check one only)

- □ 01 More than 25,000 Employees
- □ 02 10,001 to 25,000 Employees
- □ 03 5,001 to 10,000 Employees
- □ 04 1,001 to 5,000 Employees
- □ 05 101 to 1,000 Employees
- □ 06 Fewer than 100 Employees

⑦ DURING THE NEXT 12 MONTHS, HOW MUCH DO YOU ANTICIPATE YOUR ORGANIZATION WILL SPEND ON COMPUTER HARDWARE, SOFTWARE, PERIPHERALS, AND SERVICES FOR YOUR LOCATION? (check one only)

- □ 01 Less than $10,000
- □ 02 $10,000 to $49,999
- □ 03 $50,000 to $99,999
- □ 04 $100,000 to $499,999
- □ 05 $500,000 to $999,999
- □ 06 $1,000,000 and Over

⑧ WHAT IS YOUR COMPANY'S YEARLY SALES REVENUE? (check one only)

- □ 01 $500, 000, 000 and above
- □ 02 $100, 000, 000 to $500, 000, 000
- □ 03 $50, 000, 000 to $100, 000, 000
- □ 04 $5, 000, 000 to $50, 000, 000
- □ 05 $1, 000, 000 to $5, 000, 000

⑨ WHAT LANGUAGES AND FRAMEWORKS DO YOU USE? (check all that apply)

- □ 01 Ajax
- □ 02 C
- □ 03 C++
- □ 04 C#
- □ 05 Hibernate
- □ 06 J++/J#
- □ 07 Java
- □ 08 JSP
- □ 09 .NET
- □ 10 Perl
- □ 11 PHP
- □ 12 PL/SQL
- □ 13 Python
- □ 14 Ruby/Rails
- □ 15 Spring
- □ 16 Struts
- □ 17 SQL
- □ 18 Visual Basic
- □ 98 Other

⑩ WHAT ORACLE PRODUCTS ARE IN USE AT YOUR SITE? (check all that apply)

ORACLE DATABASE
- □ 01 Oracle Database 11*g*
- □ 02 Oracle Database 10*g*
- □ 03 Oracle9*i* Database
- □ 04 Oracle Embedded Database (Oracle Lite, Times Ten, Berkeley DB)
- □ 05 Other Oracle Database Release

ORACLE FUSION MIDDLEWARE
- □ 06 Oracle Application Server
- □ 07 Oracle Portal
- □ 08 Oracle Enterprise Manager
- □ 09 Oracle BPEL Process Manager
- □ 10 Oracle Identity Management
- □ 11 Oracle SOA Suite
- □ 12 Oracle Data Hubs

ORACLE DEVELOPMENT TOOLS
- □ 13 Oracle JDeveloper
- □ 14 Oracle Forms
- □ 15 Oracle Reports
- □ 16 Oracle Designer
- □ 17 Oracle Discoverer
- □ 18 Oracle BI Beans
- □ 19 Oracle Warehouse Builder
- □ 20 Oracle WebCenter
- □ 21 Oracle Application Express

ORACLE APPLICATIONS
- □ 22 Oracle E-Business Suite
- □ 23 PeopleSoft Enterprise
- □ 24 JD Edwards EnterpriseOne
- □ 25 JD Edwards World
- □ 26 Oracle Fusion
- □ 27 Hyperion
- □ 28 Siebel CRM

ORACLE SERVICES
- □ 28 Oracle E-Business Suite On Demand
- □ 29 Oracle Technology On Demand
- □ 30 Siebel CRM On Demand
- □ 31 Oracle Consulting
- □ 32 Oracle Education
- □ 33 Oracle Support
- □ 98 Other
- 99 □ None of the Above